D1605975

Women of the Civil War South

ALSO BY MARILYN MAYER CULPEPPER

*All Things Altered: Women in the Wake of
Civil War and Reconstruction*
(McFarland, 2002)

Women of the Civil War South

*Personal Accounts from
Diaries, Letters and
Postwar Reminiscences*

Compiled by
MARILYN MAYER CULPEPPER

McFarland & Company, Inc., Publishers
Jefferson, North Carolina, and London

LIBRARY OF CONGRESS CATALOGUING-IN-PUBLICATION DATA

Women of the Civil War South : personal accounts from
diaries, letters and postwar reminiscences / compiled by
Marilyn Mayer Culpepper.
   p.   cm.
Includes bibliographical references and index.

ISBN 0-7864-1695-5 (softcover : 50# alkaline paper)

   1. United States—History—Civil War, 1861–1865—
Personal narratives, Confederate. 2. United States—
History—Civil War, 1861–1865—Women. 3. United States—
History—Civil War, 1861–1865—Social aspects. 4. Women—
Confederate States of America—Biography. 5. Women—
United States—Biography. 6. Women—Confederate States
of America—Social conditions. 7. Confederate States of
America—Biography. 8. Confederate States of America—
Social conditions—Sources. I. Culpepper, Marilyn Mayer.
E484.W66   2004
973.7'82'082—dc22   2003017187

British Library cataloguing data are available

Cover image: ©2003 Clipart.com

Manufactured in the United States of America

McFarland & Company, Inc., Publishers
 Box 611, Jefferson, North Carolina 28640
  www.mcfarlandpub.com

For Tom and
my parents

Table of Contents

Introduction

Historians can provide expert, carefully reasoned analyses of the Civil War years. It is, however, the letters, diaries and reminiscences of the people living through those tumultuous years that tell the real story of the people and their times. In reading those personal experiences, for the moment you are there, riding the waves of rapture and rancor, plenitude and poverty, fearlessness and fear, serenity and suffering.

Keeping diaries enabled Southern women to express freely their innermost thoughts, their annoyance over the conduct of the war, their humiliation over their straitened situation, and their hatred of the troops of occupation, Northern schoolmarms, and the reversal of their former slave-master relationships. These same topics were also discussed in letters to family and friends. Memoirs, of course, are subject to realignments of facts and clouded memories. They are, however, reminiscences of events that months, years, or even decades later still occupy an important place in the writer's memory.

Tens of thousands of Rebel and Union soldiers kept diaries and wrote letters and memoirs. Far, far fewer writings of women have been preserved. Most of those that have survived tell the story of the women on the homefront. Unfortunately, most of the diaries were plantation women, who represent only a small, select group of Southerners.

The women introduced in this volume include Southern women from different walks of life, different areas of the country, and different perspectives—those of mature women as well as insights from a fifteen-year-old girl. For the most part the stories of these women are culled from unpublished diaries, letters and reminiscences.

For most Americans—certainly for those familiar with *Gone with the Wind*—the words "blockade running" conjure up images of Rhett Butler and his cavalier activities, procuring necessities for the Confederacy and enormous profits for himself. In Chapter One, Mary White describes blockade running from a different perspective—that of a passenger

1

engaged in the exciting and often frustrating struggle to make it to England through the Federal cordon of ships around Wilmington, North Carolina. Although Mary and her family were not seeking the financial rewards that brought blockade-runner owners and captains overnight riches, the spirit of adventure prevailed in her dramatic experiences aboard the North Carolina ship *Advance*.

To date little has been written about life in academe or about the families of college and university faculty members caught up in the tremendous upheaval of institutions of higher education in the South during the war years. In Chapter Two, Josie LeConte sheds considerable light on that aspect of Southern living.

Life in the South during the war years was precarious at best; however, life in the greatly divided border state of Missouri involved participation in two wars—the great Civil War and the incessant fighting between factions within Missouri. In Chapter Three the reader discovers Confederate sympathizers for whom life in Boonville, Missouri, became so perilous that they were forced to seek refuge elsewhere.

Like that Boonville family, tens of thousands of Southerners left their comfortable homes and embarked on a desperate search within the South for a place out of harm's way. One of those women was Sarah Duval, whose trials and heroism are detailed in Chapter Four.

Winchester, Virginia, was said to have changed hands some 76 times during the war—on at least one occasion, four times in one day. The women diarists of the town, both Confederate and Union partisans, tell us about the repeated turnovers in Chapter Five.

Overall, the women's diaries and letters had much in common. First, there was usually some mention of the weather, which, of course, often determined travel, church attendance, visiting, gardening, berrying, and laundering (i.e. clothes-drying potential). Often there was a catalog of illnesses among family, friends, and the community. Sometimes there was concern over "a great deal of fever about the village"; other times there were cases of mumps, measles, scarlet fever, bilious fever, dyspepsia, "chronick diari," typhoid fever, dysentery, pneumonia, toothaches, congestive chills, swollen feet, boils, stomach problems, shaking or congestive chills, falls, and horse-and-buggy accidents. Vague descriptions of "Helen and Ella being quite unwell," or "John being in a wondering state of mind," or comments that "our community has been visited by the fever," indicated maladies perhaps not understood by the diarist herself.

Considerable space in both letters and diaries was devoted to a record of the day's or week's sewing: baby dresses "with insertions and bunches of little tucks," chemises, drawers, calico dresses, handkerchiefs, skirts, jackets. Long hours were also spent at the loom or counting stitches on clicking needles. Food preparation was another constant: With or without the help of servants, many women made catsup and pickles and canned innumerable jars of beans, berries, peas, pears, cherries and corn.

More important, however, than the homey notations of cooking, sewing and housekeeping were the glimpses into lives torn asunder by four years of turmoil and suffering. In Wilmington, North Carolina, the last southern port available for running the blockade, Mary White, as well as the famous spies Belle Boyd and Rose Greenhow, found the experience daunting—for Rose, disastrous. Josie LeConte offers a grim picture of the burning of Columbia, South Carolina, the complete disruption of a prominent college, and the birth of a new university. Nancy Jones lived in fear amid the violence that rocked the border state of Missouri, in a town where close friends and neighbors were murdered and her young son was taken prisoner by the Yankees. Sarah Dandridge Duval bears witness to the courage and stamina necessary to survive the itinerant life of a refugee. In Winchester, Virginia, Union and Rebel women lived together in enmity in a town seesawing back and forth between Federal and Confederate troops of occupation.

Through the diaries, letters and recollections of these five women, the reader sees the war from a variety of challenging perspectives. For the most part these women lived in towns, not on huge plantations with hundreds of slaves. Among those represented are academicians, border state residents, refugees, and exiles. The women vary in age and each was at a different stage in her life. One was a teenager, another was a grandmother. One woman had teenage children and a son serving with the Confederate forces; another was engaged in the challenges involved in bringing up very young offspring in refugee quarters. One was a widow with no children of her own. Mary White lived in Warrenton, North Carolina, where her father was a businessman, a store owner. Josie LeConte, her husband a member of the faculty of what was then South Carolina College, later to become the University of South Carolina, traveled in academic circles. Nancy Jones lived in a border state, the immensely troubled Missouri, where in Boonville her husband was also a merchant, though he "played at farming" in his retirement. Sarah Duval and her family were refugees living near Richmond, Virginia. Mary Greenhow Lee and her extended family lived in the hotly contested town of Winchester; that is, until they became exiles, sent "through the lines" by Gen. Philip Sheridan for their repeated annoyances. Although Sarah Duval and Mary Lee both lived in Virginia, their locations and situations were extremely different.

Today, camcorders, video and audio tapes, and cameras can help preserve vivid images of a people and an era. During the Civil War years women had only the written word to tell the story of their lives and times.

I have, therefore, made extensive use of quotations as I endeavored to portray their struggles in their words rather than my own. My goal has been to keep my observations and comments to a minimum and to let the women speak for themselves. Readers are encouraged to draw their own conclusions.

The diaries and letters are quoted but not reproduced in their entirety. Apart from adding a few paragraph breaks and some periods to facilitate reading, I have left the writers' spelling and punctuation essentially unchanged (although some were inconsistent in their spelling over the course of their writing). I have occasionally substituted the word "and" for the writer's original ampersand, especially in Chapter One. I have employed the intrusive ellipsis sparingly. I should point out that my repeated use of the designation "Southerners" refers to white Southerners.

I also wish to make clear that the racist remarks do not reflect my views, but those of many white Southerners in the extremely racially divided society of the 1860s. I would prefer to eliminate the racist language in the diaries, but to do so would be historically dishonest about the era. Unfortunately, those prejudices influenced the thinking of many white Southerners at that time (and are still detectable in the racial biases that continue to plague America today).

The bibliography is a select list of sources that I have quoted. It does not list all of the 600 sources I consulted.

It is my fervent hope that through this book, the reader will come to know some courageous women living in different circumstances from the traditional stereotyped plantation mistress of the Civil War era. Perhaps the reader will make some new Southern friends whose words will add to a greater understanding of the unique women of the American Civil War.

For almost ten years now I have paid lengthy visits to these five women and their families. Over the years, they have grown to be intimate friends rather than sterile names in a research file. The charming young Mary White and I quickly struck up a friendship founded on the camaraderie of the love of adventure and travel (despite my experiences being on cruise ships rather than on blockade runners). Josie LeConte welcomed me into her academic circle of friends, knowing that my husband and I each spent over four decades as members of the Michigan State University faculty. Nancy Jones shared with me a great love of family and a delight in the fact that I count her great-great-granddaughter and namesake among my very special friends in the town of Lansing, Michigan. Sarah Duval was immensely pleased that I was continuing to expand her recollections of '64 that she had started so many long years ago. At first Mary Lee fumed over the fact that I was a Yankee, but upon learning that my husband was a native Mississippian, all was forgiven. I truly will find it a great loss that our daily visits have come to an end.

I am most grateful to a whole array of archivists and library personnel, particularly Rebecca Ebert, archivist, at Stewart Bell Jr. Archives at the Handley Regional Library in Winchester, Virginia; Mrs. Giannasi and Rebecca Tol at the Library at the United Daughters of the Confederacy in Richmond; John and Ruth Ann Coski at the Museum of the Confederacy in Richmond; Susan Snyder at the Bancroft Library at the University of California, Berkeley; the staff at the Earl Gregg Swem Library at the College of William and Mary in Williamsburg, Virginia; Henry Fulmer at the South Caroliniana Library at the University of South Carolina; Jane Arnold, Kristen Lee and Jack Jones at Michigan State University. Dr. Peter Berg along with Gerry Paulins were tremendously important in making a host of Civil War materials available for me at the Special Collections Library at Michigan State University.

For over a decade Frances Pollard and Janet Schwartz at the Virginia Historical Society have been incredibly resourceful and responsive to my requests. Without Nancy Berger in Lansing, Michigan, there would have been no Chapter Three, for it was she who so generously shared her great-great-grandmother's Civil War letters with me and contributed important details about the Nancy Jones family history. My good friends Carolyn Hoagland, Christy Nicholds, Dorrie Souder and Marilyn Wanger carefully proofread, questioned, encouraged, reacted and listened. Martha Niland and Mary Jane Wilson also provided support and assistance.

I am greatly indebted to our family friend and computer guru, Larry Giacoletto, who never once failed to answer with expertise and good humor my hundreds of incessant questions and SOS calls. Another family friend, Dr. Richard Bates, helped me immensely by clarifying some of the late 1860s medical practices.

I wish to thank Lester D. Stephens, author of *Joseph LeConte: Gentle Prophet of Evolution*, who was most generous in taking time from his busy schedule to provide me with special information about the LeConte family, material that I would never have had access to but for his help. James P. Beckwith, Jr., of Durham, North Carolina, the great-great-great-nephew of Mary White, kindly filled in details of the White family and was of tremendous help in sharing special pages of Mary's diary that were lacking in my copies.

The real hero of all this, of course, is my wonderful husband, Tom, for whom late dinners, delayed vacations, and mountains of books and manila folders have become a way of life. Without his advice, his insights, and his incredible patience, I would still be merely thinking about doing a Civil War book. My deep gratitude to my husband will continue as long as life itself.

One

Troubled Waters— Running the Blockade

It all seems so very strange, but we are going with Father and I hope everything will be all right.

—Mary White

Prologue

"Things were so awful here and Mother and he [father] suffered so much being separated and our baby sister Lizzie died while he was away, so he promised Mother he would never leave her again." Thus began the diary of Mary J. White,[1] detailing her family's departure (her parents, brothers Andrew and Hugh, and sisters Kate and Sue) from their home in Warrenton, North Carolina, and their valiant efforts to run the Union blockade through Wilmington, North Carolina.

Life for John White, Mary's father, had been increasingly frenetic. His own remarkably successful business as a dry goods merchant in Warrenton had been coupled with his appointment as a special agent assigned to procure badly needed supplies abroad for distribution to the North Carolina soldiers. The demands of his business, combined with his work for the Confederacy in England, added up to ever greater periods of time spent away from his home and family.[2] The tragic death of Mary's little sister, Lizzie, during Mr. White's absence brought Mary's mother's world crashing down around her. In absolute desperation Mary's mother pleaded with her husband to either abandon his work on behalf of the Confederacy or to take his family with him to what she hoped would be a far more tranquil, stable life in England. Mr. White opted for the latter alternative and the family began packing for their journey to Wilmington, North Carolina, and what would no doubt involve a precarious run through the Union blockade.

The observant Mary's faithful and factual recording of life in and around Wilmington (by that time the South's chief import-export center) during the summer and fall of 1864 provides vivid details of a crucial period during the latter months of the Civil War. True, battles are won primarily on the battlefield; however, the soldiers must be armed and fed and clothed. Many of the supplies for the Confederate armies—the "hardware," as munitions were called, as well as medicines, food and the material for uniforms—came through the blockade from Europe. The sale of Confederate cotton, exported from Wilmington and sent through Bermuda or Nassau en route to England, helped provide the wherewithal for the supplies and support of the army. Blockade running, as historian Stephen Wise explained, had become "the lifeline of the Confederacy." There were those who considered Wilmington to be the most important city in the Confederacy with the exception of Richmond. Researcher Dawson Carr added: "They may be mistaken; toward the end of the war, Wilmington might have been the most important."[3]

One recalls that one of President Lincoln's first acts on April 19, 1861, in his plan to crush the Rebel forces was to set up a blockade of the Southern ports.[4] In the early days the effectiveness of the blockade was almost laughable, as about thirty Federal vessels attempted to patrol some 3,000 miles of coastline. A few days later, the President added North Carolina and Virginia shorelines (500 more miles) to the blockade area, thus augmenting an already impossible assignment. To further complicate matters, the tiny bays and inlets along the southern coastlines provided covert landing spots for small craft carrying both unneeded and much needed goods. These blockade running ventures, however, were minor in comparison with the large scale operations being conducted in and out of the major seaports of Charleston, Mobile, and Wilmington.

Over time, however, as more blockaders were added to strategic areas and more ports (New Orleans, Fort Hatteras, and Norfolk, for example) succumbed to Union control, the war was unquestionably shortened by the Federal blockaders' growing ability to check the importation of manufactured goods and supplies so vital to the Confederacy's conduct of the war.

Just as important as stemming the South's source of guns and munitions was curtailing the exportation of cotton, an all-important source of revenue for Southern planters and the Confederate government. In addition, the blockade created scarcities, which in turn raised prices, brought on inflation, and helped create deprivation and unrest in the South. As Bern Anderson pointed out, "It is significant, however, that the Union Army's major victories did not occur until the South was suffering from shortages imposed by the Union blockade. By creating these shortages the Union Navy ensured the ultimate victory of its cause."[5]

On the other hand, the Civil War was prolonged for months or even years by the blockade runners' ability to penetrate the Union blockade. In fact, so important were the supplies sent in through Wilmington that Gen. Lee took it upon himself to remind William Lamb, the commander at Fort Fisher, that the cargoes sent up the Cape Fear River were absolutely vital to the continuation of the war.[6]

As the war progressed, and after a period of divisiveness, the Confederacy finally realized that its fate critically depended on importing manufactured goods and supplies for the army through the blockade, and, as a consequence, the Government's concerns over blockade-running were accorded new priorities. Recognizing the advantages of conducting a blockade-running business of their own, sans middlemen and greedy mercenaries, the Confederate Government set about purchasing and operating at least three or four ships, in addition to also maintaining part ownership in other vessels.[7] A common practice was for the Confederacy to buy ships in England, staff them with Confederate officers, and then send them out with a British captain and under the British flag as required by English law. Once out of English jurisdiction, however, the crew pulled down the Union Jack and sent up the Stars and Bars.

Supplies from Europe underwent a sort of "transshipment" process, whereby stores were first sent from England via larger, slower vessels and then reloaded in Bermuda or Nassau onto faster, smaller ships for the run through the blockade.[8] According to one report, in the two-month period late in the fall of 1864, "6,000,000 pounds of meat; 1,500,000 pounds of lead; 2,000,000 pounds of saltpeter; 546,000 pairs of shoes; 316,000 blankets; 69,000 rifles; and 43 cannons" were sent into the Confederacy through Wilmington and Charleston.[9]

Quickly sizing up the vital importance of blockade running in ensuring the welfare of North Carolina's fighting men, the state's far-sighted Governor, Zebulon Vance, soon after assuming office, jumped into the blockade-running arena and set about buying and operating ships that would carry rifles, oil, coffee, medicine, farm implements, as well as thousands of pairs of shoes and untold numbers of blankets and overcoats for soldiers.[10] In fact, North Carolina's ships became so successful that the state's soldiers were reputed to be the best outfitted and supplied troops in the Confederacy.

Indeed, the state's runners were so enterprising that at the end of the war in April 1865, North Carolina had on hand "92,000 suits of uniforms and great stores of blankets and leather." Oversupplies incurred during the war were given over to the government, which in turn meted out the surplus to other states.[11] Without question, the Confederate government and the North Carolina blockade runners were unbelievably successful; however, they were constantly in fierce competition with private businesses who were out to make big money and let the devil take the hindmost.

It was Mary White's father, John White, who played such a prominent role in arranging the financing of the North Carolina blockade runners. Appointed by Governor Zebulon Vance as Commissioner of Purchases, John White worked with Thomas M. Crossan, a former naval officer who was charged with procuring and outfitting a ship to be used as a blockade runner. (According to James P. Beckwith, Jr., a great, great, great nephew of Mary White, it was John White's brother-in-law, John Key, an engineer, who had a shipyard across the Firth of Forth from Edinburgh and who outfitted the *Lord Clyde*, for service as the *Advance*, to run the Federal blockade.) In purchasing ships for the Confederate navy or for blockade running, buyers were primarily concerned with cargo space, speed and light draft of water.[12]

In November of 1862 Mary's father had gone to London and arranged for the sale of $1,500,000 in North Carolina cotton bonds. Bond purchasers could collect seven percent annually or could redeem the bonds for so many bales of cotton to be delivered to the Wilmington docks. With the money (over $300,000 from bonds and gifts from Confederate sympathizers) John White bought supplies which were sent back on June 28, 1863, on the recently purchased North Carolina ship the *Lord Clyde*, which was re-registered and renamed the *Advance* soon after its arrival in Wilmington.[13]

As Hatteras Inlet, Port Royal, New Orleans and other Southern ports fell to the Union forces, Wilmington, North Carolina, became one of the South's most important ports. Its proximity to the neutral ports of Nassau and Bermuda, the protection offered by the huge guns maintained at Confederate-held Fort Fisher, and the shallow waters in the Cape Fear River, made Wilmington an ideal port for importing and exporting goods. Thus, the Whites were well advised to make their way to Wilmington and there to chance getting through the Federal blockaders and on to Bermuda and England.

The popularity of Wilmington as a point of departure was based on its advantageous location, particularly its short distance to Nassau (570 miles) and to Bermuda (674 miles). In addition, at the mouth of the Cape Fear River, some twenty miles from Wilmington, Smith's Island provided two possible channels of escape (or entrance). The two navigable routes thus made the area ever more difficult for blockaders to protect. At Smithville, just before the island, captains could rest momentarily and size up the best avenue of escape, either through the Old (also called

Western or Main or Southern) Inlet channel or through the more popular New Inlet channel. Smithville provided an ideal scouting position for the blockaders, as both entrances could be clearly seen. At New Inlet the big guns of Confederate-held Fort Fisher served as all important protection for the blockade runners, while Fort Caswell helped protect the waters around Old Inlet.[14]

During the early days of the blockade, the Federal government, as noted, was ill-equipped with vessels or experienced seamen to stem the flow of blockade runners streaming in and out of the Cape Fear River to Wilmington. At the beginning of the war the Confederate States Navy was practically nil, and the United States Navy numbered only about ninety ships, fifty of which were essentially obsolete. In addition, the U.S. Navy was crippled in its attempts to secure adequate personnel for the blockade squadrons by its depletion of 322 officers who, with the beginning of hostilities, resigned to serve with the Confederacy. Furthermore, the bounties offered by states and various localities to volunteers to join the army served to fill its ranks rather than to supply the navy's needs. Even though eventually the navy did offer special inducements to lure men into its branch of the service, in time it became necessary to draft seamen for service with the navy. As a result of acute shortages of officers and seamen some warships were prevented from sailing.[15]

Furthermore, the infinitesimal number of ships assigned duty in the area were constantly being forced to abandon their stations near the mouth of the river to return to port for repairs, for supplies, and for coal, which left almost clear sailing for the blockade runners. Despite constant appeals for more vessels, as late as November of 1863 only sixteen Federal steamers were assigned to patrol the Wilmington area, and that marked an increase of merely six ships over the ten of preceding years. The early blockading efforts were looked upon more or less as a joke. In time, however, the Federals became cognizant of the tremendous amount of contraband that was being run in and out of Wilmington, and more ships were added to the North Atlantic Blockading Squadron, thus considerably increasing the blockade runners' chances of being captured. In time, the Federals developed a system of attempting to secure the entrances to Wilmington by way of a series of three deployments of ships. First, a line of shallow-draft gunboats hugged the shoreline as close as possible with orders to send off rockets to warn of incoming or outgoing runners. Beyond that cluster, a second line of blockaders had orders to chase any vessels sighted. Finally, additional blockaders were stationed near the edge of the Gulf Stream to pursue blockade runners who made it through the first two lines of defense or who were attempting daylight entries or exits.[16] In December of 1864, thirty-three to fifty Federal blockading ships were patrolling the entrances to Wilmington, "a number approximating the entire strength of the U.S. Navy at the beginning of the war."[17] Even four months earlier in August this tightening of the blockade brought on serious consequences for the Whites.

The U.S. Navy's inability to set up a completely impenetrable blockade over so vast an area lured hundreds of intrepid Southerners, along with Englishmen and seamen from other countries as well, to risk imprisonment and even death by attempting to run the blockade. In many cases patriotism and loyalty to the Southern cause were merely secondary considerations in comparison with the opportunities for huge profits (as much as 300 to 1,000 percent) and high adventure. Ship owners boasted that if they could safely make one round trip, bringing in merchandise and taking out cotton, they still would make a profit of at least 100 percent, even if the ship and a second cargo were lost.[18] Tom Taylor, for example, bragged that his ship, the *Banshee*, made eight successful round-trip runs before it was captured by the Yankees. Despite the necessity of writing off the ship as a total loss, shareholders received a 700 percent return on their investments.[19] Despite monthly expenses of about $80,000 dollars, a blockade runner evading capture for two round trips could count on returns of some $170,000.[20]

Earlier in the war, the ships had brought in primarily arms, gunpowder, cannons, knapsacks, medicines and even personal essentials such as toothbrushes and shoes. The sale of these manufactured goods turned profits ranging from 500 to 1,000 percent of their cost. One ship, for example, carried in twenty-six Scottish lithographers, one assumes to help in the manufacture of new Confederate currency.[21] On the docks at Wilmington, the ships were hurriedly unloaded and quickly reloaded with cotton to be sold in Bermuda or Nassau.[22]

Greed, however, soon overcame any remote sense of patriotism on the part of many foreign shipowners, and seeing the opportunity for enormous profits, they sent their vessels into Wilmington carrying only gold, which was traded in Wilmington for Confederate bills ($100 Confederate for $1 in gold). Using Confederate currency, the ship captains or their agents then bought up cotton (at eight or ten cents a pound), and after maneuvering through the blockade, sold the cotton in Nassau or Bermuda for over a dollar a pound, netting them astronomical profits.[23] Blockade runners indifferent to the Confederate cause transported luxury items such as women's clothing, sugar, French champagne, Paris perfumes, thread, paper, ink, specialty foods, coffee, and dress materials. Some manifests included hundreds of barrels of brandy and wine. Among the merchandise brought in through the blockade was a specially ordered toupee for what must have been a very vain, bald-headed Confederate.[24]

Looking for support for their cause, Confederate officials pointed out the fortunes to be made as they sought to entice Londoners to join in the blockade-running operations, and Englishmen leaped at the bait. According to the United States Consul at Liverpool, "Members of Parliament, mayors, magistrates, aldermen, merchants, and gentlemen are all daily violating the law of nations. Nine-tenths of all vessels now engaged in the business were built and fitted out in England by Englishmen and with English capital, and are now owned by Englishmen." The figures included both the large English ships and the smaller ships plying Confederate ports.[25] England's Lord Russell was quoted as caustically remarking that Englishmen would, "if money were to be made by it, send supplies to hell at the risk of burning their sails."[26]

Even some British women cashed in on the opportunity to make some fast money and bought up fashionable frocks and luxury items to send through the blockade—to be sold for exorbitant prices to unscrupulous purchasers in the Confederacy. The drain on high-style women's clothing as a result of the blockade made the owner of a new bonnet the envy of her contemporaries.

Blockade-running companies and individual adventurers vied with each other for profits. Among the most important blockade-running companies was John Fraser and Company of South Carolina, whose senior partner was George A. Trenholm, later the CSA's Secretary of the Treasury following Christopher Memminger's resignation.[27] Trenholm's company was so influential as to be called by many the "bankers of the Confederacy." Its Liverpool branch was Fraser, Trenholm and Company, a group of men favoring the Southern cause. A second company, Exporting Company of South Carolina, headed by William C. Bee and often called simply the Bee Company, also played a vital role in the blockade running. According to one authority, "A great number of battles were fought principally with the guns and ammunition, the shoes, food, and clothing brought into Southern ports by the Bee Company."[28] In Wilmington, J. M. Seixas of the Confederate War Department supervised the speeding of the incoming war supplies to the front-line troops and also oversaw the shipments of cotton to England.[29]

Hundreds of runners confessed that they "never had it so good." And small wonder, for captains often received five thousand dollars or more in gold, and pilots were paid from three to four thousand dollars per round trip. Added to their basic pay, the men, often English seamen, were given from five to ten bales of cotton to sell for themselves and often bounties for successful runs. (It should be remembered that although the blockade runners were of prime importance to the survival of the Confederacy, it was also true that their insistence on being paid in gold or cotton helped contribute to the Confederacy's dwindling gold supply and the incredible inflation that pervaded the Southland.)

Actually, the blockade runners were not the only ones to profit from the blockade cat-and-mouse game. Their adversaries, the Union seamen, could now and then come in for some monetary rewards. Obviously, preventing important cargoes from entering or leaving Wilmington was the most important goal of the Union navy; however, there was always the prospect of "prize money" for the crews who captured an enemy vessel. Although one half of the value of the ship and her cargo was turned over to the government, the other half was divided among the crew with the stipulation that it be shared with any ship "within signaling distance."[30] The capture of ships coming out of Wilmington that were laden with cotton yielded huge profits for the crews of the Yankee cruisers. It is interesting to note that a ship mentioned in Mary's diary, the *Hope*, was overtaken by the *Eolus* on October 22, 1864, after a sixty-five mile chase. The *Hope* proved to be one of the most financially rewarding captures of the war. Prize money of $13,164.85 was awarded the acting master of the *Eolus*. The assistant engineers got $6,657 each, sums which "amounted to more than four years' pay for all of them." The seamen received over $1,000, and even the cabin boy, whose regular pay amounted to the munificent sum of less than $2.50 a week, received $532.60.[31] Following their capture, blockade-runner ships were usually given a cursory overhauling and put to work as blockaders for the Federal government.

"Off and Away to Wilmington"

It was a somber little gathering in Warrenton that August in 1864 when the Whites assembled at the back of their home to whisper their last good-byes to the tiny cemetery's lonely residents. About sunset, the night before they left home, Mary and her family "gathered at the little graves at the back of the garden where Mary's little sisters, Sallie and Lizzie, were buried along with her first niece, little Pattie." Despite the excitement of the trip, Mary seemed to be experiencing a slight sense of trepidation as she, along with her father, mother, brothers Andrew and Hugh, and sisters Kate and Sue, made ready to leave. Although their adventure seemed so very strange, Mary put her trust in her father, confident that everything would be all right.

For fifteen-year-old Mary, there was the sadness of parting with longtime friends from school. It took little time, however, for the plucky teenager to be caught up in the excitement and adventure of the trip. First, there was a brief stop for sightseeing in Raleigh. Awed by the panorama of the city, Mary described their visit. (Her Rebel sympathies were evidenced in her prideful comments on the display of captured flags and banners.) "In the afternoon we went through the Statehouse.

It is a magnificent building, entirely of granite from the North, surrounded by a grove of large, beautiful trees. In front is a bronze statue of Washington. In the Senate Chamber is a Yankee flag, which was their garrison flag at Plymouth, N.C. It was captured by our troops in June 1864 and contained, it is supposed, about 200 yards of cloth. The whole room is hung around (and also the Commons Hall) with banners, most of them captured from the enemy, but some of our battle flags with holes shot through and the staffs shot away so they had to be mended with iron, each side, to hold the flag. Some have nearly all the color faded out and it is very evident that they have been through desperate struggles. In the Commons Hall, there is a full length portrait of Washington, beautifully done, and in the Senate Chamber there is an engraving of the marble statue of that hero, that was in front of the Statehouse before it was destroyed by fire."

That evening, from the vantage point of their rooms at the Yarborough House, Mary and her mother "sat at our window and listened to several speeches at the Court House, just opposite. The first speaker was a candidate for sheriff of Wake County, a real Holden man, and I kept hoping someone would knock him over. After that a Vance man got up and took the Holden man down considerably. Several others spoke after that and we left them speaking, when we retired."[32] (Not surprisingly Mary's political preferences sided with the latter speaker. It was Governor Vance, of course, who had appointed her father as Special Agent for the State.) Actually, it would seem there had been precious little time for sightseeing, for during their two-day stopover in the capital, the Whites appeared to have been welcomed by a steady stream of callers: relatives and friends to visit with the family, military officials to confer with Mr. White.

The upcoming election appeared to be creating quite a stir in Raleigh during their visit. Mary explained in her diary: "There is great excitement on the street this morning, the election is going on but no one seems to think that Holden will be elected. Cousin Tom White and Dr. Hogg called, and Willie Syme was here to see me this morning, and Rebecca Williams to see Kate and Sue." Quite aside from the family's visitors and her election observations was Mary's lament: "I saw a party of deserters pass the hotel yesterday. I was very sorry indeed for them. It made me feel so sad to think how dreadful is the punishment for their crime."

Following their two-days' respite, Mr. White shepherded his little entourage on to Wilmington, where according to Mary they "arrived safely the same night about 10:00 o'clock." As Mary emerged from the train she discovered that Wilmington was no longer a "straggling town built on sand hills," as pictured in antebellum days. Almost overnight

Wilmington (a town of 4,000 in 1861), had mushroomed into a "city" pulsating with seamen, speculators, and a sordid criminal element. At this point Wilmington boasted several churches, a waterfront customhouse, a large town market house, and a town hall complete with classical Corinthian columns.[33] By way of industry, Wilmington was busily engaged in the manufacture of salt, civil and military clothing, soap, candles and swords. Turpentine had become an important export and the acrid smell must have permeated certain areas of the city. Across the river one of the first steam cotton presses in the South compressed the cotton into bales half the size of the traditional bales, thus enabling ships to double the amount of cotton carried. During the war two large shipyards had been constructed in Wilmington. The *North Carolina* had been built in 1862 and the *Raleigh* in 1864.

By the summer of 1864, however, Wilmington had become the gateway to Europe, a town overrun with adventurers and speculators out to make a fortune. Thieves, drunkards, and murderers roamed the docks; fist, gun and knife fights were nightly occurrences. Successful blockade runners found themselves rolling in money, some of which they lavished on liquor, women, and riotous living.

Fortunately, the Whites were spared the seamier side of the city when, upon their arrival on August 5, 1864, in the midst of a thunderstorm, they were met at the depot by Mr. White's friend, Mr. Parsley, one of Wilmington's leading citizens and a devotee of the Southern cause, who "carried" them to his home. There, "he and Mr. Nutt, his father-in-law, entertained us most hospitably. The ladies were absent, but the two gentlemen did everything that could be done to make our time pleasant."

Although Mary did not mention it, many male residents believed that the vast influx of seamen and unscrupulous speculators had rendered Wilmington an unfit, unsafe place for their wives and children and had therefore sent them inland, to safer, saner territory. Indeed, Wilmington was swarming with speculators from far and wide and representing all nationalities eager to bid on the auctions of luxury goods brought in by the blockade runners. (The famous blockade runner William Watson believed it was the commission merchants—brokers and agents for both inward and outward cargoes—who "without risk or danger" were the biggest moneymakers in the business.)[34] Robbers and murderers rendered crime and violence ubiquitous features of the day and night as the rogues preyed upon hapless townspeople, transients, seamen—and themselves. Blockade runners eager to squander their newly acquired riches on extravagant living sent the prices of accommodations, goods, and basic supplies skyrocketing. Inflation zoomed upwards of 1,000 percent on certain items.[35] Unquestionably, Wilmington had become an increasingly expensive place in which to live. And, of course, an outbreak of yellow fever, such as the one that devastated the city in 1862, was always a threat. Perhaps for some or all of these reasons, "the ladies were absent."

It must have proved a fascinating sight the next day for Mary to take in the frenzied activity along the Wilmington docks as stevedores, caught up in the Herculean task of loading and unloading the ships, wrestled with gigantic bales of cotton and enormous crates of rifles or clothing or sugar. She would have seen numerous ships bobbing at anchor simply biding their time waiting for a moonless night and a golden opportunity to make a dash past the Federals' cordon of ships at the mouth of the Cape Fear River.

News during the late summer and early fall of 1864, although Mary did not comment on it, did not augur well for the Confederacy. Mobile Bay was under the control of the Federals; Sheridan was bearing down on the Shenandoah Valley, and by September 2nd, Sherman was in possession of Atlanta. As the Whites were attempting their run, the North had steadily increased the number of vessels used in blockading activities.[36] The scene had changed dramatically during the latter months of the war, and the waters around Wilmington were becoming ever more precarious for the blockade runners.[37]

At the time of the Whites' planned departure, fifty ships, "some of them the fastest in the service," patrolled the two entrances to Wilmington (and yet the blockade runners continued to maneuver their steamers through the Union blockade!).[38] Had Mary White's family been attempting to run the blockade a year or perhaps even months earlier, they no doubt would have had a much easier time. In 1861 the chances of a blockade runner being caught were about one in ten, but by 1864 the odds of being captured had escalated to about one in three.[39] Surely Mary's father must have been convinced that if only one ship out of three was caught, it meant two-thirds of the runners got through.[40] The Whites, of course, planned to be aboard one of the latter vessels.

Mary's father had prudently made arrangements for the family to sail aboard North Carolina's ship, the *Advance*. (Some Southerners even referred to the ship as the *A.D. Vance* or the *Ad Vance*, although originally, according to several authorities, it was supposedly not named in honor of Governor Vance). Mary described it as "a very fine steamer 235 feet in length, and 22 in breadth." (Actually, it measured 236 feet by 26 feet.) Mary might not have known that by 1864 the *Advance* had already earned an impressive reputation as a remarkably fast ship and as an extremely successful blockade runner.[41] It was also distinguished for its regularity. One observer remarked that "indeed it was common to hear upon the streets the almost stereotyped remark, 'Tomorrow the *Advance* will be in,' and when the morrow came she could generally be seen gliding up to her dock with the rich freight of goods and wares so greatly needed by our people."[42]

Mary did not choose to note that the *Advance*, as the *Lord Clyde*, had formerly operated between Glasgow and Dublin, and had been purchased by the state of North Carolina for about $175,000 (some sources indicate $120,000). It had been converted into a blockade runner, and with the help of Mary's father, in charge of procuring supplies in England, the *Advance* was busily engaged in the tremendously successful business of running cargoes of cloth and equipment for North Carolina soldiers into Wilmington and carrying out enormous shiploads of cotton for eventual delivery in England.[43] It was only logical, then, that Mary's father would arrange passage for his family aboard the North Carolina ship with which he was so personally involved.[44]

Following their overnight stay with Mr. Parsley, on August 6, 1864, Mary and her family bade their host good-bye and eagerly boarded the *Advance*, lying at anchor in the Cape Fear River, ready for their run through the blockade. Their journey would take them a few miles down the Cape Fear River and then through the gauntlet of Federal cruisers and out to sea. Immediately, the little group set about exploring the ship, checking out their minuscule quarters, studying the river, and chatting with their fellow passengers.

As they surveyed their shipboard accommodations, Mary admitted that the steamer had been "fitted up splendidly, for passengers [during its Glasgow and Dublin run], before it was put to its present use." In its conversion to a runner the ship's "saloon was removed and cotton bales put in instead and the accommodations for ladies are very poor." (This paring down of passenger amenities was typical. Actually, very few of the ships were built or re-built to accommodate passengers. However, from two to six people, usually Confederate agents or speculators, somehow squeezed into incommodious quarters on many of the vessels entering or exiting Wilmington. Since cotton was the number-one export from the South, ship owners made every effort, such as the removal of lounges, to pile in as much cotton as possible. One runner commented that expert stevedores packed the cotton bales so closely "that a mouse could hardly find room to hide itself among them."[45] Many of the ships were so heavily loaded with cotton, sometimes with as many as twelve hundred bales weighing from five to six hundred pounds each, that they seemed like giant floating cotton bales bobbing about the waters.)

As the money poured in, blockade runners were often heard to say: "Here's to the Confederates that produce the cotton; to the Yankees that maintain the blockade and keep up the price of cotton; and to the Britishers who buy the cotton and pay the high price for it. So three cheers for all three—and a long continuance of the war and success to blockade runners!"[46]

Accurate statistics are lacking, but without question thousands upon thousands of bales of cotton were shipped out of Wilmington by the Confederate government and by private companies and individuals. Some months saw over five thousand bales leave Wilmington.[47] In 1864, when the Confederate government restricted the importation of luxury items and began requiring that all private blockade runners provide half their cargo space for cotton on behalf of the government, North Carolina ran headlong into big problems.[48] Based on the *Advance*'s spectacular records, North Carolina determined to branch out, and through the sale of a half interest in the *Advance*, the state succeeded in purchasing part interest in four other ships owned by Alexander Collie and Company of England. The transaction made North Carolina part owners with the Collie Company, a commercial firm, of the new acquisitions (the *Don*, the *Annie*, the *Hansa*, and one vessel yet to be built.) Under this partnership, the vessels were classified as private runners and thus were subject to the half cotton cargo restrictions. Governor Vance's impassioned arguments that the ships were not essentially private blockade runners were to no avail.

The First Attempt

All was in readiness that night—or so everyone thought. Unfortunately, "time and tide wait for no man," and the Whites' first attempt to sneak through the blockaders proved a dismal failure. Mary despaired: "We expected to run the blockade that night, but there was some mistake in the ship's papers and before they could be corrected, we were too late for the tide and had to cast anchor and lie there all night. Our family and Mrs. Boykin's went ashore and spent the night. Mr. Parsley said we shouldn't try the poor hotel accommodations, so we went to his house and spent the night there and started again the next morning about eight o'clock for our ship."[49]

Running the blockade demanded a wily captain, an astute pilot, and a lot of luck. The tides, as the Whites soon discovered, were not the only perils confronting blockade runners entering and leaving Wilmington. The weather, choppy waters, contrary currents, dangerous shoals, and shifting sand bars at both entrances of the River added to the risks. Allies, of course, were darkness and the absence of any sound. Runs were scheduled for dark, moonless nights; a moonlit night automatically necessitated the postponement of the run.

In an effort to decrease their visibility, blockade-running ships were painted a dull gray, lead color, or bluish green. To avoid detection, some captains wore slippers. Seamen on deck were covered with sheets, and crew members whispered as they attempted to snake their way through the blockaders. Even the hatchways and binnacles were covered.[50] A sailor with a lantern or even a lighted cigar was in danger of being shot dead on the spot if caught by one of the ship's officers. Whenever possible, ship captains much preferred to burn anthracite coal rather than semi-bituminous coal, the former emitting almost no smoke.[51]

Speed and maneuverability were crucial factors and, as the war progressed, improvements in naval engineering and design contributed to the evasiveness of the runners.[52] Wooden sailing ships quickly became obsolete, and in their place were new sleek vessels, steam propelled, with drafts of no more than twelve feet, with telescoping smokestacks and expanded room for storing the all-important coal.

Upon threat of capture, captains, in acts of desperation, ran their ships aground or set fire to them and quickly made their escape with their crews rather than allow their cargo to fall into the hands of the Federals.[53] In order to lighten their load, captains of necessity ordered the dumping of hundreds of bales of cotton, these floating "snowballs" also serving to impede the progress of enemy ships. Turpentine-soaked cotton thrust into the boilers could be counted on to contribute a sudden, all-important burst of speed.[54]

A captain's cunning in maneuvering his ship through the darkness kept blockaders constantly on the alert. "Nowhere," according to historian James Soley, "was the work of the blockade more arduous and difficult than at Wilmington."[55] Duty aboard a blockader could often become dull and tedious and, yet, a moment's distraction or a "sleepy-headed Yankee" on watch and the enemy could be long gone.[56] True, the blockaders had the advantage of guns and rockets. Blockade runners, classified as merchant ships, were unarmed, lest they be deemed pirates, the consequences of which were, of course, severe.[57]

As the Whites prepared for their next attempt to make it down the river and out to the open seas, Mary's father was well aware that the *Advance* had already experienced several narrow escapes. A few weeks earlier in July of 1864, daylight overtook the *Advance* as she was attempting to enter the river through the New Inlet channel. Suddenly, she was spotted by the blockaders and a hail of gunfire rained down upon the hapless ship as the Federals followed in hot pursuit. All looked hopeless, but with a sudden burst of speed and the camouflage of the smoke from the salt works on shore, the *Advance* made it to the protecting guns of Fort Fisher and into port. Another time she was grounded near Fort Caswell and stranded for two days. Fortunately, the rough waters prevented the Union cruisers from nearing her, and she soon unloaded enough cargo to enable her to steal into port.[58]

Foiled Again!

The second attempt looked promising for the Whites; however, Mary again registered disappointment: "We confidently expected that night to go through. We passed Forts Fishers and Caswell and went well for a time but finally got aground. We were soon off again though, and cast anchor when we had gone as far as was thought prudent to go that day [in the daylight], which was opposite Smithville and nearly between that village and Fort Caswell."

Mary described the optimism that had prevailed that night: "On the night of the 7th all was excitement on board, supper was over, the machinery all oiled, steam gotten up and everything in readiness for the run. Finally the order was given to heave the anchor and when that was up, the lights were extinguished. We then went below, stood on the stools looking over the side of the ship, and were watching the water sparkling, when the vessel got fast aground and all their efforts to get her off were unavailing for some time. We had just nerved ourselves up and were expecting to go through, but after awhile they succeeded in getting her off the shoals and ran back to the old place opposite Smithville. We were going on deck (which was covered with an awning and filled with cotton), between the bales of cotton, when the firing commenced, which would have been in about an hour if we had kept on. But as the tide was not high enough we have to wait until tonight, the 8th, and make one more effort. But they all seem to think it is hardly probable that we can go as the tide will be lower than last night."

Although the *Advance*'s difficulties were frustrating to the Whites, the problems were far from unusual; running aground on the shallow bars and shifting sands at both inlets gave captains and their pilots gigantic headaches. It was a well-known fact that the *Advance*'s size and heavy draft were her chief drawbacks as a blockade runner. The latter made her much more vulnerable to running aground on the sand bars and, of course, prevented her from carrying as much cargo as some of the other ships.[59] Mary noted that the *Helen* also ran aground the same night: "About the time we started last night, the *Helen*, which had been living by us all day, went off also, she stuck fast on the sand and we passed her, but were soon in the same condition and now it was her turn to get ahead. She went forward some time and it was thought that she was safe but she came steaming back after awhile and is lying, anchored, near us now. I suppose she will also attempt to get through again tonight."

Waiting—for murky darkness, for tides, for precisely the right moment to make their departure—involved long, tedious hours of inaction for Mary and her family. "It is very monotonous on shipboard lying still but much pleasanter than I expected," Mary admitted. Fortunately for the Whites their fellow travelers proved most compatible. "Mrs. Boykin is a very nice lady and all of us are very much pleased with her. Her husband also seems a very pleasant gentleman and Hugh plays nearly all the time with Howard, their only child, a little boy 8 years old."

The tedium, of course, provided time aplenty for Mary to record her observations made from her vantage point aboard the *Advance*. As the Whites' ship moved through the channel, Mary noted: "We passed a good many obstructions in the river, which were put there for the purpose of entangling the Yankees, if they should try to get to Wilmington." (The South was ingenious in its placement of obstructions in defense of the approach to Wilmington. "Torpedoes," metal cylinders filled with powder and detonated from the shore, and powder charges designed to explode upon impact kept nervous Yankee blockaders at bay.)[60]

Sometime later, Mary watched as "the wreck of a Yankee cruiser came floating up the river and the men on this ship fished up a good many pieces. It got ashore and to keep it from falling into our hands, it was blown up by the enemy."

By way of passing the time, the officers of the various blockade runners engaged in considerable sport—and competition—among themselves. Mary recounted the bet made between the captains of the *Little Hattie* and the *Advance*. "The *Little Hattie* went out the night that we intended to go. There is a wager made between that ship and the *Advance*, which is that the ship that gets to Bermuda in the shortest time is to have given to the Capt. $10,000 and the same amount to be divided among the crew. Capt. Wylie is confident that he will win and I suppose the Capt. of the *Little Hattie*, is sure that he will get it."[61]

During their long wearisome hours of waiting, the Whites found themselves surrounded by a flotilla of ships in quarantine, anchored for days at a time to be declared free of the murderous yellow fever, which was assuming epidemic proportions in Nassau and Bermuda. One runner complained of having twice been quarantined for fifty days at a time.[62] "Not far behind us is the *Mary Celestia* just from Bermuda, in quarantine," Mary observed. "It is reported that the yellow fever is at Bermuda and a man died on board the *Mary Celestia* this morning, it was thought from yellow fever." Later, she added, "Three more cases of yellow fever were reported on the *Mary Celestia*."

Yellow fever posed a constant threat to ship owners and their crews, as well as to both the permanent and temporary residents of Wilmington, Smithville, Bermuda, and Nassau. In 1862 it was thought that the crew of the *Kate* helped transmit yellow fever from Nassau to Wilmington. Within a matter of weeks following the *Kate*'s three day stopover in Wilmington, the city was gripped in an outbreak of the deadly fever, and by October some fifty new cases a day were being reported.[63] During that summer and fall the epidemic took the lives of 446 of Wilmington's 3,000 inhabitants within three months. One citizen pictured Wilmington as desolate and forsaken as shops closed, businesses curtailed their operations, and hundreds of citizens fled the city in terror. The Wilmington newspaper downsized its publication to one page a week, trains stopped running, the mail service was suspended, and food shortages left hundreds in dire need of sustenance. The lack of medicine and the high cost of whatever food supplies were available added to the suffering of the fever victims.[64]

The fever also took a fearful toll in Nassau. There, the famed blockade runner, Tom Taylor, told of having attended the funerals of three close friends in one day. On yet another day, he watched "seventeen funerals pass my house before breakfast."[65] During one run, twenty-eight of Taylor's crew of thirty-two were ill with the fever, and of that number, seven died.[66] Small wonder frightened authorities in Wilmington set up stringent quarantine restrictions for ships entering the port.[67]

Hope Springs Eternal

As the Whites grew increasingly restive from the confines of their ship, Mary despaired, "If we don't go out tonight [August 8th] will have to wait about a fortnight for another moon, which will be very tiresome." And, as luck would have it, once again the Whites were frustrated in their attempt to leave when concerns that the tide would be too low became a reality. Earlier that afternoon, Mary must have recognized the vulnerability of their situation when a sailor "went up to the top of the mast and looked around reported that there was eight large blockaders in sight." She later wrote: "The tide, however, did not rise high enough, so we made no attempt to go out. The *Helen*, which had been lying near us all day, went out, and as no guns were heard and no news from the ship, it was supposed that she escaped uninjured."

The next day, August 9th, Mary pointed out: "It is thought, as we did not get out last night, we will try once more tonight, which will certainly be the last time. Last night the *Annie* came safely from Bermuda and it is just in sight of us."[68] Apparently, the situation aboard the *Mary Celestia* had worsened, and a compassionate Mary empathized: "We saw a small boat carrying a coffin to the yellow fever boat, so another of the poor fellows must have perished. How sad it is to look over there and see them ... signaling to the shore, which is their only means of communication and think that the poor fellows suffer and die and have no efficient nurse to attend them."

Up the Busy River—Again

On their final attempt (August 9th) before moonlight would rule out any possible run for several days, the Whites' plans were foiled when once again the *Advance* missed the channel. The next day Mary explained to her diary: "Last night we made a last effort to run the blockade and were over the rip, and it was thought that [we] would get out without any difficulty, but they did not steer properly and we missed the channel and fastened in the sand. The engines were worked and everything done that could be done, but there was no getting off and we had to lie there all night with eight large blockaders in sight. We were so near off the sand bar that the bow of the vessel was in deep water. This morning, as soon as the tide rises high enough, we will go back to Wilmington and stay there until the nights get dark again."

After considerable maneuvering, and with the help of the tide, the *Advance* was finally able to free itself from the sand bar and return to Wilmington: "All the passengers came ashore, our family to Mr. Parsley's again. This morning at nine o'clock we expect to go to Smithville with Dr. Boykin's family [Mrs. Boykin and their eight-year-old son, Howard] to stay until the *Advance* sails. Smithville is a small village about thirty miles below Wilmington on the Cape Fear River." (Probably the Whites' move to Smithville was prompted in part by their desire not to impose upon Mr. Parsley's hospitality indefinitely. In addition, finding suitable hotel accommodations in crowded Wilmington would have been difficult, if not impossible. Furthermore, by the late summer and fall of 1864, food and lodgings had become incredibly expensive in Wilmington.)

"On our way to the shore, day before yesterday," Mary continued, "we passed Dr. Kane's old ship the *Arctic*.[69] It is the one in which he went to the Arctic regions and is now lying in the Cape Fear River used as a receiving ship. Yesterday evening we, all except Father, took a long walk but did not see many pretty residences. This morning Mr. Parsley took me out to ride and showed me the cemetery.... I saw grey moss growing on the trees. It is beautiful but, oh, so sad."

At night the Whites could probably see the huge fires from the large salt works near Wilmington. Salt, used not only as a seasoning in cooking but also as an important requisite in the preservation of meat, was a precious commodity in the South. As a solution to the scarcity, Southerners resorted to digging up the floors of their smokehouses and boiling and skimming the dirt and salt until the residue salt came clean. The army and Southerners without smokehouses had to rely on salt works set up along the South Atlantic coast that manufactured salt by boiling it from seawater. The Federal blockaders could also see the fires and now and then sent nuisance missiles into the area.[70]

"Let Them Eat Cake"

The war and the blockade runners had drastically changed life, not only for the residents of Wilmington, but also for the people of Nassau and Bermuda. The towns had became boomtowns and the price of goods soared as the runners blew their pay on liquor, food, women and gambling (although not necessarily in that order). Mary's father John surely knew something of the high living of some of the transients—and actually of some of the officials—even if Mary did not. At Fort Fisher, Mrs. Lamb's life, as the wife of the commander at the Fort, was clearly not all danger and privation; however, it surely was not the life of seeming luxury described by Georgiana Gholson Walker, wife of the Confederate States agent in Bermuda. Maj. Walker's assignment to care for and forward supplies to be transferred to and from the Confederacy, and to procure coal for the blockade runners, may have been extremely stressful; however, his problems were given but slight attention in Georgiana's diary. While their fellow countrymen were fighting and starving on the battlefields, duty in Bermuda for the Walkers seemed not too distasteful. In Smithville, the Whites were speculating about where their next meal was coming from, yet Georgiana's days were replete with attendance at dinner parties, musicales, and evening entertainments of tableaux, theater and concerts.

Bermuda evidenced a strong Southern sympathy, and Confederate supporters and young naval officers were entertained by Bermuda's younger set at scores of parties and dances. There appeared to be a constant parade of friends, dignitaries, and government officials brought in by the blockade runners. The bill of fare for a dinner hosted by the Walkers for the Archbishop of Halifax and attended by Clement Clay, among others, seemed a far cry from the deprivations suffered by most Southerners in May of 1864:

Turtle Soup
Boiled Fish—Boiled Potatoes—Cucumbers
Fillet Boeuf au Champignons—Oyster Pates
Mutton Chops, Tomatoe Sauce—Croquettes on Rice
Roast Saddle Mutton—Boiled Chickens—egg sauce
Asparagus—Green Peas—Tomatoes—Baked Potatoes
Duck with Truffles
Plum Pudding—Cocoa-nut Pudding Tartlets
Salad—Macaroni Omelette—Cheese—Bread & Butter
Ice Cream—Fresh Peaches—Ambrosia—Jelly
Blanc Mange—Bananas—Oranges—Citron—Strawberries
Table set "a la Russe" *Dishes all handed*
Champaign—Sherry Madeira—Claret
Cherry Cordial—Noyau—Curacoa

Mrs. Walker recorded the profuse compliments of her guests on her "entertainment," and hoped that by detailing her menu in her diary that "it may serve as a useful hint to me some of these future days."[71] And such were the sacrifices of the family of the Confederate States agent in Bermuda!

Nassau, too, was "*coleur de rose*," in the words of Hobart Pasha.[72] There, seamen were spending their money like the proverbial "drunken sailors"—which many of them in actuality had become. Naturally, prices were exorbitant when a successful blockade runner could earn in four weeks more than the governor's salary. Southern sympathizers, Northern sympathizers, hotelkeepers, businessmen, prostitutes, all were out to make a fast buck.[73] "What jovial days they were," Tom Taylor remembered. "Every night our dinner table was filled to its utmost capacity, and once a week at least we had a dance." (Taylor's twenty-eight trips through the blockade had made him one of the most financially successful runners in the Confederacy.)[74]

◌◌

Wilmington, as noted, was experiencing an astronomical escalation in prices, brought on by the daring blockade runners who were making vast sums of money and spending it in port. One captain admitted: "I never expect to see such flush times again in my life.... Money was almost as plentiful as dirt." Captains, crews, and speculators often lived in luxury, their newly accumulated riches having sent prices skyward.

The inflation that in 1864 ran rampant throughout the Confederacy also affected the financial scene in Wilmington. Boots sold for $500, coffee and tea went for $100 a pound, a barrel of flour cost $500, and an overcoat, $1,500.[75] As a result, rooms in Wilmington had become scarce and pricey and, therefore, the Whites sought out more modest lodgings in Smithville to wait for more advantageous sailing conditions.

Even at Smithville, however, accommodations were difficult to obtain, but finally, somewhat Spartan quarters were secured for the families. In antebellum days Smithville had been a popular summer resort, but owners had moved away from the noise and turmoil of the river traffic and left their once elegant homes to the ravages of nature and renters. "This morning," Mary explained, "we left Wilmington at nine o'clock on the *Cape Fear* (a small steam boat), and arrived in Smithville about 2. We stopped at Mrs. Stewart's, a boarding house on the shore, stayed there an hour or so and then went to our quarters, just back of the boarding house. The house we are staying in belongs to a family named Cowan. It was their summer residence, but they have not been up in some time. It is a very comfortable house with six rather small rooms and three piazzas."[76]

Even though the house proved adequate, the Whites found the dinnerware sadly wanting: "It is very amusing to see us sitting down to our meals. Dr. Boykin's family and ours have six small sized tea plates, the same number of knives and forks and one teaspoon between us. We have one cracked dish and have been putting the sugar and salt, and pepper on the table in the papers until this morning, when on an exploring expedition, a cracked dish and an old broken teapot was found. These were very valuable and immediately washed and the teapot filled with sugar and the top with salt." Waiting for a moonless night proved tiresome for the ship's captain as well, and Mary commented: "Capt. Wylie came down with us today," and then added, "The *City of Petersburg* came in this morning."[77]

Two days later, still at Smithville, and still waiting, Mary commented: "Father and Capt. Wylie have just left for Wilmington. Father expects to go home [to Warrenton] before he returns. He expects to be back the last of next week.... This evening, Tom, the boy who waits on us, went bathing in the river with the boys and they thought it was a great frolic, but the people down here say there are a good many sharks in the river, so I don't think that Mother and Mrs. Boykin will let them go any more."[78] (The concerns about the boys' swimming in the river were apparently well founded. Mary must have cringed a couple of weeks later when one of the sailors "caught a shark about two feet long and it was a most savage looking thing, with two rows of teeth in each jaw.")[79]

As the days dragged on, the Whites' stay in Smithville began to seem like an eternity. It appeared a pitch-black night would never come. Mary complained, "I don't know what would become of me if I had no books to read." The whole family appeared to share Mary's despair—"It is so monotonous here, every day passes alike."[80]

If boredom and frustration were not enough, a scarcity of food was added to their woes. Actually, the Whites were quite fortunate, for some of the area's residents were in even more dire straits and subsisted on "blockade meals" of "milk, one wheaten biscuit and a bit of honey."[81] As their situation worsened Mary despaired: "The *Cape Fear* came up just a minute ago; Dr. Boykin, Hugh and Tom have gone to see if there are any provisions on board for us. They just returned and say there are none. We are *entirely* out of bread and don't know where to get any."[82]

Determined to make the best of their situation, the Whites tightened their belts, and finally, just as they were exhausting the last of their provisions, supplies arrived and the family took hope again: "Yesterday we had to borrow some bread for our supper from Mr. Morse, the pilot of the *Advance*, but as Tom was going after it, he found a shop where biscuit could be bought, three for a dollar, so he got enough for supper and breakfast this morning. The boat came down today and brought

abundant supplies of bread, bacon, pickles, corn meal, lobsters, tomatoes, water and musk melons, etc. etc. etc."[83] (It should be noted that
C.C. Morse was considered one of the most reputable and experienced
of the Cape Fear pilots.)

Word of the yellow fever epidemic in Bermuda augmented the
Whites' worries: "This morning the pilot of one of the ships lying in the
river died of yellow fever [possibly Anderson of the *Mary Celestia*]. Ships
that came in the last few days, say that yellow fever is raging in Bermuda,
so the *Advance* will not touch there but proceed to Halifax."[84]

At Smithville, the days continued to blur into an uneventful routine
of walking, reading, visiting, and monitoring the activity at the waterfront: "This evening Brother Andrew took Kate, Sue and myself out for
a walk. We did not walk very far, it was so very sandy. We went to the
margin of the river and counted ten vessels lying in quarantine near here,
besides an old ironclad which they say is worthless from the number of
barnacles which have fastened to the bottom. Mrs. Blount, the Quarter
Master's wife called this afternoon."[85]

Expectations about sailing were repeatedly thwarted. On August 17,
1864, Mary observed: "Kate and Sue had a visit this morning from Mrs.
Blount's two little daughters, who seem to be very nice little girls. Tom
has been busily engaged nearly all the morning making little boats for
Hugh and Howard. They intend going down to the river this afternoon
to sail them."

For Mary, letter writing, reading and sewing helped take up some
of the slack: "Yesterday morning, I mailed a letter to Aunt Bet [the sister of Mary's mother].... I am now reading 'Scottish Chiefs.' I think
Cousin August gave it to Willie Muse when he was in Scotland. I have
nearly finished it and like it very much indeed. This afternoon however
Mr. Hyman called and gave me a handkerchief to hem for him, which
employed me some time. Capt.Wylie came down by boat today and
brought us several water and musk melons."

In a sudden turn of fortune, the next day the boat brought in fresh
supplies: "We got plenty of fresh bread, old bacon, beef and vegetables,
which were very gladly received, especially the corn, tomatoes and cab-
bages. Capt. Wylie left this morning for the *Advance*. He took tea with
us last evening and made a great deal of fun at our table and supper."
(Captain Joannes Wylie was a Scotsman who had come over with the
Advance from Glasgow.)

Now and then the boredom was relieved by an unexpected serenade
from a trio of lively musicians. "Last night we had a most delightful serenade," wrote Mary. "The serenaders were a Mr. Everett and his violin,
and two Mr. Laniers, from Georgia, one with a flute and the other a guitar. They played Ben Bolt, Bonnie Jean and two very spirited waltzes

besides one or two tunes which I do not recollect. I don't know when I enjoyed anything so much."[86] The next day, however, activities at Smithville resumed their habitual snail's pace. Nevertheless, proper manners prevailed and Mary told her diary, "This morning, Mother and Mrs. Boykin went out to return a few calls." Unfortunately, the day proved to be a lonely one for Mary, who continued: "Sue and Kate are at Mrs. Blount's. Hugh and Howard have gone to the river to sail their boats, and I am left alone."

The next evening was again enlivened by a charming serenade— that is, until adversity cut short the entertainment—"Last night our serenade was repeated but one of the strings on the serenader's guitar snapped and we did not have as many tunes."

Waiting for a Boat

Spirits soared, only to plummet once again as the family watched their ship approaching the next day. "This morning between ten and eleven o'clock, we saw the *Advance* coming down beautifully from Wilmington, but she stuck on the bar and had to remain there till the next high tide, which was a little after seven, when she got afloat, came opposite this place and anchored."

Mr. White's hurried trip home to Warrenton had proved fairly unproductive; however, on his return to Wilmington and Smithville he brought with him an eagerly devoured packet of letters. "Father and Mr. Morris came ashore in a small boat while the *Advance* was aground," Mary told her diary. "Father had been home but only stayed two hours there, and then Sister was in bed with a sick headache. He saw Cousin Nannie White there, and brought back a package of letters, one for me from Lou Spencer and one from John and a long one from Sister. Letters for Mother from Willie, Sister and Aunt Bet, also a letter from Willie to Sister, which Sister sent Mother. Also letters for Father from Aunt Sarah and Uncle William."[87]

August 21, 1864, was a Sunday. According to Mary, it was "about like every other day down here. Capt. Wylie came ashore but was so restless that he didn't stay here a minute, scarcely. Last night, the serenaders, who are signal officers, were on duty just a little in front of this house, so they could not come here but played where they were and three or four ladies came and had a dance on our front porch, though they were perfect strangers to us."

A new surge of enthusiasm swept through the little group when on August 22nd at about ten or eleven o'clock, Mary and her family boarded the *Advance* for what they were certain would be a successful run. Yet, despite their feverish excitement, Mary's diary entry that day carried with it a note of apprehension: "Another attempt will be made tonight to run the blockade. There are thirteen steamers in now. About eight large Yankee ships are so near that they can be distinctly seen with the naked eye, but we will not encounter them as we go in the opposite direction, but there are five where we will have to go."

That night the Whites set out once again, and once again the ship ran aground. As the moon rose, hopes were dashed, and that attempt also was aborted: "Last night at about half past eight we started off to make the attempt. We went very well until we got to the inner bar and there, as usual, we got aground and while they were vainly attempting to get off, the moon rose and shone very brightly and then of course we were effectually prevented from trying any more. However, after awhile, we got off and put back to Smithville, where we are lying this morning. Mother got *very* sick indeed while we were fastened in the sand bumping at such a tremendous rate, but she is well, or nearly so, this morning. Father and Mr. Carter (the purser), have gone ashore to Wilmington to see about having some of the cotton taken off and more coal put on."[88] (A combination of shifting sand, a preponderance of Yankee cruisers, and possibly an overload of cotton, were essentially responsible for the *Advance*'s unsuccessful attempts to leave the mouth of the Cape Fear River. At one time, possibly on that trip, the *Advance* unloaded 300 bales of cotton in an attempt to get over the bar.)[89]

Still, the little group was not without hope. Surely the next day would see them on their way! "It is thought we will lie here until tomorrow night," Mary wrote, "when another attempt will be made to go by the wretches. A blockader was lying on the outer bar, just ahead of us last night and, if we had gone that far, we would have had to come back, so it seems fortunate that we did not go. But really it is very trying to make three attempts to run out and get fast aground, to say nothing of the wearisomeness of staying nine days at Smithville."[90]

Not only was it very trying, it also must have been very frightening for the Whites as they watched other ships leave port only to encounter the sound and fury of the guns and rockets fired from the Federal cruisers. The Whites must have shuddered at the gunfire accompanying the unfortunate departure of the *Lillian*, which had come down from Wilmington to run the blockade. "The *Lillian* started out last night and it was thought [she] got through safely, but it is not certainly known yet. We stayed on the cotton bales to see it go out, saw the Yankees throw several rockets, then saw the flashes and heard the reports of fifteen guns."[91] Actually, the *Lillian* did not get through safely that night. The ominous sounds of gunfire heard by the Whites foretold the capture of the *Lillian* (also spelled *Lilian*) on August 24, 1864, by the *Keystone State* and the *Gettysburg*. Later, following a Prize Court settlement, the ship became a part of the U.S. Navy, and was "sold to private interests February 23, 1866."[92]

To be sure, Mary and her family hoped the Yankee blockaders were getting the worst of the firing heard from Fort Fisher the day before; however, Mary announced sadly that the noise was merely target practice: "Yesterday afternoon, Forts Caswell and Campbell commenced firing. Fort Fisher fired twice and the other two about a dozen times. A little boat with a cannon came steaming up and we were very much excited. [We] thought they were firing at the Yankees but, much to our disappointment, found that they were firing at a target."[93]

The next night the Whites eagerly scanned the river convinced "that one or more ships would come in, so we stayed up and about ten o'clock the first gun was heard, six or seven reports followed, but no vessel could be seen coming in, however this morning there was one discovered near Fort Fisher. It either came in last night or started out and had to come back."[94]

A near fatality contributed to that evening's suspense: "Last night while we were in the wheel house, looking out for the guns, we heard a splash in the water and very soon were startled by the cry of 'a man overboard.' We were, of course, very much frightened and ran down to see what was the matter. It turned out to be one of the stewards who fell over right at the stern. Ropes were thrown out to him but he did not regard it, but swam as hard as he could and reached the paddle box very soon, swimming against the tide and with all his clothes on. Father and Capt. Wylie have gone ashore. This morning the man who fell overboard is feeling badly. He had an ague last night."[95]

During the next night, the *Hope*, loaded with 2,000 bales of cotton, met with almost certain disaster when she ran aground near Fort Fisher. She was quickly spotted by the Yankees, who immediately began firing. When the dumping of much of the *Hope*'s cargo of sugar failed to alleviate their perilous situation, the terrified crew members leaped into lifeboats in a desperate attempt to escape through the hail of gunfire, much of it probably emanating from the protective guns of Fort Fisher. Chaos prevailed, and Captain Wylie of the *Advance* was recruited to help restore order among the badly frightened seamen.

On August 26th Mary detailed the *Hope*'s narrow escape: "Last night a *quantity* of guns were heard and the occasion was not known until this morning, when it was found that the *Hope* was aground under the guns of Fort Fisher. The *Hope* had never run the blockade before and crew did not understand the business. The vessel got aground near Fort Fisher and a couple of sails were raised on board to assist in getting her off. The Yankees saw her then for the first time and commenced firing into her rapidly. The crew thought all was over and deserted the ship. One shot only struck the vessel that knocked a hole in the deck about the size of a man's fist. The blockaders were fired on from Fort Fisher which kept them off in a measure. Meanwhile, the men in the boats were in more danger than if they had stayed on the ship, for a ball struck near one of the boats and nearly filled it with water."

The practice of overloading the vessels with cotton and sugar in the interests of ever greater profits served to complicate the problems of maneuvering the sandbar. The *Hope*'s success in jettisoning the sugar saved the day for the ship. "This morning, however," Mary wrote, "the men came back and telegraphed for two boat crews to be sent from this vessel, which was done. They reported when they came back that pineapples and ice were very plentiful. They brought back 18 barrels of sugar. A good deal of sugar had to be thrown overboard to lighten her. They got her off, however, and came down here to quarantine ground about twelve o'clock today. It is a tremendous vessel, carrying 2,000 bales of cotton, double the cargo the *Advance* carries, and does not draw as much water as the *Advance*, but this is thought to be the most trustworthy boat at sea."

Thanks to help from the *Advance*'s captain, the *Hope* made it to safe waters, the rescue mission having further enhanced Capt. Wylie's reputation for seamanship. "Capt Wylie," Mary explained, "has just returned from the *Hope*, bringing us some pineapples and bananas which were *very* acceptable. Capt. Wylie says the officers did not do their duty on the *Hope* and the crew became unmanageable and they could do nothing until Capt. Wylie came, when he brought the men to order, made them do as they ought and very soon they brought the ship off. The Capt. was so mortified at not being able to control his men, and so grateful to Capt. Wylie that he threw his arms around his neck and wept like a child."

Nightly the river pulsed with excitement as the Whites, surveying the scene from aboard the *Advance*, speculated on the success or failure of the ships stealthily plying the river. "The privateer, *Tallahassee*, formerly the *Atlanta*, is also reported to have come in last night," Mary observed. "The cause of this [return of the ship] is not known as she was off the coast of Newfoundland destroying little fishing boats by the wholesale, when last heard from. The *Mary Celestia* went out last night and we watched for guns and rockets but saw none so concluded that it got by without being seen."[96]

Some important but at the same time comical lessons in rowing offered an afternoon's diversion for Mary and her family. "This afternoon, we were amused some time at the new boat's crew, whom Mr. Carter was teaching to row. They were George Little, Willie Muse and several others who were about their speed. Willie Muse rowed very well but poor George, after some preliminary flourishes, caught a crab with his oar and finally snapped it. It was very amusing to see them rowing, every oar would come down separately, but when they went to cross the oars and draw up the boat was the funniest time of all.... However, they improved wonderfully before they finished and Mr. Carter says they will row very well with a little drilling."[97]

According to Mary's predictions Sunday, August 28th, was likely "to be more dull than any other day"; however, the sighting of a torpedo boat provided an unexpected flurry of excitement. "This morning we saw a little torpedo boat coming down the river. It went to the old gunboat, and had the smokestack painted white, so it was inferred that it would go out tonight but it seems very doubtful. It looks about the size or very little larger than some of the boats that belong to the ships. Only three or four men stay on it. It is a regular little steam propeller, has an iron rod projecting from the bow to the end of which the torpedo is attached. When they get it near enough to the Yankee ships, the torpedo is made to explode by pulling a string I think and the vessel is blown to pieces. It is of course as dangerous as it is possible for anything to be. I think any one who would trust himself on board must have very little regard for his life." The next day Mary explained: "The little torpedo affair has been trying to see how it could carry its torpedo. The torpedo is coni-cal shaped and covered with copper, this is carried on the end of a long iron rod, which projects out of the tube in front. It looks at a distance very much like a very long snake just above the water."[98]

No small amount of zest was added to the day when fresh fruit was acquired from the *Hope*. Mary wrote, "Mr. Porter's crowd went aboard the *Hope* this afternoon and brought us some pineapples and limes."

Not only did deserters seek passage on the outgoing ships, but also young boys running away from home and contemplating the high adven-ture of "going to sea" sneaked aboard and hid among the cotton bales. Mary noted: "A little boy came aboard today, who ran away from his parents in Halifax to join the *Tallahassee*. The Capt. did not know he was on board but the boatswain concealed him until they had left port. He is to be carried home on the *Advance* whenever that goes, which is to be hoped it will do at some future time."[99]

Day followed dreary day for Mary as she and her family waited for a dark, moonless night. On August 30, 1864, Mary caustically captioned her entry, "Near Smithville," confessing, "I am so tired writing *Advance* that I thought I would write it this time Near Smithville, though they are both the same place.... There is no telling when the little torpedo boat will blow up anything as she is lying very quietly by the side of the old gunboat here in the river, but she once blew up a tremendous ship, the

Minnesota, so she may give them another lesson. An attack on Wilmington is daily expected. There are nineteen blockaders in sight of here, one a turreted monitor."[100]

The next day, still aboard the *Advance* waiting for tides and darkness, Mary returned to her diary keeping: "This is Father's 50th birthday.... I have nothing to record today of interest except that Mr. Wilkes Morris returned from Wilmington and brought us some elegant biscuits, which were a great treat, as they were the first eatable ones that we have had since we left home. I wrote a letter to Sister today, in which I once more stated that we would run the blockade tonight, but the pilot has just sent a communication saying it would not be safe to attempt such a thing for it would be high tide on the bar before dark, so we are all down in the mouth again."

It must have been unnerving for the Whites the following day as, "one of the sailors, George Holt, and the watchman whose name is Taylor, brother to the 1st Engineer, left the ship." Mary opened the reason for the departures to speculation—perhaps they, too, tired of waiting for the right moment to sail.

Successive attempts to set sail during the next few days were foiled by low tides, the illness of the captain and the navigator, and the presence of Yankee gunboats directly in their path. Problems brought on by the war and the conscription of able-bodied men into the army further added to Mary's father's anxieties. Mary detailed the attempts with growing desperation.

September 1, 1864, held great promise for the *Advance*'s departure. The next day, Mary wrote, "Last night we got up steam about twilight and started out. We went spendidly, got over the rip as nicely as possible without touching at all and thought we would certainly go through, when the first officer discovered something on the bar, and when the glasses were used, a large blockader was distinctly seen lying exactly in our path. She saw us and flashed her light, so *of course* we had to put back to Smithville. It was supposed to be a monitor, as no masts were seen, and if it was, we would have had to pass so near to her that she could have been blown to atoms. On our way back to Smithville we passed the *Coquette*, just going out, but she soon came back also."[101]

Ill fortune continued to plague the Whites' attempts to leave the country. That same day, additional bad news arrived from Warrenton: "Mr. Hyman came on board yesterday evening, bringing Father a dispatch from Mr. Arrington, which said the Secretary of War would not allow him to remain at home to attend to Father's business and that his overseer was in the army, so I don't know what will become of things at home."[102]

The Curse of a Friday Night

On board the *Advance,* hopes were again renewed: "They say we will try again tonight, in spite of its being Friday night." (Sailors were prey to numerous superstitions, such as the curses incurred from sailing on Fridays or transporting a corpse on board ship.)

"I have just been up on the bridge looking at the Yankees," Mary reported. "Saw about half a dozen vessels towards Fort Fisher." Further ominous signs included her notation, "Capt. Wylie had a chill last night and is quite unwell, and also Dr. Boykin, but I reckon they will be well tomorrow. A good many of the men have had slight bilious attacks but got over them in a few days, contracted while lying in Wilmington, they think." (It would have taken little imagination to pinpoint the source of the illnesses. The men were fortunate that the pervasiveness of Wilmington's filth and corruption did not bring on far worse ills than chills and bilious attacks!)

Neither sandbars, nor darkness, nor blockaders prevented the Whites from getting out to sea the next night. Instead the real culprit was Captain Wylie's indisposition: "Last evening we got up steam, heaved the anchor and were *just* on the point of starting, when Capt. Wylie had a telegraph sent ashore for a physician to see him, said he was *afraid* he might not be well enough to navigate today if we got out to sea and consequently just had all the steam turned off and the vessel anchored again. This was the greatest disappointment of all. I believe the *Coquette* also got up steam and was all ready to go, but when she heard our anchor go down, in two minutes her anchor was down also. It is reported that her pilot is sick and I suppose she desires to run out with ours.... It is reported that the *Lilian* was taken in the Gulf Stream, and the *Mary Bowers* ran against some obstacle going into Charleston."[103] Tempering their disappointment, however, was some good news: "Capt. Wylie and Dr. Boykin are both better today."

With a new navigator to guide the *Advance* through the channel, things began looking up once again for the Whites, and then: "Last night we got up steam and got out. As Capt.Wylie is still unwell, we took another navigator to steer in case our Capt. should have a relapse.... I say we got out, that is we got beyond the bar, and the range lights[104] were not set, so we had to turn back. We intended turning and trying again, but the ship was so hard to turn that she had to be anchored and let the tide swing her around. She got around and started out again, but by the time she got to the rips the tide had gone down so much that we could not cross them, so were back again for the night. The *City of Petersburg* missed the channel and got so far aground that she had to stay there until morning and was slightly injured."[105]

By that time Mary and her family were thoroughly disheartened: "Last night was a splendid night to run the blockade, just about dark enough, rather hazy and a little wind. The *Coquette* went out and no guns were heard, so it was thought she got out safely. The *Lynx* came in the night before last."[106]

Neither sandbars, nor tides, nor range lights, nor illness prevented the Whites' seventh attempt to run the blockade. This time a collision waylaid the Whites once again. With so many blockade runners in port, many of them lying in quarantine, it was a wonder there were not more collisions. At about that time Mary had counted thirteen ships in port either in quarantine or awaiting favorable blockade-running conditions. That night one more page was added to the litany of woes encountered by the Whites that fall. In the inky dark of night, the *Old Dominion*, which was also attempting to get out that night, rammed the *Advance*, ripping a three-and-a-half-foot gash in the vessel and further delaying any attempt to leave. For a time the horrified crew and passengers feared the ship was sinking and that everyone would surely drown. Fortunately, the damage was less than expected, but, of course, it was back to Wilmington for the Whites and repairs for the *Advance*.[107]

Fear and confusion gripped both experienced seamen and the little group of excitable travelers as the ships collided: "Last night for the seventh time an attempt was made to run out. We got to the rips, got aground, had just backed off and were going at half speed, when the *Old Dominion*, which had started a little after we did, actually ran into us. Mother and the small children were down between the cotton bales, while Mrs. Boykin and I were on top of them. The *Old Dominion* came along at full speed. One of the stewards, who was on the cotton said, 'Look at the *Old Dominion* she's coming into us, get a hold, get a hold,' and with that he tumbled off. Mrs. B. and I were much nearer the shock. We thought he was in fun and stayed up there."[108]

"We saw the boat coming but thought, of course, that they would take care and not run into us, but the first thing we knew there was a most fearful crash. I tumbled down between the cotton but not before I had seen the bulwarks giving away. All was in the greatest confusion. No one knew what was the damage. We feared we were sinking and hastened to the boats. We were all ready at the Captain's boat to jump in. On our way there I stepped in some water which some one had spilled on deck and, of course, that nearly took away what sense I had left. I thought the ship was filling very rapidly indeed if the deck was wet then.

"The bow of the *Old Dominion* was very sharp and strong, but our ship was so strong that it did not run in until it had scraped the length of three feet and a half, and the hole, which was *quite* large enough for a man to get in, was made just at our door, so that we cannot open it on account of the pieces of timber knocked against it. The strong timbers were twisted into the smallest splinters, but the hole was 18 inches above water."

Fortunately, the ship could be repaired, but the accident left passengers and crew in a state of shock. "We came immediately back to Smithville and are going to Wilmington this morning," Mary wrote. "Everyone was kind to us, Capt., sailors and all. Nobody was hurt, so we ought to be very thankful. They say if this had not been such a *remarkably* strong vessel, it would most certainly have gone down. As it was, it would have sunk if the lick had been a little higher up. They are at work on it now and think it will be ready to go out [on the] 8th. We have not gotten over the excitement yet, as it was so dreadful."

By now Mary's father was beginning to have second thoughts about removing his family to England: "Father has gone ashore to see if he can engage rooms for us all in Wilmington, for a day or two. He has not decided whether we will all go home and stay there or go out. While we were going out last night, we saw the flashes of fifteen Yankee guns, but could not hear the reports on account of the noise of the wind and our wheels. It was thought they were firing at a ship coming in...." Still benumbed by their near escape when the *Old Dominion* struck, Mary surmised, "Looking at the hole now, I don't think I could have been scarcely five yards from where the O. D. struck."[109]

Finally, after Mary's father had located accommodations for them (which probably would have been expensive, noisy and uncomfortable), they were just about to settle in when the ever-hospitable Mr. Parsley, "sent Father word that if he did not bring us to his house he would be very angry, so we went there, and are there still. This evening we got a whole pile of letters from home directed to London."[110]

The following day, from her observation point aboard the *Advance*, Mary once again surveyed the impressive array of blockade runners: "This morning at about twelve o'clock, we came down to Smithville and anchored at our same old place. The *Will-o-the-Wisp*, the *Helen*, the *Owl* and the *Lynx* and another vessel are lying here in quarantine, having just come in."[111]

The new day brought new hopes—and the addition of a mysterious new passenger: "We have a character on board now to take out of the country, who is strongly suspected of being a spy. Indeed, I believe the people who know all about it feel certain that he is one, but not having positive proof to hang him, they sent him out of the Confederacy. He says he is an Italian, has been in this country about twelve months, but he speaks the English language very fluently indeed with scarcely any foreign accent. His name is Dr. Lirgo." (Mary was probably referring to the spy Antonzini, discovered aboard the *Advance* when she was captured on September 10th. His offer to provide information about bridges in the Confederacy made him an extremely attractive commodity to the Yankees. A letter from Edwin Stanton, Secretary of War, to Gen. Ulysses Grant, written September 12, 1864, read: "The *Santiago*, one of our blockading squadron, captured a few days ago the blockade runner *Advance*, from Wilmington. On board of the *Advance* was found an Italian named Antonzini, who was brought into Hampton Roads yesterday on the *Santiago*. He was found double-ironed, had been condemned to death by the rebel government for treason, and was being deported to Bermuda, his punishment having been commuted. This morning Mr. Fox brought me a letter from Antonzini, offering to give information for the destruction of bridges on the Danville road. I have requested Mr. Fox to have him sent direct to you from Fortress Monroe.")[112]

Bars and Sandbars

On September 7th, neither sandbars, nor blockaders, nor range lights, nor illness, nor collisions caused that evening's debacle. Alcohol and merry-making turned out to be the culprits responsible for yet another delay. The Whites were at their wits' end. "Last night as our pilot, Mr. Morse, had been ordered on board another ship, another pilot was detailed to carry us out.[113] He got on a spree and was not notified he was to go out on the *Advance* until about an hour before time for him to come on board. So when he did come, the guard had to wake him up and bring him on board as drunk as a fish, so far gone that he could not stand. So of course, we could not risk ourselves with him and have to wait until tonight."[114]

The discouraged, dreary little group of travelers, headachy and cross with further delay brought about by the inebriated pilot, were about to call it a night. Just then, "after we had just found that we could not go, and of course were in no very pleasant humor, suddenly distant music struck on our ears." Mary explained: "The same gentlemen who serenaded us so sweetly in Smithville, came out in a small boat and went round and round the ship very slowly, playing most beautifully. The tune next to the last was Home, Sweet Home, and they went off playing Dixie. Capt. Wylie thanked them for it and one of them replied in a few words. It seemed to do everybody on the ship good, but my head aches too much today to write more about it."[115]

Although conditions looked advantageous for the Whites' ninth attempt to run the blockade (neither sandbars, nor illness, nor alcohol proved deterring factors), the captain suddenly discovered the *Advance* was about to be surrounded by three Yankee gunboats, and ordered a hasty retreat to Smithville. In Mary's words: "We got to sea that night and the pilot had just given the vessel up to the Capt. when it was discovered that we were about to be surrounded. Three Yankee ships in front of us threw up rockets and one was on our side not more than five hundred yards off, so our ship immediately put back and went with the speed of the wind until out of their reach. We anchored at Smithville the remainder of the night. It was remarkably calm, there was scarcely a ripple on the water and our paddles could be heard a mile and a half off. All idea of going out was given up for the night until about 12:00 o'clock, it looked a *little* more favorable and they determined to try it.

"The next day, the 10th, about eleven o'clock the *Advance* left Smithville for New Inlet. The Capt. said that was the last night of the moon and they had either to go out or be blown up. She was anchored in sight of the Yankees all day. Every one thought it would be so perfectly desperate that Father and Dr. Boykin took their families off."

By this time Mary's father, realizing that the Federals had greatly tightened the blockade around the Cape Fear River, was convinced it would be foolhardy, particularly with so many blockaders in sight, to risk the lives of his family by attempting to slip through the cordon of Federal ships. The dejected Whites, resigned to the abandonment of their plans, finally gave up in desperation, left the *Advance*, and again took up temporary residence at Mrs. Stewart's boarding house: "We went to Mrs. Stuart's [Stewart's?] in Smithville, who keeps a kind of public house. She took us in and we got dinner. In the afternoon we went to the wharf to try to prevail on Gen. Whiting to let us go to Wilmington on the *Cape Fear* (a river boat) as there were no passengers except himself, and staff, and Gen. Beauregard. But he very promptly refused us and persuasion did no good. So we journeyed back to Mrs. Stuart's again, weary and disheartened. She very kindly let us have lodging for the night."

Meanwhile, the *Advance*'s Capt. Wylie determined he could wait no longer for more auspicious conditions and cautiously pulled up anchor and nosed the *Advance* through the maze of boats clogging the river. The Whites, despite their grave disappointment, surely must have found consolation in the safety of Smithville as they listened to the Federals' guns opening up on the *Advance* as she departed that night.[116]

Still in a state of shock, no doubt, from having so narrowly escaped the shelling of the *Advance* by the Federals, the Whites appealed to Commodore Lynch, who "let us have the *Equator*, flagship of the squadron down there, to take us to town the next morning early."

Then followed the Whites' long, tedious trip back to Warrenton. "At the wharf, we parted with Mrs. Boykin," Mary wrote, "who started for her home that night. We went to Mr. Parsley's where we got dinner and started home on a freight train at four o'clock. We got breakfast in Enfield about 11:00 o'clock the next morning, and arrived at Weldon at half past twelve not having changed cars at all from Wilmington. At Weldon we got two rooms, three beds and some water, which was absolutely *all*, for we had not a morsel to eat, nor a towel even. We left there a little after four o'clock in the morning and arrived at home a little after eight.... Father went to Raleigh yesterday; he came back today. He expects to go out on some other vessel the next moon, but it is very doubtful about taking his family."

The poor unfortunate Whites! Or were they not the lucky Whites? The *Advance*, carrying 410 bales of cotton, did succeed in getting out that night—just hours after Mary's father removed his family from the ship. But in short order the *Advance* was sighted by a Yankee war ship, the *Santiago de Cuba*, which dogged the ship for some ten hours before finally capturing it.[117]

Mary and her family were stunned to learn of the capture: "A few days after I last wrote in my journal, we were shocked by hearing of the capture of the *Advance*. She was captured on Saturday, Sept. 11th, off Cape Hatteras.[118] All we know about it is simply the announcement of its capture taken from a Yankee paper. We were very much grieved at its fate but very glad indeed that we were not on board. Father has decided not to take us with him as blockade running is so dangerous now. We have since heard that everyone on board the *Advance* was released on professing to be British subjects except Mr. Neal, Willie Muse, Mr. Field and Mr. Bynam would not profess to be what they were not. These four were carried to prison, but all were released on account of their health, except Mr. Neal." (For diplomatic reasons most foreigners were not imprisoned; therefore the affirmation or pretension of being British citizens.)[119]

Numerous authorities were convinced that the *Advance*'s capture resulted from its inability to obtain anthracite coal and that its use of bituminous coal and the consequent emission of black smoke had alerted the Federals. There had been constant feuding between the North Carolina officials and the Confederate Ordnance Department over the allocation of the "good coal." The *Advance* that night had been allotted only the inferior soft coal. Even the Captain of the *Santiago de Cuba* admitted that his ship would have been unable to overtake the *Advance* had she not been burning soft North Carolina coal.[120]

North Carolina deplored the loss of the *Advance*, but was cognizant of the fact that it was becoming increasingly difficult for ships to make it through the blockade. During June, July, and August of 1864, blockade runners were suffering a ten percent loss of ships, which increased to a twenty percent loss between September 1 and December 10, 1865.[121]

Following her capture, the *Advance* was sent north, purchased from

Prize Court and became a part of the Union navy. Under the name the *Frolic*, the vessel was returned to the Cape Fear River, this time under the Union flag, and was later said to be used by the Federal government in the capture of Fort Fisher.

You Can Go Home Again

Life became considerably less harried for the Whites as they settled back into their home in Warrenton, North Carolina, following their frustrating attempts to get through the blockade. However, the Confederacy's desperate need for guns and food became ever more acute, and on October 26th, Mary's father returned to Wilmington and Smithville. From there he successfully made his way to Bermuda and then to Halifax and finally on to England on his mission to secure supplies for the North Carolina soldiers. Yellow fever was still a threat, and although Mary's father did not go ashore in Bermuda, he apparently contracted the dreaded fever.

Mail, of course, was sporadic and in many cases non-existent, and Mary's family spent agonizing days and nights worrying about the health and well-being of Mary's father. For months at a time there were no letters from Mr. White: "Father left home on Oct. 22nd, and we remained. He wrote us on the 26th [October] on board the *Virginia* at Smithville that he expected to go out that night and as we have heard nothing from him since he sailed, which has been almost a fortnight, we suppose, of course, he is safe. He hated *very, very* much to go without us and we also would have given anything in the world to have been with him, but he thought it best that we should not go, as an attack was expected daily on Wilmington.... He arrived at Bermuda on the 28th, and did not go ashore but stayed on board the *Virginia* that night and started for Halifax the next day."[122]

For long stretches of time there was precious little news about Mary's father. Although on the way from Bermuda to Halifax, Mr. White was taken extremely ill, apparently with yellow fever, Mary's mother was greatly relieved by a letter from a friend assuring her that he was out of danger. "Still we were miserable," Mary wrote, "until three days after when we received a short letter from Father himself, saying that he had been very ill but hoped to be up soon. We heard once more from him at Halifax, and again from London [on December 24th], then Charleston and Wilmington fell and we have not heard since. Our poor country is so overrun with Yankees now that I expect we will hear soon.... We have no mails now, and no communications with anywhere. But there is no news to hear except from Johnston's Army. I expect the Yankee lines will have the trains running by here in a short time."[123]

Little more than four months after the capture of the *Advance* and the Whites' return home, Fort Fisher fell (January 15, 1865) to the Union forces, and the importation of supplies for the Confederate troops essentially ceased.[124] The occupation of Wilmington, the Confederacy's last major port and source of war materials, by the Federals on February 22, 1865, served as an important step in bringing an end to the war.[125]

Anxious Days Ahead

There are considerable gaps in Mary's diary following her return home. However, her scattered entries interspersed with news of her father provide a colorful collage, portraying the problems that confronted a loyal Rebel family after the war. Anxiety over the health and safety of Mr. White, the collapse of the Confederacy, the ravages of the stragglers of both armies, the appointment of William Holden as provisional governor, all made for days of anguish and uncertainty for Mary and her family.

In her April 16, 1865, diary entry, Mary attempted to resign herself to the defeat: "Petersburg fell on Sunday April 2nd, and the next Sunday Gen. Lee's Army, numbering only 8,000 men, surrendered at Appomattox Station to Gen. Grant. The whole Army was paroled and the officers were allowed their side arms. A great many of Lee's soldiers were rejoiced at his being compelled to surrender but the ones who were true to their country were very much distressed indeed. Nearly everyone seems to think that the struggle is over now. I can't realize that the '*Army of Northern Virginia*' is no more, the Army that all our hopes were based on! That it should have been compelled to yield to overwhelming numbers and resources is no disgrace. For four long years they have struggled for liberty, and if the precious boon *is* denied them they have the melancholy satisfaction of knowing that they fought well for it and richly deserved it." Tens of thousands of Southerners shared the convictions of Mr. Arrington, Mary's brother-in-law, that "the South will yet gain her independence." Mary explained: "It is impossible he says, for so many noble lives to have been lost in vain. It may be years first but he thinks we will yet be free. The soldiers say 'We are not subjugated; but considerably scattered.'"

Although the Whites made a desperate effort to put the four years of struggle and sacrifice behind them, there were still more anxious days ahead: "Willie was sent off a few days before the surrender with a detail of a hundred men and has not been heard from since. It is supposed that he is a prisoner…. We are very uneasy about him indeed." (Willie, Mary's brother, William Jones White, had been serving with the Confederacy as quartermaster in the 1st North Carolina Cavalry.) Later, Mary rejoiced: "Willie arrived at home today, was not captured as we supposed but fared a great deal worse than he would have done had he been taken. He came very near being taken several times on his way home, got scarcely anything to eat on the journey and when he reached home, he was so worn out and haggard that he scarcely looked like himself. His regiment is disbanded for the present." (Willie's return to his home was typical, of course, of the tens of thousands of Southern soldiers, who wound their way home, living on handouts from compassionate farmers along the way and grateful for the welcome shelter of a haystack or a barn for a night's sleep.)

Amidst the bleak despair over the collapse of the Confederacy were a host of immediate worries including the fate of President Davis and the future of the South following the assassination of President Lincoln. Financial problems loomed with the catastrophic demise of the Confederate currency and the very real possibility of the confiscation of the Whites' home and property. The bummers, the stragglers from both armies, however, posed the greatest threat to life and property for the Whites and tens of thousands of their countrymen. Less fundamental but still annoying was an issue that Southerners considered a further infringement of their rights: the insistence by the Federals that Southerners cease offering up prayers for President Davis.

Although President Davis had his detractors, for many Southerners he was their president, and following his hasty departure from Richmond, there were growing fears as to his safety and his ultimate fate at the hands of the conquerors.

"We are all very uneasy indeed about Pres. Davis, we fear he will be caught and hung," Mary told her journal. "We know nothing of his whereabouts. We heard though that he came very near being captured at Greensboro, indeed they did get his gold." On May 22nd following the capture of Jefferson Davis, Mary worried: "Poor Pres. Davis, we have seen the particulars of his capture and that of his family in Georgia. He said that he never would be taken, but would die fighting but he was surprised and taken before he had time to offer any resistance. I am so much afraid they will hang him, and then oh! what will we do! That will be the saddest loss for our poor, ruined, oppressed country."

With the disruption of lines of communication, even by April 22nd, a week after Lincoln's death, news of the assassination was garbled and unconfirmed in many parts of the South—certainly in Warrenton. "It is reported that Lincoln is dead," Mary wrote, "but I don't know whether to believe it or not. They say that he was at Ford's theatre in Washington and in a part of the play that Booth had to have a pistol, he loaded it and shot Lincoln. Another account says that while they were all enjoying the entertainment and triumphing over Lee's surrender suddenly the gas was all turned out and a promiscuous shooting and stabbing took place during which Lincoln was killed and Staunton and his son and Seward wounded. We saw a *Richmond Whig* last night of the 14th which said that Sec. Seward was in a very critical condition, could not take solid food but had to be kept alive with stimulants. They feared he would have erysipelas from his injuries. It did not mention how he was injured, but I presume he was in reality wounded at the theatre."

Three days later, Mary continued her distorted account of Lincoln's assassination. "The report of Lincoln's death is confirmed. It is not thought now that Booth killed him. Some one stabbed him in his box at the theatre.... The general feeling here seems to be one of sorrow at his death for the people think that old Andy Johnson will treat us worse than Lincoln. Seward and his son also were stabbed the same night Seward Jr. died, but his old Daddy after getting so low down that he had erysipelas and had to be kept alive with stimulants is actually *getting well*!"

Southerners, naturally, had little love for Lincoln. He was a Northerner and his Emancipation Proclamation had, in theory, attempted to deprive them of their chattel property. For four years the Southern press had savagely vilified Lincoln in editorials and cartoons. Now to hear of Lincoln's being eulogized in impassioned panegyrics throughout the North was a bit more than many Southerners could tolerate. Mary and her family were no exception. After perusing a copy of the *New York Herald*, an infuriated Mary fumed in her May 2nd diary entry: "I never heard so much praise bestowed on any mortal in my life as he had lavished on him. Nearly every house in New York was draped with mourning in every conceivable way and I know the people did not feel sorry at all scarcely for in describing the decorations of the houses, after saying how agonizing the grief of everyone was, it said that admiring crowds surrounded one house that was draped very artistically. That showed how much the crowd was mourning their loss. Some of the mottoes on their houses I think were really blasphemous. I recollect that one was 'Fear not Abraham, I am thy shield,' actually a quotation from the Bible. One of the ministers said in his sermon that Lincoln's murderer was worse than Jesus Christ's! Another motto was 'Servant of God, well done; thy course is finished thy victory won.' Another 'Too great for earth, thou has gone to thy rest in Heaven and left a nation weeping.' And he was not even a professor of religion that ever we heard of. 'In mourning tears the nation's grief is spent; mankind has lost a friend and we a President.' It sounds like they were ridiculing him I think."

Mary prided herself that a fast day for Lincoln on the first of June "was not observed at all here. On the contrary we all dined as heartily as possible. I am certain I never ate so much at one meal before."

Rumors were scarcely limited to Lincoln's assassination and Booth's capture. Word was circulated that Mrs. Robert E. Lee had died; Mary, however, was skeptical. "The dear old lady has been an invalid, confined to her bed a long time, and I wouldn't be surprised any day to hear of her death. Yet I do not believe it now for it was traced back to Sherman and he had no business taking her name on his lips much less knowing anything about her death."

Financial concerns kept the Whites and most Southerners on tenterhooks. Confederate currency had become absolutely worthless, not even worth digging up if it had been buried, good only for pretend-money for children to use in "playing store." Barter became a practical solution. Mary despairingly noted the problems created by a valueless currency in day-to-day living: "The people in town stopped selling anything for Confederate money some days ago. It is not received at all. This morning at Church there was a collection taken up, but although the plates were running over with bank bills, it was all not worth a cent. I don't know what people are to do for very few have any specie of consequence. The only good part about our being in the Yankee lines is, that after they get trains running all over the country we can hear from father. It is indeed 'an ill wind that blows nobody good!'"

In her concluding diary meditations Mary revealed a rather gloomy, pessimistic outlook for the future: "President Johnson has issued a proclamation, confiscating nearly every Southerner's property, and after their property is confiscated, they will not be even allowed to vote. Father is included in one of the classes he specifies as subject to confiscation. I don't expect to have a home long. Holden is now Provisional Gov. of N. Ca."[126] In one of her last entries Mary became increasingly worried about their property being confiscated. An officer sent to investigate their situation met with appeals from the Whites' friends and agreed to wait to present their case to higher authorities. "We have heard nothing of him since," Mary wrote, "and hope that 'higher authority' was kind and generous enough to let us have our home."

Coupled with financial burdens, the Whites and other Southerners lived in mortal fear of the bummers, the stragglers from both armies that plagued the countryside, conjuring up deep-seated anxieties that became constant companions night and day. "Bummers are doing terribly all around here," Mary reported. On May 5th she told her diary: "I saw a bummer pass yesterday. Two citizens caught him with his gun cocked ready to shoot a man. [Some]one rode up, knocked his gun out of his hand, and brought him to town and put him in jail.... This bummer had been to Bob Speed's and destroyed all his furniture etc. He said there was about a dozen more scattered around here."

"We have been in constant dread of raids through this part of the country for the last month," Mary despaired. "At one time we were almost sure that Sherman's army would pass through here, but now he is after poor Johnston, and I reckon will hardly turn out of his course to come here. Stragglers from Lee's army and paroled prisoners are passing at all hours of the day and night." It was great good news, however, when Mary announced: "Mr. Arrington and three other paroled prisoners arrived here yesterday evening."

At least a modicum of the Whites' apprehensiveness concerning the devastation being wrought by the fiendish gangs of ruffians who were roaming the countryside was temporarily assuaged by Willie's good fortune in securing a guard for their home. On May 3, 1865, Mary breathed a sigh of relief: "Yesterday, afternoon late Willie brought us a guard from down town. The corporal who posted the guard also stayed here. They were both very decent, well-behaved men.... Neither of them seemed to exult over us. They thought we were a noble people to fight them as long as we have and both agreed in saying that Gen. Lee was the greatest general in the world."

Now and then, touches of humor helped relieve the tension rife in a world gone out of control. It was a scene of merriment according to Mary's diary when "one of the guard's horses was put in our stable and sometime during the night, one of our horses reached over from his stall and bit the Yankee horse and pulled out part of his mane. Next morning, when it was found out, Cousin Kate Lewis, who is full of fun, said in a most demure way to the Yankee, 'I hope you will excuse our horse. He didn't know the war was over.'"[127]

Although a guard served to ward off wanton destruction by bummers at the Whites' home, more isolated areas suffered repeated raids by the diabolical thugs. The home of Mary's Aunt Bet was the scene of one of the confrontations that terrorized the area's residents: "Two bummers went out to Aunt Bet's yesterday, just before sunset, beastly drunk, carried a jug of whiskey with them. She with her children and the teacher crept out at the back door when they were in the front porch, and went over to Uncle Joe's. After supper she sent a servant over to see what they were about. He came back and said they were making dreadful threats, said they had a large body of men who would run to them if they blew a whistle, and rushed out of the yard, he thought to get their horses. She was afraid of being found, and so about nine o'clock they went to Penny and Larry's where they spent the night and came here this morning. Uncle Hugh heard of them in the night, mustered twenty men and went after them." (Fortunately, the men left before a confrontation took place and Aunt Bet and family went into town to stay with Mary's family.)

At about the same time, Mary related the horrors of the visit of two bummers who attacked "old Mr. Ichem Bennet ... who is about seventy years old. They treated the old man very badly, threatened to kill him and plunder his house. In fact they had seized him but he twisted his wrist around some way, got away and shot one who fell dead. The other man Mr. Bennet shot at him but he does not know whether he struck him or not." Expecting the worst, Ichem was hauled into the provost marshal's office where a sympathetic officer listened to his account of the shooting and finally admitted that Ichem was right to have defended himself and, in the interest of preventing futher bloodshed, provided Ichem with a guard.

Guards helped whenever possible to curtail excess foraging and malicious destruction as tens of thousands of Union troops marched through Warrenton. On more than one occasion, Mary was awestruck. "I never saw so many men since I was born. It looked to me like a million though it was in reality only fifteen thousand." At one point (May 2nd) Mary condescendingly described the scene: "I was down to see Bettie Hunter this morning and while there I saw Gen. Howard's staff come in. They were very nice looking men but nothing to compare to our generals!" Although the guards were well behaved, according to Mary, they "look very common indeed."

Schools were canceled and curious citizens gathered on porches to watch the interminable lines of "bluecoats" parade through the town: "We had a porch full of people today to see the Yankees pass. The sight was a fine one so many men marching along so beautifully to the music with their important flags etc. Yet it was a hateful sight because they were *Yankees* and if we felt so badly seeing them pass what must have been the feelings of those who have had their *all* killed by the miserable wretches."

Southern women proudly claimed their reputation for feistiness as a badge of honor. Mary and her sister, for example, thoroughly enjoyed taunting any Union officers who happened to roam too near their home: "Just now [May 2nd] as seven or eight officers were talking here at our fence Sister ran in the parlor, threw up the window and played 'Dixie' just a loud as she could. The *gentlemen* finished their conversation and then rode on as if they did not hear her, but I know they did, for they could not have helped it to save their lives." Mary could scarcely have been surprised when one of the Union guards admitted "that the women of the South were harder to conquer than the men."

Interspersed among Mary's details of daily living were telltale diary entries that, although often brief and tangential, provided insights into the chaos that pervaded life in the South following the war. Emancipation, as might be expected, created tremendous confusion for former slave owners as well as newly freed blacks. At the first opportunity, hosts of blacks immediately distanced themselves from their former masters; others sought, at least temporarily, the security of food and shelter provided by their former owners. "Eight of Uncle Joe's [servants] left him last night," Mary told her diary. "A good many servants from this county have gone off on mules and horses. I don't think any of ours will go though." Mary noted, "We are all very willing for them to go if they want to, but as certain as they do they will repent it." Later when the Union officers came to inform the blacks of their freedom, a realistic Mary worried that unskilled "servants" who formerly had been so entirely dependent upon their masters might have a difficult time eking out a living on their own.

As the armies passed through Warrenton, scores of servants gathered up their possessions in anticipation of following the army to freedom and a well-earned life of leisure. On May 2nd Mary explained: "Capt. Duncan made the darkeys a speech Sunday. They had collected down town in crowds to see the Yankees, but when they were called in the courtyard to hear the speech some thought they were to be enlisted and made off as fast as possible. Others who were in wagons, whipped their mules and went off in fine style. Capt. Duncan told the servants that they would be free in a short time, but in the meanwhile they must work as they had always been doing, that it was out of the question to think of following the army for it would be impossible to feed them." It was a discouraged, despondent crowd that trudged back to work to await further instructions from their benefactors.

Northern entrepreneurs were quick to seize upon opportunities in the Southland—in the cotton fields or in merchandising—and later in politics. In Warrenton, Mary told of the army's passing through the town on Wednesday; the next day, the guard left, and on Friday two Northerners came in "to set up store."

Amid all the turmoil of racial strife, minstrel shows drew huge crowds at the Thespian Club. Financially ruined owners sold their homes to incoming carpetbaggers; other Southerners casting a dismal look around them headed to Europe, to the North, to Mexico, or to the vast, untamed prairies of the West to begin life anew.

Loyal Southerners smoldered over the Federals' insistence that church prayers no longer be offered up for President Davis. Mary was exceedingly disappointed that their minister, the Reverend Hodges, did not pray for the president on Sunday, April 30th. "We were glad after we heard that he omitted to pray for Davis that we did not go [to church]. I don't think he ought to have left out the prayer for there were no Yankees here then and he hadn't been forbidden to pray for him."

Because of the threat of further violence from bummers and stragglers, Warrenton, as did most Southern towns, set up local defense companies. "Willie joined it," Mary noted, adding, "They all had to take the oath." This was the loathsome oath of allegiance to the Federal government, abhorred by Southerners who resisted renouncing all their Southern loyalties and pledging faithfulness to the government they had so recently and so fiercely contested. "I hear an officer will be down this week to administer it to all the rest."

Buried treasure hidden for months or years from Yankee eyes was exhumed as shocked owners tallied up their losses: "Mr. Arrington had a large box disinterred which had been buried two months ago to keep it from the Yankees, and I never in my life have seen such a sight. The box contained two watches, all Sister's jewelry and silver. The silver, every piece was as black as tar, every jewelry case, and everything of the sort, decayed and fallen to pieces. And there never was such an odor scarcely.... Everything in it was dripping with water, the watches full, Sister's handsome set of coral jewelry with nearly all the color taken out.... They have been rubbing two days on some of the silver with preparations and have succeeded in getting a few things bright again."

News of Father at Last!

Finally on May 10, 1865, a circuitous report confirmed that Mary's father was alive and well. The family was euphoric, for even second- or third-hand reports were far better than having had almost no word for over five months: "Mrs. Willie Palmer wrote to Mother the other day to let her know that Mrs. Carter had received a letter from her husband in Liverpool, dated March 10th, which said that Father was not in Liverpool, but was very well. We were delighted to hear, for the last news we got was a letter from Cousin Charlotte, written Dec. 24, 1864."

At long last, during the latter part of May, more than seven months after Mr. White's departure for England, the Whites "received a letter from Father a few days ago dated Mar. 15th. He wrote only a page and sent that open to a friend in New York to be sent by truce but the friend contrived [to send] it to Cousin Andrew somehow, in Petersburg, who sent [it]out to us. We were *delighted* to get it, especially since it contained the good news that he and John were well. He said he was boarding with Cousin Charlotte and she was as kind and affectionate as a daughter."[128]

Apparently, not only the White family, but even Governor Vance had been unable to communicate with Mr. White for several months. The insurmountable intricacies of communication at the war's end are underscored in a page taken from the *War of the Rebellion* records. Following the capture of Wilmington, Governor Vance had directed instructions to Mary's father in care of the Collie Company in London informing him of the capture of Wilmington and "the consequent stoppage of our blockade-running business.... Nothing remains," the governor advised, "but to close up our affairs as completely as possible and wait for a change.... Our goods on hand, whether in Europe or the islands, I leave to you to dispose of in any way deemed best...." The directive continued, "Not being able to export any more cotton, of course, it becomes us to exercise the most rigid economy." The governor hoped that Mary's father would keep his own expenses to a minimum and would be able to collect a thousand pounds sterling apparently owed the state from the Confederate government for freight brought in on the *Advance*. John's family was well, the governor noted, but admitted that he had not heard from John himself since Halifax.[129]

Mary's final entries in her 1864-1865 diary seemed to indicate that the members of the White household were attempting to get on with their lives. For the moment, Mary was experiencing a short hiatus from school: "I don't go to school now. Several of the girls have some eruption called, by the doctors 'prurigo,' but it is so much like the itch that Mother was afraid for us to go any longer. I have school a short time every day, hear Kate and Sue their lessons, and let Sue spell a little. They don't seem to have much *respect* for their teacher," Mary confessed, "don't get the lessons I give them unless they think proper, but I get along very well with them."[130]

And with this somber note Mary's "wartime" diary concluded. There was a postscript, however, by Mary (then Mrs. E. R. Beckwith) that was penned many years later, in 1930, from her home in Petersburg, Virginia, when she was over eighty years old: "I seem to have stopped the diary very suddenly. If I ever wrote any more just then, the leaves must have been scattered, as well as dry in all the vicissitudes of all these years. I really had no thought when I wrote it, of ever keeping any of it, but somehow it just seems to have survived. Father and John came home soon after though for I have Father's passport dated London 1865, written in French and signed by Charles Francis Adams."

Perhaps Mary's father had begun to feel hopeful after President Johnson's proclamation of May 29, 1865. According to the president's proclamation almost all former Confederates who would take the oath of allegiance to the Federal government were to receive amnesty and pardons and their property was to be restored. Unfortunately, persons worth twenty thousand dollars or more, a class which one assumes included Mary's father, were exempted from the amnesty. Soon, however, President Johnson began issuing special pardons "in wholesale lots." Many former Rebels could obtain pardons by simply applying to the president in person, or even by mail. By the early part of 1866, Johnson had abandoned his plans for confiscation.

On May 29, 1865, Johnson also announced his reconstruction plans for the creation in the South of loyal state governments. In North Carolina, W. W. Holden was appointed provisional governor and ordered to set about reorganizing the state government and writing a constitution, devised by loyal delegates, which would be acceptable to the United States government. Needless to say, this posed immense problems for Johnson, Holden, and North Carolina.

A Memorable Visit

Surely one of the most important events in Mary's postwar years, a description of which perhaps became detached from the dairy and lost over the years (or perhaps was never recorded by Mary herself) was the memorable visit to Warrenton of Gen. Robert E. Lee and his daughter, Agnes. Several versions, although not in Mary's hand, reveal a fascinating story. In the spring of 1870, as Mary was returning to Warrenton from a visit to Petersburg, she was met at the depot by her brother Willie. As she alighted from the train, Mary excitedly whispered in her brother's ear: "Brother Willie, General Lee is on the train and going to get off here!" And, indeed, it was the famous general who, en route to Savannah, was stopping to visit the grave of his daughter Anne Carter Lee. (During the war, in 1862, Anne, her three sisters [Mary, Mildred, and Agnes], and their mother had been spending the summer at Jones Springs [Warren County, White Sulphur Springs] in the hope of obtaining at least some temporary relief for Mrs. Lee's persistently painful rheumatism. Their stay took a tragic turn when suddenly Anne became extremely ill with what doctors diagnosed as typhoid fever and within weeks had died.)

Eight years later, in 1870, the Lees, eager to avoid unnecessary publicity, had made no advance preparations for their graveside visit. Without a moment's hesitation, Willie approached the Lees, welcomed them to Warrenton, and begged them to accept the hospitality of his parents during their stay in Warrenton. One can scarcely imagine the surprise and delight of the White family as Willie opened the front door and announced, "General Lee and his daughter are going to be our guests for the next few days."

Mary's sister, Sue White Pretlow, later recalled: "The only vehicle available at that hour to take them to Warrenton was, Mr. O. P. Shell's hack, it was covered with black oil cloth and on one side was painted in large white letters—Fare 50 cents Divines less.... That old hack was glorified after that night. Mr. Shell would not have changed places with the king upon his throne, as his team jogged over the three miles of rough clay road into Warrenton with General Lee as his passenger."[131]

Warrenton, of course, was agog over the news. Word spread like wildfire, and by the next morning every Warrenton garden was stripped of its blossoms, which were heaped in the carriage to accompany the general on his visit to Anne's gravesite. The general had requested privacy and solitude, and in conforming to his wishes, Warrenton citizens lined the streets in a heartfelt but mute tribute to their great leader.[132]

Agnes Lee, in writing to her mother (unable to accompany her husband and daughter because of her delicate health), told of their gracious reception in Warrenton. Following their night at the Whites' home, the Lees "drove with Captain White's horses to the cemetery. Mrs. White gave me a quantity of beautiful white hyacinths, which she said were for you, too." Apparently, both the general and Agnes felt "It was a great satisfaction to be there again." In her letters Agnes repeatedly referred to the kindness of the Warrenton residents, noting, "Indeed, I wish you could travel with papa, to see the affection and feeling shown toward him everywhere." General Lee, in a letter to his wife, confessed, "My visit to dear Annie's grave was mournful, yet soothing to my feelings, and I was glad to have the opportunity of thanking the kind friends for their care of her while living and their attention to her since her death."[133]

A Return to Normalcy?

With the passage of time social life began to revive in Warrenton. A theater group was formed, a reading group emerged, and life began to assume some degree of normalcy. Regarding the "Book Club," Elizabeth Pitchford admitted that although she was a faithful attendee, "...it's done to meet together to amuse themselves. There is not much reading done."[134] The demonic activities of the Ku Klux Klan, however, manifested themselves in Warrenton. Klan warnings were posted about town and ominous looking graves were dug in an attempt to frighten Negroes as they made their way to the polls. The blacks, however, refused to be intimidated by the Klan and exercised their franchise to advantage by electing one of their own to the state Senate and two to the state House of Representatives.

The frigid reception accorded the Yankee troops of occupation prevailed in Warrenton as well as throughout the South. One widow reaped the contempt of most of her friends and neighbors as she injudiciously befriended a Federal officer. Some detractors thought she "had set her cap for the captain." Mary was outraged by her conduct, "I wish he would take her off with him, but before she goes I should like for her to be given a good coat of tar and feathers, for she richly deserves it." In time, perhaps Warrenton's size or perhaps simply the genial nature of her people resulted in a more amicable reception of Yankee soldiers than in most other areas. Yankee merchants, or more precisely Yankee goods and supplies, were welcomed by the townspeople. The postwar years, however, took their toll on the town. By 1870 Warrenton's prewar population of 1,520 totaled only 941, and the county's farmland, valued at $3,338,899 ten years earlier, was reduced in value to $1,608,848.[135]

Although the exact date is unclear, by at least 1872 Mary resumed a sporadic diary keeping. Unfortunately, only a few pages survive of Mary White's diary written in 1872 during the postwar years, when she resided with her parents in the family home of Ingleside in Warrenton, North Carolina. From these brief pages, however, it is clear that the family Mary described in her earlier writing remained a close-knit group. In numbers that would stagger most twentieth century readers, Mary's family welcomed friends and family members for overnight, weekend, or month-long visits. Mary's sister, Hannah (married to Samuel Peter Arrington, of Petersburg, Virginia), made a yearly summer visit to Warrenton. In her September 24, 1872, diary entry Mary lamented: "We are all blue today—the house has a very deserted and desolate look. Sister, with her five children and two nurses & Pattie and Sid Watson, left this morning. The latter two have only been with us a week." (Hannah's family had apparently been with them for over three months. Pattie and Sidney Watson were the children of Hannah's sister-in-law.)

Even the Whites' apparent houseful was augmented by additional friends and relatives, who merely visited for a week or two. Mary remarked: "This has been a very pleasant summer. Kate White was with me some weeks. Virdie and Cousin Nannie were out a while too. Cousin Sallie with her three little ones were here too.... We had a house full all summer. It seems to me that almost everybody's friends from a distance came in to see them this summer. We begin to look forward to next June as bringing sister and the children. Mother and Father say that as long as they live they will claim them every summer. So far they have come, but this is only the third summer since they moved to Petersburg."

In the few surviving pages, Mary recorded her duties of "waiting" (serving as a bridesmaid in a wedding party), helping with the preparation of food for their flood of company and her parents' thirty-fourth wedding anniversary dinner, and participating in church activities and family birthday dinners. In November, once again, Mary's diary entries stopped, perhaps lost or destroyed, or perhaps to be discovered years from now in the dark dusty recesses of someone's old trunk. We do know, however, that Mary met, probably during one of her frequent visits with her sister Hannah in Petersburg, and married Edmund Ruffin Beckwith, the grandson of the famous Edmund Ruffin, a Rebel zealot who had fired one of the first shots of the war at Fort Sumter. The Beckwiths made their home in Petersburg, Virginia, and were the parents of three children.

Epilogue

In summary, of about 1,300 attempts made by 300 steamers to run the blockades, 1,000 were successful. The Federals captured about 136 ships, and they or the ships' captains were responsible for destroying about 85 more. According to Wise, the average blockade runner made a little over two round trips.[136]

In a final accounting years later, Governor Vance announced in a speech, delivered in Baltimore in February of 1885, that he had collected and distributed via blockade-running steamers, taking out cotton and bringing in supplies: "large quantities of machinery supplies, 60,000 pairs of hand cards, 10,000 grain scythes, 200 barrels bluestone for the wheat growers, leather and shoes for 250,000 pairs, 50,000 blankets, gray wool cloth for at least 250,000 suits of uniforms, 12,000 overcoats (ready made), 2,000 best Enfield rifles (with 100 rounds of fixed ammunition), 100,000 pounds of bacon, 500 sacks of coffee for hospital use, $50,000 worth of medicines at gold prices, large quantities of lubricating oils, besides minor supplies of various kinds for the charitable institutions of the State."[137] Held in trust for the holders of the warrants on which the supplies had been purchased were 11,000 bales of cotton and 100,000 barrels of rosin. Although part of the cotton was destroyed before the end of the war, Governor Vance declared, "the remainder, amounting to several thousand bales, was captured, after peace was declared, by certain officers of the Federal army."[138]

Both Fraser, Trenholm and Company and John Fraser and Company of Charleston were forced into bankruptcy following the defeat of the Confederacy and the Federal Government's refusal to pay off the debts of the Confederacy. The English Alexander Collie Company, with which Mary White's father had worked so closely, also lost immense sums of money. Anticipating a Confederate victory, this company had put its profits into new ships and North Carolina cotton bonds. Furthermore, there were reportedly 16,000 bales of Collie cotton that were confiscated at the war's end by the Federals. When neither the British Navy nor the Brazilian government expressed any interest in purchasing its vessels, they were finally sold to private interests.[139]

Mary White's observations about her ship, the *Advance*, and the other ships anchored in the Cape Fear River during their stay in Wilmington and Smithville, were accurate and informative. They presented a colorful picture of the hazards encountered in running the blockade:

the anxieties of the officers, the crew and the passengers; the problems of tides, enemy cruisers, the weather, fog, sand bars, yellow fever, drunken officers, and accidents; and the shortages and uncomfortable accommodations endured by the travelers at Wilmington and at Smithville (now known as Southport). The ships Mary described were real ships, some of which survived the war, like the *Helen*, the *Little Hattie*, the *Old Dominion*, and the *Virginia*. Others met a sad fate: the *Mary Celeste* (or *Mary Celestia*) sank while leaving St. George harbor, and the *Hope* and the *Advance* were captured.

It should also be noted that captains, pilots, and seamen were not the only courageous souls aboard the blockade-running ships. A goodly number of women displayed their mettle and resourcefulness when the vessels on which they were passengers came under fire. At least one skilled blockade runner in later years doffed his cap to some of the South's courageous women: "The devotion of the women of the Confederacy, and their heroic conduct during our struggle for existence, will always be held in grateful remembrance by the veterans of the Lost Cause. In my career as a blockade runner I chanced to see several instances of nerve displayed by them, which would do honor to an old soldier." The captain told of one woman who refused to be relegated to her cabin and remained on the bridge throughout the enemy gunfire: "She never left the bridge until we were safely anchored under the guns of Fort Caswell, and I think she was the coolest person on board the ship."[140]

Capt. John Wilkinson, reputed to be one of the ablest of the blockade runners, also had some kind words to say about women in his memoirs: "Indeed we rarely made a trip either way without as many as could be accommodated, and many ladies among them. My observation of the conduct of the fair sex, under trying and novel circumstances, has convinced me that they face inevitable dangers more bravely and with more composure than men. I have frequently seen a frail, delicate woman standing erect and unflinching upon the deck, as the shells were whistling and bursting over us, while her lawful protector would be cowering 'under the lee' of a cotton bale. I pay this humble tribute of admiration to the sex, but a cynical old bachelor, to whom I once made the observation, replied that in his opinion their insatiable curiosity prevailed even over their natural fears!"[141]

Another runner, Capt. Usina, expressed similar sentiments about the bravery of the female sex when he related his experiences with a bridal couple who were passengers on his ship, which had been selected to transport important dispatches to Europe. During the ship's uneasy maneuvering through the enemy gunfire, the groom had secreted himself on a load of cotton "while the bride was standing quietly nearby." As Capt. Usina wrote, "I said to her: 'Are you not frightened, Mrs. B?'

'Yes. I am frightened,' she said; 'This is terrible, but we are in the hands of the Almighty.' You can imagine the respect I entertained ever after for the gentleman who, with such an example before him, displayed such arrant cowardice."[142]

In 1862 the famous Capt. John Newland Maffitt, one of the most famous of the blockade runners, sent his daughter Florie from Nassau to Wilmington aboard the *Nassau*. As a result of the captain's inexperience, the ship was captured by a Federal cruiser under the command of Capt. George Walker. During the shelling prior to the takeover of the ship, an undaunted Florie surveyed the fireworks from a hazardous position on the open deck, that is, until ordered below deck to her cabin where she continued observing the action through her porthole. The crew later confessed that Florie even urged the captain not to surrender. Told that the ship's cargo of tons of powder could explode at a moment's notice, she "exclaimed with tears in her eyes that her father would prefer her being blown up rather than have the steamer fall into Yankee hands." Following the ship's capture, Florie was sent to New York where Capt. Walker, commander of the Federal ship that had seized the *Nassau*, helped secure her release. Capt. Walker, it turned out, had been an old shipmate of Florie's father before the war.[143]

A few days after the Whites' aborted departures, the *Lynx* (cited by Mary in her September 4th entry), as she was attempting to run the blockade through New Inlet, became the scene of considerable excitement when she was spotted and chased by three Federals. A passenger on board, Mrs. Louis DeRosset, later described the harrowing chase: "Immediately the sky was illuminated with rockets, and broadside upon broadside, volley upon volley, was poured upon us. The captain put me in the wheelhouse for safety. I had scarcely taken my seat when a ball passed three inches above my head, wounding the man at the wheel next to me; a large piece of the wheelhouse knocked me violently on the head." In very short order a barrage of gunfire had perforated the ship below the water line, and suddenly the captain found the *Lynx* sinking beneath him. Capt. Reed immediately made for the shore; however, the prospects of saving Mrs. DeRosset and her infant in the rough waters of the night looked bleak indeed. As the crew frantically scrambled to lower the lifeboats, the tiny vessels crashed against the side of the *Lynx*, and then hit the water with a splash that nearly inundated them. The seamen might have become unhinged, but not Mrs. DeRosset, who calmly watched for the precise moment, jumped into a seat in one of the lifeboats in its precipitous descent into the inky waters, and amid the pitching and rolling of the little boat, bravely stood up and with widespread arms caught her baby tossed to her by a seaman from a deck ten feet above.

Greatly impressed with her ultimate composure, the crew sent up three hearty cheers as she set off in the eerie darkness. Fortunately, light from the burning ship (abandoned and destroyed to prevent the Federals from appropriating the ship or her cargo) helped guide the little boat to shore where after a long wet, cold, and hungry wait, Mrs. DeRosset and her baby were rescued and returned by ambulance to Wilmington.[144]

What Georgiana Gholson Walker feared would be a perilous trip down the Cape Fear River from Wilmington and through the blockaders, as she traveled to join her husband (a Confederate States agent) in Bermuda, turned out to be an amazingly uneventful trip. As she explained in her diary, her fears about the voyage vanished as she and her three children watched the preparations for sailing. "The port holes were all closed, & blankets hung over them, the sky light covered, the lights all extinguished, except one which burned dimly in the Captain's room; the letters & papers & Government Dispatches were all collected & deposited in a weighted bag…. The captain was very considerate in his attention to me, & not only many minutes after we were fairly off, he came down to the saloon door to say, 'We have passed *one* blockader, Madame.' Shortly after, he reported another & another, & after the lapse of about two hours, I had the satisfaction of hearing that the entire fleet had been passed & that we were, therefore, comparatively safe, for which I felt profoundly grateful; & my mind was at once possessed with the happy vision of soon beholding the light of my Husband's face again." A rough passage and seasickness marred the voyage; however, four days later, four happy Walkers safely docked at Bermuda.[145]

On the shore at Fort Fisher, a fearless Daisy Lamb surveyed the hairbreadth escapes as the ships darted in and out of the River, and watched in awe the pyrotechnic displays that lighted the skies as the Federals opened fire on a runner and the guns of Fort Fisher responded with protective shelling. Mary White would probably have heard about Daisy's husband, Col. William Lamb, the commandant of Fort Fisher, who had transformed a weak, almost defenseless fort into the "largest and mightiest coastal fortress of the Confederacy," a fortification often referred to as "the Gibraltar of the South."[146] She might also have heard about Daisy, who renounced New England in favor of rebeldom following her marriage to Colonel Lamb, and succeeded in earning accolades for her coolness under fire and her gracious hospitality to the scores of Confederate officials, blockade runners, and newspaper correspondents who visited the Fort.

Although Mrs. Lamb's father begged her to seek safety for herself and her children with him in the North during the war, Mrs. Lamb returned to Providence, Rhode Island, only briefly before securing permission from Secretary Stanton to pass through the lines to rejoin her husband. At first, "home" consisted of one room atop the pilot's house adjacent to the fort, until finally a small house, called "The Cottage," about a mile's distance from her husband's headquarters, was built for them. Wary of the ever-present threat of an attack by the Federals, whereby the Lambs would be forced to make a speedy departure, Daisy kept their eating utensils, furniture, and personal possessions to a bare minimum. Life for the Lambs was punctuated by countless dignitaries, who came to confer with Col. Lamb, and even unexpected dinner guests were made welcome on a moment's notice. In the early years of the war, Mrs. Lamb's cupboards were bare, as were most cupboards in the Confederacy; however, once the blockade runners partook of Mrs. Lamb's charming dinners, they flooded her with delicacies brought in on their future trips. Often homesick and lonely without female companionship Daisy dodged the shot that sometimes rained down around her and courageously remained with her husband right up to the time of the Federal fleet's appearance and the attack on Fort Fisher.[147]

A host of famous people passed through Wilmington and the blockade including the mother of James Whistler. In 1863, thanks to the help of Governor Vance, Mrs. Whistler obtained passage to England and, while there visiting her son in Chelsea, she posed for the painting we know as "Whistler's Mother." Even John Wilkes Booth was said to have run the blockade several times en route to Canada. Although he did not, of course, venture through the blockade, President Davis visited Wilmington to inspect the city's defenses in November of 1863.

Two notorious spies, Rose Greenhow and Belle Boyd, both attempting secret service work for the Confederacy in Europe, passed through the blockade at Wilmington. Had Mary and her family been delayed a few more weeks in Wilmington, they surely would have been caught up in the details of Rose Greenhow's death. Carrying secret dispatches for the Confederate government and two thousand dollars in gold, Rose attempted to return from Europe aboard the *Condor*. As the ship was approaching Wilmington, a severe storm and Yankee gunfire ran the *Condor* aground. Rose, hoping to avoid capture by the Yankees, leaped into a lifeboat that unfortunately capsized in the choppy waters of the channel. Rose was drowned. Her elaborate funeral in Wilmington commemorated the passing of one of the Confederacy's most enterprising heroines.

Another courageous Confederate spy, Belle Boyd, on May 8, 1864, endeavored to make it through the blockade. The record of her experiences aboard the *Greyhound* as it attempted to put out to sea had a familiar ring to it. The decks were overloaded with bales of cotton; lookouts scanned the river for the approach of the enemy; there was no talk above a whisper. By morning, however, the Federals had spotted them, and the chase was on. In order to pick up speed, bale after bale of cotton was dumped overboard, as well as a keg containing twenty-five thousand dollars in gold. In short order, however, the *Greyhound* was overtaken and boarded by a handsome Union officer, Samuel Hardinge. Thereafter, a fascinating story of romance enfolded with the courtship and and marriage of Belle and her Union "captor."[148]

Without question the blockade runners were vital to the longevity of the Confederacy. One writer called running the blockade "perhaps the most successful, large-scale campaign attempted by the South."[149] Some historians estimate that the Union blockaders' inability to curtail the activities of the blockade runners prolonged the war by one or even two years. For the captains and crew, there were fortunes to be made, and as the famous blockade runner Hobart Pasha confessed, "there was a thrilling and glorious excitement about the work."[150] Indeed, blockade running constituted high adventure that appeared to have fascinated, at the same time that it frightened, captains, their crews, and their passengers as well.

The Fate of the Ships Cited in Mary's Diary

The *Annie* became a part of the U.S. Navy when it was purchased from prize court after it ran aground near the Cape Fear River on November 1, 1864. Prior to her capture the *Annie* had made it through the blockade sixteen times. The *Annie*, heading for Nassau, was carrying "540 bales of cotton (weighing 700 pounds per bale), 30 tons of pressed tobacco, and 14 casks of spirits of turpentine." In addition, the ship had $50,000 in gold and a number of Confederate bonds. The gold and the bonds were jettisoned overboard when the officers from the capturing ship, the *Wilderness*, boarded the *Annie* to claim their prize. Needless to say, the Yankee officers were enraged when they discovered their loss of the $50,000 (Horner, 113–126; Wise, 288; Carr, 178).

The *City of Petersburg*, owned by the Virginia Importing and Exporting Company, survived the war (Wise, 293).

The *Coquette* continued to operate as a part of the J. R. Anderson Company until December 1865 (Wise, 294).

The *Elsie* was captured on September 5, 1864, near Cape Fear (Wise, 297).

The *Helen* survived the war (Wise, 304).

The *Hope* was 281 feet by 35 feet and on October 22, 1864, was captured near the Cape Fear River (Wise, 305).

The *Little Hattie* survived the war. About two months after the Whites' disappointing adventures on the Cape Fear, the *Little Hattie* narrowly escaped capture as she made a daring, daylight dash into New Inlet through a cordon of eleven blockaders. Her escape was a humiliating embarrassment to the Yankee blockaders, and served to prove that the blockade runners had not lost their talent for evasiveness (Carr, 27–30; Wise, 309).

The *Lillian*, or *Lilian*, was captured on August 24, 1864, near Wilmington, and became part of the U.S. Navy after being purchased from Prize Court. The *Lillian*, as a U.S. Navy ship, was involved in the attack on Fort Fisher (Wise, 309). Both the *Lillian* and the *Owl* at one time were commanded by the famous John N. Maffitt, who resigned from the U.S. Navy to cast his lot with the South, where he had spent his boyhood.

The *Lynx* was leaving New Inlet Bar when sighted by Yankee blockaders and fired on. In an attempt to turn back, she ran aground and was burned by her crew on September 25, 1864 (Wise, 310, and Horner, 224).

The *Mary Bowers* ran into the wreck of the *Georgiana* while attempting to enter Charleston Harbor and sank on August 31, 1864 (Wise, 312, and Horner, 223).

The *Mary Celestia* sank in St. George Harbor, Bermuda, September 26, 1864, after running into a rock (Wise, 312).

The *Old Dominion* survived the war and was returned to England (Wise, 222).

The *Owl*, a blockade runner for the Confederate government, survived the war (Wise, 315).

The *Santiago de Cuba* captured the *Advance* in September of 1864 and also was on the scene in the capture of Fort Fisher.

The *Tallahassie*, formerly the *Atlanta*, was sold to the Confederate navy in July 1864. Renamed *Olustee* in October 1864, and two months later renamed *Chameleon*, it was used at various times as a blockade runner and at other times was converted to a commerce raider. The ship survived the war and was given to the U.S. by the courts in 1866 (Wise, 155, 199, 289).

The *Will of the Wisp* sank in February of 1865 outside of Galveston.

❡ *Two* ❧

Poverty and Pride

Yes! Everything is gone, but poverty and pride—*poor handmaidens—for with our poverty* our pride—increases.

—Josie LeConte

Prologue

Few Southern families were left unscarred by the Civil War; death, destruction, and deprivation were all too frequent visitors. Most Southerners, of course, were farmers, small yeoman farmers interspersed with a limited number of large plantation owners. Much of the Civil War research on women, therefore, has centered on the lives and work of wives, mothers, daughters, and sisters of men engaged in agriculture. One group of Southerners often overlooked by Civil War historians are academicians who floundered when their colleges closed during the war and who during the chaotic postwar years, suffered many of the economic difficulties experienced by their fellow countrymen.

The war exacted a heavy toll on Southern schools and colleges, and most were disbanded as the war progressed for want of teachers and students. In short order the supply of teachers became severely depleted as thousands of teachers resigned their positions to volunteer (or be drafted) for service with the Confederate army. As for students, whole classes laid aside their books and left en masse to join the men on the battlefront. South Carolina College at Columbia, for example, closed its doors in 1862. Enrollment had dwindled to only forty or fifty students in the spring of 1862 and by June of that year the entire student body had left. Among South Carolina College's faculty were John and Joseph LeConte, two eminent scientists, who along with their families discovered that the upheaval of war and the chaos which followed the fighting posed serious problems for academicians as well as farmers, physicians, lawyers, and clergymen.

61

The struggle for survival, although certainly less desperate than that of many of their fellow Southerners, is vividly detailed in the letters of Mrs. John LeConte (Josie), mostly to her sister Mary (affectionately called Mollie) in the North. The collection of hand-written letters, found in the Manuscripts Division of the Bancroft Library at the University of California at Berkeley, presents yet another dimension to the study of the lives of women in the South during the 1860s. Material from Joseph LeConte's books about the demise of the Confederacy *'Ware Sherman*, his *Autobiography* and its introduction by his daughter Caroline, and his daughter Emma's diary, *When the World Ended*, all serve to help illumine Josie LeConte's letters.[1]

The distinguished LeConte brothers resided with their families in faculty housing on the College campus in Columbia. In many respects the LeContes' backgrounds, mutual interests, and neighborliness made them almost "one family." Young Johnnie, Lula, and Julian, children of John and Josie LeConte, and Emma, Sallie, and Caroline ("Carrie"), daughters of Joseph LeConte and his wife Bessie, were not only cousins but also the closest of friends. Josie's sister, Mary Graham, to whom most of Josie's letters were addressed, had come to Columbia to regain her health before the war and once the fighting started was unable to return to the North until after the war. Naturally, she would have known many of the people and places Josie referred to in her letters.

These close family ties may perhaps best be explained with a brief background check. As a teenager Josie (Eleanor Josephine Graham) had become acquainted with John LeConte, a Liberty County, Georgia, native, in New York, where he was completing his work for his M.D. at the College of Physicians and Surgeons. The couple probably met at the New York City home of John's uncle, Maj. John Eaton LeConte, living at 46 Walker Street where Josie's mother was employed as a housekeeper. Mrs. Graham, a widow of a "good background" who was in "straitened circumstances" following the death of her husband, was accompanied by her two young daughters, Josie and Mary (Mollie), and the threesome were apparently treated as members of the family.[2] In 1841, Josie, sixteen years old, and John, twenty-two, were married. The couple then returned to Georgia where John practiced medicine for about four years in Savannah before accepting a position on the faculty of Franklin College (later to become the University of Georgia). John resigned his position in 1855 and, following a short stint as a "Lecturer on Chemistry" at the College of Physicians and Surgeons in New York, returned to the South to fill the chair of Physics at South Carolina College in Columbia.

John's brother, Joseph LeConte, also a Georgia native, received his M.D. in 1845, married Caroline Elizabeth Nisbet ("Bessie") in 1847, practiced medicine for a brief time in Macon, Georgia, studied with Louis Agassiz, taught at Oglethorpe University and at the University of Georgia, and in 1857 joined his brother John on the faculty of South Carolina College.

The LeConte families were well accepted in Columbia society; friendships abounded. There were dinner parties, fairs, tableaux, neighborly visiting, faculty gatherings, intellectually stimulating programs and talks, and guests who came for overnight or for a fortnight. Josie's brother-in-law, Joseph LeConte, maintained that "The society in Columbia at that time was one of the most refined and cultivated I ever knew, making it a delightful place for my wife and family." Life was comfortable and secure, that is until the guns sounded at Fort Sumter, shattering lives and dreams and anything remotely resembling peace of mind. Students leaped to the aid of the Confederate forces, leaving books and classes and professors (those too old to enlist) in their wake.

When South Carolina College closed down in 1862, the two LeConte brothers, in support of the South, turned to various wartime scientific pursuits for the Confederate government. During the latter part of the War, both men were employed in the Confederate Niter Bureau at Columbia—John as superintendent and Joseph as chemist, both with rank and pay equivalent to that of a major in the Confederate Army.

༄

The excerpts from Josephine LeConte's letters, augmented by material from the diaries and letters of the extended LeConte family, open a window on the incredible changes taking place in the lives of Southerners as the war ended and the days of Reconstruction closed in.[3]

Following her marriage to John LeConte in 1841, Josie wholeheartedly embraced the South and its culture and unstintingly devoted herself to her family, to the promotion of her husband's career, and to the family's emergence from their wartime trials. Josie's letters serve as a bridge between the last days of the Confederacy and the tumult of the early days of the postwar era.

In Josie LeConte one sees a defiant, determined woman of the 1860s; a woman passionately dedicated to her family, her friends, and her neighbors; a spirited woman deeply committed to supporting her husband and family through "good times and bad." (Josie's niece, the zealous Emma, reflects a younger, even feistier version of her Aunt Josie.) The charm, wit, and perseverance that so characterized Josie were put to the test as she suffered the deprivations brought on by the war. She watched in horror as Columbia went up in flames around her and shuddered over the plundering and insolence of Sherman's "bummers" as they bedeviled Columbia. In the postwar world Josie struggled to secure food and clothing for herself and her family while attempting to preserve at least some vestiges of dignity and pride in a world gone mad. Josie joined the majority of Southerners in their utter abhorrence of the Union soldiers of occupation and the officials of the Freedmen's Bureau, and unreservedly concurred in the universal southern distaste for greedy carpetbaggers, the requirements of the Loyalty Oath and the compulsory prayer in Southern churches for the president of the United States.

As thousands of white Southerners, with even less provocation than the LeContes, flirted with plans to abandon the South with all its economic and racial trauma and embark on what they envisioned would be a less stressful life in Mexico or Brazil, so too did the LeContes. The upheaval of South Carolina College, the dearth of adequately prepared students caused by the war, the LeContes' financial straits and the precarious future of Josie's husband and brother-in-law's academic careers combined to prompt Josie and her family to entertain serious thoughts about relocating to Mexico.

For the most part the LeContes' problems resonated with those of most former Confederates. The LeContes' situation, however, differs considerably from most traditional postwar accounts. For the majority of Southerners living in a predominately agricultural section of America, land and labor problems became their primary postwar concerns. In contrast, both John and Joseph LeConte's problems focused on their academic futures and, thus, the support of their families. (Actually, the LeContes had inherited plantations in Georgia from which even a meager income would have helped to tide them over in emergencies. That property, however, became so entangled in labor problems that the LeContes' absentee landlord's efforts were to no avail and even a minuscule return trickled down to nil.)

Under South Carolina College's proposed postwar reorganization curriculum, the prospect of teaching elementary science and agricultural courses to ill-prepared students was anathema to the LeConte brothers, both nationally renowned scientists. Since most Southern colleges were in much the same state of turmoil as South Carolina College, a position in another Southern college offered little advantage. Northern colleges, where the LeContes would have been snapped up in an instant were it not for their Confederate sympathies and their partisan participation in the work of the Confederate Niter Bureau, closed their doors to both men. In the final analysis, it would appear that most Southerners, were they farmers, lawyers, bankers, preachers, or teachers, were suffering the same anxieties—the dire prospects of a grim, uncertain future. This then is the story of a unique emergence from the chaos of the aftermath of the war to a life of fulfillment in California, as viewed from the relatively unexplored perspective of women caught up in the academic life of their husbands and fathers.

ை

To intimate that the LeContes' problems began with the rampage of Sherman's troops through Columbia in February of 1865 would be a grave misrepresentation of their wartime deprivations, hardships, and anxieties. To say that their problems greatly escalated at the time would be far more accurate.

As the Federal troops neared Columbia in February of 1865, its residents, including both LeConte families, were well aware of the possible fate that awaited their city, considered by Northerners as the home of the "firebrands of the Confederacy." Retaliation for South Carolina's "having started the war" was sure to come. It became crucial, therefore, for the LeConte brothers to remove Confederate supplies from the Niter Bureau to prevent their being seized by Sherman's troops.

Just hours before the approach of Sherman and his men, a "stop over" that left the city a smoldering wasteland, Josie's husband, their son Johnnie, her brother-in-law Joseph LeConte, and Capt. Allen J. Green, the former commander of the military post at Columbia, upon advice from Confederate military authorities, frantically packed whatever could be gathered up from the Niter Bureau and attempted to escape before the onslaught. Along with the men went the Negroes and their families who worked on the niter plantation, as well as much of the LeConte families' clothing, linens, and silver.

No doubt Joseph LeConte spoke for his brother as well when he later wrote of their heartbreaking parting with their families in his *Autobiography*. "That was the saddest night of my life. Our imperative duty was to save, if possible, the government property in our care, and it would have been worse than useless for us to have remained, for as we were all officers, we should certainly have been taken prisoners. And yet it was hard to leave in the hands of the enemy all that we loved most tenderly. I worked all night packing, the ominous words of Mr. Davis [a Union friend] 'I fear to tell you what scenes will be enacted in Columbia,' ringing in my ears, and the solemn booming of guns giving them fearful meaning and emphasis."[4]

A wrong road, mud, and Sherman's men poised to pounce on Columbia foiled their escape and left them in the midst of the Federals and less than twenty-five miles outside of Columbia. In a long letter written on February 18, 1865, to her soldier son Julian, serving nearby with the Confederate forces, Josie recapped the sad fate of the expedition. "Oh Me! What hours of agony and suspense I have endured since you left me on the morning of the 15th," Josie anguished. "On the 16th your father left, in company with Capt. Green and your Uncle Joe carrying with them a large amount of baggage. I sent off every stitch of Lula's

and my body clothing—all the blankets towels, table linen, sheets." Josie
continued to detail a long list of pitchers, trays, bowls, curtains, and silk
dresses that had been packed off with the bureau equipment: "They had
not gone over 25 miles when they were overtaken by a party of Mor-
gan's command and turned over to the provost guard.... Your father and
brother were by the waggons keeping watch while your Uncle Joe and
Capt. Green were out scouting. The alarm being given your Uncle and
Green had time to escape but your father and brother were taken prisoners." "All our effects were then broken open, a bonfire made of all our
clothing but the valuables were all carried off," Josie told her son.[5] "Your
father had a gun put to his head and his watch demanded which he gave
up at once, but a Capt. Craft coming up took the watch from the soldier
and put it in his pocket to keep for your father. The next day your brother
was paroled, and allowed to come home. He brought with him a good
deal of the funds belonging to the Bureau and as he was leaving the camp
the officers tossed my velvet cloak to him knowing it belonged to his family." Deliriously happy over the return of her son, Josie, of course, was
beside herself with worry over the whereabouts of her husband. Despite
Johnnie's assurance to his mother that his father was being well treated,
Josie had grave doubts about her husband's release: "They try to console me that your father will soon be paroled but I have my doubts. They
[the Federals] labored so faithfully to get your Uncle and Capt. Green
and at times their escape was so miraculous that I fear they will visit their
chagrin on him."

To her family Josie bravely vowed she would not despair if only her
husband were returned—and she added with malice toward some—the
Confederates would "whip Sherman." To be sure, Emma and her family were also frantic with worry over the safety and whereabouts of Joseph
LeConte.[6]

And the Yankees Came

During the absence of both John and Joseph LeConte, William T.
Sherman and his men descended on Columbia. (Estimates put Sherman's forces at about 65,000 soldiers, who were trailed by thousands of
civilians—bummers, deserters, and renegades.) Innumerable eyewitnesses later testified as to the absolute havoc that prevailed in Columbia
that fateful night. Soldiers emboldened by vengeance, stragglers drunk
with alcohol and predisposed for mischief and violence, newly created
freedmen exulting in their instantaneous deliverance, some two or three
hundred Federal prisoners recently escaped from the enemy and eager
to retaliate for their brutal treatment, thieves, thugs and predators bent

on vandalism and villainy all combined to create a scene of terror and absolute bedlam.

Responsibility for the holocaust that leveled much of Columbia, destroying some 1,386 homes and stores and about 366 acres on February 17, 1865, has been hotly disputed over the years by generals, civilian eyewitnesses, and historians. Loyal Southerners, of course, blame "that pyromaniac Sherman and his Hellhounds." Others believe the conflagration began when Confederate authorities, as they evacuated the city, set fire to vast numbers of bales of cotton in an effort to prevent their falling into the hands of the Federals. The fires quickly spread and rapidly devoured the city.[7]

One group of eyewitnesses and numerous latter-day historians contend that the large quantities of liquor left by the departing Confederates and gleefully seized by thirsty Federals and newly emancipated blacks were essentially responsible for the drunken mayhem of the night. Still others are convinced the worst villains were the stragglers that accompanied Sherman's army. All sides do agree, however, that a violent windstorm that night helped fuel the inferno. All sides further concur that the burning of Columbia, devastation and destruction that rivaled or superseded that of Charleston and Richmond, further fueled Southerners' hatred of the already despised Yankee.[8]

Although scores of diaries and reminiscences graphically testify to Columbia's devastation, one of the most vivid descriptions (referred to only briefly in this chapter) is that written by Josie's niece Emma, daughter of Bessie and Joseph LeConte, and published under the title *When the World Ended: The Diary of Emma LeConte*. Yet another colorfully detailed report of the city's near annihilation was that of Josie's daughter Lula in a letter to her friend J. W. Walker. Lula was convinced that the conflagration "was premeditated and intentional, the soldiery went too systematically to work, there was too much 'method in their madness' to attribute to drunken fury."[9] Even Josie herself, in the following excerpts from a continuation of her February 28 letter to son Julian, gravely corroborated the myriad eyewitness accounts of the pandemonium of that fiery February night.

As Sherman's troops entered Columbia, Josie looked on contemptuously. In no time: "The stars and stripes were floating over the Old State House. In a few seconds more the same thing happened to the New [State House] but what delighted my eyes was to see their battle flag blown right in two as they attempted to raise it. The wind springing up at the same time prevented their flaunting them in our faces. With effect— the whole of Logans Corps 25 thousand men passed by our door about 4 o'clock with their various bands of music and flags." Well aware of the deprivations suffered by Confederate troops during the last months of the war, Josie registered surprise at the well fed, smartly uniformed Union troops. "I hardly ever saw a more hardy, vigorous set of men, well clothed and fine equipments in all respects."

"About six in the evening their work of destruction began," Josie reported. "The city was fired simultaneously from all points and certainly a night of more awful horrors I never passed or conceived of." For the moment Josie's fears about Julian, who was fighting with his unit just outside of Columbia, were somewhat allayed when a young sergeant stopped at the gate to tell Josie that Julian was still safe, although "the fighting was still going on when he left."

It seemed almost certain that both LeConte homes (located on the South Carolina College campus) would be consumed by the flames. Josie and Bessie's inability to obtain any word from their husbands and their mission to save the supplies of the Confederate Niter Bureau from a Yankee takeover served to compound each woman's fears for her own household. Soldiers supposedly assigned to guard the houses appeared to offer little protection and instead taunted the owners as they attempted to extinguish the sparks.

Shortly after word of Julian's well-being, Josie explained: "Dr. Carter called to give us some encouragement. We prevailed upon him to remain which he did. From that time until he left for his native city Augusta, he proved himself a most devoted friend. Nothing could surpass his generous self-sacrificing care of us and to him we owe our preservation."

"For a long time we were in imminent danger from the flames all around as the Piazza caught," Josie told her son, "but Dr. Carter was faithful, in watching the embers and extinguishing [them] as they caught. To show you what villains those Yankees were they screamed out to him from the street what was he putting out the fire for? Now recollect this was from the guard that was stationed around the house to protect it."

Sometime about eleven that night, Josie continued, "a furious knocking at the front door tempted me to go and open. As we ladies did so, a fellow flushed with wine and every other evil passion stamped upon his face sprang in and would have immediately commenced pillage but for the ubiquitous Carter who demanded his business in such an authoritative manner that the fellow abashed at seeing a man where he only expected a number of lonely women—turned upon his heel and pretended he only came to give assistance. Carter at once ordered him to furnish it which he acquiesced in after a while by sending *two* men."[10]

The night seemed endless, Josie reported, as they continued to struggle against the fiery embers, while on the lawn below a throng of vengeful bluecoats appeared to rejoice in their travail. "All night long from the Piazza and roof we women fought the flames and there were times when the panes of glass were so hot that you could not rest your hand there for any time, but still we fought—and there stood that sea of upturned faces of Logans corps [Federals stationed about the campus] with not a spark of sympathy for us." As the night progressed their plight became ever more precarious and Josie confessed, "We were absolutely in their power and bitterly did we grieve over it."

The water having been cut off, the LeContes and their fellow Columbians were faced with a Herculean task of putting out the fires. Daughter Lula joined her mother in deploring the insolent attitude of the Yankee soldiers who exerted not the slightest effort to restrain the troops: "Meanwhile, as the flames rushed angrily on carrying every thing before them and while thousands of defenseless women & children were running wildly sweeping through the streets having saved nothing but the clothes upon them, these creatures calling themselves men stood idly by, laughingly exulting in the misery and desolation they had created."[11]

Not surprisingly, Columbia women were incensed by brazen Yankees who jeered, "Was that not a grand old fire?" and "What a queer people you are!" One soldier taunted women, saying, "You women must be very hard-hearted. I have never seen one of you cry." In attempting to secure a guard for her home, Mrs. Campbell Bryce pleaded with the Yankee officials, "If you have mother, wife, or sister pray God they may never be called upon to suffer the anguish and terror the women of Columbia have been called upon to endure since the occupation of our city by your army."[12]

The deluge of reports as to the personal conduct of the Yankees during those hours of chaos ranged from downright demonic to "curiously civil." Obviously some unprotected women were subjected to more abusive contact with their foe than were others. Although "our ladies were insulted on all sides by vile language," Josie reported that she had "not heard of any violations." Naturally, many of the women were offended by the drunkenness, the ruthlessness, and the profanity of the Yankee soldiers; however, others testified to their being "curiously civil." One woman commented: "Some of the soldiers of Sherman were demons, [while] others were very humane." "As far as I could learn," she continued, "no actual personal insult was inflicted on any lady besides rude and violent attempts to search them for gold."[13]

In spite of their needling of Southern women, Yankees often admired their spirit and spunk. And the women of Columbia, true to their reputation for feistiness, consistently rose to the occasion. In response to an inquisition by Yankee soldiers about her loyalties, Mrs. Campbell Bryce assured them she was indeed rebel through and though and quickly seized the opportunity to chastise them for invading the South. A little taken aback by her plucky response, the soldier, nevertheless, applauded her answer: "Madam, I like the spirit in you.... So many women tell us, 'We were always for the Union....' We did not believe them...." Furthermore, it was difficult for the Federals not to admire Mrs. Bryce's ingenuity in having the wheels removed from her carriage in order to prevent its expropriation. No amount of coercing could prod her to give out the wheels' hiding place. Finally the soldiers gave up, admitting, "It is such a d—d good Yankee trick she deserves to keep it."[14]

At the John LeConte home, on Saturday following the night of madness, the morning light brought a slight reprieve from the menacing flames, and Josie lay down for a moment's respite. "I threw myself upon the bed to rest when tramp, tramp, tramp, resounded through the house," she wrote. Clearly the fiendish destruction of homes and property had not been abandoned. "Upon rising," Josie lamented, "found that half a dozen fellows had entered the house from the kitchen declaring the house was on fire, rushed up to the garret pretending to put out the fire when lo and behold they tore up this time and deliberately set my house a fire."[15]

The fire was extinguished. However, as the morning progressed, it seemed the fate of the buildings was still in jeopardy, as men bearing incendiary supplies made their appearance on the campus grounds. "About 11 on Saturday morning after that awful night," Josie wrote, "they brought all the combustible materials for burning the College, but by the prompt measures of Dr. Thompson [physician and friend] who denounced them and the active measures of the commanding generals the buildings were saved, not however before some of the torch bearers tasted of cold steel. I am sure it was the presence of *their* own men in our Hospital that saved it, nothing else."[16]

According to Josie, the torching of the Ladies Hospital unfortunately brought disaster for the building and some of its intoxicated "patients." Josie's re-creation of the night's savagery in her letter to her soldier son turned positively grisly at times. "They burned the Ladies Hospital," Josie reported. "Fortunately all the sick were removed to our Hospital during the day except the corpse of one dead man. During this carnival of death and destruction a number of their own men sought a bed there as their beastly intoxication could carry them no farther. These were burned up. As the flames progressed they could be seen tearing their hair and screaming for help, but help there was none. And when the building fell in they all perished. Instantly the yells of delight filled the air. Frantically they advanced, severed the heads from the bodies, caught them up on their bayonets, and danced around to the tune of 'damnation to the rebels' little dreaming that they were their own men."[17]

Of even greater concern to the townspeople than the villainy of Sherman's men was the threat of stragglers, the criminal element who trailed the armies, men whose reputation for unmerciful pillaging and destruction struck fear into the hearts of even the bravest of souls. "We were in great terror lest when the main army disappeared we should be burnt out by the stragglers who had vowed vengeance against our house and the College buildings. Our house they seemed to have a particular spite against for no other reason that I can now see but that we kept so within doors with every door and blind shut tight—they thought this defiant and of course were itching to get at the inside of it!"[18]

During the night's rampage hundreds of residents were left homeless, turned out into the winter's cold to watch their houses engulfed in flames, their furniture, clothes, pictures, valuables destroyed before their very eyes. William Gilmore Simms, who was sheltering in Columbia, vividly described the aftermath of Sherman's stopover. More than 8,000 persons were subsisting on the meager rations being distributed by the authorities, he reported. "Half of the population, male and female, have been robbed of all the clothes they had, save those they wore, and of those many have had overcoat, hat & shoes taken from them. Watches & purses were appropriated at every corner: and the amount of treasure & wealth, in cloth, gold, silver & other booty borne away by the Huns & Vandals of the Century is incomputable.... All is wreck, confusion & despair."[19]

The horror stories of the night beggar imagination. As a result of overexposure and stress, one expectant mother caught a cold that turned into pneumonia which eventuated in her and her newborn infant's death a few days later. One resident begged for help from Mrs. Campbell Bryce, who had succeeded in stashing away some provisions and had cleverly hidden her stock of chickens, ducks and turkeys in her cellar. The poor man despaired that the day before he had been worth over $100,000 and, "today I have nothing for my wife & child to eat, nor have I the means to procure it." In short order Mrs. Bryce's lower level poultry compound was quickly depleted as word spread and hungry Columbia friends and neighbors in the same destitute condition appealed to her generosity.

Resuming anything resembling a normal life in a city that had been half consumed by flames was an impossibility. Essentials such as wood and food were in scant supply. Communications with the outside world were severed. Railroad cars and tracks were wrecked, telegraph lines were down, livestock had been seized or wantonly slaughtered. As one woman explained, "There was no money; commerce went by barter. There were no lamps or candles; one read or sewed by firelight or went about with a torch."[20]

Miraculously, the LeContes' homes and most of the buildings in the college compound were saved. The fact that several of the college buildings had been converted into hospital quarters where both Confederate and Union men were being housed, as Josie pointed out, no doubt contributed to their survival. The LeContes themselves were probably saved from further disturbance when they agreed to house several Yankees. "We did so," Josie wrote, "and had no occasion to repent our bargain. I cannot say they were gentlemen but they certainly treated us with every courtesy by not intruding upon our privacy."[21] Even Lula, for the moment, repressed her intense antipathy for the bluecoats and surprisingly found herself praising a colonel who "took up his quarters with us. Although a Yankee I shall always bear testimony to his gentlemanly conduct. He merely occupied the Library, did not take even his meals with us, never intruded on the family, and altogether showed a consideration and delicacy which I had not expected & for which I shall always feel deeply grateful...."[22]

Josie could scarcely believe their good fortune in escaping the flames. Both Josie and daughter Lula "felt that in saving our home we were immeasurably more blest than thousands in our own town. You would not recognize our once beautiful town in the mass of ruins which now greets your eye on every side; scarcely a fourth of it now remains,"[23] Josie wrote her son. "The picture of misery and woe of our beloved city is indescribable. Nothing remains intact, but the campus grounds, Theological Seminary, the new State House, which they hadn't the powder to blow up, female college—and the Catholic church. Our Episcopal church (Christ Church was burnt) the baptist, methodist and presbyterian churches—all were more or less damaged and every effort made to burn them but failed thro the exertions of their friends. One or two rows of buildings skirting the town are all that are left by that vandal horde."[24]

The fact that the old State House had been destroyed was of small consequence to the zealous Lula. For Lula it had been irreparably desecrated when the soldiers had raised their "hated" flag atop it in triumph. It was "with a feeling of intense loathing & hatred" that Lula watched the flames envelop house after house: "Still the fires spread, the State House caught and the flames rushed heaven-high. This I had expected and did not regret, for after having been polluted by having the stars and stripes float over it, I think I myself would have applied the torch if Yankee malice had spared it."[25]

Josie and Lula were indeed correct in reporting the utter devastation of the city. Furthermore, it took months and even years to restore Columbia to its former beauty. The process of resurrecting the city from the ashes demanded time, money, and manpower. Months later journalists traveling in the South pictured for their Northern readers a once beautiful city, huge areas of which had become a wasteland. "It is now a wilderness of ruins. Its heart is but a mass of blackened chimneys and crumbling walls. Two thirds of the buildings in the place were burned, including without exception, everything in the business portion. Not a store, office, or shop escaped; and for a distance of three fourths of a mile on each of twelve streets there was not a building left." An irate Columbian exploded: "They destroyed everything which the most infernal Yankee ingenuity could devise means to destroy." The man continued, "Hands, hearts, fire, gunpowder, and behind everything the spirit of hell were the agencies which they used."[26]

Another observer pointed out that Sherman had burned some two thousand and seven hundred bales of Mayor Gibbes's cotton, a loss "of more cotton than any other individual in the Confederacy." Apparently Mayor Gibbes took his losses in stride and instead poured out his animosity on Sherman for leaving the city in such destitution. For five weeks afterward, according to Mayor Gibbes, "twenty-five hundred people around Columbia lived upon nothing but loose grain picked up about the camps, where the Federal horses had been fed."[27] Since all the shovels, spades and rakes had been stolen or wrecked in the neighboring communities, sixty-five dead horses and mules destroyed by soldiers and stragglers were left to rot for six weeks on the outskirts of Columbia before they could be disposed of. Only "a wilderness of crumbling walls, naked chimneys and trees," Trowbridge reported, remained to "attest the wealth and elegance which one night of fire and orgies sufficed to destroy."[28]

In a few short days, almost as suddenly as they had appeared, Sherman and his troops marched out of Columbia leaving a benumbed, desolate populace in their wake. The townspeople remained paralyzed from shock as they surveyed their homes, stores, and churches that had been transformed into rubble overnight. Residents counted eighty-four out of one hundred twenty-four blocks, including the city's entire business district, that had been consumed by flames. Some five hundred buildings were destroyed.[29] Josie, Emma, and Joseph LeConte each responded to the eerie stillness that pervaded Columbia following the departure of the Federals and the "immense droves" of blacks, as well as hundreds of white residents and refugees who moved out with the army. According to Emma's calculations the population of 30,000 had dwindled to only about 7,000.[30] "You wonder," Josie mused, "as you pick your way among the ruins what has become of the people and where have they gone to? You can walk miles about our city and never meet a soul. The sense of loneliness and desolation is intolerable."[31]

It was small wonder that Josie concluded her letter to her son Julian on February 28 with an impassioned plea for revenge against those fiendish Yankee soldiers. "God bless you! my own precious boy and when the opportunity offers, strike a blow that that accursed race shall feel in defense of your desolated home and unhappy Mother."[32] John Trowbridge, a postwar journalist-traveler in South Carolina attested to finding in South Carolina "a more virulent animosity existing in common people

against the government and people of the North than in any other state
I visited. Only in South Carolina was I treated with gross personal insults
on account of my Northern origin."[33]

A Safe Return

While the soldiers and stragglers were reveling in their devilry, Josie's
husband and her brother-in-law, Joseph, struggling to move the Niter
Bureau supplies to safer territory north of Columbia, were frantic with
worry over what might be happening to their families in town. Following the Federals' ambush of their wagons, as noted, Josie's husband,
John, had been taken prisoner and Joseph LeConte had escaped by hiding in the woods. Both men obviously were prevented from coming to
the aid of their families in Columbia.

During their absence, both LeConte families were suffering acute
anxiety over the fate of John and Joseph at the hands of the Yankees.
The uncertainties over the Niter Bureau excursion coupled with the terror of the burning and ravaging of their city must have been overwhelming at times for both LeConte families. Lula, along with her
mother, anguished over the terrible suspense of not being able to hear
anything definite from her father: "I try to bear up and be cheerful on
Mama's account, for she is so sad, but there are times when I am heartsick with misery at the thought of how long a time may elapse before we
see Papa again. Papa a prisoner, and Jule [Lula's other brother, Julian,
on active duty with the Rebel army] so situated that we are unable to
hear from him, the future does indeed seem a blank."[34]

Finally, following a lengthy and precarious game of cat and mouse
with marauding Federals, Joseph LeConte succeeded in eluding his
would-be captors and returned a few days later to his greatly relieved
family—and the blackened ruins of Columbia.[35] As he made his way
through the center of town, Joseph LeConte was stunned to discover,
"Not a house was standing and I met not a living soul!" The fire had all
but obliterated the heart of the city.[36] Amid the "embraces, kisses, weeping" the family marveled over the details of Joseph's seemingly miraculous escape, and Joseph in turn listened to the fiery ordeal of Sherman's
occupation of Columbia in his absence.[37]

A short time after his brother's return to Columbia, a haggard and
weary John LeConte also arrived home safely on March 7, 1865, having
finally been paroled by the Union authorities. One can well imagine
Josie's elation. Emma was specific: "Aunt Josie's joy was unbounded and
her excitement brought on a severe palpitation of the heart."[38]

Needless to say, both LeConte families were jubilant over the safe return of the men; however, many of their valuables had gone up in smoke when the Yankees torched the wagons that were to have carried their possessions to safety outside of Columbia.[39] The lack of clothing, as a result of the blockade and the scarcity and exorbitant price of yard goods, had already become a major concern throughout the South. Unfortunately, Josie and daughter Lula had lost almost all of their clothing in the Yankees' capture of the wagons and were left with two dresses each and "hardly a change of underclothing and not an article to begin Summer with." Replacements would be difficult and expensive to obtain, Emma noted, "when even calico is from $25 to $30 a yard."[40] Actually, clothes were the least of their worries. Food, blankets, and firewood were far more important considerations. It was a distraught Josie who admitted, "The house that covers us—a limited supply of provisions, and some funds are all that we are now worth."[41] In the weeks that followed, the LeContes' desperate need for food, as well as that of hundreds of other Columbia residents, presented ever-increasing problems. Often the LeConte families were supplied by the food brought back by the servants from their pillage of the smoldering stores—as well as from other questionable sources. Josie's faithful servant Annie helped to feed them "from the plunder acquired when the stores were thrown open." Even Emma saw it as quite a reversal of roles to have their servants providing for them![42]

A Shattered Dream

Less than two months after Columbia's February 17 nightmare, Lee's surrender at Appomattox left Southerners dazed and reeling with disbelief. Their entire world had been upended, their hopes dashed. Josie's niece, Emma LeConte, despaired: "The fall of the Confederacy so crushed us that it seemed to me I did not care what became of me. It is impossible not to feel rebellious and bitter. It is impossible not to feel that it is unjust and cruel. And so I had better not write about it at all— only personal and family matters, if I can keep back the expression of what fills my heart and thoughts."[43]

Loyal Southerners had long held fond hopes for a wild, exuberant celebration over the final defeat of the Union forces and the achievement of Confederate independence. A devastated Emma no doubt reflected the sentiments of the all the LeContes as well as their fellow countrymen when she wrote: "That was to be a day of wildest joy, when the tidings of peace should reach us, and the thought of that time used to lighten our hearts and nerve us to bear every trial and privation. Then we determined, after our independence was acknowledged and the time came for

Gen. Lee to disband his army, to go on to Richmond to see the glorious sight, to see the hero take leave of his brave victorious men. The army is disbanded now—oh! Merciful God!—the hot tears rush into my eyes and I cannot write."[44]

The assassination of Lincoln on April 14, 1865, and the capture of Jefferson Davis on May 10, 1865, all but finished off Emma's hopes for the Confederacy. Still there was always that remote possibility that the "South would rise again," by way of collaboration with France or England against the Union, or as a renewed resistance after a few years' respite: "I was studying my German when Father came in and told me. I laid my head on the table without a word. I did not cry—the days of weeping are past—but, ah! the heartache—the only thing left to hear now is the surrender of the army in the West and that must come pretty soon. I think I have given up hope at last, at least for the present. We will be conquered. Only in the future can we still hope, either for a foreign war in which we can join enemies of the United States, or else that after years of recuperation we may be strong enough and, wiser by experience, to renew the struggle and throw off the hateful yoke. The only other chance is that by their oppression and insolence they may drive the people to guerilla warfare and be wearied out at last."[45]

In May the safe return of Josie and John's son Julian from the battlefields eclipsed both families' despondency over their shattered dreams for the Confederacy. (To Emma, Julian had always seemed more like a brother than a cousin.) One day, in a matter of seconds, a seemingly ordinary evening was transformed into an extraordinary evening. As both LeConte families were strolling a few blocks from their homes, embarked on a nighttime inspection tour of the rubble left in the wake of the Federals' demoniac visit, suddenly, out of the darkness appeared a shadowy, rough looking figure "with knapsack and blanket roll on his back." It was Julian, exhausted and footsore from blisters that made each step torture. The glorious, tearful welcome that followed, Emma explained, "may be better imagined than described." In moments to be relived in memory as long as life itself, Julian and his father immediately turned back home for a joyous reunion with Julian's mother.

In the days that followed, in an attempt to make up for the gaiety so long abandoned during the war, the young people gathered nightly for dances and parties galore. Emma told her diary: "We enjoy having the boys back and in spite of all depressing influences, have pleasant days. Young people cannot be depressed *all* the time. There are eight of us altogether, between the ages of fourteen and twenty-four, and it is nice to have the boys home even if they are returned like this."[46] The absence of "refreshments" at the gatherings was of little consequence; however, other scarcities were more sorely missed. Emma's description of her sisters' dancing party at their home should bring a smile to almost any reader's face: "Lawrence came and played for them on his violin, which, however, was minus one string—a deficiency that could not be supplied— and some of the music in consequence [was] rather curious."[47]

Now and then the young people's pleasure seemed faintly tinged with "the guilt of survival," an understandable response, it would seem, as they remembered the tragedies that had befallen so many Southern families. The partying, in part perhaps an attempt to repress painful memories of friends sacrificed to the cause, was recorded by Emma: "Accordingly, Monday evening the whole contingent from the other house [Josie and John's home] came over and we had a jolly time. Tuesday evening was, if anything, even livelier. Our spirits seemed to rise at the sound of the piano and we went into it with a vim, especially Cousin John. How long it had been since any of us had danced! It did seem heartless, perhaps, but we could not help enjoying it, and it seemed such a relief to throw off the trouble and gloom for a little while—and it was only among ourselves."[48]

Emma's father documented his daughter's account of postwar partying: "I never knew so much real social enjoyment in Columbia as in the years 1866 and 1867; society was really gay, the necessary result of the rebound from the agony and repression of the war. My daughters were then 'in their teens,' and for their sakes we entered heartily into the general gaiety. As everybody was poor the gatherings were almost wholly without expense, and therefore frequent; the hostess simply furnished lemonade and cake and the young men a negro fiddler."[49] Caroline LeConte remembered the refreshments as being even less munificent, as consisting solely of a bucket of ice water. However, she, too, recalled the levity and the ladies dancing in calico or cheap tarlatan.[50] Years later an alumnus recalled: "In addition to the lectures and the attendance on the legislative sessions, the young people got up dances, plays, concerts, tableaux, masked balls, and other entertainments, as the times seemed to grow better."[51]

Of all the gatherings the most popular postwar LeConte entertainment turned out to be the Shakespeare Club, organized by Joseph LeConte for his daughters and nephews. Each member was expected to have read or reread beforehand the play to be discussed during the evening. Prompted by a question from Emma's father, one participant reported: "Many bright and witty things were said, and sometimes philosophic ideas of weight cropped out.... Yet there was a great fund of fun drawn on at more than one of those meetings, especially if one of the lighter comedies chanced to be the theme of the evening."[52]

From Riches to Rags

In the weeks and months after the war, families throughout the South welcomed home, as did the LeContes, long-absent loved ones in various stages of health or infirmity: some men hale and hardy, some physically worn and mentally dispirited, unable to ever resume a normal life again. In the months to come millions of Southerners found food and clothing hard—sometimes impossible—to come by. Millionaires had become propertyless paupers; professionals discovered that potential clients, patients, students were unable to scrape together the wherewithal to pay for their services. Farmers returned to fields ravaged by battles and horses and troops; farm animals and equipment had been lost to theft and impressment. Storekeepers lacked both stock for their shelves and customers with money to buy whatever paltry goods they could offer for sale.

Many of the wealthiest men in the South were struggling to buy back their homes that were being ruthlessly auctioned off for back taxes. One prominent Columbia family put their property up for sale but retained four of their best cows in order to sell milk to buy food to sustain them. That sale, Josie commented sadly, would not begin to pay one hundredth of that family's debt incurred during the war. One woman was so destitute that she allowed herself but one cracker in twenty-four hours.[53]

A letter from Josie's friend Dolly Dill testified to the widespread reversals of fortunes following the war. From New Orleans, Dolly wrote, "Our wealthiest citizens have returned from exile with nothing, and even those who remained here unless they took the oath and went on with their business, which very few of them did, are not much better off. Men who retired on fortunes of half a million and upwards are now glad of places as clerks at 150 dollars a month or even less. But I do not want to give examples of what I mean when I say the people are all poor, for Heaven knows dear old Carolina is behind more of their southern sisters in honorable instances of the same kind."[54]

The war and its aftermath had generated grave problems for the LeContes as well. Years later Caroline (Carrie) LeConte remembered that after the war, although they were very poor, they "had a large pasture behind the house and two good milch cows, Hook and Crook. My mother sold extra milk to the garrison, and we lived by hook or crook."[55] Of course, there was no money for nonessentials such as toys—Carrie's doll was a skeleton in the University Museum, "beautiful," in Carrie's eyes, and "beyond comparison and worthy of all affection."[56]

Reimbursement for LeConte claims from South Carolina College, amounting to $3,125 for each family, could have greatly helped to alleviate the families' financial woes. Efforts to secure this back pay, however, were to no avail. A discouraged Josie lamented, "I never labored as hard in *my life* to get our claims ... acted on *early*—but it was all in vain." There had been vague promises by the authorities to compensate the LeContes eventually, but "not at present"—a time when the money was most sorely needed. "Don't think of me," Josie told her sister resignedly. "I am determined not to grieve any longer over what I can't help."[57] Josie's repeated "So it goes!" a phrase which punctuated her letters, reflected her ultimate frustration over their situation.

Again and again Josie assured her sister Mollie[58] how delighted she was that her sister's life in the North was pleasurable and devoid of the problems and straitened conditions that plagued the South. Even so, there appeared a wistfulness, bordering on envy, that permeated her words. On February 4, 1866, she wrote: "It is such a source of happiness to *me* to think *you* are enjoying yourself, and there is happiness *somewhere!*" Josie confessed that she had almost forgotten the meaning of the word "happiness." "In the hard life ... that we poor Confederates are all undergoing... the grim grip of necessity that clutches one by the throat can't be shaken off. The endless want too!! the *most* vexatious—being of course the Stomach, which is a customer that requires *prompt attention and short settlements.*"[59]

The LeContes, as did most Southerners, experienced a dire need for some source of income. Southern banks had sickened and died. Confederate bills and bonds were now worthless. People clutched at almost any means of support. During the latter part of May, Emma noted: "Poor father is looking very badly, too, and is very much troubled. He can get no employment and not one cent of money in the house. He hopes when the railroad is completed there may be some trade and business here and he can then get work, but that will be quite a while yet."[60]

Fortunately, John LeConte, through a bit of maneuvering succeeded in procuring a boat which had formerly belonged to the Niter Bureau for his brother Joseph. This enabled Emma's father to secure some small income for both families by plying the river and bringing in supplies to Columbia for a tenth of the corn, which he shared with his brother's family and Capt. Allen J. Green.

In June, Brig. Gen. Alfred S. Hartwell sought out the LeContes.[61] During their talks, Joseph LeConte remarked in embarrassment that the running of the boat was a "piddling sort of business.... The fact is General, the subsistence of two families depends on it." It was only then that the LeContes' acute lack of food and clothing became clear to the General. Hesitantly, for fear of giving offense, Gen. Hartwell, aware of the LeContes' prestigious academic reputations, offered the families a loan of "as much money as they wished." (The General was acting on behalf of several northern LeConte colleagues who wished to help extricate the two scientists from their financial difficulties.) Hartwell's generous proposal was summarily rejected. Emma was incensed: "Of course this offer was declined. As long as we can keep body and soul together, Father would not borrow from anybody, but to be under obligations to a *Yankee!*"[62] To beg for charity or to borrow from Yankees was unthinkable for the LeContes.

Even in defeat the LeContes were proud people who steadfastly resisted lining up for handouts from the U.S. government. Nevertheless, Josie LeConte resented the naiveté (or indifference) of several of her husband's academic colleagues in the North who seemed to be unaware of (or indifferent to) the true plight of the faculty at South Carolina College both during and after the war. One acquaintance had casually inquired as to whether they at South Carolina's university were in a "suffering condition." "If so," the colleague suggested, "they should receive assistance!!!" Josie poured forth her anger in a letter to her sister. "What a stupid question and how strange it sounds, as if we should make a parade of our poverty to solicit *Massachusetts charity!!* They must have heard by this time what our condition was, and if disposed to send anything—have done so—taking it for granted that people—*so completely robbed*—hardly anything that they could send would hardly come amiss. Yes! Everything is gone, but *poverty and pride*—poor handmaidens—for with our poverty *our pride—increases.*"

Although Josie in time was forced to admit that voluntary contributions from Northern *friends* might be acceptable, she clearly revealed a loyal Confederate's reluctance to demean herself by begging for charity from arrogant Northerners. In fairness, Josie did credit the gentleman from the North with "meaning well" and added that he and one other couple "are the only ones from that section of the country that *I* personally would consent to accept a favor."[63]

Unsympathetic relatives also evoked reproach from Josie. Months after the war Josie deplored a close relative's lack of knowledge—or lack of concern—as to the shortages and deprivation being experienced by the South Carolinians. Josie's underscoring evidences her annoyance. She reported that the woman had written that "She had never in any way felt the war and that if *she had only known how we were suffering* she could *so easily have helped us. At present* their funds were rather low to *aid us much in that way now!!!*"[64] Perhaps Josie's irritation revolved around her conviction that "outsiders" should have known—and responded to—the gigantic postwar financial problems of most Southerners.

Even in days of deepest want Josie insisted that begging for gifts from gloating Northerners was abhorrent; however, free will offerings from family and friends and even solicitous strangers (as differentiated from charity) would be gratefully accepted. Josie urged her sister to seek help from some of her wealthier friends to obtain "blankets, flannels—or clothing of any kind. Warm clothing is the *great want*." Mollie's response was immediate, and in a few short weeks Josie was ecstatically reporting the arrival of a series of boxes from her sister. A chest full of blankets proved to be the most cherished gift of all. Josie's gratitude was not surprising as thousands of Southerners were shivering through the chilly days of winter, their blankets and carpets having long ago been sent off for use by the soldiers at the warfront.

"*But of all the things sent,*" Josie exclaimed, "nothing was so *welcome* as the blankets—I can never tell you *how we have suffered from want of them....*" An enthusiastic Josie continued: "Now the cold winds may whistle. I defy everything—wrapped in these dear sweet blankets. All my cares and troubles shall be forgotten in the remembrance of so good and thoughtful a sister."[65] Again and again, in letter after letter, Josie expressed her profound gratitude for the blankets: "Oh you can't begin to tell the *comfort* those blankets have been to our household. I *bless* you every night for them and *sigh* when the morning *comes*, when they and I must part."[66]

During the raw winter months, Columbians, along with their shivering compatriots, lacking warm clothing and wood for fireplaces, became sun worshippers as they rationed their supplies for the chilly days ahead. "It would make your heart ache to see them seeking the warm sunshine on pleasant days," Josie observed, "the great desire being to save wood for the cold ones."[67]

The arrival of two boxes from Josie's sister during the summer of '65 prompted a flurry of excitement for all the LeContes. Despite the somber heading, "Among the ruins—Columbia, S.C." the tone of Josie's thank you letter was jubilant: "You cannot begin to form the faintest idea of the joy that filled our hearts at their advent. Such a screaming for hammers, hatchets, *anything* to force an entrance into this 'eldorado' of old time luxuries. How my eyes feasted on the barrel of sugar and bag of coffee! I tell you I feel *now* ever so rich—rich in a sisters love—in her kindness—thoughtfulness and unstinted generosity. Yes! Mollie I do bless you every moment of my present existence which God only knows is sad enough and there are but few things left to remind us of happier hours.... My heart still troubles me a great deal but with returning strength that may annoy me less. Oh me! From what a load of doubts—care and trouble your means have saved me!! And it must be such a happiness to you to feel that *you* have *saved us* from *positive want.*"[68]

Sharing what little one had following the war was an almost universal practice among Southerners. There was always someone less fortunate. Upon at least one occasion Josie enjoyed a surfeit of goods and immediately felt conscience-bound to share her good fortune with friends and neighbors: "I set about me as soon as the box came to divide the contents in such a manner so that other homes should be blessed. Streaks of *sunshine* are rare things now a days, and I believe it to be a sacred duty if *one* happens to be blessed that they shall light up the corners of other suffering hearts. I accordingly set enough aside for Christmas and New Years—dividing the rest to be equally divided.... I assure you there was many a smiling face and many a hearty 'God bless her.'" As one of the recipients remarked, "Isn't it a joyful thing to be able to *give* in these *days*."[69]

As the boxes grew in number and contents, Josie repeatedly instructed her sister to record her expenses, and promised to reimburse her as soon as their fortunes improved: "There is one thing we shall never forget, and that is *our indebtedness* to *you* pecuniarily. Oh Me! What a timely blessing it has proven, and how often I remember you in prayer."[70]

A new dress was an event during the war years. New clothes were few and far between, and women wore patches and homespun as badges of honor. Purchasing luxuries secreted through the blockade was severely frowned upon by loyal Southerners. Small wonder Josie was delirious upon the receipt of several bolts of dress material from her sister: "Everything that *you sent* was beautiful—the silks are perfect shades and will make up so effectively. Lula's eyes looked longingly at the handsomest organdie and I let her have it. She wore it with her new mantle last Sunday—her appearance was quite regal. She is perfectly wild over her new things and has them all made up already—struts the balcony with a very defiant air and maintains the presence of the detested Yankee makes her feel no longer demoralized!!!!" Josie thanked her sister effusively for her many gifts and laughingly announced that she now had "any amount of beautiful things *you* sent me for my back—but we have no money in our pockets!!!"[71]

Never, however, were there quite enough luxuries to satisfy everyone. On one occasion Josie's niece Emma confessed that a long awaited box proved disappointing. A carton from the North to the John LeConte family and shared with the Joseph LeContes contained no new frock for Emma or her sister. Instead there was "a white tulle bonnet trimmed with pale lilac (!) which not only goes ill with my complexion, but is most strangely out of harmony with my other clothes." Nevertheless, Emma was delighted to see *new* clothes: "It was a sight to our eyes to behold new dresses! Just to touch an organdie, and silks! The freshness of them! How really beautiful they looked. How many years it seemed since we even dreamed of a new frock finer than homespun or at most calico! She had promised Sallie and me a new dress apiece, but luckily I had built no hopes upon her promises for I knew she would need all she had to supply Aunt Josie, so I was not disappointed, but poor Sallie was bitterly so. She had dreamed of a white dress to wear to her little dances."[72]

The gift of a felt hat to Emma's father from Mollie was more enthusiastically received than Emma's lilac bonnet: "I was surely glad of that, for certainly his old one was most disgraceful. A new hat, though, looks rather odd with his old clothes." Emma bewailed her father's shabby suit and his drab appearance: "Oh, that abominable old suit! It hangs lankly on him, innocent of any fit, and of such dingy hue. His skin is tanned by exposure last winter, and hair, face and garments all seem nearly the same color. It is well a gentleman nowadays is not judged by his exterior."[73]

Unfortunately, with the passage of time the LeContes' situation continued to worsen, and Josie sought to help the family's finances by selling her jewelry, advising her sister that she would be sending two diamond rings for her to sell. "I am indebt to everyone," Josie confessed. In the midst of Josie's litany of troubles, however, came a most surprising request. Perhaps it was only wishful thinking, or perhaps daydreaming, that caused Josie to appeal to her sister for a favor totally out of keeping with her family's dire financial circumstances: "Do price in the city for me what a set of chinchilla furs would cost…. I suffer so from the cold that I am obliged to get something of the kind this winter…." She continued by asking for a book on fashions, "the best kind I can get."[74] The request was mystifying and in marked contrast to her pronouncement in the very same letter, "The suffering we have all gone thro beggars description—the future looks equally black."

Despite her own straitened condition, Mollie continued to send boxes to her sister. More importantly, however, certainly for the residents of Columbia, was Mollie's work in enlisting sympathy among her New York friends and acquaintances for the desperate plight of the late Rebels. Actually, several groups were already at work in New York on behalf of their former enemies. However, other Northerners, their animosity for the South and her people as yet unabated, begrudgingly and only with considerable prodding donated paltry sums to Southern relief. From Westchester, New York, Mollie recounted her visit to Mrs. Judge Roosevelt, "who is doing all in her power to relieve the suffering South." "She tells *me it is dreadful up hill* work," Mollie wrote," on account of the bitterness of feeling *on both sides*. The Northern women feel that the Southern women do not appreciate their acts of kindness and charity."[75]

Now and then, in her attempts to secure supplies for South Carolinians Mollie was caustically rebuffed by hostile New Yorkers: "In some places I was met by the remarks, you Southerners have given us a great deal of trouble but if you promise to behave yourselves and stay in the Union we will do something for you. So I *promised to stay in the Union* which I *could do very safely* as there is none yet." Mollie confessed that she would do almost *"anything for the South."*[76]

In response to Josie's request for medicines for the sick who were being cared for by the various benevolent societies in Columbia, Mollie sought out a doctor to put up a box of medicines. "He asked me what kind of medicine you requested at the South," Mollie wrote, her sense of humor showing. "I told him I did not think you wanted *Epson Salts* or Castor Oil but I would say quinine and Iron. Was I right?"[77]

Both Mollie and Josie nagged recipients of the boxes of supplies from the North to send thank yous to the donors, and, as might be expected, more than one Southerner choked on her words. In hindsight, one of Josie's elderly friends admitted that her note had been "quite garrulous tinctured with a little vein of bitterness called forth no doubt by long suffering" and her ill treatment by Sherman's men.[78]

With most families sharing their homes with relatives, friends or even strangers—in a Samaritan effort to provide assistance for those less fortunate, or as a source of income and survival—Josie felt fortunate to be able to have their home to themselves: "We are getting wonderfully European in our daily mode of living. Nearly every house having a different family on every floor both in this city and Charleston. They look *upon me* as awfully extravagant to live by myself. If you were to pop down upon us now, you would think you had gotten onto another planet—so changed is everything—and everybody."[79]

The Dark Days of Reconstruction

For vast numbers of Southerners the Reconstruction years were even more horrendous than the preceding four years had been. Joseph LeConte recalled: "After the war came what was worse than the war itself, the occupation by Federal troops and the humiliations necessarily attendant thereon. This, of course, we expected. But far worse was the arrival of 'Treasury Agents,' those vultures hovering over the rear of the army of occupation, sniffing for carrion, hunting for property to confiscate, taking accusations of any and all kinds, especially those by irresponsible blacks."[80]

Perhaps the briefest of summaries of some of the important aspects of the years of turmoil and change in the South following the war will serve to refresh memories concerning the period known as Reconstruction. Following the war, one recalls, the Radical Republicans embarked on a supreme effort to make over the South, to make it more democratic. Lincoln's plans for *reconciliation* and *restoration* were scuttled in favor of the Radicals' goal to *reconstruct* the South—her institutions, her people.

This coercion served to further antagonize an already embittered populace. The years 1865–1867 came to be referred to as "Presidential Reconstruction," in contrast to the passage of a series of far more draconian Reconstruction Acts in March and July of 1867, which introduced the period called "Radical" or "Congressional" Reconstruction.

Early in the summer of 1865, in preparation for the readmission of Southern states into the Union, President Johnson appointed provisional state governors, ordered state conventions to be held and required that slavery be abolished, secession be repudiated and Confederate debts abrogated. In June of 1865 Benjamin Perry was appointed provisional governor of South Carolina. Perry's appointment was generally well received, and even Josie sent a letter congratulating him: "I cannot begin to express the relief and happiness that these tidings have inspired us with."[81] In his efforts to cement North-South relationships, Perry immediately urged the people of South Carolina to take the Amnesty Oath, or, if excluded by Johnson's May 29, 1865, Proclamation, to apply for pardons. Among the several classes excluded from amnesty were "high civil and military officials of the Confederacy, governors of insurrectionary states, and those owning taxable property valued at more than $20,000." Those classes could seek special pardons by applying to the president. (In South Carolina there were some 638 persons excluded as a result of the property exemption. In comparison, in Virginia 2,070 were excluded, in Georgia, 1,228, and in North Carolina, only 482.)[82] Under Perry's direction elections were held for delegates to the State Constitutional Convention and the convention was convened on September 13, 1865, in the Baptist Church in Columbia.

Although Josie generally approved of Provisional Governor Benjamin F. Perry, she wrote to Mollie that the attempts to rework South Carolina's state constitution were "ruining *it I think* by making it more democratic." According to Josie, "This pleases ... Perry who you are aware is a thorough people's man—he said in his message the other day that in ten years from this we may look on all this suffering and our utter destruction as a blessing in disguise!!!! Did you ever know such a crazy Union man. I tell you he is a Yankee at heart!!!"[83]

Actually, Governor Perry's prediction in a message to the Convention that "In less than ten years we shall realize in the loss of slavery a blessing in disguise, to ourselves and our children," was made in reference to emancipation.[84] However, the extended elaboration of his vision of a future for South Carolina that would be "bright and glorious" could easily render Josie's interpretation valid.

Josie probably was also referring in part to Governor Perry's speech reported in the *Chicago Tribune* on July 22, 1865, in which Perry spoke in defense of President Johnson: "It has been said, and repeated all over the Southern States that the South has sustained a great loss in the death of President Lincoln. I do not think so." Perry was convinced, as were certain other Southerners, that President Johnson was much abler and firmer than Lincoln, that he was a Southern man rather than a Northerner, was acquainted with the institution of slavery, and would with faithfulness and ability serve the nation.

In Governor Perry's eyes, prospects for the future of the South appeared far less gloomy than others had envisioned. His plans for the people of South Carolina focused on improved North-South, as well as black-white, relationships. Governor Perry again predicted that "in ten years the Southern States will be happy and prosperous again." The planter and farmer, Perry was convinced, "will find that his net profits are greater with hired labor than with slave labor. Every landholder can rent his farm or plantation for one-third of the gross products. This is more than he now makes net, after subsisting his slaves. In truth, very few farmers in this region of country make anything except by the increase of his slaves. The idleness and vagrancy of the negro, in a free State, may be a nuisance to society. It must be corrected in the best way we can. I have no doubt, in nine cases out of ten, freedom will prove a curse instead of a blessing to the negro. No one should turn off his negroes if they are willing to remain with him for their victuals and clothes and work as they have heretofore done. They have had no agency in bringing about the change which has taken place, and we should feel no ill-will towards them on that account."

"Mr. Chairman," Perry continued, "as much as we feel the humiliation and degradation of our present situation, and deeply lament the losses which have befallen the Southern States, yet we should be happy to know that this cruel, and bloody war is over, and that peace is once more restored to our country. This is a great consolation amidst our wants, distresses and humiliation.... It is to be hoped that in a very short time civil government will be restored in South Carolina; that law will once more reign supreme over our State, and that life, liberty and property will be protected everywhere, as they heretofore have been."[85]

In her September 17 letter Josie summarized the tone of the September meeting of the South Carolina Constitutional Convention and the attitude of countless unregenerate Southern women: "The Convention is in full blast composed of a very calm, dignified body of men who feel the deepest sorrow and humiliation at the downfall of our Confederacy but who are resolved nevertheless to succumb to their condition with dignity." She noted that three members opposed the vote to repeal the Ordinance of Secession. "Many thought this trio *wrong* in opposing or throwing any obstacles in the way to the immediate return to the

Union, but they had the thanks of the women who as the Yankees tell us are the most rebellious set of beings they ever heard of...."[86]

The convention did succeed in repealing the Ordinance of Secession, and a new constitution was produced. The qualifications for suffrage, however, denied the vote to Negroes. Furthermore, Governor Perry's statements, such as, "This is a white man's government and the white man's only," raised the hackles of Northerners and resulted in a rain of criticism. In the elections held the next month, James L. Orr was elected governor. During his term of office the Black Codes were enacted, which tremendously restricted the activities and rights of blacks and reduced them to a servile role, reminiscent of their days in bondage.

Unfortunately, the new state constitutions throughout the South reflected the re-emergence of the old white antebellum planter class, a development clearly the absolute antithesis of the Radical Republicans' plans for restructuring and democratizing the South. Fearing that Southerners were not truly "reformed" and were bent on returning to the good old antebellum days, albeit with a free (although still subservient) class of Negroes, Congress refused to seat the newly elected delegates from the Southern states. (Tennessee, however, ratified the Fourteenth Amendment and was readmitted by Congress in July of 1866. South Carolina, to the contrary, voted against ratifying the Fourteenth Amendment, which granted citizenship to Negroes.)

The Radical Republicans, wary of Johnson's leniency, secured the passage of the two Reconstruction Acts in March 1867 that declared the existing Southern governments "provisional only" and called for the division of the ten states into five military districts each presided over by a commander. States would be admitted to Congress only after new constitutional conventions were held, with delegates being elected by citizens "of whatever race," and only after new constitutions had been framed allowing for Negro suffrage. The all-important requirement, however, focused on each state's ratification of the Fourteenth Amendment.

Under the Reconstruction division of the South into districts, North and South Carolina constituted Military District Number Two, over which Daniel E. Sickles was appointed military governor. Five months later Sickles was replaced by Major General E. R. S. Canby. In the fall of 1867 registrations for the election of delegates to the new Constitutional Convention indicated 46,346 registered whites and 78,982 registered Negroes. In the election that followed in November, South Carolina voters elected 48 whites and 76 Negroes.[87]

A Defeated South

Clearly, the postwar South was consumed by anger and humiliation over the defeat. Resuming anything but a strained relationship with the victor required time and patience and usually humility on the part of the defeated party. Being forced into a speedy reunification with one's former enemy, under dictatorial terms of the reunion, and involving the complete upending of one's politics, lifestyle, and social relationships, naturally met with vehement resistance on the part of Southerners. Josie LeConte's letters reflected much of the turmoil and bitterness prevailing throughout the South following the war.

One of the chief grievances of Southerners everywhere centered on their immense loathing for the Yankee troops of occupation. As can well be imagined the soldiers were given a cool reception by Columbia residents. Josie, as did most Southerners, deeply resented their presence: "As soon as the states get organized again it is hoped and prayed that the military will be removed. Their presence has a very demoralizing effect upon everybody.... Nearly all of the Yankee officers are going to return and drive their stakes in this town. What they can see to fancy, or expect, but to be outcasts in society, I cannot conceive, but they candidly confess they admire the state—*her people* and climate—and above all her *spirit*. This is all they see—for they get the entree *no where*."[88]

Hatred for the Yankees died slowly—actually, never, in the minds and hearts of many loyal Southerners. Josie's prediction that the occupation troops would be ostracized from Columbia society proved all too true, and even residents who befriended Union soldiers of the occupation found that they in turn suffered alienation from their former friends and neighbors. Somehow, men became more forgiving of their former enemies than thousands of proud, spirited Southern women, who viewed with utter contempt the presence of overbearing Federals in their midst. Joseph LeConte explained that although the gentlemen of Columbia were friendly with the commandants appointed to oversee the occupation troops, "the ladies were inexorable." As he wrote, "Nothing would induce them to recognize the officers and their wives; they were tabooed. I became quite friendly with some of the officers ... but I could never induce my wife to invite one of the gentlemen to the house for a social meal. We men exchanged visits, but the friendship went no further."[89]

Josie caustically depicted the disdain felt by the citizens of Columbia for their Yankee "overlords." One Northern colonel returned with his wife and teenage daughter to Columbia where "they teach the blacks at the Oddfellow Hall." "Not a soul notices them or any other Yankee in our midst," she wrote. "The only amusement they seem to have is riding on horseback with a forlorn Yankee attendant. Conscience! How our people loathe the very sight of them." Later Josie added: "When I said not a soul noticed them [the Yankee soldiers of occupation] I forgot Mrs. Leland, whom you remember is an English woman—she boards Ames and Haughton [Yankees] at 25 dollars a week—each—they also furnish the wood—and many other things besides their rations—which is a great help. In Dr. Lelands imbecile condition I suppose it is the most remunerative employment she could get. She has sacrificed her friends in this way as they will not visit her while there is a probability of encountering one of them. I can hardly blame her for she does not feel on this question like the true Southerner does."[90]

In New Orleans, Josie's friend Dolly Dill shared Josie's annoyance with the Yankee troops of occupation and the Northern carpetbaggers: "They are universally shunned. On the street, in the Hotels, at the places of amusement, the line of demarcation is as strict and unvarying as though they belonged to another race of beings. No one speaks to a Yankee, no one looks at a Yankee, or in any way notices him if they can help it." Six months later Dolly wrote: "How I do wish that we could see the last of them in our Southern land! I cannot get used to the sight of their ugly blue coats, and that still more hateful flag flaunting in one's face at every turn. They have gained no admission at all into society here...."[91]

Niece Emma LeConte resolved to avoid *any* physical or verbal encounters with the "obnoxious" Yankees: "The first time I went out to my German it was almost amusing. There was a sentinel at the Campus gate and, as I had the same invincible horror of passing him that one would have to a very loathsome reptile, I thought I would go through Aunt Josie's yard into the street. But when I got beyond the gate I saw there were two standing between me and the side gate.... So I doubled my veil, raised my parasol and passed swiftly and boldly between them for they were several yards apart. I had grown a little more used to them after several days, but I still feel a shudder when I pass within twenty yards of one.... This morning, though, I went through with the rest of the family going to Church and was obliged to pass so near one who was sitting on the ground that I had to hold my skirts back for fear my dress might accidentally touch them. Listen! They are beating Tattoo now—that disgusting Yankee Doodle. And they have dress parade every morning, just opposite the Campus."[92]

Later Emma declared: "These Yankee officers who behave like gentlemen—if Yankees *can* be gentlemen—take it rather hard that they are treated so coldly and allowed no social intercourse with the citizens. Horton [probably Colonel Nathaniel Haughton] especially seems to feel it that he is cut off so absolutely from the society of ladies. Great Heavens! What do they expect? They invade our country, murder our people, desolate our homes, conquer us, subject us to every indignity and humiliation—and then we must offer our hands with pleasant smiles and invite them to our houses, entertain them perhaps with 'Southern hospitality'—all because sometimes they act with common decency and humanity! Are they crazy? What do they think we are made of?"[93]

In another paragraph Emma continued her diatribe. "The negroes throng around them and they affiliate pleasantly with their colored brethren—even affectionately. They lie beside them on the grass and walk the streets with the negro girls, calling them 'young ladies'—and why not? Doubtless they recognize in them not only their equals, but their superiors. *Perhaps* negroes *may* come in contact with them with out being degraded, but I doubt it, for the negro is an imitative race. He has been elevated to some extent but will quickly retrograde in associating with such white people as these."[94]

Sparks usually flew in confrontations between Yankee officers and feisty Columbia women. Naturally, Yankees made few friends among residents with taunting, demeaning remarks like some of those attributed to General Ames. The general, however, appeared to have met his match in Mrs. Singleton, whose rancor characterized the deep-seated animosity harbored by thousands of her compatriots. Josie shared the encounter with her sister: "General Ames who is stationed here asked Mrs. Singleton the other day '*Now that we have conquered you*!! how long is it going to take to conquer the *hate* of you proud women of Carolina.' Drawing herself up to her full height [she retorted,] 'Ask my *great, great, grand-children* that question. Do you think that these children,' pointing to her little ones, 'will ever forget the wrongs done to them and theirs—No Sir! Nor their childrens children. It will be the duty of every Southern mother to perpetuate this hate, and leave it as a *sacred* trust to generations yet unborn'!!!!!!"[95]

Mrs. Singleton was merely one of countless indignant Southern women who not only snubbed and ignored the Union soldiers assigned to military occupation in the South, but who became verbally, sometimes even physically, contentious, particularly when personal rights and property were at stake. Even the heretofore self-composed Josie refused to meekly submit to Yankee trespassers who were invading their stable. In fact, Josie was irate: "I have become so desperate by their continued encroachments upon our rights—that I keep myself half cocked all the time and shall fight for my castle even at the risk of being put in the guard house." In a letter Josie recreated the scene for her sister: "London tore in my room the other morning—'Missus de Yankey in de stable wid a long sharp knife tearing up de debbil dere—what mus I do?'"

Josie's anger reached the boiling point: "I went there—demanded *his* business which *he* evidently thought was none of mine—and ordered him instantly off of the premises (officer too!). He looked very defiant—and

I worse—but I stood my ground. Presently I saw his crest droop and he remarked 'I came in search of a prisoner whom I thought might be in here.' 'If that was your business Sir why didn't you ring at the front door in a gentlemanly way? You could have passed then unmolested.' 'What did you suppose I was after,' said he—'did you think I came to steal?' 'There's no telling what you witches are after' said I, 'for there's no place this side of heaven for you—begone!! and let me see no more of you *here* or I'll have a corporal of the guard after [you] and have *you arrested* for you know as well as I that you have no authority for trespassing upon private families'!!!!!!!!"[96]

The outburst apparently served to ward off further intruders on the LeConte premises. "Not a Yankee has approached me since!!" Josie prided herself. "How the family did enjoy the scene and my vexation. Lula declares I am demoralized! and that my friends will never give me credit for an even tempered disposition, if I see much more of the 'blue bellies'!!!!"[97]

Unfortunately, as Josie pointed out, the troops assigned to protect Columbia residents were often the perpetrators of the crimes they were sent to prevent. Not only Josie's family but also Josie's friends and neighbors were victims of intrusion and theft by Yankee soldiers. "Do you remember old Dr. Trezevants daughter, a lovely girl of 18 summers who has heart disease?" Josie asked her sister. "A few evenings ago about dusk a loud rap at the door called her to it. Two Yankees approached and demanded entrance. She asked the object of their visit—they told her '*to search.*' She told them she was alone and they could not be admitted at that time. They then used awfully insulting language to her where upon she attempted to close the door. They then struck her with their pistols—*which broke her arm*!! She fainted and they marched off." "They attempted the same game with my quarters," Josie boasted, "but I *fought them* in good old Saxon."[98]

Josie was further outraged over her friend Mrs. Reynolds' losses and the vindictive actions of certain Yankee soldiers: "Poor Mrs. Reynolds came to see me *in despair* the other day. It seems, a large coop of very fine chickens had been sent to her—she stepped out to give an order to have some killed for dinner when she observed a Yankee negro in the act of carrying a number off to some Yankee officers at the foot of the garden. She remonstrated with them upon the outrages. 'Can't help it said they—we bought forty yesterday—and can't find but ten this morning—and we intend to go into every yard where there are chickens, and take the same number from them, besides these are very fine ones and we shall have them.' *They did not leave her one*!!!"[99]

Once the college began operations again, Josie feared a serious physical confrontation might very possibly develop between impetuous students and harassed soldiers. "I am in daily expectation of the students and [soldiers] locking horns," Josie wrote. "While they are enjoying their meals [they] taunt them with insulting language and are endeavouring in every way to force them into a fight."[100]

The sight—even the very thought—of a Yankee marrying a Southern girl infuriated loyal South Carolinians. Josie was annoyed with a Southern family who had abandoned the South for New York City during the war and there had played the role of "Confederate Carpetbaggers" by buying up property and reaping huge profits in the real estate market. In addition to Mr. Brown's financial successes, Josie reported, he had found a rich husband for one of his daughters, and the family returned to Columbia in order to orchestrate the wedding in true Southern style. Unfortunately, the "Yankeeized Southerners" were ostracized by local residents, especially when it was discovered that not only the groom, but all the groomsmen, would be Yankees. "And sorry an affair it was," Josie claimed. "The day was dismal beyond measure." The arrival of the Yankee wedding party dressed in what the locals considered ludicrous wedding attire set off innumerable rounds of tittering and snickering, which in turn infuriated the groomsmen. Embittered Columbians, according to Josie, "screamed out 'they are nothing but miserable Yankees. What business have they down here marrying our Southern girls. Let them go back where they came from.'" Southern hospitality was noticeably absent during the wedding reception as "not a Southern girl would look in their direction."[101]

Now and then, of course, there amazingly surfaced the story of a "nice," or at least a "not quite so horrid," Yankee. Josie found some charitable words to say about an incident that probably took place at one of the fairs Josie repeatedly mentioned. It so happened that a young widow had lost everything except her house and two solid silver pitchers. In an effort to save her house by raising the necessary five hundred dollars, the widow seized on the idea of raffling off the pitchers at five dollars a chance. As luck would have it a Yankee held the winning ticket, and just as he was about to claim his prize, a gentleman rushed forward, saying, "You cannot have the heart to keep those heirlooms from that distressed family for the miserable pittance of five dollars—let me return you *your* money, and let me return the Pitchers." An embarrassed Yankee gave back the pitchers to the widow, and, according to Josie, "tears were all she could bestow and they fell plentifully...."[102]

Carpetbaggers and scalawags further contributed to the list of Southern woes during Reconstruction.[103] Josie wrote contemptuously of one man who encouraged "the darkeys *against* making contracts with their former masters—and at the same time offers every inducement for them to go on one of three plantations *that* he has rented (or more truthfully seized) upon which he has a force already of two thousand negroes!!!!!"[104]

Yet another opportunist garnered Josie's wrath by buying up huge quantities of cotton in Augusta, Georgia, that was to be burned in anticipation of the arrival of Sherman's troops. When Sherman's attack failed to materialize, the man realized an "immense fortune"—and the everlasting enmity of the locals.[105]

Josie's invectives seemed merely to echo the anger and frustration of countless postwar Southerners over their Yankee subjugation: "The injustice and oppression in this state exceeds any thing you can conceive of. If you complain, no attention is paid to it. If you resist—the corporal of the guard is called, and you are placed in the guard house, and this done by a set of vulgar Western hog drivers—hog bandits ... tag rag scum of creation that havent the first instincts of a gentleman."[106]

Understandably, the Radicals and the federal government were less than enthusiastic about being criticized for their operations in the South, and not a few Southerners were clapped in jail for speaking out against the government. Josie became worried that some of her outbursts written to family and friends might have fallen into the wrong hands. The erratic mail system that had prevailed during the war continued in the months following Lee's surrender, and, of course, the safest way to insure letters getting through was to send them with a friend bound for a particular town or city. "I cannot tell why you have not heard from us," Josie told Mollie. "We write *constantly* but it seems an utter impossibility to get letters thro'—except by private opportunities."[107] Even then there were risks involved. Josie admitted that she was "in a peck of trouble" over an incriminating letter that might have gone astray, a personal letter in which she detailed her personal views on postwar conditions and people. The opening of those letters by unsympathetic Yankees could have brought serious problems for the LeContes.

The emancipation of their Negroes resulted not only in gigantic financial losses for former slave owners, but also in enormous problems in securing steady, reliable workers for their fields and in their homes. The Radical Reconstructionists' rash promises to the blacks of lard and livestock, and their avowed aim to make citizens and voters of blacks, provided the utmost challenge for both races.

The liberation of "servants"/slaves at the time of the burning of Columbia saw hosts of blacks leave their former owners, some willingly, some unwillingly, to trail Sherman's army, there to be sustained by food and promises. Apparently, three of the LeContes' former slaves "were carried off," Josie reported, one so fascinated by "the gypsy life of the army," that he planned never to return: "It seems a Yankee fancied him and stripped a fellow to rig him up, put boots on his feet and gave him a pony, and the last seen of him he was flying round in grand style."[108]

Too much rain, too little rain, bad seed, weevils, and most particularly labor problems produced giant headaches and innumerable crop failures for cotton planters following the war. The freedmen, with news of their emancipation, flocked to the cities to find a new life and new opportunities. Some construed freedom to mean they would never have to work again. Some waited in vain for their "forty acres and a mule." Some understood freedom to mean working a day here or there to put a little food on the table. Some thought freedom meant that their former owners were fully responsible for providing their food and clothing for the year provided they were willing to pick a little cotton in August. Others realized that their freedom offered a golden opportunity to achieve a life of independence, to provide sufficiently for their families, to enter into contracts where they had at least some input as to the conditions, the hours and the remuneration for their work. The free labor market was fraught with confusion for workers and employers alike.

Cotton, Josie was convinced, was no longer "king." Furthermore, cotton "was doomed" and, according to Josie, was not being planted anywhere. The blacks refused to work, Josie maintained, and the white property owners were unable to control labor. "Neither will work at it—the former because they don't like the work," she insisted.[109] (Actually, Josie's observations about cotton planting were not entirely accurate. Cotton was being planted in many areas; however, as noted, the weather, the army worm and labor shortages were not conducive to bumper crops. In fact, the South's postwar labor problems at times seemed insurmountable.)

Valuable holdings of land in Liberty County, Georgia, posed even more problems for the LeContes. Josie's husband and his brother were scientists, college professors and not cotton planters; however, even a small income from the Georgia estates which they had inherited from their family would have been most welcome. Bummers and Union soldiers had ravaged their properties in late 1864 and early 1865, and it was questionable whether a sizable number of former slaves, who had voluntarily left with or been seized by Federal troops, would return to the plantations to work.[110]

Would the land be taken over by the federal government? Could the newly freed blacks be induced to pitch in to help restore the farms and raise a crop sufficient to sustain life, or to provide even a trifling income for the owners? Josie was skeptical. "The Negroes wont work faithfully—but have all returned and are at the places.... The cotton has been entirely ignored by the negroes. They won't plant because it is too troublesome and requires too much work...." Josie had hoped to obtain some small return from the cotton in order to help pay son Julian's college expenses. She continued: "What I tell you about cotton on our places is the same on all that I can hear of—there has not been a seed put in the ground. The planters minds are made up on that point. Those few who do, intend keeping it South for their own consumption."[111]

The return of the freedmen to the LeConte Liberty County estates, noted in Josie's July 14 letter, was not necessarily typical of their reappearance on other plantations. One friend of the LeContes who had just returned from the coast reported, "at one place of his fathers, where there were 120 negroes there are but 30 living. So on all the other places. The mortality under Yankee rule has been frightful in the extreme."[112] Another gentleman wrestling with the hassles of hiring workers found himself the loser. Hiring white laborers turned out to be as chancy as employing blacks. The ex-slave "will only work upon compulsion," he complained to the LeContes. "He cannot be relied on as a labourer— hence the cotton captive has departed from us. Cheap cotton cannot be made by white labour in this country. Its no use to argue the question. The choice hands are all going and will continue to go west whither they can be more profitably used."[113]

This same disheartened planter was busily engrossed in plans to become an ex-planter: "I have hired a few hands this year and think it will be my last effort to *plant*. I will hereafter rent my lands to white tenants and only keep a few to victual the household and keep up our humble establishment. I have made up my mind if a man can make out to live honestly & comfortably and educate his children *probably* it is as much as he can expect. The day of growing rich, living luxuriously and all that is past."[114]

The scarcity of money after the war rendered most owners unable to pay wages to their workers. The numerous systems of sharecropping that were employed throughout the South met with varying degrees of success. Sometime later, Josie observed, "Many of the darkeys are coming to their senses, and are willing to make contracts, but the majority *work one* week—and *sleep* the next."[115] (It should be remembered that thousands of blacks across the Southland continued to work diligently and conscientiously for their former masters for a share of the crop. What the freedmen really wanted and needed—and often demanded— along with their freedom, was at least a small plot of ground of their own to farm, independent of or in conjunction with, work for their former owners. In drawing up contracts, landowners were often obliged to provide small garden areas for the sole use of the families of freedmen.)

The LeContes' Liberty County property continued to fare poorly. Most of the 1865 cotton crop was lost to theft and to the inability to get the remaining cotton ginned and shipped to market. Apparently little could be done about cotton thievery, as nothing could be proved, and "Stealing goes on worse than ever," Josie's sister-in-law, Jane Harden, complained. With the complete disruption of the railroads as a result of the war, cotton could be sent to Savannah by wagon only over rough, perilous roads. Furthermore, drivers could not be trusted to deliver full loads or in some instances any cotton at all.[116] When John LeConte's corn was divided in the fall of 1865 on a sharecropping agreement, the former bondsmen rebelled against allotting John half the crop, and instead, in what almost became a full-scale riot, they singled out a field hand's portion as his share. Eventually, John was given half of the corn that was in the barn.[117]

Theft was rampant, and Jane begged her brothers to come to Liberty County and take care of their property. As there was "no security for anything," John and Joseph's uncle was selling off everything he could from their places. Unfortunately there had been left "very little of anything."[118] Jane urged John to get a white man "to *live* on your place or *rent* it to a white man" if possible in Columbia. "You would find it almost impossible to get one here."

As the solution to their labor problems a great many Southerners placed their faith in the importation of Chinese, German, and Scandinavian workers—a plan that met with little success, however. In desperation Southerners fell prey to the temptation to sell their land and look for a new source of income. Newspapers were filled with ads for immense tracts of land for sale at bargain prices. Josie's sister-in-law wrote that planters in Liberty County were being advised to keep their land for "by next year Coolies will be brought from China, who can be had at a low price, and who understand the cultivation of cotton & rice and are not affected by climate."[119] However, she admitted, "It seems impossible for any one here to form any plan for the next year.... The state of things here is truely distressing—we don't know what it will come to in a few months tho, if better laws are not established for restraining the negro. Now they are continually having white men arrested & carried to the Freedman's courts in Savannah where although continually convicted of the grossest falsehood, their testimony is taken, as equal to a white man's. It is a source of continual annoyance to the men in this County."[120] Borrowing money was out of the question, for, as Jane explained, "all business is done in *cash*."

John's effort to rent out land to the freedmen proved a disastrous plan when the workers refused to pay up at the stipulated time. Relatives who attempted to make a go of the estates finally washed their hands of the project; a cousin who took over the business arrangements failed miserably. The 1868 crop netted John twenty-three dollars and Joseph sixty-five, apparently the "last money the LeContes ever earned from their vast landholdings."[121]

Racial Strife

Prospects for South Carolina's future were anything but rosy. In August 1865, two LeConte visitors, who no doubt typified millions of Southerners, as well as Northerners, expressed dire predictions as to the future of the South. Josie explained that two friends stopped in to see them who had just returned from a long interview with the bankers-brokers-and-jobbers of Wall Street New York. Josie wrote, "I tell you the developments are rich in the extreme. Oh said they! after closing the doors *tightly*—if we could only put the negroes back where they *were before* and have one good crop of cotton we would be saved—but as it is we are all going to *hell* as fast as the country can drive us!!!! The crash they feel is coming but they hope to stave it off as long as possible. They don't think it can possibly go beyond next spring. He says you would be amazed at the shifts people have to resort there to live."[122]

As 1865 waned, Josie and several family members sleepily awaited midnight: "As the minute *hand* touched the hour, everyone was engaged in prayer.... Never was a more fervent prayer put up than I did in the appeal to the throne of Grace that *we should never behold such* another [year]! I felt so happy that it was gone."[123]

With the passage of time Josie became increasingly more discouraged over their situation in South Carolina and the efforts of the Radicals to grant citizenship and voting rights to blacks. Radical Republicans' attempts to cultivate ex-slaves and indoctrinate them along party lines engendered fear and resentment (of both Radicals and blacks) on the part of white Southerners. Shock waves had reverberated through the Southland over the surprising number of people who "have gone over to the Radicals *body and soul.*" Josie warned, "The complexion of our political affairs grows beautifully worse day by day—things must be a great deal worse *for us of the South* before we can begin to see daylight. I tremble for the future of our poor land—for it is very evident the negro is the 'Goddess of Radical reason.'"[124]

Needless to say Josie was infuriated that blacks in such large numbers were being elected to high state and federal offices. One should recall that during the Radical regime black men were allowed to vote, while many white Southerners were disqualified—and women had to wait some five decades before being accorded the franchise. Countless loyal Southerners, however, held their disfranchisement as a symbol of integrity, proud that those who so courageously gave their lives for the South could never accuse them of having aided or abetted the Radicals.[125]

The possibility of a government dominated by ex-slaves greatly alarmed Josie and her fellow countrymen: "None of our gentlemen but look forward with *terror* to the Negro legislation of the next few years that is unless Johnson thro Grant comes to our relief. The negroes are very conscious of their power and are determined not to relinquish without a hard struggle. We are now in the employment of negro magistrates, with an almost certainty of all the other municipal offices being filled by them. They have complete possession of everything *but the churches....*"[126] (Revisionists have been quick to point out that although blacks were influential in politics during Reconstruction, they were never in complete control.)

Always, of course, there was the latent fear lurking in Southerners' minds of possible black uprisings and the massacre of whites. This was particularly true in South Carolina, where blacks outnumbered whites. Many former Confederates fervently hoped the days of Negro ascendancy would be numbered and that the whites would once again assume their antebellum role of superiority. Then, of course, vindictive whites would see to it that blacks would be made to suffer the consequences of their attempted equality. Josie predicted, "We are now anticipating great trouble this winter with the Blacks—It *has begun already.* I assure [you] the prospect before us for the next year is *awful.*"[127] A few weeks later, Josie continued: "Many here look forward with terrible apprehension to next winter—from the insubordination of the negroes. Some horrible massacres of families have already taken place.... Their firm belief is that Massa Linkum gave them the seacoast of South Carolina and Georgia to form a negro republic for themselves and when the Yankees go, they dont intend to let one damn Confederate boss it over them!!!! The consequence will be, that as soon as the civil authority is established again—cuffeedum will be firmly taken in hand—and the destruction unless they come to terms *at once*, will be awful in the extreme. Our gentlemen are in such an exasperated frame of mind from their repeated acts of insolence that they will give no quarter when overt acts call for redress."[128]

The antebellum and wartime subservience of blacks was difficult for most white Southerners to relinquish. Blacks in their newly acquired independence and equality were often considered "uppity" and "impertinent" by their former owners, and the potential for racial riots, if not outright massacres, continued to plague Southerners. Northern agitators, they were convinced, seemed bent on stirring up trouble. "The miserable wretch Thompson that tried to get up [a] row here, told them [blacks] that whenever they met *us* on the side walks *they* must drive us into the gutters—and various other incendiary speakers which had had a bad effect upon them and made their manner very insolent of late."[129]

In late July, Dolly Dill's letter corroborated Josie's fears of possible violence or Negro riots. Dolly detailed her husband and her father's attendance at a meeting of Radicals in New Orleans, during which they were infuriated by "having heard some most inflammable appeals to our colored population, which made them both certain that trouble must very soon be the result."[130]

Resentment over the behavior of blacks following the war was almost universal. The departure of longtime "servants" in a quest for independence angered many Southerners who considered them "ungrateful wretches." For others, their leaving proved a blessed relief in having fewer mouths to feed. Emma complained: "Jane left us yesterday, having only informed Mother the day before of her intended departure. She was a great nuisance.... I wish she [Emma's mother] could clear out the whole of them—we have them to feed and get very little out of them in return."[131]

Josie, along with her niece, deplored the sudden exodus of "servants" throughout the South: "The negroes on Jane Harden's place have behaved insufferably—every house servant leaving them without a moments notice—Jane and Johnnie have had to do all the cooking, cutting wood—drawing water—while Annie and Ada attend to all the house work—making beds—cleaning knives—Cornelius practices all he can to keep them in other necessaries not made on the place—A few weeks ago they determined to send the Negroes off the place—Johnnie went to Savannah to try and get Emigrants to fill their places but the expenses necessary for starting the plantation were so heavy that they have abandoned that idea, and he is now going out to Dublin to take charge of a school at a salary of eight hundred dollars a year!!! Dublin is a small out of the way place in Southeastern Georgia—the mother and Ada go with him as assistants. 'How the mighty are fallen'...!!!! *No one* excites my commiseration like Jane her whole life seems such a blight."[132]

Among her own servants Josie discovered both loyalty and defection. One assured her repeatedly that no Yankee promises could ever lure him away from the family. "'Talk to me about Yankee *free me—no free t'all*. I wouldn't gib *my missus up* for all de Yankees in de world'!!!" Josie wrote. Another former servant, Josie sensed, was yearning to return. Josie resisted the temptation to take her back, but promised her that "She must never want for any thing while I lived. I would share the last crust with her—poor thing how she wept."[133]

Young Emma LeConte was particularly displeased with the activities of the newly freed blacks. Her tone was caustic as she recounted details of the grand celebration by the black residents of Columbia on July 4, 1865—their first real Independence Day. After briefly observing from her doorway the fireworks sent off from the common opposite the campus, Emma withdrew into the house: "I could not stand it. It was too humiliating and made me realize our condition too keenly. When the pyrotechnics were exhausted, the band ceased and the negroes were left to make their own music. Hundreds of voices singing strange negro songs and hundreds of feet dancing weird negro dances made a terrible noise. They were still dancing when Col. Haughton returned about twelve o'clock and put an end to their frolic, when we were able to sleep."[134]

In a similarly disparaging voice, Josie also offered her version of the 1865 Fourth of July celebration in Columbia, pointing out that the newly freed men had requested Colonel Haughton to provide a hearse in order for them "to bury slavery." This the Colonel refused to do, and, furthermore, fearing trouble, he also refused to allow them a cannon and a hundred rounds of ammunition to help celebrate the day.

Ceremonies got off to a rousing start at ten that morning in the college chapel, Josie reported. The gathering included "every negro in the town," and this meant, Josie complained, that "all our ladies had to do their own work." Following the chapel service the revelers moved on to a splendid dinner which concluded with ice cream. The entertainment, Josie commented, cost "a thousand dollars in gold for you must know they [the blacks] are the only ones that have money." According to Josie, Colonel Haughton soon ordered all the well ropes cut when it was discovered they were poisoning the water. Finally, a band concert, followed by the firing of a few rockets, brought the evening to a close.[135]

A Future Riddled with Problems

The flood of Northern teachers who came South following the war to help teach illiterate black children to read and write created yet another annoyance for many Southerners. The objections were not necessarily about the educating of freed people, but rather about the infiltration of "gloating Yankees" attempting to change the system. The Northerners' familiarity with their students and with the freedmen irritated most white Southerners. "The school marms in the town," Josie complained, "utterly defy public opinion—*ride* and walk with negro men at any and all hours."[136]

Although vast numbers of Southerners thought the teachers' efforts would be ineffectual, others applauded the women and smiled at the children's reactions to their new roles as students. Josie reported to her sister her conversation with Alice, apparently one of the black housemaids. Asking Alice how they were getting on with the Yankee schoolmarms, Josie re-enacted Alice's response: "'Berry well I believe Missus! But dey lick like de mischief! de big ones say dey dont mind it, so dey lurn dem somethin but de little ones dont like it ... when our noses do leak dey wipes it wid der nice hankercher dat is full of nice ting (perfume) and dey kiss de latta's [mulatto's] but dey wont touch de little black ones in dat way.'!!!!!"[137]

Southerners' contempt for the persistent influx of "insufferable, arrogant northerners" also extended to various staff members of the Freedmen's Bureau.[138] In their work attempting to assist the Negroes in their adjustment from slavery to freedom by protecting the rights of freedmen, overseeing labor contracts, and securing justice in the courts, Bureau officials earned the enmity of most white Southerners. The Freedmen's Bureau officials had their work cut out for them. As one writer explained, it "would have taxed the combined capacities of a social service worker, an administrative official, a labor conciliator, and a judge."[139]

The former Rebels were quick to accuse the Bureau officials of overstepping their authority, of insufferable partiality to ex-slaves, of incompetence, of a powerful liaison with the Republican Party. The work of the Bureau was subjected to ridicule and the officials were *persona non grata* in Southern society. During his tenure as a Freedmen's Bureau administrator at Greenville, South Carolina, John De Forest was snubbed by members of the South Carolina aristocracy. "To my native infamy as a Yankee I added the turpitude of being a United States military officer and the misdemeanor of being a sub-assistant commissioner of the Freedmen's Bureau."[140]

Josie was irate over the uninhibited intermingling of the Freedmen's Bureau "feminines" and Columbia's newly freed blacks. "You ought to see the operations of the feminines attached to the Freedmen's Bureau," Josie wrote. A local home, she related, was "seized for the headquarters," and the newly freed blacks were allowed to hold dances in the basement for an entrance fee of one dollar and a half. Naturally, Columbia residents were shocked when at one of these "balls," the Bureau "feminines" joined the blacks in square dances. In turn, the black ladies were decidedly unenthusiastic about sharing their partners with Freedmen's Bureau women, a situation which erupted in at least one tumultuous brawl. Two weeks later—these "white feminines" joined in the round dances. Josie was aghast. "Great Heaven! Think of such a thing in this state!!!! Now they parade the streets in open day light with the negro men...."[141]

In language that reads more like that of the latter twentieth century than that of the nineteenth century, Josie denounced the motives of the officers and "feminines" of the Freedman's Bureau: "Greed of gain is all that activates them and they screw it out of the poor negro in every way. If they consult Ely on any point no matter *how trifling* they have to pay the fee *right down*."[142,143]

Josie's friends also appeared to share many white Southerners' loathing for the Freedmen's Bureau. From New Orleans, Dolly Dill wrote Josie: "I hope the Freedmen's Bureau has had the same downfall in S. Carolina that has overtaken it here. The Rev. Mr. Conway who was at the head of this Bureau when we arrived, and who had 'nigger on the

brain' in its most virulent form has lately been removed by order of Johnson, and his place filled by one Gen Fullerton who cant seem to hustle
out fast enough the occupants of confiscated property, whether they be
black or white. Many a poor Confed (or as they call them here 'Con-
feds') has within the last two weeks stepped back into a house and property which he had long ceased to regard as his own, tho' many of them
sell out at once or rent, not having the means to keep up the old style of
things. Mr. Yank, however, generally contrives to carry off with him, a
writing desk, or a handsome clock, or a favorite chair, or some article of
luxury or convenience to which he has taken a fancy."[144]

Their new relationships with blacks and the sometimes defiant,
aggressive attitude of their former "servants" would entail considerable
adjustment on the part of Southerners over the years. However, Josie and
untold numbers of other Southerners, despite their reluctance to recognize them as equals, were deeply concerned about the problems facing
the newly freed black men and women. After years of maintaining a
somewhat paternalistic care for their Negroes, many former slave owners were apprehensive about the ultimate fate of the newly emancipated
blacks. The sudden liberation of four million unskilled, uneducated, inex-
perienced blacks promised gigantic problems for the entire country. In
December of 1865 Josie wrote: "Equal sufferers are the poor Negroes.
God help them—! Thousands will perish this winter from cold and starvation before our eyes and yet we can't help them." The LeContes
lamented that at that time they had all they could do to keep body and
soul together and unfortunately had precious little left to share with others. "*I assure you,*" Josie wrote, "*our own struggles to exist occupy all our
thoughts and time.*"

The detested Loyalty Oath constituted yet another trial for Southerners to bear. Taking the oath of allegiance to the U.S. government was
a loathsome, humiliating task for many Southerners—and absolutely
inconceivable for thousands of others.[145] The oath required swearing to
"faithfully support and defend the Constitution of the United States and
the Union of States thereunder" and to "abide by, and faithfully support, all Laws and Proclamations" made during the rebellion. Those who
would not subscribe to the oath were not permitted to vote, conduct
business, practice law, pursue their pre-war careers, or even obtain a
marriage license. There were those who refused to take the oath, believing it negated the deaths of their fathers, sons or brothers in the war.
Some were convinced there was no alternative but to pledge allegiance.
Still others considered a compulsory oath not binding. For some, to take
the oath or not to take the oath involved a serious struggle with their consciences.

Josie was heartsick upon visiting a friend and seeing the poor woman struggling to cultivate the soil with a table knife in order to "make a garden." Suddenly her friend Mrs. Pope burst into tears. Her husband was under strict orders not to conduct business of any kind and the couple was at a complete loss for money for food and clothing. (Mr. Pope apparently had refused to sign the Loyalty Oath, or was being discriminated against as an owner of more than $20,000 of property, or was a civil servant before the war and was therefore unable to take the Iron Clad Oath, which stated that one had never given "aid, countenance, counsel or encouragement" to persons engaged in armed hostility against the United States.) An embittered Josie detailed for her sister Mrs. Pope's wretched health and obsessive fear of starvation: "These are moments, when I am fearfully rebellious and find it difficult to say and feel in all *sincerity*— 'thy will be done.' I will ask myself—what have *we* done, or *she* done, that should make *us* to cruelly suffer, when the authors of all our misfortunes are glutting over, and really thriving—upon our untold misery? However the battle *is not over yet*—much as they may desire reconstruction and a republican form of government. Its gone! never to be resuscitated in our day or generation."[146]

Emma LeConte found an outlet for her views on the Loyalty Oath in her diary: "They are administering the oath here now and almost everyone is obliged to take it, for unless they do they are not allowed to engage in any occupation, nor to travel beyond the limits of the town, nor will they be protected against violence or injustice of any kind. Aunt Josie says, and I suppose they reason in the same way, that she would take it as a mere form forced upon her and therefore not binding on her conscience, and that she would break it as readily as she would take it. But I cannot feel that way and I do not see how I could do it unless really starving. Father, too, feels that it would be a most painful necessity that would compel him to such humiliation. Well, I do not suppose it will be required of women, and I hope Father will be spared the swallowing this bitter pill on account of his being a paroled officer."

"I saw a copy of the oath yesterday," Emma noted. "It requires you to repudiate all allegiance to the so-called Confederate States and only permits loyalty to your own state so long as that state is not opposed to the United States, thus putting allegiance to the U.S. Government *above* that to the *state*. You then have to swear allegiance to the U.S. Government, binding yourself in the most solemn way to uphold it under all circumstances, and all this is sworn without mental reservation or secret evasion, 'so help me God.' Who could take such an oath as that? It is a tyrannical measure to force it upon the Southern people. Ministers are not allowed to preach without taking it and I hear Mr. Shand has had to submit to it."[147]

During the war it had been the practice of many of the Southern churches to omit the prayer for the president of the United States and instead to substitute a prayer for the president of the Confederacy, Jefferson Davis. Once an area was taken over by the Federals, however, the military authorities insisted that the prayer for the president *of the United States* be reinstituted in the service. This, of course, as an abrogation of religious freedom, caused a rain of protests from devout parishioners—and even from confirmed atheists. Emma, therefore, took issue with General Hartwell's threat to close down the church: "The next thing he did was to go to Church. After the service he wrote a note to Mr. Shand saying he had observed the omission of the prayer for the President of the United States, and that Mr. Shand would be pleased to use it hereafter or he would be under the unpleasant necessity of closing his Church. (Closing a Church at present means giving it to the negroes.) A few days after, he left for a week or two. Mr. Shand went to Col. Haughton about it. The Colonel told him he was very sorry, but since the thing was brought before him officially, he was compelled to carry out his orders. 'I have,' he said, 'abstained from going to Church ever since I have been here because I understood the prayer was not used and I did not wish to interfere with your religious worship.'"

"The next Sunday," Emma continued, "Col. Haughton went to Church and the prayer was used. At the first words the congregation rose from their knees. Mr. Shand hurried through it as if the words choked him, and at the end not one *amen* was heard throughout the Church, not even from the minister who was assisting at the altar. Cousin Lula says she felt her blood begin to boil as she heard that villainous wretch prayed for! Did ever anyone hear of such tyranny as forcing a *prayer* on people? What has the government to do with the Church? There is no union of church and state in this country."[148]

Charitable "Entertainments"

By the end of the war there were tens of thousands of widows and orphans struggling for survival, and untold numbers of returning soldiers utterly debilitated by the war and destined to live out their remaining months or years in rocking chairs or hospital beds. Despite their own pressing problems, Josie and her extended family realized there were always those less fortunate. Considerable time and effort on the part of the LeConte women in both families were spent helping with various charitable "entertainments" held in Columbia. The Soldiers' Aid Societies that supplied the mountains of bandages and clothing for distribution to front-line and hospitalized Southern soldiers during the war years were quickly transformed after the surrender into societies devoted to helping provide assistance for the thousands of physically or mentally disabled veterans and their families.

Actually, it was the women of the North who became famous for their gigantic fairs, held both during and after the war in many of the large northern cities. Ingenuity coupled with incredibly long hours of difficult work turned those extravaganzas into huge moneymakers for the United States Sanitary Commission and soldiers' relief. The South, also, was swept up in the fair mania. During the war, however, as a result of the disruption of lines of communication and the paucity of goods available, those fairs were usually conducted on a much smaller scale than the mammoth affairs produced in Chicago, New York, Boston, and Philadelphia.

Just a month before the Federals raged through Columbia, the city had staged an elaborate bazaar in the state house that raised $350,000 for the Confederate cause.[149] Although the fair was originally scheduled to have remained open for two weeks, unfortunately, the proximity of Sherman's men necessitated a shortening of the bazaar's run. Nevertheless, most of the Confederate states were represented by booths which, Emma noted, were "loaded with fancy articles—brought through the blockade, or manufactured by the ladies." The prices seemed exorbitant. "How can people afford to buy toys at such a time as this!" Emma exclaimed. "However, I suppose speculators can. A small-sized cake at the Tennessee table sold for seventy-five dollars."[150]

All of the LeContes seemed to be caught up in the city's endeavors to raise money for the soldiers during the war and for the veterans after the war. Josie's executive ability proved a valuable asset to the fund-raisers, and her letters to Mollie were enthusiastically punctuated with details of the various postwar fairs, concerts and tableaux. For at least one benefit Josie was given sole responsibility for the tableaux. Although she expressed some reluctance about her involvement, she also welcomed the assignment as a temporary release from their postwar gloom: "I despise all these swindling operations—but have been dragged in on account of loneliness and a desire for some little excitement that can make us forget for a while the blackness of our political fortunes."[151]

Columbia audiences were delighted with Josie's tableaux, "gotten up" as a means of helping raise money "to clothe the soldiers' orphans in the town." "Our tableaux passed off most successfully, and we realized hundreds of dollars after all expenses were paid," Josie boasted.[152] In no time word of their financial triumphs spread to Virginia. There, executives preparing for a large fair in Richmond eagerly sought to enlist the help of the South Carolina women. Once again Josie became immersed in helping to arrange a South Carolina table for the Richmond event. A tempting offer came from the Richmond women to pay her expenses if she would go to Richmond and preside over that table. Although she admitted she would have loved to she was unable to join the Richmond ladies, as she complained, with the lament of all women since—and including—Eve, that she had "nothing to wear." Even husband John was involved in the work of the Virginia fair, the proceeds of which were to go to the care of the thousands of Confederate graves at Hollywood Cemetery in Richmond.[153]

The Academic Scene

Even elementary schools, as well as education in general, suffered for want of teachers and money during and immediately following the war. Most Southern schools were in a non-existent, or at best, a chaotic state during the war years, and the education of younger children was temporarily abandoned or taken over by older sisters in a family. Emma was given the responsibility for teaching her sister Sallie, a task which she believed would reap an added bonus in helping her prepare to earn a living for herself should the need arise. "I have decided to review arithmetic and algebra with a view to possibly being able to get an assistant teacher's place.... It may not be necessary for me to get work and I may not be able to get it, but the review can do me no harm in any event." Emma noted that her own French lessons were paid for in provisions "at the rate of ten cents an hour." Even with such modest fees, however, Emma was uneasy about how long she could continue, as the LeConte funds were "diminishing very fast and we cannot tell where more is to come from."[154]

Josie was hard put to know where to turn in order to obtain adequate schooling for her sons. Their unrelenting antipathy for Yankees prevented Josie and her husband from even remotely considering sending their children to northern schools. She instructed her sister: "*Never* speak of a northern institution to us! John would rather see the children *dead*, than enter one of them. You ought to have seen how he *raved* the other day when I hinted at it...."[155]

Hiring a tutor for their children appeared to be the best solution to the education enigma for many Southerners, but unfortunately there was always the problem of compensation. Unable to come up with the money for the services of a tutor, Josie worked out an arrangement with a young scholar that enabled him to live with the family in lieu of a salary: "Mr. Bice is now domiciled with us as a private teacher for my boys. He is exceedingly anxious to pursue his law studies—his means are of course nothing and withal very desirous of coming to Columbia to live. I told him I could not give him a salary but that if he chose to become a part of our household and would consider his board equivalent to his labor I would be very glad to obtain his services. He jumped at the offer at once. John has given him the use of his apparatus room so that every morning about 9 o'clock they march to their labors. I consider myself most fortunate in securing his services *especially* for Johnnie."[156]

Following the war, South Carolina College, as did most Southern institutions of higher education, underwent immense changes. John Trowbridge pointed out that conditions at South Carolina College after the war patently illustrated the devastating effect of the war on education in the South. In Columbia a pre-war student body of two hundred and fifty students had dwindled to eighteen. Pre-war state appropriations of sixty-five thousand dollars to the College had shrunk to eight thousand dollars, and the professors were not seeing any of that paltry sum. According to Trowbridge, "One, a gentleman of distinguished learning, said he had not had ten dollars in his possession since Sherman visited them."[157] It was decided to enlarge the College by adding a law school and a medical college, so as to make it a university.

In October of 1865 Governor Perry urged the opening of the College and its conversion into a university. Officials believed that returning veterans needed a practical education in order to find gainful employment in the postwar world. The traditional classical education had considerable merit, they agreed, but now students strapped for money and often inadequately prepared for college because of their four year stint in the Confederate Army, should be offered a realistic preparation for business, mathematics, engineering or a particular profession. Two months later a bill for the reorganization of South Carolina College into the University of South Carolina became law. John LeConte served as chairman of the School of Natural and Mechanical Philosophy and Astronomy, and Joseph LeConte served as Chairman of the School of Chemistry, Pharmacy, Minerology, and Geology.[158]

The General Assembly's appropriation of $8,600 in December of 1865 provided a beginning, although a somewhat tenuous one, for the new university. Unfortunately, at that time there was no funding made available for back pay for faculty members, and under the new system, professors' salaries were reduced to $1,000, about half what they had been before the war.[159]

On the credit side, however, professors were allowed to engage in outside work to supplement their meager salaries and were provided housing and the income from student fees. "Our College is a thing of the past," Josie explained. "It has been converted into University. On its new career which it enters upon next Monday, let us wish her a 'God Speed.' We get *now* our houses free of rent and one thousand dollars a year from the State—besides the fees which are 25 dollars a ticket, for the next two years—*if we remain*. The difficulties of getting along will be great—after that the position will be *very* remunerative. Neither John or Joseph would feel it *this* year if the Fresh's and Soph's studied their departments—but these will comprise most of the new students."[160]

Inadequacies probably best describe the festering problems that beset the burgeoning University of South Carolina immediately after the war. Foremost, of course, was the inadequate financial support for long-neglected repairs of campus buildings and faculty housing[161]; for books for the library, which was open only on Tuesdays, Thursdays, and Saturdays; and for the acquisition of new equipment or the replacement of old laboratory instruments that had been stolen or lost during the war. (Case in point: three new books comprised the total acquisition for the library in 1866.) The theft of a telescope prevented the teaching of astronomy for several years; laboratory equipment sent out of the city in anticipation of Sherman's invasion of Columbia was subsequently lost, a situation that immensely complicated the teaching of science classes.[162]

Inadequately prepared students, many of whom had spent four years in the Confederate army instead of in college preparatory schools, slowed class instruction down to the lowest common denominator. Even entrance exams had to be abolished for a time. In 1866 the only entrance requirement was that the youth be at least fifteen years of age. (Many students, of course, were older, owing to their service with the Confederate troops.)[163] The relaxation of requirements drew fire from a frustrated faculty and multitudes of other South Carolinians. As many of the requirements for students at the university became more relaxed, a great many tradition-bound segregationists were unnerved by a section of Article X in the 1868 constitution which read, "All the public schools, college and universities of the State, supported in whole or in part by the public funds, shall be free and open to all the children and youths of the State, without regard to race and color."[164]

Fears that Negroes would be admitted to the university served to discourage enrollments. In February of 1869 the legislature passed a bill stipulating, "The University shall not make any distinction in the admission of students or the management of the University on account of race, color, or creed." Members of the faculty, parents, students, and South Carolinians in general grew uneasy about the ultimate fate of the university as rumors persisted that the college was soon to be closed.

The financial difficulties of the university resulted in "hardships and mortifications" for the professors, many of whom began to look to "greener pastures" or a possible change of careers. Nervousness increased as the number of students dropped to fifty-seven in the 1868-69 year, about half the number of students as in the preceding, 1867-68, session. In his *Autobiography* a distraught Joseph LeConte fumed: "The prospects for the South were gloomy in the extreme. I bore the iniquities of the government as long as I could, but when the negro legislature began to talk about what they were going to do with the University, I thought it time to quit."[165]

With the resignations of important faculty members and their replacement with Northerners, concerns over the future of the university deepened. There was a rumbling of criticism from citizens steeped in the classics that students were getting only a smattering of knowledge and that the reputation of the once-distinguished university was quickly degenerating into that of a second rate high school.[166]

It certainly must have come as no surprise to anyone that the scarcity of money, experienced by even the antebellum wealthy, would result in a dearth of students. In the postwar South obtaining an education, for many young men, was often of secondary importance to helping one's family secure the basic necessities of life. Although there were district scholarships available, few students took advantage of them. "The prospects of the University are quite gloomy," Josie declared. "The people in this state have suffered *so* terribly that they are not able to send [their children to the University of South Carolina]. Those *who have the means* send them to European universities. It is believed by financiers that this state *alone* sacrificed twelve hundred millions in the struggle."[167]

When a new elective system for choosing classes was introduced, few students selected the important but less popular and more difficult courses. In an attempt to attract more enrollees, professors were required to expand their regular course offerings with practical short courses. Often these were in areas outside the professor's areas of specialization and necessitated considerable extra work. Josie quipped "unless *we leave here*, it is *all work*, and *no pay!*"[168]

Thus ran a partial list of the frustrations awaiting a faculty that has since been described as "one of the best ever assembled in South Carolina." University fees were twice as much as those in 1860, and in January 1866, only about twenty students were on hand for the opening of classes.[169]

Within months people began referring to the university as a dismal failure. There was even a proposal to shut it down for a year in order to regroup and to reassess the university's future. Fears of a take-over of the university by the Radicals coupled with plans to replace white professors with blacks and concerted efforts to open the university to all students without regard to race or color, discouraged student attendance and added to the anxieties of an already apprehensive faculty. Professors had had their fill of struggling to teach students lacking even a decent high school education. The idea of prostituting their academic and professional degrees in trying to teach what they deemed elementary school subjects was extremely distasteful to the members of the faculty.

Although the LeConte brothers' financial difficulties were somewhat relieved as their salaries resumed with the reopening of the university, this appeared merely a temporary solution, for, as evidenced in Josie's letters and reiterated in Joseph LeConte's *Autobiography*, escalating problems at the university along with Yankee occupation and Radical Reconstruction contrived to make life onerous and unpleasant for the LeContes. Joseph LeConte admitted that he had been well satisfied with Benjamin F. Perry as provisional governor. (Perry had formerly served for many years on South Carolina College's Board of Trustees.) However, the LeContes, as well as thousands of other South Carolina residents, soon found life unbearable in the midst of carpetbaggers and scalawags: "When the permanent government was organized in the presence of bayonets, with a carpet-bag governor, scalawag officials, and a negro legislature controlled by rascals, things were very different, and at last became simply intolerable." Joseph LeConte continued: "The iniquity of the carpet-bag government was simply inexpressible."[170]

Many other Southern colleges were undergoing similar hardships, and to move to another struggling Southern university probably would have had few advantages for the LeContes. Both John and Joseph LeConte were renowned scientists and, had it not been for the stigma of the LeContes' service and commitment to the Confederacy, hundreds of northern colleges would no doubt have grabbed up such notable scientists.[171]

Continued dissatisfaction led the LeContes to give serious thought to leaving Columbia and even prompted Josie to seek some kind of employment herself: "This action [inability to recover back pay] compels us now to look earnestly about us for another home somewhere where John's talents can be made remunerative. Poor fellow his troubles and cares are breaking him down rapidly. In the meantime I shall look about me and see what employment I can get that will keep us from starvation a condition that we are fast verging into."[172]

Emma LeConte also fervently hoped she could find gainful employment to help with the family's financial crunch: "I wish I could get some employment *now*, anything, no matter what. If only I could make a little money—ever so little—just to help Father a little bit."[173]

With their situation becoming increasingly more desperate, the LeContes even considered conducting a fashionable private school in which both families would participate: Josie's husband, John, would teach philosophy, brother-in-law Joseph would take over the chemistry department, and Josie, her daughter Lula and niece Emma would handle the English classes.[174]

As her husband's health continued to decline, the result of his mounting problems, Josie undertook a vigorous campaign, through letters to friends and relatives, to help her husband find a more agreeable, more remunerative position, yet one "suitable to his tastes." Josie was a greatly admired favorite with her husband's colleagues. His friends were her friends also, and her correspondence was voluminous.

To Leave or Not to Leave

Moving out of the country, away from the turmoil, as did so many Southerners at the end of the war, held forth great promise, and for months emigration was the subject of endless discussion in both LeConte households. At the end of the war, one recalls, thousands of Southerners in all walks of life discovered it impossible or unbearable to resume their pre-war life. Some even refused to make an attempt at readjustment. Economic problems, fear of reprisals by the vindictive Radicals, concern over the status of blacks, confusion as to the future of the South, financial opportunity and a host of other reasons enticed thousands of Southerners to move westward. Several thousand more left the country and settled temporarily, or even permanently, in Canada, England, Mexico, Cuba, and Brazil.

Although many of their friends were leaving Columbia to take up residence in Europe, Josie was reluctant to pull up stakes: "In fact all the best people are quitting the country which I think is premature. I am anxious to wait for two years and if affairs dont mend then goodbye forever! John is anxious to go at once but I am not willing until I can see some opening. They are making every arrangement to open the College in January. If we receive our back pay we will be set up at once and I can then send Julian to England under the care of the McCords who leave at the time or Mrs. Denck."[175]

Several months later Josie was becoming increasingly discouraged over their situation at the university: "Everything looks so dark and gloomy and we find it so difficult from *our* stand point to discover the *first ray of sunshine* as to render it impossible to mature very present plans. For a time we will content ourselves by remaining and seeing what can best be done."[176]

Wildly enthusiastic reports from friends in Mexico, a popular spot for colonization, sorely tempted the LeContes to join their friends and to seek a new life for themselves. Josie confessed to her sister, "...so weary *am* I of these terrible struggles for existence that I have become thoroughly disgusted with the country and am moving Heaven and Earth to leave." She continued, "I have almost made up my mind to persuade *our* colony to go to Mexico—*great inducements* are offered to men of talents from *the South*—if we conclude to do so we will take with us upwards of 500 persons, among them the first military as well as Scientific talents of our Soil.[177]

"If our Prof's can secure positions before going, I shall not hesitate one moment—there seems to be no doubt about it. From all I can hear but that their services will be most acceptable in which case *we shall all leave here ... next November*. I can't mention names ... but you will be surprized when you hear who they are.... Such numbers of *our friends are already there*—and so many going—that we shall not feel like strangers there, and the bitter memories we take with us will only serve to bind us the closer together."[178]

Josie admitted she had given some thought to going to Russia, "but my winters experience give me the shivers whenever I think of such an inhospitable climate...." She assured her sister, "Of one thing *you* can be certain, *we will* go out of the country—*somewhere*—circumstanced as we are now *our existence is intolerable*."[179]

The colony at Cordova, Mexico, was particularly alluring to Josie: "General Price's settlement at Cordova is said to be having a glorious time of it. A great many of the wealthiest Missourians-Tennesseeans and Louisianians have joined the colony.... I should prefer living in the city of Mexico 'tho I should not object to a fine coffee plantation at Cordova for it is in that settlement that we should prefer pitching our tents." She added that she had been reading everything she could lay her hands on and had "come to the conclusion it is the right place for us."[180]

Information about Mexico would have been easy for Josie to come by for American colonization in Mexico was receiving a big play in magazines and newspapers at that time. Writers extolled the opportunities for Southerners to "lessen the unpleasant remembrances of the past and to deaden the pangs of defeat" by emigrating to Mexico. In a letter given wide circulation in the press, the Confederate naval leader Matthew Fontaine Maury, who had been appointed Imperial Commissioner of Immigration by Emperor Maximilian, beckoned his fellow countrymen to join the Cordova and Carlota colonies, where he assured them an agreeable climate, cheap labor, congenial surroundings, and opportunities for huge fortunes awaited. "Corn, cotton, coffee, sugar and tobacco all do well here," he promised, and land can be purchased "at any price from a few cents to a few dollars per acre." A Louisiana gentleman, Maury pointed out, had set up a coffee plantation and was realizing a profit of some sixteen thousand dollars a year. The possibility of introducing classes in science conducted in English at the University of Mexico no doubt held special interest for the LeContes.[181]

For months Josie's determination to leave the country waxed and waned. Now and then her enthusiasm cooled a bit, perhaps as the result of wariness, perhaps due to a fleeting ray of optimism concerning prospects of the university—and of the South itself, or perhaps because of Josie's fondness for Columbia, their friends and the invigorating campus scene. Without question, Josie loved Columbia and South Carolina. She confessed: "Glorious little state that she is—how I shall grieve when we leave her shores! If it was possible to live here, I should not dream of going—but we can't starve and time's flying."[182]

Niece Emma and her family shared the John LeContes' interest in possibly leaving the country. A shortage of funds, however, presented a problem. "If we could only leave the country—will we ever have the means to do so?" Emma anguished. "How could we ever raise the money? We dream of this and make plans to emigrate—but the means are lacking now. We will have to wait. But I would rather work hard for my daily bread than live in luxury under Yankee rule."[183]

Despite his enthusiastic letter in *De Bow's Review*, Maury came to be skeptical about the proposed emigration of the LeContes to Mexico. The LeContes' spirits were considerably dampened by a discouraging letter in which Maury reported that conditions did not augur well for a move.[184] (How fortunate it was the LeContes did not take up residence in Mexico! Even Maury himself left Mexico and settled in England for two years.[185] By the spring of 1867 the Cordova colony was "a thing of the past," its demise carefully detailed in Andrew F. Rolle's *The Lost Cause: The Confederate Exodus to Mexico*.)

Years later, Josie's niece Caroline recounted the LeContes' dilemma: "Such an escape [emigration] was often considered by the family of Joseph LeConte, but our father was loath to leave his native land. Meanwhile, at the North, the most eminent men of science were working, hand and foot, to obtain positions for the two LeContes, John and Joseph. But in the latter part of the war these brothers had been experts in the manufacture of war supplies for the Confederacy, and now, outside of the ruined South, every academic door was closed against them. My mother was wont to say that my father could not have gotten a position in a primary school."[186]

"The clouds darkened," Caroline recalled. "The South Carolina legislature, through its negro board of trustees, was taking the first steps to declare the chairs vacant and to convert the University into a school for illiterate negroes. Now, indeed, emigration was imperative: England, Mexico, Venezuela, Brazil, were all discussed in turn."[187]

For the LeContes it began to look as though there was no alternative but to emigrate—somewhere. And yet times were to grow even more grievous for John and Josie LeConte with the death from advanced tuberculosis of their daughter Lula on March 21, 1868. Their grief plunged the bereaved parents into a deep depression from which they found it almost impossible to extricate themselves.

Sunshine at Last

Finally, at long last there appeared a glimmer of sunshine. Word was making the rounds in academic circles that California was in the process of starting a new university near San Francisco. Louis Agassiz, the world-famous naturalist and a long friend of both families, sent word to the LeConte brothers urging them to apply for posts on the faculty, and promising to "back them with strong letters." Ah! but would they stand a chance at the positions? Was California far enough away that the record of their service to the Confederacy would not be held against them? Would their Confederate background immediately disqualify them? In very short order senators, representatives, and regents were deluged with letters of recommendation from the country's top scientists praising the LeConte brothers as "the best men they could obtain in this Country to fill the Chairs of Physics and Chemistry at the University of California."[188]

Numerous influential men in California were queried as to the LeContes' prospects. At least one authority was asked, "If upon examination, Dr. LeConte [John] should be found competent to fill a position in the University, would it be an objection to him in your mind, if you knew he was a Southern man with Southern principles and had taken part in the late rebellion?" The reply was immediate and tremendously encouraging: "Not in the least. I want the South represented in the University. I want professors from all parts of our country. I have no prejudice against any section. If I had been in the South in 1861, I have no doubt that I would have been in the Southern army…. No Sir! The politics of Dr. LeConte will never be considered by the Regents when his name comes before them."[189]

To some people California seemed the "end of the earth," the "jumping-off place of creation." One enthusiastic supporter, however, along with notice of his endorsement, counseled: "The change, tho' painful, will, I think, be the best for yourselves and your children, and perhaps for the cause of humanity. The South can never again be what it was. New habits, new thoughts and new men will have sway. You would no longer be in unison with the times were you to remain, and, therefore, your energies would be best employed in a new sphere and under new conditions."[190]

Soon the LeContes' impressive credentials prevailed and in November of 1868, John LeConte was elected to the chair of physics at the

University of California. Two weeks later Joseph LeConte was appointed to the chair of geology.[191] Acceptances, with "sincere gratification," were immediately dispatched. Once again life for the LeContes was transformed almost overnight. The suffering and bitterness of the war years and Reconstruction would soon become a thing of the past—the land of opportunity awaited them.

Epilogue

General George B. McClellan had been the University of California's first choice as president, but with his rejection of the offer, John LeConte was made acting president. As it was all-important for him to assume his new responsibilities as soon as possible, Josie's husband borrowed eight hundred dollars from his brother and quickly arranged passage to California via Panama. Joseph LeConte and his family (minus Emma, who had married Farish Furman five months before their departure), accompanied by sister Jane and her daughter, chose to await the completion of the transcontinental railroad. Caroline LeConte later wrote: "My father waited only to see that the way was reasonably safe. Then not knowing very well what was before, but dreading that which lay behind, he packed up his effects."[192]

Being extremely short of funds to pay for the expensive railroad trip west, Joseph LeConte and his wife Bessie were ecstatic when John repaid Joseph the eight hundred dollars he had borrowed for his journey to California. The train trip was a thrilling experience, especially for five-year-old Caroline, although she registered great disappointment that the train's guard of Federal soldiers was not called upon to put down at least one Indian attack. They hurtled their way across the plains, Caroline reported, sometimes at speeds of "sixteen miles an hour."[193]

Upon their arrival, they were met by John LeConte and escorted to the spacious home of millionaire Charles Webb Howard, who for a paltry sum had turned over his home, servants, and garden to the LeContes while he was traveling in Europe. Ah! This surely was the Promised Land!

It took little time for both LeConte families to become deeply enamored of California, the University, and the people. Josie wrote her sister, "Nobody thinks less of you for being poor but you must come determined to work and if you have decided talent and *will work*—you get well paid for it."[194]

Josie quickly learned, however, that San Francisco and Oakland breezes could prove embarrassing for a lady, as she wrote that winds "whistle thro every rickety joint of your frame work. As for *legs* and underclothing *I blush for my sex at every turning point.*" She warned her sister, "In heavens name have *shot* put in all your dresses before you leave New York."[195]

California, at that time, was famous for offering golden opportunities, the place where people "picked up gold in the streets." Young Carrie had believed the expression literally, and on their first excursion around Oakland the little girl became greatly preoccupied with constantly bending over to study the streets. When her father chided her for lagging behind and examining the sidewalks, Carrie could scarcely conceal her disappointment: "'Papa, where is the gold that people pick up in the street?'"

"But the gold came," Carrie remembered. "It came with my father's first salary. He beckoned the family into my mother's room. Then pulling out the money, piece by piece he flung it down on the bed. 'Gold!' he shouted. 'Silver!' he proclaimed. And then throwing up one hand, fingers outspread, and with a thrilling cry: 'Money!' The women with cries of delight were fingering the strange-looking yellow and whitish roundels that could buy anything from land and houses to boots and shoes."

"My father commenced paying back what he had borrowed," Carrie continued. "Christmas came on apace and with it a huge box of toys. 'Why, Papa,' Carrie exclaimed, 'I never heard of Santa Claus before! Why didn't Santa Claus come to the little boys and girls in Columbia?' I looked up and wondered why my father's and mother's eyes were filled with tears."[196]

The University of California welcomed its first class of students in September 1869. Joseph LeConte was standing behind a table as the first student to enroll approached: "Clarence Wetmore stepped forward. Dipping a pen in ink, the Professor handed it to him, saying, 'You have the honor to be the first student to register in this institution that is destined to be one of the very greatest in the country.'"[197] (The University of California opened its doors in 1869 with "thirty-eight students, eight professors, and an income of about $30,000.")[198]

Josie's husband soon retired as acting president in order to devote full time and attention to the department of physics. In 1876, however, John LeConte returned to administrative duties when he was elected president of the University of California. According to Josie's sister-in-law, Jane Harden, "Josie was, and is now the happiest woman you ever saw. What she has wished for years past has come at last." Josie's pride in her husband was also reflected in her sister-in-law's letter to her daughter: "My brother John has been elected President of the University. I am glad of it, for he richly deserves it and no more suitable one could have been selected. Commencement day was a time of much pleasure and gratification to me. John appeared in his official capacity, in public for the first time. Much honor was done him on the occasion which he bore with self possession & calm dignity. His address to the Graduating Class was one of the best I ever heard. On Commencement day, my two brothers John and Joseph were the most prominent men on the occasion."[199]

John LeConte served as president of the University of California until 1881, when he again stepped down to continue his work as professor of physics, a position which he held until his death in 1891. Joseph LeConte served the University from 1869 until 1901. Throughout the years the LeContes' loyalty to the University never wavered. In Carrie's words, "This is the University which, when every worthwhile academic door was closed against them, saved the LeConte brothers from exile to a foreign land."[200]

Devastated by her husband's death in 1891, Josie lived out the next three years a lonely, melancholy figure. In December of 1894, while Josie was sitting in the warmth of the fireplace, reading and dozing, a section of newspaper slipped from her lap, was ignited by the flames which quickly spread to her dress and engulfed the charming, beautiful Josie.[201] Josie had eluded the flames that consumed Columbia in February of 1865; in one tragic moment, almost thirty years later, however, flames finally succeeded in claiming their wily victim.

Family and friends were exuberant in their tributes to Josie. "She had constant adorers from all classes," her niece Emma remembered. "The callow college boys fluttered around her like moths," Emma wrote admiringly, and John's colleagues "bowed at her shrine."[202] One author commented that at various scientific meetings, "Such men as Bache, Peirce, Henry, and Agassiz vied with each other in doing her homage. Her fame in social circles equaled that of her husband among men of science."[203]

Surely one of the most eloquent testaments to Josie's character and influence was Joseph LeConte's praise of her in his memoir of his brother, read before the National Academy of Sciences in April of 1894, in which he noted that aside from the early influence of his father, "No other influence so greatly affected the whole course of his life as that of his wife. Mrs. John LeConte was a woman of rare intelligence, spirit, and vivacity and of great force of character, united with queenly beauty and great social influence. He never undertook any enterprise or made any change of life without her advice and counsel. Their mutual devotion was as perfect as human devotion can be, and continued with ever-increasing strength to the very end.... The moral effect of such a wedded life who can estimate? Surely it is the most powerful of all influences in ennobling and purifying human character. If character is formed in childhood, it is ripened and refined by a happy wedded life."[204]

CI *Three* IƆ

A Precarious Existence

In what a deplorable condition is our great country, once so prosperous,
united and happy, now in a state of anarchy, confusion and ruin, and
when, where or how, it will end God alone knows.
— Nancy Chapman Jones

Prologue

The precarious existence of a family living in Missouri during the
war years is revealed in the letters (1861–1865) of Nancy Chapman Jones,
of Boonville, Missouri, to her recently married daughter, Mary, residing
at that time in San Antonio, Texas.

Missouri, one recalls, proved to be a volatile trouble spot throughout the Civil War. A bitter rivalry existed between Confederate rebels
who actively favored the state's secession and Union loyalists who insisted
that the state remain in the Union. As a border state, its government
ostensibly siding with the Union but potentially capable of being over-
thrown by Southern sympathizers who would then vote for secession,
Missouri was handled with kid gloves by the federal government. Lincoln's Emancipation Proclamation, of course, applied only to the states
"still in rebellion." The emancipation of slaves in the border states was
withheld for fear slave owners, who were already teetering in their allegiance to the Federals, would angrily switch sides were they to be summarily divested of their slaves. The Compromise of 1820 had decreed
that Missouri would be a slave state and Maine a free state, but thereafter no state north of latitude 36° 30' would be admitted to the Union
as a slave state.

The acquisition of immense new territories following the Mexican
war and the gold rush in California brought renewed conflict between
the anti-slavery men of the North and the Southern slaveowners who
wished to settle the new territories with their slaves. The Compromise

of 1850, hammered out by Clay, Webster, and Calhoun, allowed California to come into the Union as a free state but called for "popular Sovereignty" (the vote of the people to permit or prohibit slavery) to prevail in the rest of the "acquired territory." Later the Kansas-Nebraska Act, introduced by Stephen A. Douglas, repudiated the Compromise of 1820 (the Missouri Compromise) and allowed the people of newly formed territories to determine whether they would be slave or free. Kansas thus became a battleground between anti-slavery Northern settlers, pro-slavery Southerners, and Missouri border ruffians. The sacking of Lawrence, Kansas, and John Brown's massacre at Pottawatomie Creek were merely two instances in what became known as "the bleeding of Kansas."[1] The inflamed passions of thousands of pioneers who settled in Missouri permanently or sought temporary respite in their trek to more westerly territories erupted in violent collisions between zealous Union and Confederate factions.

Missouri citizens soon found themselves fighting two civil wars in the 1860s—the American Civil War and the Missouri Civil War. As a key border state, seething with divided loyalties, Missouri, from the very beginning of the war, provided the breeding ground for inflamed passions, resulting in repeated skirmishes and guerrilla warfare. Historians generally agree that Missouri soon became the scene of some of "the worst guerrilla warfare in American history."[2] According to James McPherson, "More than any other state, Missouri suffered the horrors of internecine warfare and the resulting hatreds which persisted for decades after Appomattox."[3]

In perusing Nancy Jones's letters to her daughter, Mary, one is reminded that even members of the Missouri state government were at odds with one another. The governor, Claiborne Fox Jackson (a former business partner of Nancy's husband Caleb Jones, according to Caleb's grandson), sided with the Confederacy despite the fact that a convention called to determine Missouri's stand in relation to the Union voted overwhelmingly against secession. Jackson's Confederate sympathies were clearly evident when at his inauguration on January 5, 1861, Jackson promised that "Missouri will not shirk from its duty ... to stand by the South." As Nancy noted in her letter to her daughter, when Lincoln called for four regiments to be supplied from Missouri, Jackson retorted that Missouri would refuse to send troops, would refuse compliance with what he considered to be a diabolical order. Jackson had contemptuously replied, "Your requisition is illegal, unconstitutional, and revolutionary in its objects, inhuman and diabolical, and cannot be complied with."[4] Nancy referred to Jackson's reply in her letters of April 22, 1861, and observed that large numbers of enthusiastic Boonville residents appeared to have supported Jackson's stand.

Despite deep-seated animosities a Union government eventually emerged during the summer of 1861. Jackson was deposed and he and many of his cohorts left Missouri for Arkansas. (Nancy refers to this in her June 25, 1861, letter.) Upon their departure, members of the Missouri state convention convened, declared the governor's office vacant, and a new pro-union governor and other state officials were elected. By this action a Union government prevailed in Missouri until January 1865.[5]

☙❧

Although Missourians living in the southeastern counties and in the northwestern areas of the state tended to favor Secession, many of the German residents, especially around St. Louis, held strong Union sympathies. A divided Missouri saw an estimated 109,000 (three-fourths of the state's white men) join the Union forces, while 30,000 to 40,000 fought with the Confederacy.[6] The Caleb Joneses, of Boonville, therefore, found themselves inextricably caught up in the turmoil and violence that ravaged the state. Although Caleb Jones had been born in Baltimore (1805), financial losses had overtaken the family and prompted a move to Cynthiana, Kentucky, where Caleb grew to young manhood. From Cynthiana Caleb in 1826 struck out on his own for Missouri, where he embarked on a teaching career in Arrow Rock, a small town about twelve miles out of Boonville, Missouri. Merchandising, however, promised far greater financial rewards, and Caleb Jones quickly gave up the meager pecuniary returns of teaching. Over the years there were preliminary business ventures in Arrow Rock, Bolivar and Philadelphia, and in time his development of a prosperous wholesale and retail business in Boonville, which Caleb expected to grow to supersede St. Louis.[7]

Much of the merchandise for Caleb's wholesale and retail businesses were forwarded to Missouri from several of his brothers, who were stationed in Philadelphia. By closely watching the markets, his brothers were able to purchase supplies and send them on to Boonville, where Caleb resold them for a profit. In addition to his businesses, Caleb invested in farm lands and "played at farming." According to Nancy Jones, "It took Caleb Jones, the merchant, to keep Caleb Jones a farmer." The Joneses soon became a well-established family in the Boonville community, where Caleb owned thousands of acres of fertile Missouri farmland and served as one of the incorporators of the first bank in Cooper County. Although a slave owner, Caleb "did not buy and sell slaves for a profit, but always had enough to supply the needs of the family." (In 1860 Caleb Jones owned seven slaves, two of whom were teenagers and one a young child.) Caleb's business acumen and investments apparently paid off, and by the time Caleb has amassed a hundred thousand dollars, he called it quits and retired, deeming his earnings "enough to satisfy any man."

In 1831 Caleb married Nancy Chapman, whose family had also migrated from Kentucky and who had lived for a time with her family in a fort in Howard County for protection from the Indians. Despite her hardy frontier conditioning Nancy was known for her "gentle, loving character and we [her family] were all the better for knowing her and receiving her kindness."

In the course of time three children were born to Nancy and Caleb Jones: Addie (often referred to as "Ada"), who married a prominent Boonville lawyer, William D. Muir, and lived not-too-far distant from Nancy; Mary, to whom the letters are addressed and who had recently married Justin McCarthy, the head of a San Antonio business engaged in obtaining supplies for the Confederacy; and George, whose possible conscription into the army eventually helped convince his family it was time to leave the country and escape the trauma of wartime Missouri.[8] Prior to the war a fire had destroyed the family home, situated on one of Caleb's farms, and a second home, a large brick mansion, was built to replace it. Somehow that home was never pleasing to Nancy Jones, and a third home, called Oakland, was under construction when the war came. Although it was made livable, it was never quite finished.

As background for the letters quoted in this chapter, the reader needs to know that shortly before the war, Caleb Jones, in the interests of traveling and seeing the country, had packed up his family and set out on the long overland trip by horse and carriage to Texas. In San Antonio, considered at that time the "gateway to the Southwest," the Joneses sold the carriage, sent the servants back to Boonville and settled down for the winter. It was a new world for Nancy and Caleb, who enjoyed life immensely among interesting people and in a totally different setting. It was during that sojourn that Mary met and fell in love with the young Irishman, Justin McCarthy. (The Joneses' winter in San Antonio would explain Nancy's familiarity with her daughter's surroundings and friends.) Mary had had a bevy of beaux in Boonville, but it was Justin who truly captured her heart. In the spring Nancy and Caleb returned to Boonville, and were soon followed by Justin in hot pursuit of his ladylove. In short order the couple were married in the home of Mary's sister and brother-in-law, the William Muirs.

The wedding proved a wrenching experience for Nancy and Caleb, both devout Methodists. Not only were they losing a daughter to far-away Texas, but, horror of all horrors, she was marrying an Irish Catholic! Nancy had done her best to prevent further contact between Mary and Justin, hoping that their letters would be delayed, or better yet somehow swallowed up in the irregular mail service of the times. Both parents must have struggled valiantly with their Protestant convictions in accepting Mary's choice of a husband. Apparently Nancy and Caleb reconciled themselves to the marriage on the condition that the wedding ceremony be performed "first by the Methodist minister and then by the Catholic priest." The distance between mother and daughter, Justin's Catholicism and her regret at not having known her son-in-law better, continued to trouble Nancy in the months and years to come. Several times, Nancy attempted to apologize for her lack of enthusiasm at the time of Mary's wedding.

Following a brief wedding trip to New York, Mary and Justin journeyed south to make their home in San Antonio, "right back of the Alamo." In San Antonio Justin McCarthy and his two partners developed a seemingly thriving business by buying up goods and then selling them to the Confederate government. (Surely a business arrangement that must have involved some or a considerable amount of blockade running!) Justin did, indeed, have access to luxuries soon to be in short supply in most of the South. This became evident when several weeks after their wedding trip Mary and Justin sent a trunkload of gifts, including neckties, books, hats, and caps, to the Joneses and the Muirs—and even to their "servants."

"The trunk full of presents arrived this morning and will form quite an era in our household history," Nancy wrote. "Your selections give universal satisfaction. Ada is delighted with Minnie's hat, the baby's is just the thing she wanted but could not get in Boonville. She is very much obliged to Mr. Mc for it and wonders how he ever thought of buying such a thing. George was in this morning. I gave him the cravats and your pa's book which I know will please him very much." Nancy conveyed Ada's request that "you must tell her how to arrange her hair for the head dress she does not know how to put it on. I am very much pleased with my caps. I will keep the one Mr. Mc bought to wear when he makes me a visit."[9]

Unfortunately, Justin's business at times was fraught with many of the wartime perils of risk and deception. Mary and Justin's son later recalled an incident of a double loss suffered by his father when on a trip to France racketeers bilked him out of 50,000 dollars by drawing up an exchange on a bogus French bank. Although he soon successfully established credit in Paris and purchased supplies, his huge shipment of goods was captured by the Union forces just prior to their delivery to the Confederacy. Worry over his finances no doubt helped bring about Justin's illness and his early death at the end of the war.

Missouri: A War Within a War

Through the letters of Nancy Chapman Jones to her daughter, Mary, in San Antonio, Texas, the reader is offered the opportunity to experience vicariously the uncertainty and frustrations of thousands of Missouri families struggling through those terrible years of strife. Fears for their son, for their property, for their very existence, come to life in the pages of Nancy's letters. Despite her attempt to put up a good front in an effort not to overly alarm her daughter, Nancy's letters evidence the anxieties of their precarious situation. At any moment their home could be torched; an ill chosen word here or there and they could be arrested and exiled, their home and property confiscated. Any vestige of resistance could find Nancy's husband meeting an untimely death and found floating in the river, as was the fate of their dear friend and neighbor, Dr. Main. For Missourians there was the bloodshed on a distant battlefield coupled with the barbaric guerrilla warfare on the homefront. As usual, tens of thousands of Missouri women paid the price for their husbands' allegiances and were subjected to robberies, violence and insults—the latter which they often returned in kind. Fortunately, for the most part, the sanctity of womankind prevailed and few white women were raped or murdered; however their notorious feistiness often resulted in extremely brutal treatment. A St. Louis politician predicted: "There will be trouble in Missouri until the Secesh are *subjugated* and made to know that they are not only powerless, but that any desperate attempts to make trouble here will bring upon them *certain* destruction and this [certainty] of their condition must not be confined to Soldiers and fighting men, but must extend to non-combatant men *and women*."[10]

❈

Within days after the firing on Fort Sumter, Nancy Jones chronicled for her daughter the reigning confusion over Secession and the divisiveness of Missourians. "The people here are in a state of great excitement," Nancy wrote. "The court house was crowded last Saturday. Mr. Vest made a secession speech. The palmetto flag was waving over Boonville and the secession feeling is gaining ground very rapidly. You have doubtless seen Governor Jackson's reply to the Presidents call for troops, that not one man would Missouri send in any such unholy crusade. I fear we will have need for all the troops here on our own border."[11,12]

Two weeks later, conditions continued to worsen in Boonville. "This is the fourth of May, just two months since Lincoln's inaugural," Nancy told her daughter, "and in what a deplorable condition is our great country, once so prosperous, united and happy, now in a state of anarchy, confusion and ruin, and when, where or how, it will end God alone knows. The secession feeling prevails here almoste universally and the flag waves over our town. Mr. Vest says he is for an armed neutrality untill we are well armed then he is for casting them all on the south side."[13] In her next letter Nancy despaired: "We knew a trying time was coming, but we regarded it as something in the future. It is hard to realize that it is actually upon us."[14]

Dutifully, Nancy conveyed the news of the dissension rampant among Boonville residents. Nancy bitterly registered her hatred of Douglas. "You remember how much you were pleased with the speeches made by William Douglas last winter. He has turned traitor, and is as black a black republican as can be found." Nancy also evidenced little respect for the Boonville Hogans. "Mr. Hogan is a Union man. Miss Borron and little Mary Hogan stood at their fence with boquets for all the officers, when Lyon marched by on his way to Springfield."[15]

The Civil War as a fratricidal war pitting brother against brother, was all too clearly exemplified in the case of Caleb Jones and his five brothers. "Richard and Robert Jones are both Union men," Nancy informed her daughter. "Robert was shot by a secessionist and badly wounded; he is recovering. William is a rebel. He was arrested and taken to Jefferson City, where he was detained a few days, and then released without any trial. Ben went to Kentucky about two months since. I doubt if he ever makes this his home again. John is ultra southern, and your pa is a rebel, he denies the right of secession, but thinks our grievances justify rebellion and revolution." (Caleb's cousins and nephews were similarly divided in their sympathies.)[16]

Although Nancy's husband had earlier professed his abiding allegiance to the Union, he soon began to take issue with the actions of the federal government, and following serious reflection determined to cast his lot with the South. In customary mid-nineteenth century fashion (referring to her husband, Mary's father, as "Mr. J" or "your pa"), Nancy explained to her daughter: "You know your pa has always been for peace and the *dear Union*, but he is so exasperated at the proceedings of Lincoln Co. that he is now for fighting for the rights of Missouri. He says he will leave Missouri if she submits to black Republican rule. I think we are two old to give up all, now that we are getting a little comfortable again. My Grandfather fought for American independence, he lost his property and health, in the struggle, and I am not at all inclined to run from the Lincoln rabble. I cannot believe Missouri will submit to disgrace."[17] (Nancy never abandoned her pro–Confederate views and thought it "so absurd to hear people talking about the Union, when their is, nor ever can be again, a Union of the North and South.")[18] Earlier, Nancy had written: "Mr. J did say that he would not shave again until peace was restored. He has always opposed secession, but at the same time he is an advocate for state rights and opposed to any encroachment on them."[19] (It is unclear whether Caleb persisted in his resolution not to shave; however, in a letter written in December of 1863, Nancy confessed that, along with his crippling rheumatism, her husband's "long white beard gives him a very old appearance.")[20]

Although the Joneses' neighbors, the Mains, assured Nancy that Missouri would secede, Nancy was less optimistic. "I was going to add I hope so, but as hope consists of desire and exp[ect]ation I will say I desire it but hardly *expect* it.... I trust our war difficulties will soon be adjusted. The South is in the right and right must prevail."[21]

Talk of war, of course, was the prime topic on street corners, as well as in parlors. Boonville fairly exploded with excitement; however, Nancy was realistic in recognizing the death and destruction that war would entail. "But my heart aches to think of the loss of life, the blighted hopes, and the many sad mourning hearts that will be left desolate.... I believe I am almoste a Quaker when I think of the horrors of war. Mr. J says he is as much of a Union-man as ever, but he now wants a union with the southern Confederacy."[22]

Furthermore, although many Southerners—as well as Northerners—subscribed to the notion that the war would be of short duration, Nancy held serious doubts about a quick victory. "I think so far Providence has very manifestly favoured the South. Some predict we will have peace in three months. I wish I could think we would, but I am not so sanguine. I fear there is no compromise in the North."[23]

Nancy's predictions became a reality when suddenly the war was brought to the Joneses' very doorstep. On May 10, in an effort to secure Unionist control in St. Louis, Frank P. Blair, Jr., and Brig. Gen. Nathaniel Lyon surrounded a pro–Southern state militia camp just outside the city. The militia surrendered quietly; however, as Lyon paraded the defeated militiamen through the streets, a riot broke out, and before the fighting had subsided some thirty people were killed. What seemed to be uncalled-for violence on the part of Union troops angered many Missourians.

Rumors of the clash in St. Louis reverberated around Boonville. Nancy nervously conveyed verification of the rioting to her daughter: "George has just returned from town. The news of the war in St. Louis is true, about thirty killed. Booneville is in a tumult. Mayor McDearmon was shot this evening by old Mr. Reily. The telegraph wires have been cut between St. Louis and Jefferson." With twenty-twenty foresight Nancy predicted, "I have no doubt the war has commenced with us and will be carried on to the bitter end."

Boonville was in an uproar, as was most of Missouri. News was slow to reach Boonville, and Nancy relayed the following report to Mary: Nancy's husband "went in to see what could be done to repell invasion, for the war is upon us, even now, they may be fighting in town. Mr. L., Mr. Muir, and George went in this morning. George was so determined to go, that your pa took him with him. The Governor and General Price went to St. Louis and had an interview with Lion [*sic*] and Blair, offered to suspend the military bill for the present, and disband the state troops, if they would promise not to invade the state or arm their home guards. L. and B. said the only condition of peace was the unconditional surrender of the whole state, and they would take military occupation as in Maryland, which of course will never be submitted to with out a struggle. Gasconde Bridge has been burned, and the rail road torn up to retard the progress of the black republicans. They now have to come by water which will give us more time to prepare. I believe the reception will be a warm one."[24]

Nancy's report was more or less correct. In a final attempt to prevent further bloodshed, a conference had been held on June 11 (three days prior to Nancy's letter), with Jackson and Sterling Price squaring off with Blair and Lyon.[25] Diplomacy failed, however, and the meeting erupted in verbal fisticuffs and Lyon's declaration that "Rather than concede to the State of Missouri for one single instant the right to dictate to my Government in any matter … I would see you … and every man, woman, and child in the State, dead and buried. *This means war.*"[26]

Four days later Brig. Gen. Nathaniel Lyon had pursued the rebels and succeeded in taking over Jefferson City (June 15). Earlier, Nancy explained to Mary her concern over the protection of the Capital: "Military companies have gone from this and adjoining counties, to aid in protecting the Capital against any attack from the hired assassins stationed at the St. Louis arsenal. Such usurpation of power as Gen Harney has assumed is unprecedented, or rather I suppose Lincoln has assumed the power and Gen H. is his agent. How the people of Missouri can submit to such insult I cannot imagine, yet their does not seem to be a spirit of submission. Those who talked the loudest are now as meek and quiet as lambs."[27]

The Battle of Boonville

Chased out of the capital, Gen. Price and the Jackson government retreated to Boonville. As Nancy explained: "Gen Price, the Gov, and suite arrived in Boonville yesterday. It will be the head quarters for the army and the temporary seat of Government." Unfortunately, the tenure of the pro–South forces in Boonville was of short duration, for Lyon's hot pursuit quickly culminated in the "Battle of Boonville." This mini-battle on June 17 and the defeat of the pro–South troops forced a further retreat of Price's men, sent them scurrying off to southwest Missouri, and scored another victory for the Union forces. As a result many Missourians began to reassess their loyalties.

In Nancy's report of the "Battle of Boonville," her anti–Union sentiments are clearly discernible in her sarcasm concerning Gen. Lyon's actions at St. Louis. The recurring problem of getting mail through the lines is also underscored: "More than a week of intense excitement has passed, since I wrote you and I have not had an opportunity of sending the letter." (With the disruption of the mail service, letters had to be sent by a friend traveling to Texas or through a circuitous route involving someone heading eastward who later transferred the letters to a westward traveler.) "I continue writing, however," Nancy commented, "hoping that something may occur to enable me to send them. Gen Lyon, the hero who distinguished himself at Camp Jackson, and was promoted for the murder of women and children, has his quarters at the Fair grounds. A little battle was fought 5 or 6 miles below Boonville the 17inst, the date of the battle of Bunkers hill and the burning of Charlestown."[28]

Details of the "battle" were sketchy, for as Nancy explained: "We have very little reliable news of any kind." Already the telegraph had gained a reputation as the "tell-lie-graph." Unable to provide a newspaper account, "in consequence of the suppression of the Press in B[oonville]," Nancy relied upon Madam Rumor: "The State troops had very little time to prepare. Their was some officers in B[oonville], late of the U.S. Army who were requested to take the command. They declined doing so. I presume they were unwilling to risk their reputation with such raw material. Gen Price was quite ill, and Col Marmaduke, a young graduate of West Point, took command.[29] The State Ts [Troops] had planted a few small pieces of cannon about 4 miles below B[oonville], to prevent the boats ascending. Gen Lyon burned this, and landed his boats 3 in number, 2 or 3 miles below them, and consequently drew our party from their little strong hold.

"Frank Blairs company led on the attack. They were met by Coles company of rangers whose fire toled with terrible effect, so much so as to break their ranks. 'Old Sam Cole' as he is familiarly called, is an old resident of this county, who assisted in driving the Indians away. He had a company of 1,000 men who fight in Indian style, each one being *Capt.* I believe all our Boonville *boys* belong to his company, the Muirs, Howards, and Harper. Blair in conversation with a gentleman of B[oonville] complimented this company very much. He said they fought like devils, and with a courage worthy of a better cause. Col Marmaduke drew his men (who were raw undiciplined Malitia) out in an open wheat field, with no arms but old shot and squirrel guns, to stand the fire of the enemys artillery, which any old woman knows was perfect nonsense, and just as the fight commenced ordered a retreat, which was by some very reluctantly complied with. The greater part of the State troops did not reach the battle field at all. The only company that was well armed,

was stationed at Walnut Grove Cemetery, and had nothing to do but follow the retreating party."[30]

Critical of the performance of both the high command and what
secessionists saw as an ineffective mustering of the state militia (Gen.
Price's troops were forced to retreat), Nancy called the skirmish "more
properly speaking a mob attacking the federal troops. I have not the least
doubt but the mob would have gained the victory, if they had just been
'Let alone.'" The dispirited militiamen were convinced that the outcome
would surely have been different had "Pap" Price been in command.
General Price was indeed ill, suffering from a recurrence of dysentery
or cholera, and thus missed participating in Missouri's first skirmish.
And, true, the Missouri militia, as Nancy pointed out, were poorly
equipped.

Nancy toted up the casualties as "two killed and 7 wounded; the
enemy 23 killed and about 30 wounded."[31] For Boonville residents these
losses became the first casualties of the war, and Nancy grieved along
with the stricken families. The tragic death of Dr. Quarles, one of the
two battlefield casualties, stunned all of Boonville. Nancy explained to
her daughter that following the battle, upon the return of her husband's
riderless horse, Mrs. Quarles had set out on a frantic, unsuccessful search
of the battlefield. Not until much later was Dr. Quarles's lifeless body
discovered on the battleground: "When Dr. Quarles was killed his horse
ran home. Mrs. Q went with her negro man and searched the battle field,
but with out success. He was not found until late in the day."[32] Despite
her grief, Nancy was extremely disapproving of Mrs. Quarles' brother-
in-law, Dr. Beck, for "taking quite an active part on the side of Lyon and
Blair. How contemptible that fellow makes himself on all ocasions."[33]

"Jef McCutchen was shot in the leg," Nancy continued. "It was
amputated the day after, but gangreen soon took place. It was again taken
off higher up, but poor fellow nothing could save him. He was buried to
day. How deeply I feel for his afflicted mother; the family too were very
dependent on him for support. The other wounded are doing well. They
are strangers to us, but there are mourning hearts some where for them."
The old schoolhouse, she reminded her daughter, "where you had so
many romps, and happy hours," had been taken over as the hospital and,
"a number of ladies are in attendance, as nurses." *Harper's Weekly* indicated that some eighty men and boys were taken prisoner. Of that number, nineteen were soon released and sixty-one were put on board the
Louisiana. In Nancy's version, "Lou Boyle and about 40 of his company
were taken prisoners. They were kept on a boat two days and nights and
were given a little crackers and coffee twice in that time, and made believe
they would be shot. Lou doubtless began to think, 'the way of the trans-
gressor is hard.' They, however, took the oath and were released."[34]

The presence of large numbers of Federal troops in Boonville following the "battle" sparked further antipathy among loyal Confederate zealots, particularly when "a great many citizens have been arrested, houses searched, and other outrages commited." The Federals, Nancy chafed, took over the post office, "and both printing offices are in possession of Gen Lyon. We are even deprived of a local paper."[35] (Earlier in her letter she had mentioned this suspension of the newspaper.) Commenting sarcastically, Nancy wrote: "We hear nothing by mail but what our master allows. Of one thing, however, we feel assured, that as long as we hear nothing, all things are right, for so soon as anything unfortunate to our party occurs, we will be sure to hear it."[36]

Nancy questioned the "boasted institutions of free press and free speech" as she reported to Mary: "I have not seen any correct newspaper account of it [the Battle of Boonville]. A reporter for the St. Louis Republican was here and had written the result and incidents of the fight, when Blair had him arrested, his papers taken from him, and sent him a prisnor to St. Louis."[37] Nancy, of course, was incensed when "Gus Simpson was knocked down, and a dutch Capt cut him on the head with his sword because he called them a set of robbers. Gen Lyon toled Mr. Simpson, that he would tolerate a freedom of the press in St. Louis, that would not be allowed in Boonville." She continued: "They broke the press of the 'Observer,' the editor of the 'Patriot' is with Gov Jackson. We have very little reliable news of any kind."[38]

Apparently even Nancy grew dissatisfied with Governor Jackson, despite his pro–Confederate stand. News of Jackson's withdrawal to the Arkansas border was dutifully recorded by Nancy: "Gov Jackson with about 500 men is on his way to Arkansas, rumor says to prevail upon Ben McCulloch [CSA general, former Texas Ranger] to return with him, and drive the black republicans from Missouri." Although several Boonville men left with the governor, one disillusioned follower returned after a brief stay accusing the company of having "two much whiskey, and two little dicipline." Nancy, too, registered her disappointment with Jackson and agreed, "Jackson is evidently not *the* man for the times."[39]

Two weeks later Nancy became further alarmed: "Rumor says our Gov is near the Arkansas line with the State troops. Large bodies of troops are moving from Tennessee and other points on the frontier to join them. They are also in communication with Ben McCulloch. I fear the south west will be the field of many bloody battles. The U.S. troops hold all the rail roads, and moste of the large towns in Mo. Their is from 8 to 10,000 Federal troops in the south west, principally dutch.... The convention is called to meet on 22d inst, the object is to ordain a provisional government and order an election for State officers. The convention will be surrounded by Federal bayonets during its session. I fear the

results."[40] (The convention did indeed meet on July 22, 1861, declared
the governor's office vacant, elected a new governor and continued in
authority until January 1865.)

Talk of war, Nancy admitted, "is the all engrossing topic with everyone." Reports of the escalating turmoil in St. Louis both angered and
frightened Nancy: "Gen Fremont proclaimed martial law, and had cannon planted so as to rake the streets. All secular papers that made any
pretentions to telling the truth suppressed, and a number of City officers
arrested and placed in confinement."[41]

As is obvious from Nancy's letters it was entirely possible for Missourians to hate war and bloodshed even more than they hated Yankees.
"I fear there will be great slaughter at St. Louis," Nancy predicted. "It
is generally believed that will be the next point of attack. O why will they
not stop? There certainly has been enough blood shed to satisfy the
moste blood thirsty war partisans. What dreadful loss of life there was
at Mannassas. I read an account of a Georgia regiment, all unmarried
young men of education and fortune, who went into the engagement
with 6,000, and come out with 60. In my estimation the lives of all the
wooden nutmeg yankees at the North, would not compensate for those."
Later in the same letter Nancy continued, "That we may soon have peace
with an honorable adjustment of all our difficulties is my prayer."[42]

Some two months after the Battle of Boonville, a raid on Confederate sympathizers accused of aiding the enemy further terrified the
pro–South residents of Boonville. On August 27 Nancy wrote her daughter: "Yesterday a boat bringing a number of soldiers landed early in the
morning and they began arresting citizens and plundering stores, or as
they call it confiscating property belonging to rebels who had been lend-
ing aid and comfort to the enemy. Last week several wagons were loaded
in B[oonville] with supplies for Gen Price's army, and every house that
sold them goods is proscribed. I send you the proclamation of the Federal officer, he confiscated the goods of Hardcastle, Johnson, the tailor,
Richy and Kirton, B. S. Wilson and Houx and Andrews, packing up and
taking to the boat such things as they wanted. They left this morning
taking five prisnors with them. If we have been correctly informed they
are Ben Tompkins, John Porter, Cpt Stephens, tailor Johnson and Dave
Andrews. We expected they would rob the banks, as they have done at
other places. We heard this morning one of the Banks guarded against
that by burning their paper and hiding the gold. They took with them
the steam ferry boat and every skiff, so their is no way now of crossing
the river at Boonville. I could talk to you a week telling of the outrages
commited by the home guard."[43]

Panic reigned throughout much of Missouri. The polarization of
Confederate versus Union passions erupted into violence and outrages

across the state. In a continuation of her August 25, 1861, letter, Nancy informed her daughter: "Dick Henning is in from Neosho [the seat of banished Governor Jackson's pro–Confederacy government]. He says we have suffered nothing here, compared with the south west. The country is devastated. The two armies took about 5,000 dollars worth of goods from your uncle Dick, the state troops giving *scrip*, and the others nothing, although he is a prominent Union man."[44] (And yet, those were the early days of the war. Personal animosities and guerrilla warfare quickly heated up to fever pitch.)

Boonville residents found this a shrewd time to keep ardent Confederate views under wraps. An impulsive retort or even an innocent act that might be considered partisan defiance could bring down the wrath of the Federals. Despite being aware of the possible consequences, the Joneses' friend, the irrepressible Dr. Main, refused to stifle his Confederate loyalties and was quickly seized and put under arrest. "Dr. Main went to town and was arrested twice," Nancy declared. "He was marched between two files of soldiers over to the fair grounds. The charge brought against him was that he had said he would like to have a shot at Frank Blair and he replied that he had said so. Gen Lyon said words did not constitute treason, and as it was not proven that he had committed any overt act, he was released. Soon after another party arrested and marched him over a second time. The Dr. made his bow to Gen L[yon], and said 'I hope sir you will give me your abject slave a pass that I may not be subjected to the humiliation of an arrest every half hour.' You can imagine how precise and dignified the Dr. looked."[45,46] Nancy concurred with Dr. Main's loathing of Frank Blair: "I think some patriot, ought to immortalize himself, by hanging Frank Blair, for he is the prime mover in this attack against Missouri. He has removed his family from St. Louis and is afraid to walk the streets alone."[47]

As time passed numerous passages in Nancy's letters were devoted to her disdain for "stay-at-homes" (that is those who would not enlist in the *Confederate* army): "Dr. Harrison you know was about the first one in Boonville to sport a secession cockade, and also to return from Gen Price's army and take the oath, and resume his loafing."[48]

In a gossipy March 27, 1862, letter Nancy told her daughter: "John Howard, Wilson Trent, and a number of others that have been hiding out in Saline [nearby county] to keep out of harms way were arrested by a party of home guards, and released, on their promising to go to Boonville and take the oath which they accordingly did. John is now loafing about B in the same old way. I have been greatly disappointed in him. When the war first broke out I thought John H had at *last* found something that he could do, for I was sure he would fight. I never was more mistaken. He has never been in a battle yet. He was listed lieutenant of the voluntiers in Boonville, but when the troops were reorganized at Springfield he failed to get an office which some think made him leave, and others say that simultanious with the giving out of the whiskey, John's courage oozed out."

Gloomy Days

From time to time a feeling of helplessness engulfed Nancy. In addition to Missouri's problems there were always the immediate concerns of eking out a living in the here and now. In her May 20, 1861, letter to Mary, Nancy detailed the ill-fortune of their friend (and Oakland farm tenant) Mrs. Wiggs who suffered the loss of fifty young chickens thanks to a violent rainstorm and the loss of half of her young turkeys to a ravenous hawk: "Their is but one step from the *sublime* to the *ludicrous*. I talk about things of state awhile, then come down to pigs and chickens. I suppose I may as well laugh as cry for I cannot remidy the evils. I wish I could."

In some Missourians the tumultuous times bred indecision and inertia and in others, such as Caleb Jones, led to an abrupt refocusing of attitudes. Nancy, herself, found it difficult to summon the courage to see to the completion of their new home, which could instantly be consumed in a surprise guerrilla raid. Her husband, on the other hand, was incensed over the political scene and daily voiced contempt for Lincoln and Republican rule.

"The times are so gloomy," Nancy reflected, "that one has very little motive, to make improvements, for our house may be burned by a mob, or our property confiscated. War is a great leveler, and unless peace is soon restored, all men will be on an equality in a pecuniary sense. Your pa become so much excited the other day while reading a paper, that he said Governor Jackson might have all his horses, cattle, hogs and money. I advised him to keep cool [a popular word even in the 1860s—also used most effectively by Lincoln in his Cooper Union Speech], that he would be called on soon enough. He regards Missouri as out of the union now for she ignores the authority of the President, and at St. Jo, Hannible and Boonville the people have refused to receive the newly appointed postmasters."[49] In the same letter Nancy referred to the local residents' resolute abhorrence of abolitionists. "The man appointed to the land office in Boonville is a relative of a prominent abolitionist. On his arrival a committee waited on him, and informed him this climate would not suit him and as they were so solicitous of his health he left in a hurry."

Completion of the Joneses' new home became a secondary interest as Nancy, preoccupied by the constant threat of Union confiscation or the ravages of bushwhackers, grew increasingly reluctant to devote large amounts of time and money to a house whose demise might be imminent. "I have no heart to do any thing in the way of fitting up our house," Nancy lamented. "The furniture we bought, has been standing in the hall for weeks, we have stoped all improvements, our house would have been painted, papered and furnished, and the yard fence and gate all finished, had it not been for the uncertainty of Missouri's position. Time proves all things, we must wait and see."[50]

Days and Nights of Terror

For most Missourians life was tumultuous at best during the war years. The countless skirmishes, the barbarous guerrilla raids such as those led by William Quantrill and later by Frank and Jesse James, and the savage confrontations between Union and Rebel sympathizers rendered citizens fearful and demoralized. Numerous groups of guerrillas, probably the most famous being Quantrill's Rebel raiders, terrorized Missouri and Kansas residents by swooping down on communities in surprise raids, killing unarmed civilians, randomly looting stores, particularly liquor stores, pillaging and burning homes, and making off with whatever money and jewelry they could seize. Most of the guerrillas were young men, seeking revenge for what they deemed abuse to themselves or their families by the Federals, convinced in their own minds that they were protecting Missouri citizens and contributing their bit for the Southern cause. Still others were simply impetuous young hellions imbued with a psychopathic bent for violence and murder. On August 21, 1863, Quantrill, for example, led a raid on Lawrence, Kansas, that destroyed the town and left more than one hundred and eighty men and boys dead. Naturally such merciless killings resulted in retaliatory measures by Union men. Border animosities continued to heat up when, following Quantrill's raid, in an effort to curtail guerrilla activity, Brig. Gen. Thomas E. Ewing issued his famous Order No. 11 on August 25, 1863, calling for the removal within fifteen days of all citizens in Jackson, Bates, Cass, and one half of Vernon County in western Missouri. The homes of thousands of Missourians were then torched. Some months later Ewing's draconian order was rescinded and certain loyal Union homeowners were allowed to return to their homes.[51]

The Jones family certainly was no stranger to the violence and turmoil that convulsed wartime Missouri. Caleb himself was almost killed on one occasion: "Some of the home guard come out here for oats. Mr. Jones was in the garden, and one of them laid his gun on the fence and took deliberate aim at him, but fortunately missed him. Mr. J inquired why they shot at him. They said he did not halt when they commanded him, and he had not heard any order to halt. The discharge of the gun was the first intimation I had of their being on the place, so you may form some idea of the state of things here," Nancy agonized.[52]

Deep trouble also loomed on the horizon for daughter Addie's husband, William Muir. As a staunch Southern sympathizer who refused to take the oath of allegiance required by the Federals, he quickly found himself disenfranchised and unable to vote. In desperation, after incurring the wrath of the local Union faction with his openly partisan remarks, he sent his family to Canada and moved his law practice to St. Louis. (Apparently Muir had decided to take the detested oath of allegiance and thus was able to resume his law practice.)

Amidst the confusion and strife that ran rampant throughout the divided ranks of Missourians, it was hazardous to trust anyone, even one's longtime friends and neighbors. Emotions, bitterness, and revenge overcame reason and reflection. The malevolence that pervaded Boonville struck frighteningly close to home when one night two men preyed on the good nature—or naiveté—of Dr. Main. In the fall of 1862 the Joneses' close friend and neighbor, Dr. Main, in good faith admitted two men into his home one evening, and was later hurried to the river never to be seen again—that is until his lifeless body was recovered from the Missouri River. Nancy Jones relayed the gruesome details to her daughter: "I know you will be pained to hear of Dr. Main's untimely death. Some two months since a party of men two of whom were dressed in the federal uniform went to the Dr.'s house about midnight and by representing themselves as friends gained admitance, and then took the Dr. to the river, hung him and threw him in the river. His body was recovered the second day after in the same place they had thrown him. He seemed also to have received a blow as one of his eyes was knocked out. Mrs. Main tried to follow him, but they drew a pistol on her and forced her back. The citizens dare not make an effort to ferret out the murders, because the Dr. was a southern sympathizer." Nancy was unerringly realistic in summarizing, "Things here are in an awful condition and growing worse daily."[53]

As Southern loyalists the Joneses were extremely reluctant to have their young son, George, conscripted into the U.S. Army, a possibility which became more and more threatening as time wore on. On one occasion, the spirited young George was arrested by the Federals for hurrahing Jefferson Davis. As the Federal troops passed the Joneses' farm one day, young George in a fit of exuberance retaliated with his partisan sentiments. Engaged in a search for some missing cattle, George had hurried over to the fence for a closer look at the hated bluecoats. "The soldiers were hurrahing for Lincoln and the Union," Nancy wrote, "and

George said hurrah for Jeff Davis; he says he was like the little school boy who said *it* whistled *its* self, for he was so angry at the thought of our State being over run by such a dutch rabble, that he said it before he was aware of it. One of the Cpt rode up to the fence where George was all alone and putting a pistol almoste touching his head, asked if he said hurrah for Jeff Davis. George said he did. The Cpt then ordered a guard to march him off, and threatened to shoot him if he took one step backwards. George demured a little, but says he knew how they had been shooting people in St. Louis, and as the fellow had a very *red face* he thought he would not resist, but if it was to do over again he would."[54]

"When the dinner hour arrived without George making his appearance," Nancy felt uneasy, "but [I] tried to quiet myself by thinking he had stoped at Howards mill. Mr. Jones laughs at me so much about making a baby of George that I was ashamed to confess how anxious I was. Mrs. Wiggs heard late in the evening that George was not at home. She then toled us that he returned before dinner, and had called her attention to the troops as he passed the door, that she saw him sitting on the fence, and afterwards saw him walking up the road with them, but never thought of it again until she heard he had not come home."

Naturally Nancy and Caleb were frantic over George's disappearance, and in an instinctive response to Mrs. Wiggs' alert, George's distracted father rode out to the army encampment in search of his son. "They found the troops encamped near Pilot Grove, and passed the guards without much trouble," Nancy explained. However, in the wee hours of the morning and only after repeated inquiries and considerable evasiveness, Caleb "at last found him guarded by two soldiers. They doubtless arrested him through sheer wontoness," Nancy wrote, "and would have released him as soon as *they* thought him sufficiently punished. Mr. Jones was treated very respectfully by all, excepting, the officer who released George. He taunted him by saying he guessed he would not hurrah for Jeff Davis again. Mr. Jones told him by making such arrests he was pursuing the right course to make Davis men." Needless to say, Nancy was furious: "I felt so indignant at the outrage, that I did not shed a tear until I saw the carriage coming and knew that George was in it."[55]

By the fall of 1862 the Federals' perversity in arresting George and the threat of further abuse had frightened his parents into sending him to Jacksonville, Illinois, for his schooling. Much as Nancy missed her son, she confessed, "I would not have him at home *at present* for any consideration."[56] In the same letter Nancy admitted, "Comparitively, things are quiet in this immediate neighborhood, but I am afraid they will not continue so."

Daily Hassles

As one might expect, the Federals received a cool reception from many of the Boonville residents. Ada, in one of her infrequent letters, confided to her sister: "Boonville is full of Federals, and has been ever since the first battle was fought near there. You can not imagine a more disagreeable place. The Federals do not turn aside for any one, but rudely push by ladies on the side walks, and allmost ride over them when crossing the streets. They are constantly making arrests and searching people and homes."[57] According to Nancy, young George also deplored seeing "the streets full of dutch soldiers, and in every store one or two stationed as spies. Is it not humiliating?"[58] The Federals' abrupt appropriation of horses and mules for their own purposes soon rendered Nancy "a prisoner at home." The threat of theft left her, justifiably, "afraid to go any where, for fear the mules will be taken out of the carriage."[59]

If the women of Boonville found the Federals obnoxious, that epithet was returned in full measure by the Union troops in regard to their associations with rabid, fiercely loyal pro–South women who "hoped they [the Federals] would all get killed." Some soldiers responded maliciously with insults and even violence (rarely or never rape). Others succeeded in suppressing their pent-up animosities. A Federal, for example, sent word home from Boonville announcing: "The women were the spunkiest I ever seen, and when a squad of us would visit a house we would have to take a few broadsides but our orders were to do things as civil as possible and we had to stand it as best we could but I felt several times like if I could see them strangled."[60]

The Horror Stories Continue

Letter after letter contained a recital by Nancy of the death and destruction wrought by the war: "We are in a very exposed situation here on the main road. Troops are passing almoste daily. Thousands have marched by. They take every horse, mule, ox, saddle, bridle, wagon and harness, they can find. We have so far escaped better than our neighbours, owing to our having all such things hid out. We keep nothing in the stable but Doubloon, and no one but Speed [a Negro servant] can go near him. They forage entirely upon the State Rights party."[61] Five months later Ada reported to her sister: "Mrs. M and youngest child are boarding at the Berger's. Their friends pay their board. Their negroes, furniture & clothing have been confiscated."[62] Nancy expressed immense sympathy for a Mrs. Brown who had come from Virginia to bury her mother at Cape Girardeau in the old family burying ground and upon her return "found her house burned to the ground, the negroes gone, and her daughter missing."[63]

Members of the Quarles family, who had lost a son in the first battle of Boonville, were heartsick when another son, a minister, who in good conscience could not take the oath of allegiance, was sent to Fort Warren. A Mr. Painter, Nancy bristled, was "banished to Massachusetts, for preaching a sermon on Thanksgiving day last year, that did not suit the powers that be."[64]

Having been burned out at Sarcoxie, Mat Wilson, his wife and six children, en route to Fayette "for the convenience of the schools," stopped for the night with the Joneses: "He had a very fine dwelling house handsomely furnished which, with his store house, was burned by the State militia." As for her own family a disheartened Nancy complained, "Mr. Jones has been working hard all his life and now, owing to the change in times, will hardly be able to collect money enough to pay his taxes this year."[65] Six months later she despaired, "Their is no security here for life or property."[66]

Fortunately, Boonville was spared some of the tumult and barbarity that engulfed the counties bordering Kansas, where a Missouri woman recalled the Jayhawkers "swooped down on us day and night, searching our homes for money or contraband goods." Seemingly nothing was sacred: "They frequently ran their bayonets through all the clothing in the wardrobe or through the mattress to see if there was any one concealed there. When making a dash into Missouri towns they would order the men in the town to erect the Union flag and command the women not to give food to Southern soldiers or Bushwhackers under penalty of death, telling us if we failed to comply with this command they would return and sack and burn the town, shoot the men and take the women and children prisoners."

As the number and savagery of guerrilla atrocities accelerated and after William Quantrill's group attacked Lawrence, Kansas, General Thomas Ewing issued his famous Order No. 11, on August 25, 1863, calling for the removal of residents of four counties bordering on Kansas which were thought to be the hotbed of Quantrill's guerrilla forces. Both sides immediately moved in to torch and ravage the countryside. The order resulted in a huge public outcry (for one thing, it did not discriminate between loyal and disloyal Missourians), and it was suspended a few months later. Furthermore, the order failed to curtail the savage attacks of guerrillas, who continued their mission of creating havoc and devastation.[67]

Some ten to twenty thousand Missourians were forced to flee the area under Order No. 11. Frances Twyman recalled with horror the "many scenes of misery and distress I saw on the road when people were ordered to leave their homes on a few days' notice. The road from Independence to Lexington was crowded with women and children, women walking with their babies in their arms, packs on their backs, and four or five children following after them—some crying for bread, some crying to be taken back to their homes. Alas! They knew not that their once happy homes were gone. The torch had been applied—nothing left to tell the tale of carnage but the chimneys."[68] "I try to forgive, but I cannot—no, cannot—forget," Twyman confessed. "If Tom Ewing is in heaven today his inner life must have been greatly changed."[69]

Such stories, as well as thousands more like them, were unnerving to the Jones family. Would they as Southern sympathizers be similarly targeted for vengeance?

To Leave or Not to Leave

Even before the "Battle of Boonville" and George's arrest, Nancy and Caleb gave serious thought to leaving Missouri in search of safer territory. "If Missouri does not join the 'Southern Confederacy,' we too, may take up our abode in Texas," Nancy speculated. "Time will tell."[70]

Monetary consequences, removal from family and friends, and a hazardous journey all ruled against a move at that time. By July 11 Nancy was confiding to her daughter: "Mr. Jones says let what may hapen, he is tied here for a time. In the first place we are too old to move to a new country with the hope of living to enjoy any improvements we might make; here we are comfortably situated, having a good farm, stock. Real estate would not sell for one third its value; our personal property would be a sacrifice. It is impossible to make collections, and by remaining here he may be able to realize something from debts and stocks, which would probably be lost if were to move at present; he is also unwilling to abandon the state when the services of every man is needed. A few weeks will determine the fate of Mo." Still, the possibility of emigrating was not completely abandoned as Nancy added, "Sometimes your pa says if he could realize one half the value of his property he would leave Mo. to the black republicans, and perhaps we may be compelled to leave in a year or two money or no money...."[71]

The question of whether to move or to stay continued to plague the Joneses for the next weeks and months. By the end of August, property values had continued to dwindle and Nancy remarked that when a friend "said to Mr. Jones that he would be willing to take 30,000 dollars, less, for his property now, than he valued it at the first of last Jan, Mr.

J. said he could beat him, for he would be willing to take 50,000 less for his."[72]

Although the possibility of joining her daughter and her son-in-law in Texas had great appeal for Nancy Jones, she was extremely reluctant to leave their son, George: "The greatest hindrance I have is leaving George. Like all other boys, he is exceedingly anxious to join the army. I quiet him by telling him that he is the only child we have with us now, and his father and I are two old to be left alone, that he must consider himself a *home guard* and protect us. I fear if I was to leave him he would go to the army which would not suit him at all. He is so near sighted, when much exposed to the sun he is almoste blind. He is such a great big soft baby that he could not bear exposure...."[73]

Nancy's other daughter, Ada, and her husband also vacillated over the wisdom of moving to Texas: "Mr. Muir talks of going to Texas. Ada is exceedingly anxious to go, and stay at least until things are more quiet here. If they do go they will start as soon as they can get ready, very likely in company with Mr. and Mrs. Bell. Mr. Jones says nothing less than an army can move him just now, and I must stay to take care of him and George."[74]

A Family Tragedy

In September of 1863 adversity tightened its grip on Nancy and Caleb Jones with the death of their precious granddaughter from "congestion of the liver." With a heavy heart Nancy shared her grief with her daughter: "I know your heart will ache, when you read this. She [Ada's daughter, Mary's niece] died the 11th of Sept, and was buried on the 12th, which was Mr. Muir's birth day." The death of children was a tragic fact of life for families in the 1860s. The deaths of children under the age of five took a fearful toll accounting for almost half the deaths. Whooping cough (almost eradicated one hundred years later thanks to the development in the late 1940s of a vaccine and the availability of antibiotics) proved a deadly nemesis as it indiscriminately swept through families. "Minnie, Mattie and Caleb had whooping-cough, and Matties constitution was too delicate to battle with the disease," Nancy grieved. "You know what weak lungs she had. The dear little one was so sprightly and cheerful, that we did not realize how ill she was. Mr. Muir thought Ada was unnecessarily alarmed, and said he went for the Dr. just to please Ada. Mattie was the first one to meet the Dr. at the door. She took him in the parlor and showed him Willie's likeness, toled him 'that was her aunt Marys baby, her little cousin Willie in Texas.' Ada says she never heard her talk sweeter. She was very fond of the Dr. and seemed to be trying to entertain him. She was so cheerful that I believe the Dr. was deceived, for he only advised giving her a little soda water, for an ulcer on her tongue which he said was caused by acid stomache. Ada says it must have been a kind of mothers instinct, for she felt that Mattie was dangerously ill. Wednesday night the Dr. gave her a little medicine."

"Thursday I went to see her," Nancy continued, "and when I left I thought she would be much better the next day. What poor short sighted mortals we are. The next day her pure spirit took its flight from earth to Heaven, to join her little brother Frank, she so much loved to talk about. The immediate cause of her death, was congestion of the liver."

Memories of Nancy's beloved grandchild kept flooding back unwilled. "Mattie had improved so much, and become so interesting, that she was twining herself around our hearts more, and more every day. Minnie too, seems lost without her. They went to Sunday school together, and were so much company for each other."

Clearly, Nancy was grief-stricken over Mattie's death; however, calling upon her religious faith to sustain her, she resigned herself to the will of God. "The Lord gave, and the Lord hath taken away, blessed be the name of the Lord." Mary's sister Ada was inconsolable. "Ada cannot feel resigned. I never knew any one to grieve more for a child. For a time I feared she would by her excessive grief bring on brain fever, or something worse."[75]

"You have the only good likeness of Mattie their is," Nancy reminded her daughter. "Be sure to preserve it. If you can, have a photograph taken from it and send it to Ada. She intended having Matties taken at the same time Minnies was that I sent you, but she had a sore on her face, and the artist said it would spoil the picture. It was then put off from time to time until it was too late."[76]

Sickness and disease were constant predators, especially for young children. While another villain, scarlet fever, which viciously deafened and murdered young children, was threatening Boonville innocents, Ada's children went out to stay with Nancy and Caleb at Oakland, just outside of town. Fortunately, the grandchildren remained unscathed, but such was not the case for some of the Joneses' less fortunate friends. "Mrs. Kemper has lost her oldest child with it. Last summer her two little girls died within a few hours of each other with cholera infantum. They were buried in one coffin. She has one child about five months old."[77]

Confederate Outrages

The havoc wrought by the repeated raids, atrocities and pillaging of both Union and Confederate armies and supplemented by merciless guerrilla attacks kept Missourians in a state of turmoil. Adding to the Joneses' despair were the outrages committed during the Jo Shelby raid on Boonville. Although heretofore, almost invariably, it was the Federal troops who were blamed for the confiscation of property, this time it was the Confederates themselves who were responsible for the foraging and theft. The participation of their own soldiers in the wanton destruction of property, the precise act for which they had so bitterly condemned the Federals, left the Southern sympathizers in Boonville in a state of shock. The Joneses stood aghast as they watched their produce and farm animals disappear before their very eyes: "You have doubtless heard of the dairing raid made by Jo Shelby [Colonel J. O. Shelby, known by his initials as "Jo"] in to Mo. They dashed into Boonville, robbed the stores of whatever they wanted, then come out and camped at Waverly, made their camp fires out of our fence rails, used our corn and oats, and out of a fine crop of oats only left us enough for seed, killed two fine Durham heifers, and as many hogs as they wanted, and then to cap the climax took Brownie. Your pa tried very hard to get him from them but they would not give him up.... Losing him broke up our team. A runaway negro stole our best mule and we have nothing left that will work in harness but one mule. Mr. Wiggs has an old horse blind in one eye, and of these we some times make a team for the carriage. The rebbels took a fine mare from Mr. Wiggs."[78]

Nancy again referred to their losses during the raid in a letter from Canada in 1865: "When Shelby made his raid in Missouri he camped on our farm and took all that he wanted. Gen Price did the same. His army cleared our farm of grain, hogs, horses, cattle, fruit, fence rails and every thing else they wanted. The event took poor little Jenny. Mr. Jones estimates his losses by their camping at Waverly at three thousand dollars. They took 'Doubloon' our fine young horse, worth a thousand dollars."[79]

Nancy was not alone in condemning the actions of Shelby. Even Confederate officers complained to President Davis about Shelby's raids into Missouri and his commitment to "the pirates' law of property." Colonel C. Franklin complained that Shelby's troops considered all mankind as "objects of prey," and they "rob indiscriminately friend and foe." Shelby's troops had "transferred to the Confederate uniform all the dread and terror which used to attach to the Lincoln blue," Franklin asserted. "The last horse is taken from the widow and orphan, whose husband and father has fallen in the country's service. No respect is shown to age, sex, or condition. Women are insulted and abused."[80] Such behavior, Franklin insisted, was clearly alienating much of the Missouri populace.

The Hated Oath of Allegiance

In addition to the violence, foraging, and general disruption stemming from the war and the conflict of loyalties, life in Missouri was further complicated by the need for citizens to sign the oath of allegiance. In many areas persons who refused to sign the oath were prohibited from practicing law or conducting church services. For the Joneses' friends, and more immediately for their son-in-law, Mr. Muir, a lawyer, the oath involved a serious struggle with their scruples. Citizens were faced with the momentous decision of whether to sign—to lie, to deny one's convictions, to betray friends—*or* whether to refuse to sign and to suffer the loss of livelihood and possible banishment, confiscation of one's property, or even physical abuse. Apparently, Mr. Muir was "the only lawyer in Boonville that has not taken the oath of allegiance. They are not permitted to practice in any of the courts without taking the oath.... In St. Louis Gen Halleck[81] requires all lawyers, magistrates, and ministers, to take the oath."[82] The restrictions of the oath were so stringent that few Southerners could honestly swear that they had never "given aid or comfort to Confederates, that is, never fed, or nursed, or housed, or sympathized with, or provided a blanket, a cup of water, a pinch of tobacco, a wagon, or money for a Confederate."[83] (As noted earlier, Nancy's son-in-law, following heated disputes with Unionites, dispatched his family to Canada and moved to St. Louis to continue his practice of law.) Nancy continued: "Rumor says the Revd Mr. Marvin would not submit, and left *between two days* for 'Dixie.' Judge Thompkins says he disgraced his children, by taking the oath of allegiance."[84] When the Catholic priest in Boonville refused to take the oath of allegiance, he was arrested and imprisoned, but was finally released as a result of public indignation. Nancy Jones admitted that she finally took the oath "as a safety precaution for her family."

Emancipation and the Loss of "Servants"

Life for many Missourians became increasingly more onerous with the loss of their "servants." Although Lincoln's Emancipation Proclamation was not extended to the border states, nevertheless, Nancy was well aware of the fact that in time slaves everywhere would be given their freedom. "The bill for the emancipation of slaves in the District of Columbia has passed and been ratified by the president, and I suppose the next thing will be to pass a similar one for all the border states. The future of our unhappy country looks dark and gloomy, yet we know that

'One rules who is too wise to err, and too good to be unkind,' which should support and comfort us."[85]

In time the Joneses watched their servants leave the premises singly or in pairs—some to enlist with the Union army, others to enjoy their freedom and seek a life of their own: "A recruiting office has opened in Boonville for soldiers of *African descent*, and Speed, Ike, and Willie, enlisted. Aaron would not go. Speed and Will cried like children when they left. I suppose Sally, Caroline and Ann will not leave before spring. Three hundred negroes have been sent from Boonville to St. Louis, and the office is still open and as Sally says the negroes keep *roling*. Ellis left home some time ago, and was employed as teamster. He returned a few days since quite sick, minus the money he took with him, but wiser if not better than when he left home. All but two of Mrs. Muirs negro men have left her." Nancy added, "Your pa would willingly leave Missouri, if he could sell out to any advantage, for it will not be a desirable place for a white family for the next half century."[86]

Nancy's infrequent mention of their servants had invariably indicated a genuinely friendly relationship: "Ann saw me writing and said please tell Miss Mary I want to see her *mighty bad*."[87] However, upon the departure following their emancipation of their blacks, Nancy and Caleb, as was true of most Southerners, were somewhat annoyed at the ingratitude displayed by the departees. (Apparently, the Joneses were not entirely dependent on their household help, for in July of 1861, Nancy wished Mary had "Ann and Ike with you." She continued: "If a safe opportunity offers us will send them to you. Ann is delighted at the prospect of going to you."[88]

In time all of their servants departed save one: "Aaron is the only negro we have, the others have all gone as soldiers and camp followers. Sally and Ann left the lst day of March. Wash Sally's husband come in a wagon with two soldiers drove to the door of her house and loaded the wagon with her goods and drove off leaving me sick in bed with pneumonia. Mr. Jones said nothing to them only asked them if they were there by authority and they said they were. I have hired a white girl."[89]

Nancy's World

The pervasive nineteenth century conviction that a "woman's sphere" consisted of her family, her church and her home certainly held true for Nancy Jones. Nancy lived for her family. In the days before the airplane and mass transportation, one recalls that grownup married children frequently lived next door, across town, or on an adjoining farm. It must have been a shattering experience for Nancy suddenly to be

separated by hundreds of miles from one of her daughters. The close-
ness of Addie and the delight in sharing in the lives of her children
brought untold happiness to Nancy. Mary's marriage and removal to
distant Texas was heartbreaking. Letters became the lifeline between
mother and daughter.

Nancy constantly anguished over the fact that her daughter lived at
such a distance and that, as a result of the war and the violence that ravaged Missouri, it might well be some time before they could be together
again. The thought must surely have crossed—and crisscrossed—Nancy's
mind that she might never see her daughter again. Mail was sporadic at
best, and letters often were four or six months in transit. In one of her
very first letters to her daughter, Nancy was disappointed that Mary had
not written more often while on her honeymoon in the Northeast: "I
received your letter from Baltimore this morning, and as I expected you
would write from Washington you may guess how impatient I have been
to hear from you."

In the same letter Nancy could not refrain from expressing her regret
that she had not gotten to know Justin better before the marriage. (In
those days of small towns and farm villages—and of cousins marrying
cousins—parents were usually well acquainted with a daughter's fiancé
and frequently with his parents, as well. Justin McCarthy was almost a
stranger to the Joneses.) "I hope Mr. McCarthy will bring you back soon,
and stay long enough for us to get acquainted with him," Nancy wrote.
"It seems strange for me to say I am not acquainted with my daughters
husband, but such is really the fact. I do not think I was ever in Mr. Mc's
company half an hour at any one time and scarsely knew how he looked
until I saw him last."

In true motherly fashion Nancy sent her best wishes and also a bit
of advice [for a daughter on her honeymoon!]: "I hope you will enjoy
your northern tour very much. Be very careful not to take cold by getting your feet wet this rainy weather. I am not with you to watch over
you but I cannot keep from thinking about all these things." As a parting thought Nancy suggested: "I think Mary you ought to come see us
before you go to San Antonio [en route home from her honeymoon]. I
cannot bear the thought of that Gulf. I feel as if I would never see you
any more when you get so far from me. You must be sure to write *every*
week. If you knew with what anxiety I shall look for a letter you would
not neglect it, for I cannot live atall if I do not hear from you once a
week."[90]

Despite her feelings of neglect, within days after Mary's wedding,
Nancy had a new baby grandson to alleviate her loneliness: "I am staying with Ada. She gave birth to a fine boy the Friday morning after you
left. She says you made a narrow escape, and that Mr. McCarthy will

now understand why she did not have invited company." (Mary's wedding had been a simple ceremony at Ada's home. Nancy later told her daughter that notice of the wedding had been carried in the "Observer" and that Ada, in what appeared to be a Boonville tradition, "sent a slice of cake to both the editors.")[91]

The birth of the new grandson was a joyous occasion: "The children are delighted with the babe, and Mr. Muir makes as much ado as if he was the first baby. He looks like Minnie and is named Caleb. Your pa has not seen him [his namesake] yet. I expect to go home tomorrow. Mrs. Muir is coming to stay with Ada next week. I need rest very much." Nancy continued, "I am writing in Ada's room while her and the babe are sleeping, and the room is so dark I can scarsely see the lines."[92] Nancy seemed always at the ready to help Ada with her growing family. She concluded her May 4, 1861, letter asking to be excused for her poor penmanship for, "I am writing under disadvantage rocking the crib with one foot."

Anxieties over the perils of childbirth were obvious as Nancy related the details of baby Caleb's birth: "Ada was taken sick [the pervasive euphemism for the beginning of labor pains and the birth process] Thursday evening and the babe was born at 2 o'clock Friday morning. She has been very ill, on Sunday night after her confinement she thought herself dying. Dr. Thomas was up to see her three times during the night. Until after the ninth day is considered the moste critical period. This is the 9th day and I hope she is safe, but she will require very careful nursing."

In her next letter, some two weeks later, Nancy gives the reader a brief glimpse into the postpartum medical practices of the times. By then Ada was off the critical list, but still unwell. In her next letter Nancy expressed her concern for the new mother: "I fear Ada will not be well enough to write you soon, she had been suffering from acid stomache and she thought a little magnesia would correct the ascid. A dose of one teaspoonfull of salts and magnesia threw her into moste violent pain. The Dr. gave her morphine to relieve the pain and that night blue pills and the next night calomel and opium. When I left here yesterday she was some better. Mrs. Muir will stay with her this week, she had been sitting up part of the day for more than a week. I fear she will now have a long spell of fever. She is thiner and looks worse than I ever saw her. The babe is well and grows finely. He is a beautiful child."[93]

Letters—The Family's Life Line

Getting and receiving mail often proved an exercise in frustration. For Boonville residents, mail needed to be carried by someone traveling (in any direction) to a destination where the missive could be more reliably sent on, or simply handed on, to the intended recipient. Two months after her daughter's marriage Nancy was mystified to discover that her daughter was not receiving her letters. "I promised to write you or have a letter written once a week," she wrote, "and I intend to keep my promise as long as their is any possibility of sending them. I expect to send this to Neosho directed to your uncle Dick, requesting him to mail it in Arkansas, if he had an opportunity. It is the only way I can think of at present." (That letter was handed off in Neosho and relayed, it was hoped, to Mary by "a gentleman who was going to Texas." That or a similar letter was returned to Nancy a year later, when the "mailman" unfortunately could not find an opportunity to send it on from Neosho.)

In August, after a month of not hearing from Mary, her mother declared: "It has been so long since I wrote you that I really forget the date of my last. Of course you know the reason was because there was no way of sending a letter. Mr. Thomas Tutt was in Boonville, and very kindly took my letter to St. Louis, and said he would try and get it to Memphis, by private conveyance. You last letter was the 16th June. We have not heard a word from you since, neither have we received a paper. I try to console myself by looking at your picture, and thinking you are at least well, as San Antonio is a healthy place. I am exceedingly anxious to know all about your housekeeping arrangements."[94]

The tenuous Texas postal connection and the long separation weighed heavily not only upon Nancy but upon the entire family. Mary's speedy return to Boonville was an ever-present (although unrealistic) expectation for each member of the family. Almost a year after Mary's marriage, a letter sent via a vague circuitous route through St. Louis induced a wild fleeting hope that Mary was on her way home: "When George saw the post mark he thought you was in St. Louis, on your way home, and so eager was the poor fellow to know, that he broke the envelope, but when he saw San Antonio Nov 24 his hopes vanished. He dreamed the other night that you was at home playing on the piano, and the parlor was full of company, so when he saw the post mark, he thought he was getting to be a dreamer too. *Apropos* of dreams, you know you pa has always ridiculed the idea of any one believing in dreams, but he is now like a drowning man catching at a straw. When I say in the morning I dreamed of seeing Mary last night, he will ask anxiously, how did she look? Was she well? I can appreciate his feelings so well, that I have not the heart to laugh at him, for his inconsistency."[95]

Several months later Nancy laughingly described her husband's teasing her about reading and rereading Mary's letters: "Your letters afford me so much satisfaction. The letters Mr. Greenleas brought me I was reading over about the third time when your pa come in the room. Said he are you reading those letters over again, there is nothing in them but a baby. I find he is as anxious to hear about the baby as I am, for as soon as he heard through one of the servants that Mr. Bell had come, he rode over to see if the report was true, and come back with a letter which by the way he had taken time to read."[96]

Despite the distance and intermittent mail service, Mary continued to be a sorely missed component of the family circle. Nancy reassured her daughter: "Do not think you are forgotten, for their is scarsely an hour in the day that your name is not mentioned. Minnie (Ada's little daughter) enquired why I did not send the carriage for aunt Mary to come home. She seems to think you are on a visit, and it is quite time you was coming home. This is the third week that Ada and family have been staying with us. You pa frequently says when we meet in the dining room, now, if we had Mary and Mr. Mc here we would have all our family together. How sad I feel when I realize how uncertain our meeting is, in the present distracted condition of the country."[97]

In the lives of Ada and her youngsters Mary still played an important role. In a postscript to one of Nancy's letters written almost a year after Mary's wedding, Ada declared: "I cannot become accustomed to your absence but miss you more now than when you first left home. I am so anxious to see you & Mr. Mc and the dear little *stranger* which you will be entertaining I expect before this letter reaches you."[98] Nancy noted that one of Ada's children's favorite plays is "going to Aunt Mary's house." In another letter: "The children talk a great deal about Aunt Mary's baby." With the eagerly awaited arrival of a picture of the new baby, Nancy wrote, "Ada sent me word I must bring it in for she wanted to look at it every few minutes."[99]

Even a year after Mary's wedding, following the departure after a month's visit of daughter Ada and her family, Nancy felt her loneliness creeping up on her. A reflective Nancy wondered: "This is the anniversary of your marriage. Where are you? And how are you? are questions I would gladly have answered. How much longer must I bear this suspense. I thought this time last year, that being separated from you, with the certainty of hearing from you frequently, and perhaps seeing you soon was more than I could live through, so you must not laugh at me for being gloomy at the present prospect of affairs. Every thing seems to indicate a very protracted war, of course the whole country will be ruined, and all traveling facilities lessened. If I could only hear that you were all well I could be reconciled. I try to say, not my will, but Thine be done, O God, but I fear I have a very rebellious and selfish heart. You doubtless have so many new and interesting duties to occupy your time that you cannot realize my feelings. I am cooped up in the house, and nothing to do but think about you."[100]

Later that year Nancy bemoaned: "Your pa regrets not having gone back to Texas instead of improving this farm. Our family is too small to be so far apart." From Canada, almost three years later, Nancy reminisced: "Last Monday was four years since you left me. How little we dreamed of being so long separated." Once again she repeated, "I have often said this winter if you and family were with us how happy I would be."[101]

Nancy repeatedly reminded her daughter to write weekly. "A mother is always thinking moste of the child farthest from her, and the moste exposed to danger. If you was with me, and Ada or George away, I would suffer a great deal more uneasiness about them than you...."[102] It was impossible to send a newspaper, Nancy complained, "when it is so difficult to send a letter. We can only trust in Providence and hope for better times. The darkest hour is just before day."[103] (Although the solicitude and tenderness expressed in Nancy's letters might lead one to think that Nancy favored Mary over Ada, one should remember that Ada and her family lived close by and were frequent visitors at Nancy's home, often for weeks at a time. Nancy could express her concern and love for Ada personally, whereas infrequent letters had to serve as hugs and affection for daughter Mary.)

On at least one occasion, however, Nancy admitted to her daughter, "I am *almoste* reconciled because I know you are safer there than here." Much as Nancy longed to see her daughter, she reasoned: "Dear Mary I fear it will be a *long, long* time before we meet again. You think you cannot come home this summer, and indeed under the present circumstances it would be wrong for me to wish it, because traveling will neither be safe nor pleasant." Nancy continued, "Dear Mary, knowing that you are so happy and contented, reconciles me to the separation, for I can moste cheerfully submit, to any personal privation, to secure the happiness and welfare, both temporal and spiritual, of my children."[104]

Nancy rarely penned a letter that did not include the refrain about writing weekly: "Dear Mary, I hope the mails will not again be interrupted, for I am so anxious to hear from you, to know of your safe arrival in San Antonio. To write to you, and receive a letter from you once a week is one of my greatest pleasures. If I am deprived of this how shall I pass the *long long* days."[105] In another letter: "The days are very long to me now, write, write."[106] Later: "When shall I hear from you again. It is really too hard not to receive a letter once a week. I feel like it is more than I can submit to."

In addition, in almost every letter Nancy begged Mary to come home for a visit. (A reader might deem Nancy overly possessive, but what mother isn't at least a *little* possessive? Furthermore, one must remember that for most women at that time family was *everything*.) Small wonder

Nancy marshaled all her resources to reinforce the family ties: "Tell Mr. McCarthy I think if there is any safe way of coming, he had better bring you and the *dear little one* (this following the birth of baby Willie) home and spend the summer with us. I see no use in gentlemen confineing themselves so closely to business," Nancy added flippantly.[107]

In a later letter, despite the fact that the war was still raging, Nancy seemed convinced that Mary would soon be coming home: "How strong a thing is *hope,* and how utterly miserable would we poor mortals be without it. When you left I thought I would never take any more interest in any thing earthly, and felt perfectly indifferent about our house ever being finished. My work basket I thought would have rest. Now I find myself planing and thinking about what I will make and fix up for you by the time you get home again, and how nicely I will have your room fitted up and arranged for you and Mr. Mc."[108] In another paragraph Nancy sent her compliments to Mary's husband and instructed Mary to tell him, "If he wishes to sustain the favorable impression he made in Boonville, he must not keep you away long."

In her efforts to keep the Boonville connection strong, Nancy reported: "Your friends in town and country make many enquiries about you. They all send their love to you. Miss Jo Knily says Mr. McCarthy has made one enemy here, that *she* does not like him atall for taking you away. Miss Kate Nelson thinks you deserve credit for taking the people by surprise. I had no idea you was such a universal favorite. Everyone I have met regrets your leaving Boonville."

As the wedding had been small and Mr. McCarthy's visit brief, the couple's wedding picture created quite a stir among Mary's Boonville friends: "There is a great deal of curiosity manifested by your friends, to see the man you was willing to leave all for. I believe they all agree with *you* in thinking him handsome. Is he the least bit vain? If he is do not tell him. Fanny Fern says the man is not living that is not vainer than a woman, and she sometimes speaks the truth. Mrs. Muir [Ada's mother-in-law] is so angry with you, because you would not marry Jim [her son] that she would scarsely look at it. She had it all so nicely planed in her own mind, that she cannot get over the disappointment. Ada cross-questioned her until she did admit he was *right good looking.* Jim poor fellow cannot talk about you atall. I know you will think this all imagination, but Ada sees it as plainly as I do."[109]

Perhaps Nancy was attempting to reassure herself of the merits of Mary's new husband. Perhaps she was pointing to a list of Mary's former suitors hoping that Justin would read the letters and perhaps hold his new wife in even greater esteem. Perhaps it was simply her wealth of love for her absent daughter that prompted Nancy to repeatedly refer to Justin's good looks and Mary's host of Boonville admirers.

Oh! To Be with Mary Now!

News of Mary's pregnancy brought immense joy—and consternation—to Nancy and her Boonville family: "We received your letter via
Louisville moste joyfully." (It was probably the letter announcing Mary's
pregnancy.) Nancy continued: "It is the first we have had since June, the
one you sent by express we have not received, that mode of conveyance
is prohibited. I am really glad I did not know of your illness until you
was able to write me you were well again. I would have been perfectly
miserable."[110] Not surprisingly Nancy was heartbroken that she was not
able to go her daughter during her "confinement": "Mr. Jones thinks
it would be a very hazardous trip just now, as the country between here
and Lexington is full of Federal troops and the Kansas 'Jayhawkers' are
commiting all kinds of depredations. If I can get to Texas, with any
degree of safety, either by land or water, I will do so sometime during
the winter, however, if I cannot be with you I hope Mrs. Gallagher [a
San Antonio friend] will supply my place."[111]

Advice she could not convey in person to her daughter during her
pregnancy and subsequent childbirth Nancy chose to spell out in her letters. (To be sure, Nancy's advice to Mary prior to Mary's "confinement"
has little to do with the military or political conditions during the Civil
War; however, a female reader might find interesting Nancy's suggestions
about prenatal care and the nursing of a baby.) Early on, Nancy
instructed Mary: "Exercise in the open air, without fatigue, is very necessary for you now. Do not sit down to *embroidery and stiching* as I fear
you will. Nothing is more injurious. Please tell Mr. McCarthy, I particularly request him not to allow it. Your health in after life depend very
much upon your passing safely through your first confinement, therefore I hope you will be very careful and prudent."[112]

"For fear I may not be with you," Nancy warned. "I must give you
a little advice in relation to your approaching confinement, which I hope
you will attend to. In the first place do not become low spirited, *as the
manner of some is.* Think how many have passed safely through the same
ordeal, and you must remember too, this is only the beginning of a *Bak-
ers doz.* Take as much exercise, both riding and walking, as you can bear,
without fatigue. Guard against constipation of the bowels, which is so
apt to cause fever. Your diet should be cooling and nourishing."

"And after the birth of the little *Irishman,*" Nancy continued, "put
it to the breast at once. Some ladies think they have no milk at first and
begin feeding the child, which of course makes it sick, and then they must
give it medicine, a moste barbarous practice. Ada has never had any trouble with her breast, which I think is owing to her pursuing this course,
of putting the child immediately to the breast. The second or third day

their is a rush of milk in the breast, and if the child has not been drawing it out, they are sure to become inflamed, and they sometimes rise
and are very painful. To prevent this get someone to draw all the milk
out for a few days. To prevent sore nipples begin at least a month before
your confinement, to wash the nipple once a day, either, with a little cam-
phor, or a little alum dissolved in whiskey. This hardens the skin, and
prevents them becoming so tender and sore, from the childs sucking. Do
not get out of bed until the eleventh day. Of course you can change from
one side of your bed to the other, and have things arranged about it, but
you must not get out of bed, to sit up or dress until after that time. If
Mrs. Gallagher can not stay with you, be sure to hire an experienced
nurse. Dr. Thomas does not allow Ada to leave her room for one month.
You must not laugh at all this, for I have suffered so much, through ignorance, that I want you to proffit by my experience. Tell Mr. Mc he must
take good care of you, for I am hardly in a good humor with him yet,
for taking you so far from me, and he must bring you and *all the family*
home as soon as traveling is safe again. May God bless and direct you
my dear daughter, is the prayer of your affectionate Mother."[113]

With the approach of her "confinement," apparently Mary had
become anxious about her own health and that of her unborn child.
Nancy endeavored to buoy up her spirits: "I am sorry you have suffered
yourself to become low spirited, as moste ladies do, and hope that long
before this reaches you, you will be in fine health and spirits, and so busy
nursing the dear little *one* that you will never find time for another fit of
the blues. Oh how I wish I could see you all. I know you will be a moste
devoted mother. I fear Mr. Mc will bring the same complaint against
you that Mr. Muir does against Ada. He says she makes herself a perfect slave, and thinks of nothing in the world but her children." Nancy
then quoted Mary's sister, whose philosophy in essence was the widely
held mid-century concept of "woman's sphere": "Ada says she does not
know what a married woman has to think about but her home and children."[114]

Earlier, sister Ada herself had also passed along her concerns and
suggestions: "I am so anxious to see you & Mr. Mc and the dear little
stranger which you will be entertaining I expect before this letter reaches
you." She added: "I hope you will be very careful after your confinement.
Do not leave your room under one month. Oh! How I wish Ma or I could
be with you, but that is impossible. Ma is so anxious to be with you that
she will be certain to go as soon as there is any probability of reaching
Texas. The children talk so much about you, I do not believe they ever
could forget you. The servants all send their love to you and want to see
you so much."[115]

Almost two years later, Nancy, as becomes a mother, was still offering advice, although this time in retrospect (or perhaps in anticipation of a future pregnancy): "I am very anxious about Willie. I had remarked to Ada the day before the receipt of your letter, that I was afraid he would be sick teething, as this was his second summer, and he was weaned so young. I think children have less trouble teething that are not weaned until they are at least one year old."[116]

Naturally, Mary's pregnancy was a grave concern for Nancy—as well as the whole family. Day after day an anxious mother ached for some inkling of news, and yet, as the days dragged into months, still there was no word from Mary. For six months, from September 5, 1861, to almost the end of March 1862, there was no letter, and Nancy was growing ever more frantic to know how her daughter was managing her pregnancy: "Mr. J. seemed so unwilling for me to go without him, (and he could not leave at that time, without a great sacrifice) that I was unwilling to urge it, lest something unfortunate might occur, and then I would reproach myself for it. I have been hoping, from day, to day, that some way would be opened for me to go, until I am almoste in despair. Your pa says I have but one idea, and that is going to Texas. Every snow that falls, he insists on my starting in the slay, but I think it *doubtful* about my reaching San Antonio in that kind of conveyance, I decline. The Indian troubles in the Nation makes that rout unsafe, and the 'Jayhawkers,' are worse than they have ever been. All the country between here and Arkansas is infested by them."[117] A frustrated Nancy agonized over her own personal geographical confinement.

Three more painful weeks passed until finally the sun broke through the clouds and the long awaited letter from Mary arrived. Tears of joy interrupted any further writing for Nancy that night, as she confessed, "I could do nothing but cry over it."[118]

In the weeks that followed, Nancy continued to lament her inability to go to her daughter: "You urge me so much to come to you that I know if I had received your letter in due time, I would have started regardless of consequences. Mr. J still thinks the trip almoste impossible."[119]

One forgets that grandparents in those days were not provided the wealth of "likenesses" available in the modern day plethora of Polaroids, camcorders, and throw-aways, and in April, following his birth, a precious picture of Mary's baby resulted in almost a tug of war in the Jones family. Proud grandparents circulated and recirculated the picture among relatives and friends, all the while bathing in the sea of compliments and admiration that a "showing" engendered. Mrs. Wiggs's assessment that "he dont look like a natural child, but jist like a picter," resonated particularly with Nancy. "Really," Nancy marveled, "their is something so noble looking, and beautiful, in the expression of his face, that it does look more like a fancy sketch, than a life likeness. Tell Mr. McCarthy, I fear he will be a little vain when he hears that we all think Willie more like him than you."[120] Nancy pointed out that she had had a "glass put over it, so that the children can kiss him as much as they please." A day earlier Nancy had gone to Ada's to retrieve "my baby." Ada, however, "prevailed on me to let her keep him a little longer, as Julia Johnson … was coming to see it. Indeed the young *gentleman,* has had quite a *reception,* at Ada's." "If the Prince of Wales, with his bride were to arrive in Boonville," Nancy predicted, "I do not think your intimate friends would be more anxious to see them, than they have been to see 'Mollie Jones' baby,' as they all call him. He has been very much admired and complimented."[121]

Temptation and Deliverance from Evil

Evidences of Nancy's religious convictions punctuate her letters, and her deep concerns for the spiritual as well as the temporal welfare of her family surface repeatedly. As a devout Christian Nancy unquestioningly viewed most of life's joys and sorrows as the will of God. Even the course of the war itself, Nancy was convinced, would be determined by an omnipotent, omniscient God. Early on, although dismayed by rumors of a Confederate rout, Nancy repeated: "The Lord God omnipotent reigneth and all things will work together for good to them that love him and keep his commandments." Nancy was particularly eager to have Mary affiliate with a church in San Antonio: "I hope you will join the Church soon. I know Bro Hall [Nancy's Boonville minister] would willingly send you a letter if you prefer. 'Seek ye first the Kingdom of God, and his righteousness; and all these things *shall* be added unto you,' 6 Matthew, 33rd."[122]

The following year Nancy responded joyously upon learning of Mary's having joined the church, "for the path of duty is always the path of safety. May you live a consistent member."[123] Nancy concluded her letter: "May He who Tempers the wind to the shorn lamb, guard, and direct you all along the journey of life and at last save us all in Heaven where there will be no more parting, is the prayer of your Mother."[124] (For Nancy to have to have been so exuberant over Mary's having joined the church, one suspects that Mary first joined her parents' Methodist church prior to her conversion to Catholicism.)

Later, there was deep concern over Mary's abandonment of her Methodist upbringing and her adoption of the Catholic faith. Reading between the lines, one senses a grave disappointment on Nancy's part that Mary married a Catholic. There may, however, have been additional reasons for her objections to the marriage; for instance, Nancy's admission that she had not been very well acquainted with Mary's husband.

From the start Nancy had had grave reservations about Justin McCarthy. Following the marriage, Nancy, from time to time, seems to have suffered little guilt trips for her pre-nuptial objections to Mary's fiancé. Early on, Nancy, hoping to head off any serious relationship, had stubbornly disapproved of their correspondence. Much later, in an attack of conscience, as the mails became more and more irregular, she admitted: "You know I always take trouble on interest so I imagine the postal arrangements will be interfered with and I will not get letters from you regularly, and I [will] be punished for the wicked wishes I made, when you and Mr. Mc were corresponding. I would not of course intercept a letter but I did wish moste sincerely that they would be lost or destroyed in some way."

From time to time Nancy attempted to make amends: "I know you think I did wrong to oppose your marriage as I did, nor can you ever understand how hard it is for a mother to give up a daughter to the protection and companionship of a stranger, until you have a daughter married then you will know all about it, and not till then." Other times Nancy simply cannot resist a sly reference to Mary's whirlwind courtship. "Last night long after your pa was *snoreing soundly* I lay awake thinking of you, and of the little petty trials and annoyances, incident to housekeeping. The first year is always the moste trying to a young *wife*. Ada thinks you will make a splendid housekeeper. You certainly will make a model one, if you only have half the determination to be one, that you had to marry Mr. Mc. I hope, however, you will not meet with so many trials and obstacles in the one, as you did in the other. Yours was certainly a case of 'perseverance under difficulties.'"[125]

At first there appeared to have been some remote hope that Mary's husband could be converted to Protestantism. In one of her early letters, in relaying church news, Nancy felt obliged to add a fellow churchgoer's remark: "Mr. Prottsman says he indulges a hope that Mr. McCarthy will turn protestant as William Morrison of St. Louis did, you remember he married Kate Seinney." In the end, however, it was Mary who converted to Catholicism.

The influence of her Catholic husband and being thrown in with Catholic friends in San Antonio eventuated Mary's conversion to the Catholic faith. Surely it must have taken courage and commitment for Mary to buck her Methodist background and her parents' Protestant biases and turn to Catholicism, and Mary remained a devoted Catholic to the end of her life. Although Mary's second husband, Dr. Gibson, was a faithful Methodist, their marriage ceremony was performed by a Catholic priest, and years later Mary sent her son Willie to Notre Dame for his college education and her daughters to St. Mary's. She died repeating the Hail Mary prayer and was buried in the Catholic Church.

Despite their efforts to avoid friction, Nancy and Caleb's anti–Catholicism surfaced now and then in their letters. Caleb, dismayed over the marriage, in time resignedly accepted the situation, saying, "It was right for a wife to be with her husband." In contrast, Nancy's other son-in-law, Addie's husband, William Muir, represented all the quintessential Methodist religious qualifications. Without question, his service as Grand Master of the Masons of Missouri further testified to his anti–Catholic bias and no doubt gained him considerable stature in Nancy and Caleb's eyes.

꧁꧂

Aside from Nancy's anti–Catholic prejudices, her letters bear evidence of a caring, loving, Christian-like wife and mother. Nancy's acceptance of the righteousness and justice of God's rule of the world was succinctly revealed in her conviction that "We can only hope for the best, and put our trust in 'Him who doeth all things well.'" News of church activity in Boonville included the notation: "Miss Kate Nelson joined the M.E. church on probation last Monday night at love-feast. Bro Hall is growing more popular every day. His fearless independent course is wining him many friends. He always enquires very affectionately after 'Sister Mollie.'"[126]

It was with a grateful heart that Nancy thanked "our Heavenly father, for permitting us to hear from you as often as we do." At the same time that she lamented the distances that separated the family, she acknowledged, "I know such repining is very sinful, for we have great cause for gratitude to the 'Giver of every good and perfect gift,' that it is as well with us as it is."[127]

Aware that a reunion with her daughter would be months or even years away, Nancy looked to faith and hope to see her through their separation: "We have the privilege of meeting daily at a Throne of Grace, where there is One who is ever ready to hear our petitions. How comforting the thought, '[To] the Christian, hope is an Anchor to the soul, both sure and steadfast.'"[128] Earlier she had written to Mary, "I pray that you may be kept from temptation and delivered from evil."[129]

At some point, Brother Hall must have left Boonville or been replaced, as Nancy wrote, "We are very much pleased with our new minister, the Rev. Mr. Pugh." She continued: "I hope he may be instrumental in doing much good in Boonville. He had a large congregation last sabbath, and preached a *good* sermon. The Corronation hymn was sung, which filled my eyes with tears, because I missed your voice. It is a favorite hymn of mine, and I think you sing it more beautifully, than any one I ever heard."[130] Later, in her letters from Canada, Nancy continued to profess her faith in a loving God. "We poor short sighted mortals know not what is best for us," Nancy acknowledged.[131] "God grant that we may very soon have a happy reunion, is my daily prayer," she repeated later.[132]

Attendance at the theater or a frivolous masquerade ball was frowned upon by the Boonville faithful. Nancy made special note of the fact that "The Episcopal minister and his wife, attended a masquerade ball at the Thespian Hall after easter or lent, which some of his members did not like." Daughter Mary's frequent attendance at the theater had alarmed Nancy, who was greatly relieved to learn of her daughter's growing disinterest in theatrical productions: "I am truely glad to know, that you are tired of theatricals. Distance lends enchantment to the view. I thought you would soon tire of them. Such pleasures cannot satisfy an immortal mind. The path of duty is the only path of safety."[133] Drunkenness, of course, was strictly abhorred by both churchgoers and the irreligious: "George Spear is doing worse than ever. He is laying about the streets drunk."

With secession, a shift in allegiance from Union to Confederate loyalties prompted countless Boonville parishioners to make a decided change in their traditional church prayers for their government. Nancy observed many parishioners who had previously offered up their prayers for the president with President Lincoln in mind, were soon audibly— or silently—petitioning for God's blessing on Confederate President Jefferson Davis instead. Nancy acknowledged that Mrs. Cope "says she had changed her prayer book and instead of praying for the president of the U. she prays for Jeff Davis of the southern confederacy."[134] She continued her letter, "We know not what will become of our distracted country but we do know that the 'Judge of all the earth will do right.'"[135]

Life in Boonville

Much of Nancy's time, apart from writing letters and attending to church work was spent in sewing and crocheting: "I intend making you some drawers soon. You have some made off the same piece of linen I will make them, and have them nicely done up, before I put on the triming." "They will be ready for you when you come home," Nancy added slyly. Ada, she divulged, had made some pin cushions as a present for Mary—"two large strawberrys with two or three emorys attached to them, to hang on either side of your mirror, one large pin cushion for your toilet, and one small one for the *dear little ones toilet*, and a needle book." Nancy herself had "knit you three crotchet mats for your wash stand, one large one for the basin and two smaller ones for the soap dish, and brush stand."[136] The great difficulty, of course, was getting their handiwork to Mary. "I send you some little trifles I had made for you," Nancy promised, when an opportunity for transportation appeared feasible. Ada tucked in a little shirt and had just drawn off a little bib for Nancy to overcast for little Willie: "It is to be made with a little white cord around the neck." Everyone shared patterns; however, the ever-anxious Nancy held back: "I am reluctant to send you the sack pattern for fear you will ruin your eyes."[137] In another letter Nancy announced that she had "made Willie a comfort, out of that light colored delain of yours." "It is tacked and bound with green ribbon and large enough for a *pair* of *boys*," Nancy hinted.

☙❧

To be sure, not all of Nancy's letters were full of gloom and doom. Punctuating her letters from time to time was gossip, particularly concerning weddings and the remarriage of widowers. Details of one acquaintance's marriage within a month after his first wife's death set the town's tongues wagging. (The widower's wife had died very suddenly, "it is supposed from an over dose of opium, which she was daily in the habit of taking.") "The half has not been toled," Nancy began, but then dispensed with further juicy details and concluded, "but I have wasted too much paper on them."[138] By April, according to Boonville gossip, no one had been to call on the newlyweds and they had left town in disgust. The bridegroom was incensed that his new wife was "not *appreciated* in Boonville." In another gossipy tidbit Nancy allowed that although a certain bride was "very small and dumpy," the fact that she was "very rich" apparently made up for any deficiencies in stature.

Sanctuary in Canada

As anxieties mounted over the possible conscription of George, over the very real threat that they would become victims of the guerrilla warfare that was consuming the state, and over the possible confiscation of their possessions by the Federals—or the Confederates—Nancy and her husband decided that leaving the country was the only viable solution to their problems. Canada was a logical choice as a temporary refuge: there was no language barrier, the government presented no obstacles, and in Canada they would find comfort in associations with countless other Southern refugees. The Joneses, however, as did most Southerners, soon returned to their homes following the cessation of hostilities.

Although the exact date is unclear, by September 21, 1864, the Joneses had left Missouri and escaped to Paris Station, Canada. Apparently things had gone from bad to worse in Boonville, and dozens of families had or were in the process of leaving, many for St. Louis or Idaho or Canada. Soon Ada and her family joined her parents in Canada for at least five months. In his letter in the fall of 1864, Caleb Jones explained to Mary the urgency of their flight from Missouri. "Our State is in a deplorable condition. Every crime is daily commited with impunity. Moste of our friends have left."

Nancy's husband then began to recite a liturgy of the atrocities that had taken place in Boonville: "Mr. Henshaw who bought Charlotta & children & his neighbour Mr. McClenahan were shot a few days since & many other respectable persons have been killed."[139] A few months later, Nancy documented her husband's reporting of the violence that helped convince them to leave Missouri: "Every boat and conveyance that leaves Mo is crowded with people, some running from the drafts, and others for fear of being taken as a hostage, or assessed as a Sympathizer, or killed by a bushwhacker. Your pa thinks between the Jayhawkers, and the bushwhackers, Mo will be devastated, and only a fit aboade for the lawless, for years to come. His health has greatly improved since he come here. It is, perhaps, owing to the security he feels where none dare molest or make him afraid. It is certainly harrassing to live where you are liable at any moment to be shot, or thrown into prison without ever knowing what for. After Mr. Jones left home [he had preceded Nancy to Canada, probably in June of 1864] two of our nearest neighbors were shot. Mr. Boller our German neighbor was shot to death by bushwhackers, and Robert Sloan ... was severely wounded by the pursuing party, they mistaking him for one of Mr. Boller's murderers." (Booneville residents were shocked by John Henry Boller's murder. Boller had apparently been an innocent, hard working, well-liked farmer who lived "across the road" from Nancy and Caleb. Less than three months later his son was also murdered by guerrillas, probably led by "Bloody Bill Anderson.")

"'Mr. Harper's house was stoned one night while he was at prayers," Nancy continued. "He prayed on. James Nelson, Dr. Borman, True Hickock, Mr. McPherson, and Mr. Bendels have been knocked down on the street (two of them in their houses) and beaten almoste to death. Our neighbor Wooldridge and family have gone to Idaho. Since the war all our very near neighbours have been killed, Dr. Main, old Mr. Boller and his son Godfrey, Mr. Neff [Jacob Henry Neff lived on property adjoing the Joneses' farm] and a young man living at Mr. Raileys farm was shot at by about twenty men. He has recovered minus his eye sight. I have great cause to be thankful to Him who never slumbers nor sleeps that your pa and George have escaped so well." Nancy concluded: "To me now, everything seems so little compared with human life."[140]

Realizing Mary's concerns over the fate of her parents, Caleb Jones attempted to reassure his daughter, "Do not be uneasy about us, we are ... living under the protection of the best Government in the world & have ample means to live on here or elsewhere by using due economy until the Storm Subsides."[141]

Returning to Missouri anytime in the near future was out of the question for the Joneses. "We cannot hope to return to Missouri having any assurance of living in Safety until there is a cessation of hostilities," Caleb explained to Mary. "The war waged in that State is one [of] extermination. The country is overrun with Gurellas—to whom no Quarter is shuon & they shuo none. They scalped three soldiers lately near Rouckport [probably Rocheport]. Highway robbery is an every day occurance. We are yet at a Hotel—but expect to get possession of a large House I have rented in a few days. Your Ma had her Parlor and her Chamber Furniture, Carpets, Books & moste of our valuable household goods sent here—We will have very little to purchase to fit us out comfortably."[142] (The Joneses had apparently hired a man to live in their home and sell their stock. A few months later they sold their farm home, "Waverly," to the Provost Marshal for ten thousand dollars.)

Indecision troubled any plans for the future. After the war, should they pack up and head for Mexico or Europe, return to Boonville, join Mary in Texas, or simply remain where they were? As did so many Southern sympathizers, the Joneses seriously contemplated the idea of emigrating to Mexico.[143]

Caleb Jones speculated: "We may *probably* yet become citizens of Mexico and Subjects of his Imperial Majesty Max[imilian] as I think the climate of Monteray would suit your ma better than any other I know of. We have now no settled plans and must be governed by events—which are yet to transpire. A few months may make developments which will enable [us] to determine on something definite—we, are now residing within two hours travel of Niagara falls."[144]

Epilogue

By March of 1865, seven long, anxious months had elapsed since the Joneses had heard from Mary. At last a letter containing news of the serious illness of Mary's husband made its way through the lines to Canada. Nancy replied immediately. "[Your letter] did not bring the joy your letters have always done, for we are deeply grieved to hear of Mr. McCarthy's ill health." Nancy continued: "We will now be all anxiety until we hear from you again."

No doubt both Nancy and Caleb would have much preferred to go to Texas to be near their daughter, rather than to brave the snow and ice of Canada. Nancy assured her daughter: "We would gladly have gone to you instead of coming to this bleak and frozen country, where the snow has not been off the ground for five months, but you know the penalty would be confiscation." During the long winter months, despite the fact that Ada and her youngsters had joined them in Canada, Nancy had become less and less enthusiastic about their refugee life in Canada: "This is truly the 'Botana Bay of America' for it is filled up with convicts and criminals from the U.S. and from every other country. To keep George from the draft is the only inducement we have to remain here.... We have no fixed plans for the future." Even relocation in Europe and the prospect of being with Mary held out great promise for Nancy: "If Mr. Mc decides upon going to Europe to remain any length of time, we may go too. No one is left in Boonville whose business would admit of their leaving. A few of our acquaintances, the Harpers and Howards, among them, are there yet." (Caleb, however, immediately squelched Nancy's European dreams, pointing out that their finances would not permit such a move.)[145] Afterward, Nancy and Caleb rented their newer home, "Oakland," and moved back to "Waverly," as the Waverly house "is more easily injured by renting than the other which has never been finished and to have room enough for your family and Ada's when you come home." Nancy added, "Mr. Jones has rented his fields and the grain will be sufficient for us."

Only three letters written from the Joneses' Canada retreat survive in the collection. In one of the final letters, dated Sept. 21, 1864, Caleb attempted to assess the family's financial situation. At the end of the war, while thousands of Southerners were desperate for food and a roof over their heads, the Joneses surprisingly had come through the war fairly well-off, despite their losses.

Although their situation was far from perfect, Caleb Jones wrote his daughter from Canada expressing his appreciation of their relative good fortune. "Self exiled & deprived as we are of the Society of children & friends we feel profound gratitude to the Giver of every good and perfect gift—that our lives are yet spared and we are not destitute. We trust the Same providential care will Still be vouchsafed to us & that we may yet have the happiness of being united on Earth & inseperably united in Heaven."[146]

Caleb's good fortune he hoped to share with his children and grandchildren. In the last letter of the collection Caleb Jones informed his daughter: "Mary—I have Sustained great loss—in the last 4 years—yet have fortunately been able to Save I trust a sufficiency of my property to aid—our children in Starting anew in business—I would like to Know Mr. Mc's plans & whether he will require aid, as soon as possible. I have some Cash—which has been unproductive for a considerable time—which ought either to be given to our children or invested in some paying business—If possible let us hear from you. We are all well."[147]

The collection concludes with Caleb's final instructions, and unfortunately exact dates are missing. Even in that last letter the Joneses were at a loss to know of Mary's circumstances: "We know not whether Mr. Mc has been restored to health, where you are, or what your condition may be. If we know that you was in San Antonio your pa and I would soon be with you, now the cruel unnatural war is over, and travel can again be resumed."[148]

Sometime later, however, with word from Mary concerning the death of her husband, Nancy and Caleb Jones returned to Boonville, quickly repacked and set out for Texas to rescue their recently widowed daughter and her young son and to bring them back to home and friends in Boonville.

Years later, young Willie recalled with touching detail his grandparents' arrival in San Antonio. Following her husband's death, Mary and Willie had been living at the Manager Hotel on Alamo Plaza. There, the twosome spent long tedious days eagerly awaiting the arrival of Mary's parents. Traveling conditions were uncertain, and the wait must have been interminable. According to young Willie, one of his first and most treasured memories was standing with his mother peering down the road for signs of the dusty stagecoach they so hoped would herald the arrival of his grandparents. At long last the stagecoach appeared, clattered to a stop, and the tired rumpled passengers began to disembark. What a disappointment it must have been to watch each passenger alight, yet discover no dear familiar faces. Mary must have choked back the tears as she shook her head, "'No, they are not there. They are all men.' Then there was a cry, 'Oh, there is Pa,' as he stepped from the coach, followed by Grandma, and away ran Mother to meet them, almost overcome by joy."

It took only moments for Nancy and Caleb to scoop up young Willie in proud, grandparental love and affection, an adoration that Willie returned in full measure. They "were almost a father and mother to me," Willie confessed. "I had their love and they had mine." Since the frigid winter temperatures merely added danger and difficulties to stagecoach travel, Nancy, Caleb, Mary and Willie put up at a select boarding house and sat out the winter days in San Antonio. In the spring the foursome returned to Boonville where Willie stated that he "lived very happily" amongst cousins and friends. Some four years later Mary carved out a new life for herself and her son by marrying Dr. Henry Clay Gibson.

Nancy's family circle was completed when Ada and her growing family also came back to live in Boonville. There, life blissfully took on new dimensions for Nancy who repeatedly confessed that she loved her grandchildren as much as she did her own children.[149]

☙❧

The Joneses' situation in Boonville was without question much more critical than Nancy's letters to her daughter reveal. Nancy, no doubt, was attempting to paint a cheerful picture for her daughter. Fearing to alarm her daughter over the rampant violence permeating most of Missouri, Nancy alluded to facts but sought to suppress the family's desperate plight as Confederate sympathizers in a hotly divided state. For Nancy Jones and her family, as well as for tens of thousands of other Missourians, the vicious, partisan confrontations between Northern Unionists and Southern sympathizers that raged throughout Missouri during the war presented, in many respects, almost as great a threat to life and property as did the warfare raging on Southern battlegrounds. Dr. Main and Caleb Jones were apparently marked men, and Dr. Main's murder surely must have sent shudders up and down the spines of the Jones family. The Joneses, with good reason, feared they might well be next on the hit list, for, as Nancy wrote, "since the war, all our very near neighbours have been killed." Missourians had become "prisoners in their own homes," afraid to leave for fear of loss of life and/or property.

In addition to providing insights into the cataclysmic conditions confronting Missourians during the rebellion, Nancy Jones' letters also bear testimony to the strong family ties that bonded the Jones family, even in daughter Mary's absence. They reveal the importance of letters as all-important life lines in a world gone terribly awry (many of Mary's letters she confessed to reading at least three times) and give credence to the religious convictions that undergirded life for many mid-nineteenth-century Americans. The Joneses' hegira from Boonville to Canada, and their concerns about resettlement after the war, were problems facing millions of their countrymen. Viewed as a whole, Nancy's letters dramatically document the premise that life for most Missourians during the war years, particularly for Southern loyalists, consisted of days of unabated anxiety.

ℚ *Four* ℘

"Turmoil, War and Wretchedness"

I thanked God for the fortitude He had given me.

—Sarah Duval

As the North's anaconda grip tightened on Southern territory in 1864, thousands of Southerners joined their countrymen in flight—to the countryside, to cities, to Texas, to the far West, *anywhere* to safer territory. "Those were our dark days," Sarah Duval wrote, "and men's hearts began to fail when they saw their grand leaders fall one by one." And yet, Sarah continued, "no time was afforded for vain repining."[1] Some refugees found asylum for a few weeks or a few months, only to be uprooted by the approach of the Federals and forced to move on again, their hegiras often doomed to be repeated again and again, even as many as ten times. In many respects the refugee life of Sarah Dandridge (Cooke) Duval (hereafter referred to as Sallie, the familiar name used most commonly by her family and friends) was typical of that of untold numbers of Southerners (an estimated quarter of a million) who embarked on frenzied attempts to escape the Union Army. In February of 1864, Sallie and her family, fearing their farm home in New Kent County, Virginia, to be imminently vulnerable to Federal invasion, hurriedly packed up what valuables they could and set out for what promised to be a safe haven in Chester, Virginia.

Trains, already jammed with casualties en route to hospitals, swarming with troops headed for the battlefront, or overloaded with refugees scurrying south, east, or west to less hazardous areas, rendered rail transportation precarious at best. Destruction of rail communications was a key military objective, and worries that the tracks would be destroyed and thus delay or prevent their departure, or that as a result of sabotage along the way, they and their baggage would be unceremoniously dumped

163

in some isolated field half way to their destination, compounded Sallie's anxieties. The Duvals and their New Kent neighbors were terror-stricken for fear they would be overtaken by Union forces before they could make good their escape. However, with meticulous planning, they reasoned, perhaps their departure would go unnoticed by enemy scouts or roving guerrillas poised to swoop down on them or on their partially evacuated home.

Through some devious finagling the Duvals finally secured arrangements with a sympathetic engineer who promised to signal them as the train approached their home, whereby they could then hurry onto "the cars" without being detected. On the appointed day, in the midst of a blinding snowstorm and surrounded by as many linens, blankets, china and household necessities as they could handle, Sallie and her family anxiously scanned the railroad tracks. Suddenly, the engineer's secret signal pierced the air, and the family clamored aboard the train leaving their comfortable home, Sallie lamented, for "the world of turmoil, and war, and wretchedness...."

For a few blissful weeks the Duvals' sanctuary in Chester proved relatively peaceful; however, almost overnight Sallie and her family were subjected to the multitudinous anxieties that beset most wartime refugees. Soon, the loneliness and the gnawing uncertainties of the transient life began to constitute the least of their worries. All too soon the family was overrun by enemy troops and severely buffeted about by sickness, death, confrontations with guerrillas, stragglers, and their old nemeses, the Federals.

Hopes of earlier days—that their sojourn in Chester would be merely a temporary relocation—were quickly dispelled with the devastating news that Yankee troops had burned the Duvals' New Kent County farm home. Furthermore, their new location failed to have any long-lasting salubrious effect on the illnesses that pervaded the family. Sallie was miserable: "The invalids of the family seeming little benefited by changes of air and scene, since it brought with it little peace of mind, for we had come into the midst of the most stirring events. My husband's health had grown rapidly worse and he was now so feeble that he could scarcely keep up." Despite her own family concerns, Sallie noted that they all "anxiously followed the movements of our army—as it fell back steadily from the neighborhood of Fredericksburg."

Anxiety over the illness of her husband and children kept Sallie on tenterhooks. Her worries escalated, however, when in early May a huge deployment of Union soldiers descended on Chester: "Early in May—about the 9th—we were startled by the sudden descent upon our Village of a heavy force of Federalists." Mass-hysteria shook the entire town. What to do? Where to go? Where to hide? Sallie was beside herself with fear: "There were few men among us, only here & there, an invalid unable to do service. The inhabitants were so terrified they hid themselves in every place that promised security. There was a large culvert under the double track of the R.R. through which ran a stream, now very shallow. The women near had carried boards under this & made a temporary flooring, on which they now placed their beds, boxes etc. & packed themselves & their children, leaving their deserted dwellings to the mercy of the enemy." For Sallie and her family there was no choice but to courageously tough it out at home. "We alone remained in our house, our sick people could not be moved so we did not give it a thought."[2]

"Firing was heard very near," Sallie recalled, "and the familiar musketry told us our few men were engaged. Then volumes of smoke & flames ascended from the woods a mile off." In the midst of the turmoil, yet another burden was added to Sallie's mounting responsibilities as Sallie became nurse for still another patient. A poor soldier who was dying of consumption was brought to her house and bedded in her hall. The man was "coiled up in a grey blanket the corners of which were held by a man & a woman and laid in the floor of our hall."

Suddenly, as she was attempting to minister to the newly arrived ward, Sallie's attention was diverted "to my little daughter who from terror, I supposed, turned deadly pale and seemed so faint I carried her in my arms to a sofa in an adjoining room," where she suffered a "terribly prolonged chill." As the gunfire inched closer, Sallie, abandoning all concern for her own safety, dashed across the yard to the kitchen on a mission of mercy for her daughter. A second later and Sallie herself would have been killed when "a ball whirred past me, between the house and kitchen tearing up the earth and was found a few paces off." "The dear child," Sallie explained, "had a terribly prolonged chill, but no physician was left in the Village and we used such restoratives as we could command." As the day wore on, another child, with a heavy cough and fever, soon joined the other bedridden patients.

With no physician to call upon, both nursing and doctoring responsibilities fell to Sallie. In her preoccupation with her husband, who was barely able to sit up, and her seriously ill children, Sallie found she "had little time to think of the Yankees. But the burning woods, and high wind, and above all the steady musketry not a mile off—made it a day of horrors."

"Towards evening the firing ceased," Sallie continued, "and our wounded men were brought into the Village, where they were temporarily cared for by field surgeons." The poor stricken soldiers, crowded onto the floor of the hotel and awaiting transportation to Richmond hospitals, tugged at Sara's heartstrings, and for a few moments she took time from her own nursing duties to minister to the soldiers in Chester's makeshift hospital. Sallie explained, "The children's chills were followed by only a slight fever and late in the afternoon I had pitchers & buckets of very strong tea made," which she transported to the writhing, wounded soldiers.

Sallie agonized over "the poor wounded & scorched soldiers, who had made so successful a stand against odds [and now] lay exhausted on the floor and with absolutely no restoratives." She continued: "The enemy had fallen back, but our men were apprehensive of a night attack and anxious to get off to Richmond; not until dark however did any cars arrive, but during the night the brave sufferers were carried to R'd [Richmond] and there, carefully provided for."[3]

The following two days occasioned repeated fighting near Chester, made even more deadly by the firing of the woods and the gruesome deaths of soldiers on both sides who fell victim to the flames. For Sallie the next two days constituted two days of excruciating personal agony and suffering. Surely nothing in life can be so devastating to a mother as the tragic loss of her child, and yet for Sallie her grief was compounded by her distress over a second child's life-threatening battle with pneumonia. "I cannot trust my trembling hand to write of the events of the next two days." Sallie was frantic. "While one of my children, so long a sufferer was taken away from us, and from the pains & turmoil of this life, after a congestive chill—the elder of the two had grown so rapidly ill with pneumonia that I had little time for the indulgence of grief, or thought, of our alarming situation." In her sorrow Sallie could scarcely continue: "I will not dwell on these harrowing scenes."[4]

In addition to one child's death and the near terminal illness of another youngster, there was still more pain in store for Sallie. "It was on the 12th of May. I was sitting by the side of our eldest child, who, as yet ignorant of our loss, seemed sinking into a calm natural sleep when my quick ear caught the sound of cavalry. Within hours after the little coffin had been committed to its earthy home the hastily improvised gravesite would be desecrated, trampled down by legions of iron hooves and irreverent riders." Sallie was horrified. "Raising my eyes to the curtainless window, to my horror, saw a number of mounted men riding past with flags flying. I went quickly to the window to obstruct the view if possible fearing B [her daughter] might open her eyes. Had I raised it to close the shutters, it would have aroused her, so I stood there each moment expecting to see the end of the cavalcade. Across on the other side of the lane thro' which they passed lay our garden and here in what we thought would be a quiet place, our beautiful little darling had scarcely been laid two hours before. Within a few paces of her resting place, thousands of men were now hurrying on their errand of blood!"[5]

The faith in God that sustained so many millions of people throughout the war found a resurgence in Sallie as she stood at the window: "As I stood there I had ample time to dwell on the fearful scenes of the preceding days, and I thanked God for the fortitude He had given me, and for the bodily strength which seemed born of the excitement thro' which I had passed, for I was never blest with great physical strength."

And, indeed, strength in abundance was precisely what Sallie needed, for yet another calamity was about to descend upon the family. As the cavalry stormed by, Sallie watched in dismay: "I saw, tho' I made no sound, our trusty man-servant, W'm, who had been our carriage driver, borne off, with the soldiers, and mounted on our only horse. This very reliable and faithful servant had been brought with us from the Farm together with this one horse & cart to haul wood, and to bring supplies from Richmond when needed, that we might be independent of the cars, which being so continually needed for military purposes, carrying supplies for the Army etc. it was often impossible to make use of them. I saw it all & William's rueful glance back told me he was most reluctant to go and while I stood there I remembered that we were, almost entirely bare of some of the necessities of life, & here our only stay was taken." Again, Sallie sought deliverance: "I involuntarily lifted my heart to Him who has promised to provide such things as He sees us have need of—in truth my life in those days seemed one continuous prayer."[6]

The Duvals thus became prey to a common practice of invading Union soldiers, who would force or entice "servants" to leave their masters. Unfortunately, this "tolling off" of blacks was not always a humanitarian gesture. Union forces theorized that the departure of blacks would serve to minimize the workforce in the fields and thus limit the food supply both for the Confederate Army and for civilians on the homefront. At the same time, it would help to demoralize their owners and bring a speedier end to the war.

As Sallie continued to watch from her window, she observed her friend, "Mrs. I," standing at the door of the kitchen. "Possibly, her motive in going there just *then* was, by her presence to restrain her servants & mine, who might for aught she knew, in their excitement, join the cavalcade of soldiers as they passed, this had often been done before to our knowledge. I next saw one of our men run out from the kitchen, and that he was peremptorily ordered back or to keep out of sight, for he stood with his back to the wall, where he could not be seen. Only now and then, when curiosity got the better of him, peeping round the corner of the building, and as quickly being ordered back by Mrs. I. At last making himself distinctly visible, he was called and ordered into line disappearing as W'm had done in the turn of the lane."

Two Spirited Women

The feistiness that so universally characterized Confederate women throughout the war years was soon to be personified in Sallie and her good friend (identified only as "Mrs. I"). Feeling "quite despairing," Sallie noted, "Seeing B was now profoundly asleep, and her father who had come in some time before, quietly by her side, I ventured to leave the room. As I entered an apartment on the first floor, I saw from the window Mrs. I still standing in the kitchen door, now talking to several officers on horseback. I could not hear distinctly this conversation, but the chief spokesman seemed a courtly gentleman, and apparently pleased with her unaffected simplicity of manner & her sweet face. The talk lasted some minutes when he urged his horse forward & held out his hand to her. At this, with great dignity & a countenance that I thought, expressed regret at giving him pain, she put her own hand behind her."

As might be expected Mrs. I's action was less than appreciated. "He reined his horse back so suddenly that he almost sank on his haunches, & I heard broken sentences and the words muttered—'These Southern women'—'to be expected' etc. Then the whole party rode off down the hill leaving us both gazing after them."[7]

Moments later Sallie had her turn with a Yankee. "Meanwhile during the above mentioned colloquy while I looked on," Sallie related, "a soldier of vile countenance came to my window, which was quite near the ground and pointing to the meat house, demanded of me the key. I had it in my pocket at the time, but replied, 'That is not my house, I have only been here a few weeks & have no meat.'" Still, the would-be thief persisted. "He then said 'None of your d—secesh lies. I'm going to have *meat*,'" whereby Sallie replied, "'that he could not get what I hadn't to give.'"

Insisting on knowing "whose place is this?" Sallie's predator grew increasingly agitated. "'There' I said 'is the lady of the house,'" Sallie responded, pointing to Mrs. I. "Turning & seeing her in conversation with officers, he skulked away around to the building occupied by my servants, after giving me another oath and a scowl." Later, Sallie admitted: "We happened to have an unusually large supply of flour etc. but no meat, while Mrs. I in the same building had a good many large pieces of the latter which were then a treasure indeed. My nurse afterwards told me this ruffian had made the same demand on them and they had corroborated my story, this being the only way to convince a Yankee of the truth of a statement made by a 'Rebel!'"

Having at least temporarily divested themselves of the bullies, Sallie and Mrs. I nervously surveyed the passing scene. "During many hours of this weary day the cavalry continued to pass our premises, while the Village had rapidly filled up with a large body of Infantry. The news was soon brought us by the servants that a raiding party was going to cut the Danville R.R." It was estimated there were some 10,000 soldiers, and Sallie and Mrs. I corroborated the numbers of marchers. "Certain it is, they were passing two abreast, close upon each other's heels—for several hours. This kept up until quite monotonous, but at last they all passed, & so far no stragglers from the Village had ventured up the hill to our house. They were ever cautious at first, fearing a surprise I imagine, which was natural as they were on strange ground & only 12 miles from Richmond and about 11 from Petersburg."

Later that afternoon about 4 o'clock, as Sallie and Mrs. I were chatting at the window, "We were startled by the sound of an engine approaching from the direction of Richmond—and to our dismay saw the smoke above the trees, which concealed the track from our view and thus the engine fearlessly approaching." In a matter of seconds, knowing that the train would be easy prey for the Federals, the two friends, thanks to quick thinking and resolute courage, became instant heroines. "We scarcely took time to exchange a word but ran down to the track, not 50 yards off, at the great risk of being seen by the enemy, and waved the train back." Warning the engineer that the Village was occupied, Sallie informed him of "the heavy force of cavalry which had passed our house, and its reported designation." As a result, Sallie wrote, "The old gentleman lost no time in getting up steam, and backed off, freighted with this important intelligence. The authorities had not been apprised of the occupation of the Village that morning, and the engine alone was ventured out—to see that the 'coast was clear.'" "The information of threatening danger to the Danville R.R. was of immense importance," Sallie wrote. "That same night when they reached Matoax [Matoaca?] Station they met a brave resistance from the re-inforced troops at Appomattox Bridge—no time had been lost. The next day our friends read in one of the daily papers, an account of the scene at 'Chester' when 'two brave ladies had risked their lives to save the locomotive & men,' who were so unsuspectingly steaming into the Village—but our friends little dreamed who the ladies were."

Sallie and Mrs I marveled at their great good fortune in not being detected. "The escape of that engine is inexplicable! The track makes a bend just on entering the place, and trees grew quite thickly near, but how it escaped observation I could never imagine, and how *we* escaped is equally marvelous. Our front yard extended to the road and was so much above the level, that in waving the cars back, we were necessarily very conspicuous from the Hotel not more than a hundred yards lower down, around which and beyond, the Northern troops lay. They were stricken with blindness surely, and we ran back terrified into the house, every second expecting a volley after the retreating engine and sure that

we could hardly escape their wrath. I can only state facts as I saw them
& do so with undeviating fidelity."[8]

By the next morning, life had taken on a rosier hue for the Duvals.
Sallie's prayers had been answered. Food had been provided when their
favorite servant, William, made his way back to the family on foot (and
was soon followed by the other wayward servant, Daniel). "When the
former entered the back gate he picked up and brought to me a bag of
bacon. This had evidently been thrown over into our lot by some one
weary of the load. The low park fence along which they rode for a quarter of a mile, enclosed Mrs. I's premises—the little alley, with its gate as
outlet, was the only part that we claimed. Just here the weary man relieved
himself of his load and this seemed to me, as surely sent as the ravens
to Elijah, with his 'cake of bread and meat in the morning & cake of
bread & meat in the evening.' Some who read these recollections, may
have the faith which I have, others will smile with incredulity. I can only
say this simple fact occurred, just as I state it."[9]

Over the weekend, Sallie's "two invalids seemed to be convalescing
and Sunday's sun shone out with something of cheer in it." She rejoined,
"My poor husband had gained some strength, tho' so lame he could
scarcely walk even with a crutch, but that evening departing from his
custom he managed to get down to the dining room to tea."

As Sallie's husband began to regain his health and strength, Sallie
was plagued by the persistent fear that he might be observed and taken
prisoner by the Federals in Chester. "The Village by this time was quite
full of Northern troops and though our house on the hill was somewhat
removed from them, I felt great anxiety—since repeated rumors had
come to us of the arrest of boys and old men—& fearing lest some strag-
gler should see him thro' the closed shutters, I made the slats as close as
possible."

One evening detection appeared imminent to the terror-stricken Sallie: "We had just finished supper when a horseman galoped fearlessly
around the house and before I could get the to the front-door, he was
there. I firmly held the door entreating my husband to go to his room,
but he was in so crippled a condition, that with the help of the servants
and children it was still some time—it seemed many minutes, tho' probably only seconds—before he could be gotten up stairs. The stiff limb
was hard to manage, and but for my alarm, the scene would have been
ludicrous. When at last I saw that he was safe, all of which took less time
than the telling has done, I had to surrender my post to Mrs. I—the kind
friend who was ever at my side when I wanted and needed her.

"My breath was gone and I was so alarmed for my husband. I
staggered after him up the steps. In a moment Mrs. I came to the foot
of the stairs saying in a suppressed tone 'Come quickly Mrs. D, he is a

Confederate.' I regained my strength and sprang down the steps—going
up to him, and unconscious of what I did—felt in the darkness the cloth
of his coat, as if by the very touch I could discern, the dear grey. He must
have been amused, but to my questions only replied 'Madam I am a
South Carolina Confederate and have lost my way.' Then I ejaculated in
my excitement 'Then my dear boy go away from here.' 'That is just what
I want to do—but why.' We then told him Northern soldiers had possession of the Village. He asked if there was no man on the place who
could give him some idea of the roads. I told him only an invalid up
stairs—and before I could think, he stalked unceremoniously past us up
the steps, while the servants who had assembled in the hall were entreating me for God's sake not to let him go up—as he was a Yankee in disguise
& only wanted 'Mass. Robert.' I assured them that he was unmistakeably
a Southerner, but they were greatly agitated & shook their heads saying,
I would know better when too late.[10]

   "Meanwhile the youth had made his way into the first chamber at
the head of the steps, & I followed in time to hear him say 'Cheer up,
you will have good news before tomorrow night.' After getting the necessary instructions as to the shortest road to Petersburg, and how to
avoid the Federalists, he departed with our blessing, & a division of a
loaf of bread, which he seemed glad to get, tho' he would not stop a
moment for anything else. He paid me a graceful compliment which was
worthy of a South Carolinian, and I believe from his heart and then he
galoped away as fearlessly as he had come. I afterwards learned he was
a courier from Gen'l Beauregard (who had just taken command at
'Drury's Bluff' a few miles off) to Gen'l Pickett then around Petersburg
with his divisions, ordering him to advance & cut off the retreat of Gen'l
Butler while he, Beauregard attacked him in front.[11,12,13] Just here I will
say—this circumstance of the young courier's having lost his way, & been
directed by some one in Chester, appeared in the Richmond 'Examiner'
a day or two later. How the information was picked up we could never
learn."[14]

   In directing General Beauregard's courier and alerting him to the
huge contingent of Union soldiers just a few yards away, Sallie and Mrs.
I once again shared a few moments of glory by providing an important
service for the Confederacy.

   Actually, her fear and loathing of the enemy was not so intense that
Sallie could not summon deep compassion for the incoming carloads of
desperately sick and wounded Federals. The next morning, having been
roused by the ominous sounds of gunfire from nearby engagements, Sallie reported the village "in a great state of excitement": "A church immediately opposite to our house & on the other side of the R.R. had been
used by them as a hospital. Soon we saw flat after flat, and one coal car

after another with boards laid across the top ... all laden with poor wounded men, and as they were borne on stretchers from the cars up to the door of the Church tenderly & carefully lifted off, we could plainly see the stretchers were saturated with blood. Our hearts ached to see so much suffering, for no woman could behold unmoved such a scene."

Amidst all the chaos and anguish, one heartrending scene would remain indelibly etched in Sallie's mind for as long as life itself: "I watched it all from the bedside of my little daughter who was now rapidly convalescing. Soon they seemed to find it would not be safe for them there and they commenced moving their wounded from the Church and going back towards their encampment beyond the Village. As I sat at my window I saw a man borne between two stalwart soldiers up the hill, on a stretcher. When they reached the house of one of our neighbors, the dying boy asked them to stop under the shade of a tree at her door and to get him some water. My neighbor came out with a glass and gently raising his head put it to his lips. One of the men advised him not to drink it as 'The d—secesh would as soon poison him as not.' But the poor boy had only to look into her tearful eyes, to be reassured, & without hesitancy partook of the lifesaving draught." Sallie's neighbor then "rested his head gently down and they were about to bear him on as the firing of guns was heard nearer & nearer each moment." Yet, "He heard not the sound & heeded not the danger but raised his eyes appealingly to hers & said 'Would you kiss me for my Mother?'

"I need not say she pressed her lips on his cold forehead & his impatient carriers bore him away. But the Angel of Death was hovering over him, and tho' he faintly breathed when she gave him a last-look, it could not have been many moments before he was out-of-sight & hearing of all earthly scenes & earthly sounds."

"No doubt," Sallie sighed, "there were many scenes similar to this, enacted in the long, weary days of that bloody war."[15]

Food continued to be as pressing a problem for the Duvals as for the rest of the Southland. Once again Sallie experienced an immediate response to her prayers. As she turned her attention away from the drama outside her window, Sallie faced yet another dilemma: "My attention was called from outside scenes by my little convalescent saying, if she only had some soup, or even a cup of tea & some toast, she would be so glad. Alas! This entreaty was useless and my eyes filled up when I remembered that every fowl except my precious little A's pet chicken had been taken from us several days before and my last tea & white sugar had been carried to the soldiers after the fight at 'Winfree's Farm.' She *must* have nourishment and the terrible experiences of the few preceding days had, strange to say, made me forgetful of this. I went from her room praying as I went, that something might be provided. I was going to have the pet chicken killed but where was the tea and sugar?

"Just as I reached the back door a mulatto rode up on a very spirited & unmanageable horse, both evidently under terrible excitement— the horse rearing & the man cursing. He carried a basket with great difficulty and seemed anxious to get rid of it. One of our negro men rec'd it from him, to keep, as he said, till he returned for it; it being Gen'l Gilmore's and before many moments he was dashing on furiously after the retreating Yankees, in the direction of the Village. I raised the napkin that had been hastily thrown over the contents and there before my eyes was a bowl of lump sugar and two small canisters, one of tea, and another of coffee with part of a ham of bacon, broken fragments of bread, soiled napkins, plates etc.—all telling of an interrupted breakfast. I seized the tea & sugar with a thankful heart; and told the servants to keep the rest until it should be called for."[16]

And still the manna rained down! Moments later one of the household servants, "faithful old George, came up to me from the kitchen and said 'Missus, dem Yankees, give me dis, for butcherin Mr. Winfree's calf for em & I brought it to you.' It was beautifully prepared and the dear old darkie did not know he was heaven sent.

"Some may cavil at this, but our Heavenly Father saw 'what things I had need of' and I stopped not to marvel at the almost miracle, but from the depths of my heart returned Him thanks and accepted from George a part of the gift for the child's sake. A few hours later I had the comfort of seeing her enjoy the savory soup made of it, and when she asked where it had come from I told her, the Good Father had provided it, as He did everything we needed, and always would when we fully trusted in him."[17]

That same day Sallie was again able to impart vital information— this time to two badly frightened "Blue coats": "It was now nearly midday, and all the house was wild with excitement—it being evident from the firing & tumult in the air, that the enemy was being driven as the sounds came nearer & nearer. My friend and I were standing on our front-porch, when two 'Blue coats' approached with hurried and nervous manner, begging us to tell them what to do, one of them vociferating he was 'a Scotchman and had been dragged into the service but had never fired a gun against a Southerner.' I replied that there was nothing now left to do, but surrender, pointing as I spoke to a detachment of Confederate cavalry, who were galoping up. They said they would be known by their blue coats, and be shot. I said 'take off your coats and lose no time,' turning as I spoke to go to the other door, for a better view. I lost sight of the poor scared men, and half an hour later saw them trailing along in the dust and crowd, surrounded by our men. They spied us, and called out saying, 'Your advice was good Ladies, we are on our way to the 'Libby' where I have wanted to go for two years.' I was surprised at being recognized and at the remark, my last view of them was as they tramped on with their blue-coats thrown over their arms."[18,19]

New Dangers Ahead

For a brief time the residents of the village rejoiced in a temporary tranquillity. The blessed calm, however, was short-lived. Sallie continued: "Thus ended the weeks occupancy of the Village by the Enemy, and we were left in temporary quiet, that is till about the middle of June. On the 3rd of that month the second bloody battle of 'Cold Harbor' had been fought, when Lee and Grant remained for days thereafter confronting each other. In Chester we could hear nothing from 'the front' and about the 12th I went to Richmond to see how matters stood. During the day we heard there that Gen'l Grant had crossed to the south side of James River at City Point, and that Gen'l Lee's army was 'in motion.' These movements, our friends persuaded us, threatened a repetition for us of what we had suffered, scarcely a month before. We yielded to their kind solicitations, and decided to go for a short stay among them, hoping the danger would soon be past.

"Returning home that evening we made preparations to leave the next-morning at 9 o'clock. That night an unusual number of trains seemed to pass. Early in the morning we learned they had all gone, except one locomotive & a few flats. When I first looked from my window the scene which lay before me soon explained itself."

News of another Yankee invasion sent shock waves through the town, frightening the village residents into a mass exodus from the town. Villagers, Sallie reported, were frantic in their efforts to leave: "The people in the Village on either side of the R.R. were seen running hither & thither, carrying baskets, satchels etc. while the family living on the opposite hill, were running down the steep path, several of them dragging their trunks after them."

It took little persuasion for Sallie and her family, once apprised of the proximity of the Federals, to board the waiting flat cars where they and their friends became innocent victims exposed to the murderous June sun: "Being all ready, after taking a hurried breakfast we joined the motley crew on the flats, in the burning sun of a hot day in June with nothing to shield us from its rays. The servants had provided for our comfort chairs & cushions, and as the train moved off my old nurse handed on, a plate of *fried bacon* and plain corn bread 'for the children,' her own breakfast no doubt, which she had no heart to eat. We had gone but three miles when the engine was stopped, & we were told they had orders to go no further! Filled with consternation we used every degree of expostulation in vain. Being unable to endure the heat of the sun, we all took refuge in the woods, tho' it was a pine forest & no breath of air stirring.

"We were scarcely off of the cars when two of my children were taken very sick, one of them with a chill, and I had no means of providing for the comfort of either. The people were very kind, doing all they could to alleviate the suffering & discomfort of the little ones, but the day dragged wearily enough. We were left in ignorance of how long we were to be detained here, when guns were heard in the direction of Chester, and way-farers came by telling us that fighting was going on just beyond there. As can be imagined our alarm was great, as every moment the musketry became louder and we could not tell, whether friend or foe was nearest us. The cars meanwhile had gone on somewhat further and we had no means of escape. Towards evening, the blessed news came that the enemy was driven back, and the train of cars would soon return, and take us home again. We hailed the dirty flats with delight and resuming our places, were in a short time rec'd with every demonstration of joy by the whole population.

"The aspect of things was quite different from that of the morning. Pickett's Division after a skirmish with the enemy had arrived, and all hands were busy, putting up tents, and some of the soldiers getting ready for their evening meal. On every side soldiers met our view, as far as we could see, and after the wretchedly uncomfortable day, we went to sleep, with a feeling of security we had not had for many a night."[20]

"The trip to Richmond however was not abandoned, the sick ones must have medical attendance. Being told that we could go up early in the morning on the 'ambulance train,' we again made our preparations taking our seats in time in one of the many coaches. We were detained for hours, however, waiting for the poor soldiers, who, in the Hotel, which was again used as a temporary hospital, were having their wounds dressed, and some of them suffering the amputation of their limbs.

"I will pass over the succeeding months of July and August, as, protected by Pickett's Division we felt secure from invasion, only hearing from afar the *echoes,* and among them, of the fearful mine explosion at Petersburg, which tho' meant for our destruction, wrought ten-fold more havoc among the perpetrators of the fearful deed."[21]

Epilogue

Although Sallie's husband's health was gradually restored, their harrowing experiences had taken a toll on Sallie's health: "Repeated domestic sorrows, and at last my own utter breakdown of health, compelled me to take the advice of my physician and try to reach the mountains. Just at that time Winchester and the surrounding counties were, we believed, in the hands of the Confederates, and it was thought we could undertake the journey in safety. By this time my husband's health was sufficiently restored for him to return to his duties in one of the Home Departments, and he could get leave of absence only long enough to accompany me and our three remaining children to Staunton, where he put us on the stage for Winchester paying $75 a seat for each of us, the distance being about 94 miles, my friends having been written to some time before to meet us there."

Even the trip to a mountain retreat was beset with problems for Sallie. Once again a child became ill, and the verdant beauty of the countryside was wasted on Sallie: "The journey would have been a very agreeable one, since the Valley turnpike over which we travelled lies through a country of unsurpassed grandeur of scenery—but for the suffering condition of my youngest child, who lay in my arms all day, parched with fever, and my own sad reflections and foreboding, for the idea had been whispered that the road might not be free from the Enemy."

"Our fears were soon realized," Sallie reported. "On the forenoon of the second day, after leaving Strasburg, the stage stopped, and the driver came to the door telling us he could proceed no further, as he had heard firing in the direction of Winchester, and then saw in the distance an ambulance approaching which boded no good. I urged him to go on until assured of evil, pointing to my sick child, which seemed to touch him, and also reminding him that the owners of the stage line would surely have warned him, if there had been any danger. This last argument prevailed, tho' he said the Yankees had recently seized their whole line of fine stages and destroyed them. This I urged again was a good reason for believing the owners would take every precaution to preserve them. I am sure I was never so eloquent before and the other passengers left the talking with me, and anxiously awaited the result. My persuasion had the desired effect for he mounted to his seat on the box & drove steadily on in spite of a number of ambulances which we met hurrying past all filled with wounded men. Getting no orders from his employers I suppose he felt quite safe in going on, which feeling we could not share, tho' we were glad to profit by it. As we drew near Winchester I suffered the greatest anxiety. The enemy was certainly near, would my friends meet me?" Sallie wondered, "Where should I stop? And what should I do with my poor sick child? My faithful old nurse had necessarily been left behind, and I, really sick and prostrated, felt forlorn indeed."

Winchester, Sallie discovered, was convulsed with soldiers and inhabitants rushing about in mass confusion: "As we entered the town our own soldiers were marching rapidly down the streets, the confusion and excitement among the inhabitants was very great. The stage made its way to the door of the principal hotel and looking out I saw only *men, men, men*. The sidewalks were crowded with soldiers—the porches, windows & everywhere, not a flutter of a woman's garments appeared to encourage me & relieve my timidity. The three females who had accompanied us had gotten out at the edge of town.

"At last an officer who was near, courteously came forward & took my little girl in his arms, while I with the two larger children followed. Soon the proprietor came and led the way to the Reception room. We learned that Gen'l Anderson was there with his staff, also Gen'l Fitz-Lee and all hands were busy, as these officers, with many others, must have dinner prepared immediately. So no one came to take me to a chamber and at last I ventured out to make enquiries as to the carriage I expected to meet me there and to see what the prospect was for dinner. Dinner I was told was nearly ready, and soon after the landlord came to escort me down. The repast made quite an impression on me. It was no doubt the best the times afforded, but a sorry affair. I did not count the soldiers who sat down, but together with ourselves there must have been at least twenty. There was one moderately large roast of beef, a dish of green peas (boiled in the pod, served all together, pod, peas, stems & all), a dish of corn and some bread—this was all and in passing let me add that the charges per day were $40 apiece."

Sallie's anxious questions were rewarded with even more dismal news: "When I had enquired if my kinswoman's carriage had been heard of, I was told that it was extremely doubtful whether she had horses or carriage, or even her house left as twenty-eight large mills & residences, were reported to have been burned in the Upper Valley, and that the Federalists had possession of the two principal roads out of Winchester, which was discouraging for me."

Sallie's spirits lifted somewhat when she received a special visit. "During the afternoon I rec'd a visit from a relation then living in Winchester who kindly invited me to his house, and advised me to remain there quietly, till it should be safe for me to pursue the remaining 15 miles of my journey. A friend offered to bring me the first intelligence to this effect, and meanwhile to try and secure for me a conveyance out of Winchester, when the time should come for me to go. This he succeeded in getting for the sum of $125 and Gen'l Fitz-Lee's courier coming on the third night with the news that the Enemy had fallen back from the turnpike (my route). I next morning took up the line of travel, and departed with many good wishes from my friends."

"The carriage was ante-diluvian, and the horse likewise," Sallie wrote, "so our journey tho' on a turnpike was slow. Meanwhile the driver regaled the children with a story of a lady, a Mrs. Jackson he said, who, two weeks before had hired from him a conveyance & two horses & it was believed that she and the driver had been killed, as her empty trunk, and other traces of them had been found a few miles out of Winchester concealed in the dead leaves in the woods, near the public road. Such alarming tales were calculated to make us nervous and the still smoking campfires of the Enemy, close to our road as we jogged along, greatly increased this feeling."

Finally the little family reached the home of Sallie's kinfolk: "At last we neared the spire of the mountain on which the house *should stand*, but I could see nothing but trees, and feeling unable to endure the suspense while travelling the circuitous road that led to it, stopped at the house of an old friend near which we had to pass. I there enquired & to my great joy, learned our kinsfolk had been spared. Soon we drove in the familiar old gate, and there to my great delight beheld the peaceful and unusual sight of two gentlemen sitting on the piazza, smoking, with their feet elevated nearly to the level of their heads—and so immersed in their papers, they did not hear our approach. And joy beyond words! These two gentlemen, the two young officers nearest and dearest to me, enjoying a few days furlough. But when they raised their eyes—oh joy! Our dear absent ones come back on furlough of a few days! Then the greeting.... But no words can describe the delight of that hour. All my fears dissipated & my best hopes more than realized! Such moments come rarely in the life of any."

◎◎

Sallie Duval had been remarkably perceptive in envisioning the "world of turmoil, and war, and wretchedness" that awaited her as she departed her happy home in New Kent County, Virginia, in February of 1864. Much as she hoped their relocation in Chester, Virginia would provide a far safer haven than New Kent County, Sallie was too much a realist to believe their refugee life would be a comfortable one. Sallie's experiences as a refugee were anything but unique, and in these brief excerpts the reader is offered a sampling of the calamities that befell those thousands upon thousands of Civil War women who moved—alone or with their families—in an effort to escape being overrun by the Federals. Countless refugees soon learned, as did Sallie, that their abandoned homes had been torched; that there were few areas that were not sooner or later overtaken by the Federals; that Yankees, Confederates, "bummers," stragglers, and roving bands of thugs could descend upon their property and make off with their valuables, poultry and horses without a moment's notice. Deprived of the support of longtime neighbors and friends, refugees discovered that life could become almost unbearable, particularly in times of illness and the loss of a loved one. Sallie and others like her were put to the test to enable their families to survive despite the scarcity of food supplies and the "capture" by the Yankees of the few "servants" that remained with them. For many, their faith in God alone sustained them. Spirits flagged at times, but somehow their indomitable Confederate feistiness prevailed. Fortunately, Sallie's reunion with her kinfolk provided a happy ending to her war experiences. Would that that conclusion had been true for all of Sallie's compatriots.[22]

C/ Five /Ɔ

Life in a Divided City—
Perspectives from
Winchester, Virginia

The men had all gone with the enemy and the women were all she devils.

—Secretary of State William H. Seward
speaking of the town of Winchester

Prologue

The Civil War divided a country, but it also separated people within states, within cities, within families. A case in point is Winchester, Virginia. When one examines the chaos resulting from the Civil War, one can look at Winchester, a town that is said to have changed hands 76 times, upon occasion as many as four times in one day. Although the number is disputed, and although there were certainly not 76 major battles staged in Winchester, diaries, memoirs, and facts testify to dozens of confrontations between Confederate and Federal forces. Winchester's excellent "highways" and its location near two capital cities—Washington and Richmond—made it a key acquisition for both armies. In addition, Winchester was situated a short distance east of the new state of West Virginia, west of the border state of Maryland, and south of faithful Union advocates in Pennsylvania. Furthermore, the rich farmland of the Shenandoah Valley provided much of the sustenance for the Confederate army.

As the months passed, Winchester underwent so many changeovers that Mary Greenhow Lee grew indifferent to the sounds of soldiers and galloping horses engaged in cavalry raids: "The first sound I heard this morning was the clanking of sabers & dash of Cavalry; so accustomed

180

have I become to border warfare that I did not get up to see whether they were Confederates or Yankees, but completed my morning nap.... By dinner time, all had vamoosed." "Who will we belong to to-morrow?" Mary wondered.[1]

Winchester, of course, was Confederate territory—at least some of the time—and primarily peopled with "true Southern" patriots; however, the town also included a number of staunch Unionists, who alternately cheered and wept as the town seesawed back and forth between friendly and enemy takeovers. While the Union army was in control, ardent Confederate women kept their silence or maintained a sometimes cautious, although oftentimes caustic, resistance. When the Confederates took over, it was time for loyal Union women to hold their tongues. Smothering one's bitterness was not always possible, and both Southern and Northern Winchester diarists detailed cases of an ever-increasing number of families who were harassed or eventually "sent beyond the lines."

The extensive diaries of Mary Greenhow Lee and her sister-in-law, Laura Lee, invite their readers to vicarious participation in the intimate life of two willful Southern women zealously committed to the Confederate cause.[2] For Mary and Laura there was no middle ground; the struggle for independence became a crusade they were willing to die for if necessary. Unable to don military attire and take up arms in defense of their convictions, the Lees sought to do battle with words and deeds on their homefront—Winchester.

And, indeed, the Lees were scarcely unique in their devotion to the Confederacy. The town's loyal coterie of Confederates took great pride in being "secesh" and saw their attempts to thwart Union orders and hassle Federal officers as their contributions to the war effort. Feisty and obdurate, the Lees and their partisan friends seized every opportunity to express their irritation over Yankee occupation and the hated bluecoats.[3]

The Enemy in Our Midst

Spirited Rebel women, such as the Lees, took out their hatred on the despised Yankee invaders of their sacred homes and land by verbally insulting the intruders or by coldly ignoring their very presence. (Mary Lee had a reputation for being "the most outrageous rebel in Winchester.") Women slammed their doors and shutters, wore dark veils, and refused to walk under the Union flag in their persistent attempts to avoid any and all contact with the Federals. Secretary of State William Seward was both candid and succinct in his appraisal of Winchester following a visit to the Kernstown Battlefield. "The men had all gone with the enemy and & the women were all she devils."[4]

Mary Greenhow Lee, who made her home with two of her sisters-in-law, Laura Lee (Lal) and Antoinette Lee (Nettie), and two nieces, Laura and Louise Burwell, summed up the animosity of many pro–Southern Winchester residents when she noted smugly in her diary: "...I cannot get up a feeling of fear for the Yankees; I have such a thorough contempt for them that I do not realize they are human beings & I feel able to protect myself from them. Whether this feeling will continue, I cannot tell, but in the few interviews I have been compelled to have with them, I know I have got the better of them."[5] (The preceding sentiments were written early in the war. Mary Lee's loathing of the Federals, however, certainly did not diminish over the years; instead it appeared to intensify.)

As Union troops paraded by their home Mary Lee took great pleasure in ignoring them. With an air of superiority she mused: "You would be delighted to see how little Union feeling there is here, even amongst the lower classes & the servants; they go about amongst them & then tell us what they say. I believe they are all the time expecting an attack from Jackson & when he comes I know they will run; wreaking their vengeance on the town & the Secessionists but not waiting to fight. They spend their time marching up and down Market St. [directly in front of the house]. Regiment after regiment & company after company pass every day but not a face do they see, at our house or our whole square. They gaze at the windows as they pass, while we, unseen, enjoy their mortification. It is an army gotten up for show and parade. The reports of disgruntled Federals that "they were never treated with such scorn as by the Winchester ladies," warmed her heart.[6]

When a Winchester woman contended that the Federal officers were "men of the highest social position—the very elite of Northern society, and she could not understand 'why the Southern ladies should have such bitter feelings & refuse to receive them,'" Mary was quick to respond, insisting that "she does not realize that our houses cannot be opened to the murderers of our friends & the enemies of our liberty."[7]

Zealous Winchester "secesh" took few pains to hide their rebel sympathies and instead gleefully flaunted their partisan allegiances at every opportunity. Prayer meetings, dinner parties, and even chance street corner meetings were occasions for the Lees and their friends to gather for lively Southern talk and the disparagement of the enemy. "Mat Baldwin called me & several other persons came up," Mary reported gleefully, "& we had a joyous Rebel conclave at Randall's corner in the midst of the Yankees."[8]

Antipathy for Union soldiers was even more scathingly directed to

Union women. During Union occupations of Winchester, numerous Federal officers seeking accommodations for their wives—or mistresses—stopped by "to ask if Mrs. Lee will take a gentleman and lady." "Lady!" Laura Lee exploded. "I might be obliged to live for a time in the house with some of the officers, if it was necessary, as a protection from the depredations of the soldiers, but no consideration of any kind could force me to live under the roof with a Yankee woman."[9]

Not surprisingly, the Yankees' ruthless habit of sending abrasive Confederates—or even innocent rebel homeowners—"through the lines" garnered them countless enemies among the Winchester residents. An infuriated Gertie Miller noted in her diary that Mrs. Logan and all her family were sent out of Yankee lines. "Old Milroy, his wife and brats have taken her house and all her things."[10] The occupation of Winchester by General Robert Huston Milroy, Union Commander of the Division at Winchester, was notorious for the lack of discipline on the part of the soldiers and the frequent confrontations with the townspeople as they appropriated garden produce and fence rails for their own creature comfort. The spacious home of Lloyd Logan, a prosperous tobacco merchant, had apparently attracted General Milroy's attention, and he quickly moved in and set up his headquarters there. Later that day when Mrs. Milroy was to join him, he arbitrarily sent the Logans (despite the serious illness of two of the Logan women) beyond the Yankee lines, forcing them to leave all their furniture and allowing them to take only their clothes.[11] In her April 7, 1863, diary entry, Cornelia McDonald noted: "The whole town has been shocked and outraged by Milroy's treatment of Mrs. Logan. He wanted her elegant house for his own headquarters, and cooly gave her orders to vacate it with her family. They demurred, as was natural and Mrs. Logan and her daughters were ordered to a room in the house where they were kept close prisoners all day, without even a morsel of food of their own abundant stores; and at evening a rude wagon was sent to the door, the ladies put in and driven six miles out of town, where they were set down by the roadside, destitute of everything. Her son was imprisoned in the guardhouse." Mrs. Logan's keys were turned over to Mrs. Milroy, who was informed that "in the future they were to be hers."[12]

General Milroy apparently did not take kindly to criticism, and two teachers were sent out of the lines for having written letters that were intercepted and found to contain uncomplimentary comments about the General. Cornelia McDonald was particularly distressed over the closing of one of the teacher's schools, fearing that she would have nowhere to send her son Kenneth.[13]

The theft by Union soldiers of fence rails to be used for their campfires was a constant annoyance for Winchester property owners. Mary

Lee recreated an entertaining scene from a friend's call on General Milroy to protest the seizure of the rails: "I found this morning, that the Yankee negroes left to take care of the horses in Dr. [R.T.] Baldwin's stable, had been burning our fence again, so I went over to see the result of Mrs. B's last visit to Milroy, & Dickens himself could not have pictured a richer scene. She told him John Brown was the cause of the war; he said it was a lie; she drew up close to him & looked, as only Mrs. B. can look & said in a vicious tone, "don't you say I lie" whereupon he got into such a rage, that he danced about the room & ordered her out in the most insolent manner. She slowly retreated keeping her eye on him. She acted the whole scene."[14]

As the story made the rounds of friends and neighbors, a mischievous group of women contrived to further irritate the general by entreating Cornelia McDonald, friend, Winchester resident, and artist, to paint a picture of the visit and send it to the general as a Valentine's Day present. The clever Cornelia set to work: "He had been rude to Mrs. [Portia] Baldwin, ordering her from his room, and at the same time asking two coloured, and gorgeously dressed ladies to be seated.... So I made a grey headed officer in uniform seated in a chair, and inviting two negro women to take seats, while with a frown he was repelling a handsome young lady (not Mrs. Baldwin) dressed in stripes of red and white, with grey muff and tippet. I heard he received it, and he might have done so, for he ordered a search and prosecution immediately."[15] (The fact that Milroy was depicted as being seated in the presence of standing ladies was no doubt calculated to further humiliate him.)

In a letter to his brother, Randolph Barton, son of the Lees' neighbors, the David Bartons, provided a similar version of Mrs. Baldwin's visit to General Milroy's headquarters. "Mrs. Baldwin went to Milroy complaining about horses being picketed in her yard: Milroy—Is your husband loyal; Mrs. B.—Yes, loyal to the South. M[ilroy] commenced accusing our people of bringing on the war. Mrs. B.—It commenced at the John Brown raid. Milroy—Madam you are a lion, sergeant take this woman off. Mrs. B.—Sir, I refuse to go till I am ready; she sat down and continued sitting for some time, she then arose, I am ready to go now, and off she went." "Just like Mrs. Baldwin," Randolph Barton added.[16]

Union soldiers, of course, were infuriated by the harassment and utter disdain accorded them by Winchester residents, and during one Union takeover, Laura Lee, also a passionate secessionist, denounced the Federal commandant's proclamation (similar although, fortunately, far less inflammatory than General Benjamin "Beast" Butler's New Orleans ultimatum) "that if the citizens *male & female* did not treat the soldier with more courtesy, he would not be answerable for the consequences."[17,18] The threat, of course, failed to intimidate the Lees. The provost's ultimatum, that "the ladies shall not wear sun-bonnets and aprons on the streets, because they only do it to insult the soldiers," also went unheeded by the Lees. "Of course after such an order, they are universally worn," Mary gloated. "All my household wear them & I think I shall have to adopt mine."

Yankee orders *not* to do something always served as a red flag for Mary to immediately set about defying those orders. "One Company of Yankees still in town—Genl. Averell's Head Quarters, five miles out, on the Martinsburgh road & the Provost Marshal's office at Neffstown. I heard the ladies were not allowed to go to the Hospital, so I immediately armed myself with a basket for my patients & some books for the Surgeons & went to the York. The sentinel refused to let me enter, but when I asked if he would shoot me if I went in, he said no."[19] As she was about to cross the yard, however, one of the doctors wisely dissuaded her, "fearing it would tend to more stringent measures."[20]

Not surprisingly, hurrahing enemy troops succeeded in irritating both Federals and Confederates. Randolph Barton recalled having been taken prisoner by the Federals and being marched through Winchester, in fact past the door of his own home. He surely must have rejoiced at seeing his family and friends standing in the doorway and cheering in an effort to buoy up the prisoners' spirits: "Miss Nett Lee rushed out with a cullender full of beaten biscuits and the vessel being soon emptied by the prisoners, she waved it over her head, cheering most lustily. We were the first prisoners who had ever passed through Winchester, and the severities of the war had not yet come into practice. After that, for such an exhibition of sympathy, she would have been bayonetted on the spot."[21] (No doubt the writer exaggerated as to Mary Lee's sister-in-law's possible fate; however, the act certainly would not have endeared her to the Federals.)

Winchester secesh deeply resented restrictions by the Federals, which they considered excessive and unreasonable. Cornelia McDonald was incensed when she was prevented from taking a leisurely walk on her own property. In April of 1863 Cornelia wrote, "We are being more severely dealt with by our tyrants every day. Today every shop and place of business was closed to those who would not take the Federal oath. Not even a place to get a shoe mended. We have long ceased to expect to buy."

Houses were searched repeatedly for guns, military papers, and flags, or simply as a means of flaunting Union authority. Naturally, the Lee home proved a popular site for a search. After one particularly disagreeable confrontation, Mary Lee threatened, "If they come after my flag again I will tell them I will make them one, if they will promise to plant it where I direct—on the old Capitol prison in Washington, where their President keeps Mrs. Greenhow immured, being afraid of a woman's tongue."[22]

Only hours later, there was another demand for the flag. Undaunted by Mary's denial, the soldier then told her "he thought I might have one *to sell*, that he wanted a trophy to send home; I shut the window in his face, as I could not submit to such impertience."

The Yankees were not to be denied. For some time the Federals had had reason to believe the Lees were concealing a Confederate flag "under a plank, under a certain window," and they took great delight in repeatedly searching the home. On one occasion Mary wrote: "Just as I finished dressing this morning, I saw a squad of Yankees drawn up in front of the door, & by the time I got down found the girls had spoken to them through the windows. When I went to the door I found an officer who said he had orders to search the house. I immediately consented & he tole me his Col. had been informed I had a flag concealed under a plank, under a certain window. I told him it was not true but insisted on his taking up the carpet to look. He had the sense to believe me."

Fortunately, the officer looked under the wrong window! "If he had looked under another front window," Mary admitted, "he would have found the loose plank under which so many contraband goods and other valuables had been concealed. It is evident that some one who knows of this place had given information. I knew Lal had our flag on [concealed beneath her skirts!] but I found it was Genl. Ewell's flag he was searching for. I told him common sense might have taught him that we would not keep such a flag here—that we had made one for Genl. Ewell's Head Quarters & sent to him at Shepherdstown & had not heard of it since. He was thoroughly ashamed of the whole affair. We laughed at him for reviving the stale joke of searching for flags—he behaved very well & believed what we said. He is a N. Yankee & it is a new Regt. that has not been here before. They were much more quiet last night, than those who were here before."[23]

Rumors continued to circulate about Mrs. Lee's flags. A prominent young Union woman insisted "that Mrs. Lee had three Confederate flags concealed in her house & that she could put her hand on the place in Mrs. Lee's house where Genl. Gordon's flag was hidden." "It is utterly false," Mary claimed, "but that makes no difference with the inventors or the hearers of these falsehoods."[24]

When Federal officers came to search the McDonald home for guns, Cornelia ushered them through the rooms, at one point testily spreading out the baby's clothes and asking "if they did not look traitorous."[25] Earlier, a contingent of U.S. officers had called on Cornelia asking to look through the rooms of her home with the view of making it their headquarters. Cornelia responded that she "had no objection to them seeing the rooms, but that I had very many objections to having it occupied as headquarters."[26]

All too often the soldiers made no pretense of searching a home for contraband but simply invaded a secesh home singly, in pairs or en masse. Apparently, nothing was sacred. Cornelia McDonald told of a Federal who had opened her oven door and snatched her homemade rusks out of a hot oven and attempted to carry them off—until she grabbed the soldier by the collar, holding him until the hot pan burned his hands and he dropped it. Other soldiers tried to make off with her Christmas dinner; another group broke in the windows in an attempt to force her to prepare breakfast for them all. So emboldened were the soldiers in appropriating her food and garden produce that Cornelia found she could provide food for her seven small children only by keeping their cow hidden in the cellar and secreting their chickens in the attic. Now and then, she could surreptitiously arrange for her servant to trade homebaked bread for meat, sugar or coffee from the soldiers, since secesh who would not subscribe to the Loyalty Oath were not allowed to buy food in the stores. Without a "please" or a "thank you," cavalry units took over Cornelia's yard and orchard.

To her credit, now and then Mary Lee wisely kept her temper under control. When the Federals housed some of the quartermaster's and commissary's horses in her stables without her permission, she decided "discretion will prompt me to let them remain as they have been quiet & if I turn them out, they will probably burn down the stable or a worse set will get there."[27] The persistent agitation of Yankees, however, constituted only one aspect of Mary Lee's homefront war on her hated enemy. Mary's real contributions to the cause consisted in secretly conducting an underground mail service and at every opportunity forwarding information, letters, clothing, and supplies into the Confederacy. Concealment, intrigue, and subterfuge were all part of Mary's game plan to thwart the "vile wretches."

Surely a high point of Mary Lee's war experiences in Winchester was a visit by Gen. Thomas J. "Stonewall" Jackson, which Mary deemed as recognition and a subtle token of his appreciation for her work on behalf of the Confederacy. In October of 1862, Mary asked future readers of her diary: "What do you think—all you who may hereafter read my journal? What do you think has happened to-day? I must lead you to it by degrees—I kept house, went to the Hospital & various other places, came home, took leave of Capt. Chambers, dressed for dinner, and was standing at the door giving orders to my butcher, when I saw Hunter McGuire approaching with a plain looking officer, whom I did not recognize. Imagine my delight when he introduced Genl. Jackson. I brought them in to the back parlour where Nettie & McIntosh were sitting & I will try to remember his conversation. I commenced by telling him how happy I was to make his acquaintance but I think he did not hear me. Hunter told me he was deaf, I must speak louder. He looked around (the room was looking quite nice) & said 'You do not appear to have been annoyed by the Yankees.' As my replies were merely for the purpose of drawing him out, it is unnecessary to record them. We talked of the mails & papers while the Yankees were here & I told him of how we outwitted them. Then he talked of the flag which was hanging over his head & I gave him the history. When he was leaving I begged him not to leave us to the Yankees again & he said I must talk to Genl. Lee about that. I assured him we looked to him & him alone, whereupon he said, had he his choice Winchester would be his Head Quarters. That, from him, was a great deal."[28]

Mary was ecstatic over the visit: "I never was more surprised at a visit, than at this. It was a most unexpected compliment to us. As there is no gentleman here he came entirely on our account & he would not have come merely at Dr. McGuire's suggestion, as visiting is not in his line. Altogether, it was a most agreeable episode." Earlier, in conjecturing who would be their next unexpected guest, the Lees little dreamed it would be "a voluntary visit from our brave General."[29] In May, Mary had reported Jackson's having complimented the women of Winchester and credited them with "being the backbone of the Confederacy." Somewhat later she wrote: "There is still a hope Jackson's corps will remain between us & the Potomac."[30]

ଜୀଠ

In addition to the details of her harassment of the Federals, Mary Lee's diary provides the canvas for her colorful portrayal of the Winchester scene during the war years. A quiet, sleepy town, Winchester was not. Not infrequently, Yankee threats to burn the town touched off an exodus of panicky residents headed for safer territory. Rumors of mass murders of blacks saw hundreds of slaves fleeing singly or in groups, in terror for their very lives. Band music resonated throughout the town, blaring favorite or detested enemy tunes. Thousands of soldiers filed through Winchester preceded by unfurled silken flags and prancing horses and followed by the rumbling of caissons and supply wagons. All too often there was the thunder of cannons and gunfire, and the horrendous aftermath of the bloodstained carts piled high with the dead and dying. Battlefield deaths became so pervasive that Cornelia McDonald despaired: "What a harvest Death has reaped! Where is the home that is not shadowed by grief, or the heart that has not received a blow?" Several months later she again cried out, "Scarcely a household that I know but has a vacant place, and a fireside but where there are breaking hearts and want."[31]

Southern women displayed an incredible commitment to their cause. During the early days of the war, almost no sacrifice seemed too great: lack of food and shelter, the destruction of cotton fields, homes, and personal possessions, all constituted realistic conditions of a war for independence, accepted, if not willingly, then resignedly, by women on the homefront. Death on the battlefield was deemed a heroic sacrifice made in the service of one's country.

Tragic news that would have felled less devout Confederates seemed, outwardly at least, to be stoically taken in stride by the Lees and their neighbors. In May of 1862 as the Lees were gathered on their porch boisterously cheering the evacuation of Winchester by the Federals and the reoccupation of the town by Confederate troops, word arrived of the shocking death of the son of their friend and neighbor, Mrs. David Barton. The tragedy was compounded by the fact that Marshall Barton had died in fighting on the outskirts of Winchester within sight of his own home. And yet, Mrs. Lee told her diary on May 27, the stalwart Mrs. Barton bore the news "with the most perfect composure, & staid on the porch, giving our soldiers bread and coffee as they passed...." According to Mary Lee, "Mrs. Barton staid down stairs all day Sunday, & has been all the time more wonderfully nerved up, than you could have imagined possible. She says she gave her sons to her country & that she must not murmur at the sacrifice."

Cornelia McDonald corroborated Mary Lee's account, writing that Mrs. Barton had been among the hundreds of Winchester "secesh" who were handing out food from their doorsteps to the hungry rebel forces as they marched through town. As she did so someone touched her arm and told her that Marshall had been shot. "'Bring him to me,'" she said, "and went on distributing her bread to the men." When the corpse was brought to the house, Mrs. Barton led the way and gave directions—"He was born in that room and there he shall lie."[32] Tragedy struck yet again when seven months later Mrs. Barton lost a second son at the Battle of Fredericksburg on December 13, 1862.

"In God Is My Trust"

Their church and their religion were important aspects of the lives of most Winchester women. The diaries and letters are punctuated with Bible verses and supplications to God: "God is able even yet to send us deliverance"; "I still believe God will help us"; "Thanks to my heavenly father who goodness has never failed me"; "Our God is a strong rock and house of defense."

As the Lees waited out yet another turnover of Winchester, Mrs.

Lee commented: "We live in such strange times; in a town held by our enemies—in hourly expectation of the arrival of a vanquished army, which may probably be allowed to wreak its vengeance on our town, if they have time—& without any protection of any kind, & still not afraid. In God is my trust."[33]

Church attendance, of course, was the norm, that is until controversy over the Prayer for the President turned loyal Southerners away from their churches and resulted in private prayer meetings held in secesh homes. During the war years Confederate churchgoers naturally insisted on praying for guidance for their president, that is, President Jefferson Davis. In Federally occupied areas, however, failure to pray for the president of the United States instead of the president of the Confederacy brought down the wrath of the Union officials, and churches were promptly closed. In Winchester during periods of the enforced prayer for Lincoln, the order was so abhorrent to scores of even the most devout churchgoers that many, including the Lees, held their own prayer services in the privacy of their homes. Laura Lee, as did countless Southerners, thought it ridiculous that Yankees would expect them to attend churches "where we would hear prayers for the President of the United States and the suppression of the rebellion." She continued, "We have prayer meetings twice a week at the different houses, where we pray for our own President."[34] At one meeting Mary reported, "At five o'clock our prayer meeting assembled, & to my surprise, there were more than thirty persons present.... I conducted the services, but confined myself to the prayer book prayers. I was very much gratified at the success of our little effort; all enjoyed it, & there was certainly much real feeling. You cannot imagine how strange it feels, to know we are having services in our own homes, that we would not dare to have in public; some of the Conrads [neighbors] heard some of the Yankees say, they would watch & see where all these women were going."[35]

Clearly the "love thy neighbor" commandment garnered half-hearted support from many Winchester residents, and no support at all from others. On March 17, 1862, Laura Lee confessed, "Did not go to church—fearing it overrun with Yankees." The Lees were scarcely alone in deploring the Yankees' conduct of the war and their intrusions upon Winchester residents. On New Year's Day in 1863, Portia Baldwin (Portia Baldwin Baker), wrestled with the conflict between her personal bitterness and her religious convictions: "Enemies again among us. God keep me from uncharitable thoughts or words." "Oh the wicked shelling and sacking of Fredericksburg—God did and will certainly punish for this iniquity," she mourned. "The Fed. (French) Gen. came here the first of last week and (Milroy) today. They are foot by foot and plank by plank destroying our property. They give us no privileges. God tender their hearts. I can pray for them but I don't know how to pass them, without wishing bad things. I can love them so much more, when they are far off. I am wishing them in their homes."[36]

Their religious faith no doubt helped energize the concerted effort Winchester women put forth as volunteers in the hospitals and as nurses in their own homes. The Civil War diaries of Winchester women, including Mary Lee's diary, are replete with notations of their work at the local hospitals. At first some women were reluctant to care for the sick and wounded soldiers of the enemy; however, their humanity soon prevailed, and even the staunch rebel Mary Lee cared for Confederate as well as Union patients.

Following the bloody battle of Kernstown, Cornelia McDonald hurried to the center of town where banks, jails, the courthouse and churches had become impromptu hospitals and morgues. The porches were "strewed with dead men," some of whom had "papers pinned to their coats telling who they were." There Cornelia "saw some ladies standing by several groaning forms that I knew were Federals from their blue garments." Cornelia wrote, "The men, the surgeon said, were dying, and the ladies looked pityingly down at them, and tried to help them, though they did wear blue coats, and none of their own were there to weep over or help them."[37] Similar scenes, of course, were repeated time and again as the war raged on.

Both Union and Confederate women faithfully prepared and delivered food to the Winchester hospitals and POW camps—activities that ignited frequent clashes. During some Union occupations the Lees were prevented from taking food to the Rebel hospitals in Winchester, and during one Confederate regime when 200 Yankee prisoners were brought into the town, the Union ladies, according to Julia Chase, "were not allowed to give a single thing, the Rebel guards eating the contents themselves from 2 of the baskets." Julia continued, "The Provost said there was great excitement when the Union girls took the food down, but he & others forget how invariably the Secessionist girls feed the Rebel prisoners & our officers do not prohibit them. Oh the marked difference between the two parties. The Southern people, who pretend & claim that all their army is composed of gentlemen & Southern Chivalry. Alas, how little chivalry or humanity is exhibited; it is completely disgusting."[38]

In addition to the detested prayer for President Lincoln, the taking of the Loyalty Oath to the Federal government was also considered an abomination throughout the occupied areas of the South. During Union occupations of Winchester, as was true in most Federally occupied towns, secessionist Winchester residents were required to take the Oath in order to conduct business, to travel, or to practice law. With the rapid turnovers of rule, however, at times the restrictions were enforced and a few arrests were made. At other times the Loyalty Oath was ignored. To renounce the Confederacy was, of course, an impossibility for most Southerners, particularly those who had sons or relatives fighting in the Confederate army, even more so for those who had lost loved ones on the battlefield. Taking the Loyalty Oath to an enemy government would be tantamount to disavowing their convictions and would brand them traitors in the eyes of their countrymen.

When Cornelia McDonald sought special permission from Gen. Milroy to purchase "necessaries" for her family (Rebels were not allowed to buy food in the stores without taking the oath), Milroy "said his orders were to withhold permission from everyone who would not declare himself or herself loyal to the United States government." Cornelia was incensed: "I told him it was impossible for me to do it, as it would be entirely false; and added that it could not be a matter of importance what women thought or wished on the subject."[39]

Milroy remained unmoved: "He said it was a matter of great importance and rather fiercely observed that if it had not been for the women the men would long ago given up, he firmly believed, that their pride and obstinacy prevailed over the good sense and sober judgment of the men, who knew they were fighting in vain. I said nothing in answer to his passion, knowing well how our men hated them and knowing also that they would fight to the very last rather than yield to their unjust and unreasonable pretense of authority over us." Cornelia survived by asking some congenial Yankees "to buy me things I cannot get myself because of the oath, and they do it readily, and seem glad to oblige me."[40] Somehow, Mary was able to procure some food from the enemy. As an aside, she wondered whether "condensed milk and dried eggs are known in the Confederacy. The are wonderful inventions particularly for use in a country that has been ravaged by a Yankee army & where all the finest cows and poultry have been destroyed."[41]

It should be remembered, however, that the Loyalty Oath worked both ways. When the Southerners were in control, loyal Union people objected to taking a loyalty oath to the Confederate government. During one period of Confederate occupation of Winchester, Laura Lee noted, "There is the greatest excitement here about the oath business. A great many men refuse to take it, and ten of them were sent to the North this morning, in consequence. The fate of many others is to be decided today."[42]

The efforts of Union soldiers to entice slaves to leave their owners was partly a moral conviction and partly a military effort to reduce the working force and thus curtail the production of foodstuffs for the army as well as for civilians. This pressuring of their "servants" constituted yet another Yankee annoyance for Winchester secesh. With the constant

Federal-Rebel turnover of Winchester, it took little ingenuity for "servants" to follow along or join the Union troops in possession of the town and bid a permanent goodbye to their former masters. The powerful longing of their "servants" for their freedom came as a huge surprise to many Southerners, who deemed them unappreciative wretches.

"At dinner time I found Evans [one of the Lees' slaves], was missing, & in a little while Mrs. Barton came over, in the depths of despair, as Jim had gone also." Mary despaired: "It is needless to tell you that Evans is a dreadful loss to me, in every point of view; but I have never had the least confidence in the fidelity of any negro. At such a time as this, [I] was not at all surprised. Of the ingratitude it is not worth while to speak; blessed are those who expect nothing, for they will not be disappointed. I do not grumble or fret, for I am still proud to say, it is not in the power of the whole Yankee nation to depress or crush me, or make me say I am sorry, so long as the boys are safe & so far we have heard nothing to the contrary."[43]

Laura Lee was undone by Evans' departure: "It was a great shock, for I thought if there was one who would be faithful, it would be Evans, but there are few who can withstand the temptation to be free. They do not look forward to the hardships and difficulties of a free negroes life." "Great numbers have gone today," she added.[44]

Later, upon hearing that Evans was "laid up somewhere in town, with an attack of leg," Mary was sure "he has often wished he was at home, where he was as carefully nursed as any other member of the family."[45]

"Another day of anxieties," Laura Lee wrote on March 20, 1862. "Hugh [the other of the Lees' male slaves] has been gone for two days, and today we heard he had passed through town with a regiment." On another occasion Laura Lee told of "a very annoying affair this morning with Emily." According to Laura, "She took offense at some imaginary grievance and took up her baby and walked off, saying as she could not give us satisfaction, she would go somewhere else. I followed her and told her to go back home and behave herself and not act in such a silly way. She came back very readily, and went on with her work, but I should not be surprised at any moment to find she has gone off in earnest."[46]

The loss of their "servants," of course, brought on disagreeable chores for their former mistresses. Mary confessed, "I am getting very tired of my reduced establishment & I miss Evans and Emily every hour."

"No washerwoman," Cornelia McDonald complained, "and soiled clothes to carry away; so today I tried to have a few of the children's clothes washed." Suddenly the roar of cannons nearby brought a halt to the laundry session, and partly out of fright and possibly because of exhaustion Cornelia "went in to sit down till my heart stopped beating as if it would thump its way out." Cornelia wrote: "My hand had a hole in it from the soap and the rubbing; on every knuckle. I tried to wash the dirt out of the wristbands."[47]

Washing dishes was Kate Sperry's bugbear: "I'd rather do anything than that—of all awful greasy dirty work—washing dishes is the *awfullest*—not only did I scald my fingers but splashed my clothes, broke a few plates etc.—the most *awkward* creature the town Winchester can boast I am."[48] "Tried to sew," Mary Lee admitted, "but I am so completely out of practice that I prick my fingers & make a botch of it."[49]

To be sure their ultimate freedom was not the only goal prompting slaves to leave their former masters or mistresses. Fear proved a prime motivator, as Yankee troops accelerated the departure of "servants" by spreading rumors of the wholesale murder of all blacks in the area. Later Laura Lee reported: "There is the greatest panic among the servants. The Yankees have assured them that Jackson is murdering all the negroes as he advances, even cutting the throats of the babies in their cradles. An officer told Emily that such is the case. Numbers of them believe it, and are terrified beyond belief. They have spread abroad a report too, that they intend to burn the town. Crowds have gone from here today."[50]

Oh! For Some Reliable News!

The incessant tumult, as Winchester was buffeted between the repeated Federal and Confederate evacuations and occupations, proved unsettling to say the least. Facts were difficult to come by; rumor abounded. Winchester fairly lived on rumors. As would be expected, all during the war word of Confederate victories was accepted as gospel truth by the Lees, while word of Union successes was highly suspect. Early in the war, in March 1862, Laura Lee, for example, was convinced that the Union forces were in error in taking credit for a victory at Pea Ridge. The victory, she insisted, "is really ours."[51] Years later, historian James McPherson, in contrast, called the battle "as inglorious a rout in reverse as Bull Run." As McPherson wrote, "Although each side suffered about 1,300 casualties, the battle of Pea Ridge was the most one-sided victory won by an outnumbered Union army during the war."[52]

On May 23, 1862, as the Union troops appeared to be evacuating the town, Mary Lee noted: "There is a rumour afloat that Winchester is to be burnt to-night & there is considerable panic, chiefly amongst the servants. One of the Yankee stories told to the negroes to-day is, that 'Mr. Jackson' is killing all the negroes, men, women & children; this is their last resort to frighten off those who have still remained at their homes. There was a report circulated this morning, that no one was to be allowed to triumph, or evince any symptoms of joy, or they would be shot down."[53]

As sinister rumors persisted, even the most zealous rebels now and then suffered moments of doubt and despondence. Later, in an uncharacteristic moment of faint-heartedness, Mary admitted, "I have never felt subjugated, or afraid to say or do anything I wanted, till to-day; my impulse was to hurrah for Jeff Davis, to every one who passed, but I really was afraid for the consequences." As the Federals made good their departure, Mrs. Lee sensed a dreadful battle in the offing: "My only fear has been, the retreat through this place, & of an infuriated & defeated army, & the time for it has come. Tomorrow, Sunday, I fear the battle will be fought, unless the Yankees go to-night. They are passing by this moment in large numbers. What an inexpressible relief it would be to find them all gone in the morning. I confess that I feel a little nervous to-night; are you surprised at it, or do you think me cowardly; I should be brave, if I had to act; but sitting in my lonely little room, at this late hour, I do feel so utterly unprotected, in the midst of danger. I must look above for help & strength."[54] Mary's depression was short-lived, however, and she was soon back to her feisty ways.

Enough Is Enough!

As the war was winding down, so too was the patience of Gen. Philip Sheridan and his staff. For almost four years the Lees had been doing their best to outmaneuver the Federals during the Union occupations of Winchester and make the lives of Yankee officers as unpleasant and miserable as possible. The Lees prided themselves in doing whatever they could to further the cause by secreting letters through to the South, providing information to the Confederate authorities and constantly hassling the enemy in their midst. Their activities became almost a game, in which they mentally awarded themselves a Medal of Honor for each successful venture. Finally, General Sheridan[55] had had it. He simply could no longer stand the Lees' "constant annoyance," and in February of 1865 he sent the Lees (Mary, Laura and their extended family) packing.

Somehow the Lees found it difficult to understand precisely *why* they were to be banished. They tended to forget Mary's traffic in smuggling letters and contraband to the Confederates and the family's persistent refusal to comply with certain restrictions levied by the Federal authorities. Their exile, they contended, was a severe punishment for activities commonly engaged in by other Winchester residents.

Both Mary and Laura Lee vigorously protested their banishment, insisting they were unequivocally innocent of any wrongdoing. "It is a most cruel outrage, and perfectly undeserved," Laura Lee insisted. "The only thing we have ever done against their orders, was to receive and send letters, and that is done by three-fourths of the people in the town, and the Yankees are perfectly aware of it, and know also that they cannot prevent it. They have proved it on several persons, but never punished them." Actually, Laura Lee may well have been at least partially correct in assessing the situation thus: "The true reason [for the banishment] is that we kept entirely aloof from them, asking no favors, making no acquaintances, and in fact perfectly ignoring their existence. We were among the few people who were able to do it, and Sheridan determined to punish us, and humble our pride if possible."[56]

In the weeks before their banishment the Lees seemed to have stepped up their treasonous activities. In a January 26, 1865, diary entry, Mary Lee smugly reported: "After considerable difficulty [I] succeeded in getting off a batch of letters by underground to go south. It is such a pleasure to outwit Sheridan." Early in February, Mary bragged that she was actively engaged in "distributing Southern letters—passed by Sheridan's Hd. Qrs. with my pockets full notwithstanding his stringent orders against such treason & I hear of nothing but the pique of those Yankees at not being received in our house."[57]

Numerous entries detailed Mary's afternoons spent relaying Southern letters. On February 4, 1865, shortly before their banishment, Mary confessed that a sudden thaw had made lakes of the streets and sidewalks. However, neither ice nor snow would deter Mary from her mission: "There was such an accumulation of ice in the streets that the thaw had made it like rivers. The water is up to our porch steps & I had to go several squares out of the way to go on a contraband errand, to carry two flannel shirts & a hat to be sent to the boys & letters to both Genls. Early's & Gordon's Hd. Qrs.[58] Full of treason. It was so slippery under the water that I was miserable for fear I would fall & scatter my plunder, but I got through safely." (And the Lees could not understand why they were being banished!)

Actually, it is a bit unclear whether the Union authorities knew of the Lees' "underground activities" but had their sights trained on bigger game, or whether they suspected the women were engaged in covert endeavors but had no real proof to go on. The Lees' rebellious spirit and refusal to abide by Union orders, however, came through loud and clear.

Their banishment surely should have come as no surprise to them, for months earlier Mary Lee was aware that she could be arrested, and consequently kept a suitcase packed, "ready for any emergency." There were warnings aplenty that the Lees preferred to ignore. Much earlier Mary had been forewarned when, "Mr. Burwell [probably the nieces' father] came to tell us that he had been commissioned to tell us, that we were in danger of being arrested & sent to Fort Delaware; the chief cause of offence, as far as I could ascertain, was our not walking under the Union flag."[59]

Just days before their banishment, a friend had stopped in, saying that she did not want to alarm them, "but she had just come from the Provost's Office & Parsons told her he knew of the letters that were being sent backwards & forwards & that mails were brought in & carried out to Mrs. Lee's & Mrs. Sherrard's & that the first fine day some of the very nicest ladies in town were to be sent through the lines." "I must confess it was rather startling," Mary admitted, "but I have made up my mind not to anticipate evil; it is bad enough when it comes. Who has betrayed us or whether it is merely conjecture we cannot tell."[60]

The day after the warning, Mary decided "that as this was not a pleasant day, we would not be sent through the lines—it is best to make light of such threats, though the carrying out would be a sad day for me." "My house & everything in it, except the few pounds of baggage allowed each person," she realized, "would be torn to pieces & I should never again have the means to furnish a home, but I trust to Providence to avert the evil."[61]

Sheridan, however, was deadly serious. Nevertheless, the indomitable Mary was not about to take Sheridan's orders to leave without putting up a fight. Mary scarcely drew a breath before paying a visit to Gen. Sheridan in an attempt to ascertain the precise reasons for their banishment—or probably to personally register her contempt for the general and his orders. The meeting must have been a rare scene of acrimony that neither Sheridan nor Mary would ever forget. Mary was accompanied by Mrs. Tuley.[62] In a vivid description of the meeting, Mary reported: "Sheridan shook hands with Mrs. T. & had the impertinence to offer his hand to me. I extended the tips of two fingers & then asked him what accusations he had to bring. He replied very rudely there were a plenty of charges & he ignored my request that Lal might be allowed to go to Clar[k]sburg & was as rough & low as I had imagined he was." Mary was grateful for the promise that they "should give us ample time for preparation & that I might get someone to occupy our house."[63]

"Everyone said it was a mere threat to induce us to lie & entreat," Mary wrote, "but that I would not condescend to do." Laura Lee noted that many fruitless "efforts had been made to induce Gen. Sheridan to retract the order, but in vain." Indeed, the Lees had their pride to maintain. "We would not allow anyone to ask the Union people to interact for us, as we knew it would be of no avail, and we did not choose to be so humiliated."[64]

"When I came home," Mary continued, "we sat down quietly to sewing, thinking the bad weather would delay our fate; numbers of our friends were coming all the time to sympathize & offer services, but there was nothing for them to do today. We determined to carry the silver to the Bank tonight & the two Lals & I waded through the water with it." Before they went out, however, Mary was handed "a written order that we should be sent through the lines on Saturday morning." "There were no charges made except that we had caused them constant annoyance," Mary wrote. The annoyance, Mary agreed with her sister-in-law, "being really that we would have nothing to do with them."

Mary's return home touched off a frantic effort to pack up as many of their possessions as possible or to distribute them to friends for safe-keeping. With Christian resignation, Mary accepted the inevitable, "It is terrible to have one's home destroyed with the certainty that we shall never have another, but if God permits it, it is all right."[65]

At once, the Lees "went in various directions to try to get a tenant for the house, but were unsuccessful." Mary told her diary: "Then we collected our clothes and were busy until ½ past two packing that we might have our last day free for securing our furniture, if possible. It was well we did not wait until Friday to pack, for the house was thronged with friends during the whole day. There was the greatest sympathy felt for us, and expressed in every possible way. All the smaller and more valuable articles were taken away and secured, but the heavy furniture we had no hope of removing. And as no tenant could be found, the servants were in the greatest distress. We promised to arrange that they should remain in the kitchen and left them some provisions, knowing that they could easily support themselves. We prepared provisions to last until we could reach Staunton, and packed up the groceries and other supplies to leave behind. But it was but little we could save of the things we valued most. We concluded all our arrangements late at night, and by 8 o'clock the next morning many persons arrived to see us off."[66,67]

For the Lees there was certainly no evidence of humiliation in their banishment; instead, perhaps, a certain pride prevailed, accompanied by even a touch of arrogance. In the midst of the packing, scores of friends dropped by to lend the Lees money, to sympathize, to help them load their goods into the ambulances: "Our friends came in looking as if they were coming to a funeral, & could not understand our not looking gloomy. Many tears were shed, but not by us. Even strong men wept." Despite numerous appeals to Gen. Sheridan on behalf of the Lees, he remained unrelenting. At least, Mary boasted, "it showed Sheridan how we were regarded by the community."

The Lees found their departure heartwarming: "Friends crying; the servants, not only our own, but old attaches of the family were weeping bitterly. We laughed & talked all sorts of rebel talk & the Yankees gazed in astonishment at seeing people turned out of their homes & not depressed by it."

The Lees' departure was "a perfect triumph," Laura Lee proudly announced to her diary: "Large numbers of our friends crowded around the ambulance, and many ran through the streets, following us to the Provost's office where we were to join the Sherrards. We were all excited enough to have a very cheerful parting, and the Yankees saw no tears except from our servants and other colored friends."[68,69]

Mary Lee corroborated Laura Lee's account: "Many of our friend followed us in procession down to Mr. Sherrards waving their handkerchiefs." "The Provost's Office is in the Bank," Mary explained, so they "had full view of our movements. The whole street was filled with lookers-on: citizens, Yankees, servants—altogether a most motley assemblage. As we rode being sent out of Sheridan's lines we felt very independent & said loudly what we pleased. We had two ambulances & an army wagon piled up with baggage; we had an escort of over twenty men. They were very civil except one rascally Sergeant who kept close to our ambulance listening to everything we said."[70]

The entourage had proceeded only a short distance when the Lees were unceremoniously dumped by the side of a cold, rain-swept road. The women were dumbfounded. "We had been informed we were to be sent to Middletown, 12 miles from Winchester, but when we got to the outer pickets, two miles from town (Newtown), we were stopped & informed by the Capt. we were to be put out there & our baggage to be searched."

Laura Lee added some important details to the adventure: "The officer in charge of the party said he had orders to search us and then leave us. It was perfectly inhuman. A heavy rain was falling, everything covered with snow and ice. We urged the cruelty of opening our trunks in such a place. At last he agreed that if we would give our word that we had no letters about us, he would not search, and would take us to a house in Newtown. We assured him we had none, and then we moved on."[71] Luckily the officer naively accepted their assurances that they definitely were not transporting any illegal goods, for Mary Lee later explained she had been carrying "dozens of treasonable possessions." (Deportation certainly did not in the least dampen the Lees' spirits, and even in exile the Lees continued their covert activities by immediately sending word to the Confederate army that the Yankees were about to spring a surprise raid.)

A friend wrote sadly of the Lee-Sherrard departure: "We were not a little surprised and dismayed at seeing the Lees and Sherrards *sent through* yesterday. Their train presented quite a surprising spectacle—first an escort then two ambulances then another squad & a four mule wagon containing baggage. They were fortunate in being permitted to carry so much. Various charges brought against them—one was trying to gain *notoriety* by communicating contraband intelligence &c &c. The society of W[inchester] is quite reduced & shall miss them a great deal."[72]

Needless to say, Mary Lee was delighted to learn that their removal from Winchester warranted a certain amount of publicity, even in the North. According to Mary's diary the family was greatly entertained by an article from the *New York Herald*, entitled "An Alleged Conspiracy to Capture General Sheridan." According to the *Herald* the Lees were banished for their complicity in a plot against General Sheridan. The story read: "A few days ago three Winchester families by the names of Sherrard, Lee & Burwell, were sent without our lines on the charge of disloyalty. It is alleged they conspired together to get up a sociable ball, to which Genl. Sheridan was to be an invited guest & that during its progress a detachment of Mosby's guerrillas was to seize the General, take him captive & convey him to Richmond a la Kelley & Crook. The plan was frustrated & the ladies (?) who concocted it are now in full communion with those for whom they have exhibited such a warm sympathy." A later story accused the Lees of attempting to poison Sheridan & his staff. This prompted the exasperated Mary Lee to write facetiously that she "should not be surprised if we were to be accused of murdering Lincoln."[73]

As the Lees attempted to make their way to Staunton, they were welcomed in Newtown, Woodstock, and Edinburg by old friends and new acquaintances who "did everything that kindness and hospitality could prompt to give us pleasure and comfort." "This kindness at the outset," wrote Mary Lee, "was very reassuring as we had been told that everybody in the Valley was so ruined that we must expect nothing."[74]

At one point, as Federal troops were passing, "We recognized several of the servants who have been so much in our kitchen, belonging to Sheridan's staff officers. Among them George, who ran in to the back yard to speak to us. He said he had hired himself to Gen Forsyth in order to get to Staunton. He said that directly after we left Gen Sheridan had an order posted on the house, forbidding any one to trouble anything in it. Some Yankees who came to take the stoves had to go off minus." The Lees were pleased to hear that their home had been made safe from marauders and that their tenant "has a Col. staying with her, who will protect the house."[75]

The Terrible News

By March 14 the Lees found their way to Staunton. It was during their wait in Staunton for an opportunity to go on to Richmond that the devastating news of the fall of the capital reached the Lees. Mary Lee despaired, "Can the terrible news I have just heard be true? One of the children has just come in with the announcement that a telegram has been received saying Richmond is evacuated. I have been watching for Dr. Stribling to come & half an hour has passed & I still hope there is some mistake. I have thought enough in that time to drive me crazy. If true, what awful scenes may be enacting in Richmond at this moment; the Masons—all the friends I had hoped to see so soon; have they made their escape? Then the necessity which compelled such an evacuation would compel the abandonment of Virginia & finally the sad, sad question—what shall we do? To return to Winchester—go farther north if our beloved Army is going South will be indeed a living death. But my mind is too bewildered to take in selfish plans."[76,77]

On April 4 Mary anguished: "All day yesterday I was in a state of suspense, as there was nothing but rumours to depend on & the absence of official intimation to Genl. Lomax, who has command in the Valley, gave me some hope that the evacuation was only of non-combatants preparatory to one of these terrible battles. Now in the absence of all reliable information, we can only conjecture that the rail roads supplying the army were either cut or so threatened as to make it necessary to fall back to our base of supplies. But though troubled beyond expression, I am as confident as ever that light will come out of darkness & that our cause will finally triumph, though there may be still greater obstacles in attaining that glorious end." A few sentences later, she added: "Yesterday was a dismal day; I tried every way to occupy myself—read, wrote, worked, went out, laid down, had some visitors & still it was so long & dreary. Poor Nettie; I know it will go so hard with her. I do not suppose we five will ever have a home together again.... I suppose Staunton will soon be occupied by the Yankees & we shall be again in their lines."[78]

Rumors circulated wildly and Mary Lee hoped against hope that the information was false, that the army had merely fallen back. Winchester was peppered with one rumor after another: "Fitz Lee whipped Sheridan (Thank God); that the South Side R.R. was cut, which compelled the evacuation of Richmond—that Gen. Lee was at Amelia Court House & Mr. Davis & the Government at Lynchburg."[79]

Despite the alarming reports, Mary remained sanguine that successful Confederate forces would in the end win out. "If I doubted the righteousness of our cause & our final success, I should be utterly miserable, for the anxieties for the present are as much as I can bear. The chief trouble is for our Richmond friends; they are experiencing for the first time what we have endured for three years & the increasing ferocity of the Yankees & their triumph at occupying the rebel Capital may make them even more insolent than usual."[80]

Upon hearing the news of the fall of Richmond, Mary Lee's sister-in-law, Laura Lee, was stunned: "Richmond evacuated by Gen. Lee last night, and this morning at ½ past 9 the Yankees marched in. I have no heart to write more."

Winchester was indeed in a state of turmoil. "The Yankees are coming up the Valley in large force & it is thought will be here tomorrow evening," Mary wrote. "Everything is being moved off & there is great excitement. When Sheridan passed through a few weeks since, his soldiers were allowed such license & were so insulting to ladies, that I must confess I dread their coming. There are so many causes of intense anxiety now that I feel almost overwhelmed; the fate of our friends in Richmond weighs on me most heavily—then the thousand rumours about our army."[81]

Rumors finally gave way to truth, and on April 13 Mary conceded "And now these hopes are blasted for the blow I so dreaded is struck. Genl. Lee's farewell address to the army he surrendered is in town & it would be looked on as foolhardy were I still to express a doubt as to his having surrendered in person. I am taught again that we must not depend on the arm of flesh. I had looked on Genl. Lee as the rallying point for the Army of the South, composed of Johnson's, Kirby Smith's & the remanants of the Army of Northern Virginia, but that hope is destroyed & I can only pray for strength to bear what will be the greatest trial of all, the willingness of our people to kiss the rod, not in submission to the Divine Will, but from policy."[82]

Good Friday, a grieving Mary felt, was a day "so appropriate to my feelings; the accumulated sufferings of years, added to the intense anxiety & almost hopelessness of the present crisis almost overpowered me & I found myself several times on the verge of giving way when persons spoke to me about it [the fall of Richmond and the surrender]."

Hope for that ultimate glorious Confederate victory died slowly in the minds and hearts of many Southerners. Even the surrender at Appomattox failed to completely convince the Lees that their cause was, indeed, a "Lost Cause." Their confidence, however, was beginning to wane. Mary Lee told her diary, "Even yet I do not despair; God can deliver us, if it is right; if not, give me grace to say, 'Thy Will be done.'"[83] On April 15, 1865, she continued: "All the energy & enthusiasm of my nature ... was warmed into full development for my country, my beloved Southern Confederacy. I was willing to endure any privation, to become a beggar for the future for the great end I never doubted was in store for us. But now if we fail, all has been in vain & precious blood spilt has been that of martyrs. I shall have to drag on a weary existence, struggling with dire poverty in a country infested by Yankees, for they will pervade every section like the locusts of Egypt."

Even in her diary entry of April 16, 1865, Mary Lee was still endeavoring to put up a brave front: "I shall not give up till terms of peace have been accepted by the whole Confederacy & then I believe another contest will commence to keep the Southern people whipped." However, the rumor of Johnston's surrender, she admitted, "would destroy my last earthly hope, though God is able even yet to send us deliverance."[84]

In many respects Mary Lee probably never completely accepted the Confederate surrender. The family celebrated the joyous return from the war of their beloved nephew, Robert, yet that, too, was clouded by the confusion and anguish of defeat: "Bob is looking so handsome, but it unnerved me so to see him come home 'after the war' so differently from what I had expected—no triumphs—no rejoicings. He, like most others, thinks it is all over…. Having given up the firm faith I have always had in our ultimate success, I am like a ship at sea without pilot or compass; I am tossed about 'by every wind of doctrine,' believing nothing but hoping & fearing everything. I have lost all self-control & have several times found great difficulty in restraining my fears, even when with entire strangers."[85]

For a brief moment during her fit of despondency, provoked no doubt by the collapse of the Confederacy, one captures a soulful insight into the heart of a rarely seen Mary Lee, a Mary Lee stripped of bravado, a Mary Lee feeling sorry for herself. Almost as overwhelming as the defeat was her disappointment at not being able to continue on to Richmond at that time. Having longed for "many, many years" to return to Richmond, to her many friends, to the scene of her baptism and marriage, Mary grieved, "But it is only another lesson for me to learn, that I am not to look for any individual enjoyment in this world."[86]

As in all defeats it became all-important to find a scapegoat, a reason for failure. Everyone had a candidate, and for Mary Lee it was the lack of patriotism on the part of her fellow countrymen: "I do not pretend to say where the blame chiefly rests—certainly not with Genl. Lee nor with our army as a whole; but I trace it back to the want of patriotism in our people, who instead of giving all they had, that was not necessary for their own support, to the army, have hoarded it to make money & now I hope [the] extortioner will be sacked by the Yankees."[87] Some historians theorize that during the last months of the war it was the women's lack of commitment and growing disinterest in making further sacrifices that eventually helped bring down the Confederacy. Mary Lee, however, was certainly not one of those women.[88]

Mary Lee's hatred of Sheridan remained unabated. The "ifs" of the Confederate defeat continued their torment: "If Sheridan had been checked in his onward course, this would not have happened; if these unpatriotic farmers had given up their supplies, our Cavalry would not have been disbanded & could have stopped him."[89]

Furthermore, in the days that followed, Mary Lee found the passive acceptance of defeat by her fellow Southerners utterly reprehensible. "I am far more humiliated by the evident satisfaction of the people than by the surrender of Lee's army, still I do not even yet despair. Lincoln's policy of reconciliation is the height of diplomacy & will do us far more harm than the most despotic military rule."[90]

Several days later she continued: "My heart sinks at the spirit of satisfaction that is afloat & I can only hope that it is not fair to judge all the Confederacy by what is going on here & in Albermarle—they are absolutely getting up mass meetings to send delegations to Washington to ask that Virginia may be taken back into the Union under the Constitution as it was before the War & that the Virginia soldiers shall be disbanded provided the State is not kept under military rule. I have been proud I was a Virginian till now, but since Lee's surrender, I am ashamed of the craven spirit which possesses all I see & throws a dark cloud over the hitherto untarnished name of the once proud old State—proud of its untarnished name. Our noble dead have shed their blood in vain, if the spirit of cowardly submission exists much longer. I will still believe it is but a temporary panic & that Virginians will not long prove recreant to themselves & their fallen heroes." It surely came as no surprise that Mary applauded the Stauntonites for distancing themselves from all Yankees— "I am getting quite proud of the Staunton people for their utter neglect of the Yankees socially & I hear they are very much mortified at it."[91]

The assassination of Lincoln brought with it a flurry of new rumors: "that Andy Johnson is killed & Washington & Baltimore in flames," events which Mary believed in the end would bode well for the South. The town was beset with reports that "Andy Johnson is impeached for conspiring with Booth for Lincoln's assassination," and "that the Yankees contemplate an immediate war with France." Mary Lee must have delighted in the thought: "Will it not be a righteous retribution if the North have now to suffer amongst themselves the horrors they have inflicted on us for four years." Mary shed no tears over the assassination and instead commented: "Today farther confirming the astounding news that we have heard for several days—that Lincoln is killed & Seward mortally wounded. The accounts are conflicting, but the fact is almost established. What a wonderful Providence it is & I feel it will work for our good."[92]

Apparently Lincoln's death had never been beyond the realm of imagination for many Southerners. Sometime earlier Mary had written: "Altogether our star is in the ascendant & a few weeks will decide whether we are to have peace now, or not till Lincoln's term expires, that is to say if he is allowed to live so long."[93]

Rumors continued to proliferate—perhaps because former Rebels feared vicious retaliation from their Northern conquerors. On April 22nd Mary exclaimed, "The condition of the country is more exciting now than it has been since the War. There are wild rumours afloat; that Genl. Lee & several other of our Generals have been assassinated. Our prayer that confusion might be brought into the councils of our enemies is answered."[94] Some days later Mary reported, "I hear the women of Richmond are maintaining the honor of the Confederacy—but not the men."

For the most part, life in Staunton continued much as usual—constant rounds of "visiting," afternoon teas, dinner parties. In May, Mary noted, "We have not spent one evening alone since we have been here." Writing of an evening with the Sherrards and Ella Stribling, Mary noted, "It went off quite pleasantly; no gentlemen, as those who visit here are not paroled & had to make their escape before the Yankees came."[95]

Mary's difficulty in accepting the collapse of the Confederacy was coupled with her apparent inability to accept emancipation. Following the collapse of the Confederacy, when there should have been little doubt about the future of emancipation, Mary Lee still seemingly refused to accept its inevitability. In Staunton some five weeks after Appomattox, Mary was about to take on a new cook: "I thought she was a free woman & would have acceded at once, but finding she was a slave, I went to her master, the Presbyterian preacher & told him I would not receive her without his consent, as I did not choose to employ run away negroes, as I consider all who leave their owners till the status of slavery is more fully settled." Still resolute, Mary seemed to consider it a malicious spreading of falsehoods for Union soldiers to apprise blacks of their freedom. She registered complete surprise when a servant threatened to leave, telling her that he was being offered fifty cents a day to work for another employer: "The Yankees here tell the servants they are free, I suppose as a punishment to the people for not receiving them [the soldiers]."[96]

News of the capture of Jefferson Davis sent the Lees into the depths of despair. A despondent Mary Lee wrote: "The news of the day made my heart so heavy; there is an official report that *our* President has been captured & what adds to the mortification, as well as the deep, deep distress is that it is said he was making his escape in his wife's clothes. I cannot believe it, on mere Yankee authority; surely our cup is full to overflowing but Thou, O Merciful God canst protect him even from the malice of such enemies as for our sins are now permitted to triumph over us. Our President is a pure patriot, the hope of whose reputation was drowned by the insane actions of other branches of the government. He & our army were 'sans peur et sans reproche.'"[97]

With the war over for all practical purposes, the all-consuming question of "What shall we do?" began to take shape. Should the Lees go farther north, go back to Winchester, go on to Richmond? Actually, returning to Winchester was not a viable option. One of the Lees' friends informed Mary that "on her own responsibility she had written to Sheridan & seen Hancock to ask that we might be permitted to return to Winchester. She had not heard from Sheridan & Hancock gave her a pass but said the conditions could not be made known till the time of our return. On her asking what those conditions would probably be, he said 'a parole that we would not say or do anything against the United States Government.'" Naturally the conditions were totally unacceptable to the Lees. Mary continued to chafe over their banishment. "It was so cruel of Sheridan to throw us out of our homes to gratify his petty spite; as he was giving up his command in Winchester at the time, he would not be 'annoyed' at the sight of us."[98]

❦

The constant flow of soldiers through Winchester, as noted, had quickly denuded the fields, gardens, and fences of the town's residents. Sheridan was faithful to his orders from Grant that following his march through the Shenandoah Valley, the Valley would be turned into a barren waste "so that crows flying over it for the balance of this season will have to carry their provender with them." Thousands of barns and mills, half a million bushels of wheat, almost twenty-five thousand farm animals had been destroyed by Sheridan's men.[99] (The appropriation of Southern property was termed "pressing" (impressment) by Confederates when the theft was conducted by their own countrymen; it was called "foraging" by Yankee soldiers seeking to supplement army rations, and was deemed "wanton destruction and outrageous devastation" by Southerners whose property fell victim to unprincipled Federal soldiers or army stragglers. General Sherman summed it all up with his famous statement, "War is Hell!"

Under whatever nomenclature, the constant ravaging of homes, farms, livestock and fences in Winchester and the surrounding area had left many families almost destitute. The name "Sheridan" quickly excited odium and resentment among Winchester's pro–Confederate residents.

Following the war, as a result of Sheridan's rampage through the Shenandoah, food, furniture, and clothing were hard to come by for the Lees as well as for thousands of Southerners. Mary Lee despaired of her situation following the family's displacement: "Is it not strong faith to go to housekeeping at this crisis, in a strange place, with very little money, no supplies & only a few pieces of furniture...." Housekeeping in Staunton, Mary complained, "on this small scale is more troublesome than at home with a house full, as it is almost impossible to get supplies & I have a very indifferent cook. Then again I am so utterly unnerved by the state of affairs that I have no life nor energy for anything."[100]

Thanks to the generosity of friends, however, the Lees were able to secure some furniture and enough cups and plates for the family. Even so, the Lees found it difficult to obtain nourishing food for their table. After paying an exorbitant price for bacon, Mary explained, "We can get nothing else to eat—have no butter, no vegetables, as the country people come in very little when the Yankees are here."[101]

The blockade, inflation, and the inability to obtain thread and yarn rendered new clothing a scarcity. In desperation, Mary related the following in her diary: "One of my employments has been ripping up my marriage dress to have it dyed. I had thought to keep it to line my coffin, but I thought it would be incongruous for the pine box I expect to be buried in, so I determined to use it in another form that its unique appearance might not at some future day cause amusement."[102]

The incessant house searches which had plagued the Lees in Winchester continued to haunt them in Staunton. In Winchester, one recalls, the Lee home had been repeatedly searched by the Federals in an attempt to locate a hidden Confederate flag, which upon at least one occasion was safely concealed under her niece's clothing. Now, in the Lees' exile, Mary's home was again suspect, and in May an officer arrived to search through rooms, trunks and drawers for a weapon which had been used in an attack on General Duval.[103] More than two months of exile had failed to moderate any of Mary Lee's rancor. With an air of disdain she gave him carte blanche to search the home and icily informed him that the act had surely been perpetrated by one of their own men—a fact which later proved to be embarrassingly true.[104]

"Last night our attention was attracted by the unusual number of sentinels in front of our door," Mary wrote. "They were posted about 50 paces apart, down the middle of the street & there was evidently considerable excitement; this morning I ascertained the cause. Genl. Duval was being entertained at Mr. Rush's (?) (the iron merchant), the only place where he is invited & during the evening he was shot at from the street, the ball passing under his arm. A double chain of pickets was placed round the town & no one allowed to leave their houses; every house was searched. A Capt. & guard came to search here & I amused myself not helping the officer." Mary continued: "He very deferentially apologized for his errand & asked which room he should enter first; I stood in the hall & told him it was perfectly immaterial; he still insisted

I should show him the way, but I folded my arms & told him he could go where he pleased; it puzzles them so when they are on these expeditions to offer neither obstacles nor assistance. He made a very cursory search, opened a few drawers & asked me to unlock my trunk & raise the lid but would not touch it. I might have had arms enough for an army concealed in the places he did not search. I told him we believed it was done by some of their own men & to my great comfort, it has proved to be the case."[105]

The Lees' disinclination to pray for the president of the United States persisted and several weeks into their Staunton stay, Mary reported "Mr. Latane [the Episcopal minister] closed our church yesterday, not wishing to have any trouble about the prayer. We went to the Presbyterian & my eyes were again offended by seeing Yankee Officers under the same roof with myself. I hear their pardoning office has been crowded with men eager to gain their protection. I have not ascertained whether any of the better classes are amongst the number."[106]

Two weeks later a new minister took over the Episcopal Church, with plans to commence the service at the Litany and omit the prayer. "I very much fear he will get in some trouble over it," Mary reasoned. However, the following Sunday she commented, "Our services passed off quietly; Ranny omitted the prayer; there were Yankees present & no disturbance as yet."[107]

In May 1865, the Lees continued to bristle over their situation and the restrictions imposed by the Federals: "There is a rumour the Yankees are to go on Tuesday & that they are to be replaced by negro Regts. I will not contemplate such a calamity. The restrictions now are very great; no one is allowed to be out after dark; it is a great annoyance, as the weather is warm & it would be the most pleasant time to walk & receive visits."[108]

Death, constant turmoil and anxiety took a serious toll on women during the war years. This the Lees discovered from personal experience and facts detailed by their Staunton friend, Dr. Stribling, superintendent of the Western Lunatic Asylum, who provided them with some shocking information. "A singular coincidence has occurred here today; singular & so sad," Mary wrote. "There have been three new inmates brought to the Insane Asylum, made insane by the War—all women; one of them, Miss Williams, from Clarke. Dr. Stribling says hers is one of the worst cases he ever saw."

Southern women's preoccupation and tremendous sacrifices on behalf of the Confederacy are lucidly summed up in Mary's confession: "I do not wonder at it. I feel so completely unhinged & so unequal to any exertion of mind or body. I have not thought or felt on any other subject for the past four years (except in dwellings of the past) & I remember how it fretted me to see anyone else interested in merely personal or ordinary matters, unless they were in some way connected with our armies & our country. I have such dread of beginning my new life of labour under present auspices, but I still believe God will help us."[109]

The Union Scenario

Although this book focuses primarily on Confederate women, one should take at least a brief look at the other side of the coin. Federal sympathizers enjoyed a state of euphoria during the periods of Union occupation that so vehemently fired the passionate resentment of the Lees, Cornelia McDonald, Gertie Miller, Portia (Baldwin) Baker and other "secesh" women. During the occupation of Winchester by the Rebels, Hattie Griffith, a young Quaker, who lived just outside Winchester, saw her father imprisoned and most of his factory destroyed because of his pro–Union views. Knowing that her own family and that of her uncle were constantly under surveillance, Hattie diplomatically tiptoed around her rabid Confederate neighbors: "Uncle James and Joseph are both watched all the time, and I fear we are, too. Oh, how careful we must be all the time, and yet we say nothing."[110]

In a daring act of kindness during a time when Union prisoners of war were herded by the Rebels into a field "without living quarters and with a scant amount of food," Hattie's father courageously brought in flour and saw that it was made into bread for the prisoners, which he and Hattie carried out to the men. In 1864 Hattie braved ostracism and actively served as an agent of the U.S. Sanitary Commission.

Julia Chase also observed the Winchester scene in a far different light from Mary and Laura Lee. Julia's sympathies, as did Hattie's, lay with the Federals. At times, however, despite her Union loyalties, even Julia could not resist the urge to condemn what she considered ineptitude on the part of the Federal troops while they occupied Winchester: "But, oh it was so humiliating and mortifying to see how badly our Troops manage things. We do not wonder at the Secessionist women so saucy and bold, taunting and provoking in their remarks. Great God! will the time *ever* come when these Secessionists shall be compelled to be silent, when *their men* shall be routed through our streets, and not as seems always to be the case, both on a small and large scale, the Federals beaten, retreating, routed out. Shall the Unionists ever have good occasion to rejoice to see their army successful."[111]

It was particularly galling, Julia thought, to discover Federal prisoners being forced to perform servile street cleaning duties. "Today we have been subjected to a humiliating sight, seeing Federal prisoners under guard cleaning up the street in town—Rebel dirt. Why do not their own men do it, or get the colored people. We have never seen Rebel prisoners set to work at this thing, but we hope the time is not far distant when we shall be permitted to see Rebels put to the same thing and treated exactly as they treat Federal prisoners. Oh, may we cry, Oh! Lord, how long! how long."[112]

For Julia Chase the incessant changes occurring in Winchester meant living "in the U.S." one minute and an hour later, as a result of a sudden Confederate takeover, living "in Dixie." Days of jubilation for the Lees were days of dejection for Julia Chase, and vice versa. As the Lees tallied up Union outrages, Julia Chase in turn pointed to Rebel atrocities.

The war between Union and Confederate Winchester residents raged over almost everything, from seemingly petty annoyances that set neighbor against neighbor, to the more violent clashes that involved injury and even death. As one might expect, the conflicts involved bitter verbal as well as military confrontations. Neither side, of course, held a monopoly in conjuring up schemes designed to insult and infuriate the enemy. Julia Chase's description of an evening gathering of Union ladies typifies the hostility that pervaded the town.

Julia explained in her diary that guests being entertained by a Union lady had been annoyed by Rebels "spurred on by some Secesh persons in the neighborhood ... riding up and down by the house and as they passed by making some insulting remarks about the young ladies." The Rebels continued their roguery by twice stopping and demanding to search the house for Yankees. On their way home the guests "were annoyed by these *Southern Chivalry* asking if they did not want beaux, etc."[113]

The same rowdies were bent on more mischief the following evening when, according to Julia Chase, they attempted to force their way into the Milloy's Winchester home and arrest Mr. Milloy as a Union spy. Despite their dire threats to destroy her property, Mrs. Milloy refused them admittance, pleading her husband's serious illness. A few hours later, however, the ruffians returned, pushed past Mrs. Milloy, and barged through the house in search of Mr. Milloy. Perhaps Mr. Milloy's illness dissuaded the men, perhaps their consciences prevailed, for somehow they abandoned their proposed violence and left. Julia continued: "Mrs. M's Secession neighbors are the cause again of all this trouble, and there are some such despicable creatures in our town that they do not care what becomes to the Union people, if they could have their way, should all be shot or hung, & yet these Southern people call themselves such praying people, that they are more righteous & holy than the Northern people. Oh Lord! That thou knowest the hearts of all men, whether their prayers are sincere or mere lip service, and thou knowest how long these things shall continue, how long the loyal people shall be persecuted, taunted and reviled."[114]

While the Lees were busily engaged in relaying information to the Confederate forces, there were loyal Union women who were actively conveying whatever news they could obtain to the Federals. In the fall of 1864, a true heroine, one noted in history books years later, emerged from a Winchester schoolroom to provide information of vital importance to the Union forces.

It takes little imagination to envision the chaotic information system that resulted from the widespread disruption of railroads and the mail system in the South. Rumor ran rampant and anyone with information (which often turned out to be misinformation) about troop movements or the strength of army forces was highly valued as a military informant. In September of 1864, Winchester became an ever more hotly contested area. Desperate for reliable information on the strength and activities of the Confederate forces, General Philip Sheridan sought to obtain a loyal contact in Winchester. Along with word that Tom Laws, a black vegetable peddler, had easy access in and out of Winchester came information that a Rebecca Wright, a Quaker schoolteacher in Winchester, was definitely pro–Union and could be trusted to provide any information she could glean about the Confederate forces. Sheridan jumped at the chance to contact Rebecca Wright, and Tom Laws became the willing courier of a note written on tissue paper, concealed in tin foil and carried in his mouth. If by any chance Tom were to be stopped and questioned by Confederate pickets as he entered or left Winchester, he was instructed to quickly swallow the pellet, thus destroying any incriminating evidence.

As Tom Laws knocked at Rebecca Wright's schoolroom door he was extremely nervous for fear he might be approaching the wrong Miss Wright—Rebecca's sister was pro–Confederate! Rebecca was equally nervous, fearing that this might be some kind of a ruse in a Confederate effort to entrap her and thus imprison or banish her for her Union sympathies. After delivering the note, Tom Laws promised to return at 3 P.M. for her answer. Rebecca studied the message: "I learn from Major-General Crook that you are a loyal lady, and still love the old flag. Can you inform me of the positions of Early's forces, the number of divisions in his army, and the strength of any or all of them, and his probable or reported intentions? Have any more troops arrived from Richmond, or are any more troops coming, or reported to be coming? I am, very respectfully, your most obedient servant, P. H. Sheridan, Major-General Commanding." There was an addition: "You can trust the bearer."[115]

Actually, Rebecca did have accurate information to send to Sheridan. A convalescent soldier had sought her company earlier that week

and in discussing the most popular topic of the day—the war—had inno-
cently revealed much of the information Sheridan was seeking. But to
pass on this information to Union officers would jeopardize her position
in Winchester. If news of her activities were to leak out in Confederate-
held Winchester, it certainly would result in ostracism and very likely
would lead to her and her family's banishment or imprisonment. Rebecca
was extremely distraught over her situation. At first she determined not
to respond to Sheridan's request, but a talk with her mother changed her
mind. In response to Rebecca's fear that they all might be killed by the
Confederates in retaliation for her "treachery," Rebecca's mother counseled, "Aye, that is true, Becky…, but men are dying everywhere for their
country. Thy life and my life and thy sister's life may be needed, too. I
would not persuade thee, child. Settle it with thy conscience. Let God
guide thee in this. Go to thy room and give thyself to prayer."

By three o'clock Rebecca had composed her answer, a response that
provided Sheridan with valuable information and gave him a decided
advantage in the Third Battle of Winchester. In her response dated September 16, 1864, Rebecca wrote: "I have no communication whatever with
the rebels, but will tell you what I know. The division of Gen. Kershaw,
and Cutshaw's artillery, twelve guns and men, Gen. Anderson commanding, have been sent away, and no more are expected, as they cannot be spared from Richmond. I do not know how the troops are situated,
but the force is much smaller than represented. I will take pleasure hereafter in learning all I can of their strength and position, and the bearer
may call again Very respect yours."

General Sheridan, himself, in his *Personal Memoirs* commended
Rebecca and declared, "Miss Wright's answer proved of more value to
me than she anticipated." Within days Sheridan had secured Winchester
for the Federals, who maintained control of the town to the end of the
war. Later Sheridan, himself, came to Rebecca's schoolroom to thank her
personally. In January of 1867 Gen. Sheridan sent Rebecca a gold watch,
chain and breastpin along with a letter: "You are not probably aware of
the great service you rendered the Union cause by the information you
sent me by the colored man a few days before the battle of Opequon on
September 19, 1864. It was upon this information the battle was fought
and probably won. The colored man gave the note rolled up in the tin-
foil to the scout who awaited him at Millwood. The colored man had carried it in his mouth to that point, and delivered it to the scout, who brought
it to me. By this note, I became aware of the true condition of affairs inside
the enemy's lines, and gave directions for the attack. I will always remember this courageous and patriotic action of yours with gratitude and I beg
you to accept this watch and chain which I send to you by Gen. J. W.
Forsyth as a memento of September 19, 1864."[116]

After the war when Rebecca's contribution to the Union victory became known, the local citizens spat at her and insulted her until finally the Wrights were forced to leave Winchester. Thanks to the efforts of Sheridan, Rebecca was given a job in the Treasury Department in Washington. Although she was given a gold watch and breastpin, she was never given a pension.

Epilogue

After her stay in Staunton, Mary Lee moved on to Charlottesville, Richmond, and Petersburg. Eventually settling in Baltimore, Mary Lee never returned to live in Winchester. Upon her death in 1906, her body was brought back to Winchester and interred next to her husband's in Mount Hebron Cemetery. In Baltimore, as might be expected, Mary devoted her efforts to helping to organize the Daughters of the Confederacy and to serving as secretary of the Southern Education Society, which assisted in the rebuilding of destroyed Southern schools.[117]

Cornelia McDonald left Winchester at her husband's insistence, settled for a time in Lexington, Virginia, and finally made her home in Louisville, Kentucky. Although she investigated the possibility of returning to Winchester, her former home was deemed unlivable. Cornelia McDonald died in 1909. In addition to revealing much about life in Winchester, Mrs. McDonald's diary also depicts the trials of one of the tens of thousands of women widowed by the war. Left as the sole support for five children, Cornelia gave drawing lessons, took in boarders, and taught school in a frenzied effort to feed, clothe and educate her young family. (A far more extensive account of her diary and reminiscences may be found in *A Diary with Reminiscences of the War and Refugee Life in the Shenandoah Valley 1860–1865.*)

❦

The women of Winchester were apparently well aware of their unique position during the Civil War in a town probably more trampled upon than any other town of its size. Diaries abound, particularly those of secessionists, testifying to the vitriolic partisanship that engulfed Winchester. For these women their warfare consisted of words, insults, and harassment. Some of the most outspoken women, such as the Lees, paid the price for their venomous speech and activities by being banished and refused readmittance into Winchester. Other Southern—or Union—sympathizers, endeavored to keep their cool, smoldering in silence or finding release for their pent up anger in torrid diary entries. Violent swings from Rebel to Yankee domination of Winchester became a wartime way of life, accompanied by the almost incessant fears of oppression, and a vicious confiscation and vengeance that threatened—and often succeeded—in divesting them of most of their worldly possessions. Even these brief diary excerpts picture a town peopled with spirited, determined, recalcitrant women each tenaciously convinced of the righteousness of her cause.

ℭ *Six* ℗

Death of a Cause

*One can never exaggerate the horrors of war on one's own soil. You under-
state the agony, strive as you will to speak, the agony of heart-mind-
body. "A few more men killed." A few more women weeping their eyes out,
and nothing whatever decided by it more than we knew before the battle.*

—Mary Chesnut (from C. Vann Woodward, ed.,
Mary Chesnut's Civil War [New Haven:
Yale University Press, 1981], p. 769)

Lee's surrender of the Army of Northern Virginia to Gen. Grant on
April 9, 1865, signaled the end of the world for Southerners—certainly
the end of the world as they had known it. Later, Johnston's surrender
to Sherman on April 18 and Kirby Smith's surrender of the Confederate troops west of the Mississippi, on May 26, 1865, drove the final nails
in the Confederate coffin. Upon hearing the news of the Lee-Grant meeting at Appomattox Court House, most Southerners feared the end was
in sight.

The fall of Richmond a week earlier should have clued Southerners that the Confederate army was in big trouble. Even the staunchest of
Rebels must have blanched at President Jefferson Davis's hasty departure from morning church services on April 2, 1865, when he was handed
the message from General Lee stating that his position near Richmond
could no longer be held. That day and night, the scene was utter chaos.
The president wasted no time in packing up at once and leaving the city
to the crowds of drunken civilians and deserters who had looted the
commissary depots and were reveling in the lavish supplies of whiskey.
Fires set to prevent the Union acquisition of buildings and mills quickly
spread out of control, and explosions of munitions depots and labora-
tories sent thunderbolts throughout Richmond. Pandemonium reigned
supreme. As one woman wrote, "I have heard persons say it was like their
idea of the judgment day; perhaps it may be."[1] On April 3, Federal troops

occupied the city and restored order. The following day marked Lincoln's triumphant procession through Richmond.

As the Federals marched into Richmond, Fannie Dickinson was staggered by the city's transformation. Confederate gray had been replaced by Yankee blue: "And now what a change! I cannot realize the dread fact that the hated enemy are here in our midst surrounding our homes, and daily, hourly are we to meet them, and perhaps talk with them and hear their taunts while we must be silent lest an unguarded word should draw upon us ill treatment." Later, Fannie continued: "It seemed to me the day would never end, it was so filled with strange events, strange sights and strange sounds. At our corner was stationed a Yankee guard who, as each Negro woman and child passed by, were stopped and shaken hands with most vigorously, taking the little ones into the lap and treating all to whiskey. 'Twas indeed a disgusting sight.'" The following Sunday, Fannie could scarcely believe her eyes upon seeing two Yankees in the choir and another Yankee preacher being invited into the pulpit. "I could not keep back the tears as I thought of the wrongs our people have suffered, and now how indignities were heaped upon us, in ministers coming thus like wolves in sheeps' clothing to insult us in our affliction."[2]

Other Southerners, such as Kate Cumming, took the fall of Richmond in stride, remarking, "I am not sorry, as I feel certain we shall never have peace until the enemy has possession of all our large towns, and then they will see that they have work still before them to conquer the South."[3] "All is not over," insisted the diehards.

A week later, at Appomattox Court House, a weary Gen. Lee and a triumphant Gen. Grant met to work out the terms of the surrender. Less than a week later, President Lincoln was assassinated at Ford's theater in Washington.

∞

The Civil War witnessed not only a divided country, but also a divided South. Secessionists clashed with Unionists, pro–Davis men collided with anti–Davis men, planters' goals differed from yeomen's needs, almost every Rebel had his own opinions about the conduct of the war. There were Southerners who were eager for the cessation of hostilities, as well as those, still hoping for a Confederate victory, who wanted the fighting to continue down to the last man standing. In his or her heart of hearts, no doubt everyone truly wanted peace—but peace with a triumphant Confederacy.

Actually, the surrender probably came as little surprise to the hundreds of deserters who in the last months of the war were leaving the army in epidemic proportions. There were estimates that, by late 1864 and early 1865, from two-fifths to two-thirds of the Confederate army were absent without leave. Frantic appeals to immediately return home were streaming in from distraught wives whose farms had been devastated by Yankee (or Confederate) theft of their farm animals and equipment. With fields leveled by encampments of blue- or gray-clad soldiers, and crops a disaster as a result of the wartime manpower shortage, a dramatic outcry resounded from women imploring their husbands to abandon a cause that allowed women and children to starve to death.

Still more Rebel soldiers could see the handwriting on the wall as the appalling death rate continued to climb. Atlanta had been occupied, Savannah had been Lincoln's Christmas present, Columbia had been put to the torch. More and more, it was appearing to be a no-win situation. Why should they continue to risk life and limb when stay-at-homes were lolling safe and sound on their front porches, and hoarders and speculators were engaged in making a monetary killing?

Women, who four years earlier had wished they were men and could join the soldiers on the field, were beginning to change their minds and fervently pray for peace. Some historians credit women with actually helping to bring an end to the fighting. Southern women, who in the early days of secession had so exuberantly and patriotically cheered their men into enlisting, finally began totaling up the sacrifices in lives and property and decided the sacrifices far outweighed the gain.

Furthermore dissatisfaction with the Confederate government was beginning to escalate. Jefferson Davis had always had his share of detractors (and admirers), but as the war dragged on, the former began to outnumber the latter. The Confederacy's 10-percent tax on farm produce and its impressment of horses, mules and food supplies were aggravating to even the most loyal Rebels. Catherine Edmondston had been greatly annoyed with the Confederate government when, less than a week before the surrender, impressing officers had appeared with orders to "take all the best of our team" and "all our meat save three months supply." Clearly, frustration was mounting.[4] There was growing belief that the terrible bloodshed must end.

Having lost one son, and having another son captured and imprisoned, Sarah Espy longed for an end to the fighting: "O for peace that my children could stay at home."[5] In her diary she continued: "I think *too*, that the cause is hopeless. I fear the South through the influence of her leaders has committed a great wrong. Now innocent people must suffer for it."[6]

A grateful Nettie Darneille rejoiced that the terrible bloodbath was coming to an end. Her husband "was impoverished by the war.... Losses of every kind overtook him, but while our lives were spared we tried to thank God and be cheerful." Nettie had come to realize that "Life had to be commenced over again; everyone in the South was poverty stricken after April '65, when the war ended. But oh, what joy it was to feel that peace was once more to be enjoyed, even if poverty did come with it."[7]

Gertrude Thomas was happy to see the conclusion of the strife, as she wrote, "The war is over and I lift a grateful heart to God thanking him for this much and trusting him for the future."[8] In a letter to her daughter, Sallie Bird, of Hancock County, Georgia, wrote: "The Armistice is filling all hearts now. I am thankful for a cessation of hostilities, even for a while. I hope things can be honorably settled."[9]

Although defeated, Southerners took pride in what they felt had been a heroic struggle. One woman explained: "The news of Lee's surrender was not unexpected. There was no reason to feel ashamed, for the South had fought gallantly, with great heroism. The best blood in the South was shed. There was no humility, simply tragedy."[10]

In marked contrast to the "swords into plowshares" women, there were "fight-on" fanatics, so fervently committed to the cause that for them there would be no turning back—ever. Still others had fallen victim to rabid Rebel newspaper accounts and wild rumors that unrealistically reported every battle as actually a Southern victory. True, there was always tomorrow. Deep in the heart of every loyal Confederate was the lingering hope that somehow, somewhere, one more battle, one more sacrifice, would result in success. Surely, Southern spirit and determination would eventually win over Yankee advantages of manpower and economics. After all, wasn't God on their side?

᧕᧕

With a greatly enfeebled rail service, telegraph lines obliterated, and newspapers printed half-page on wallpaper—or not at all—communication, to say the least, was difficult. Rumor had its heyday in rural areas. Even in the large cities, there was always someone with "the latest word," rumors that frequently distorted fact and alternately spread hope and fear throughout the populace.

Federally occupied Huntsville, Alabama, was inundated with rumors. Mary Jane Chadick reported hearsay that "the South is to be reunited with the North in an anticipated war with England and France"; that "slavery is to remain as it was"; "that England and France and Spain had acknowledged our independence."[11] Sarah Espy listened to reports claiming that "Johnston has captured Sherman & half his army."[12] Later she wrote, "We now hear that Richmond is certainly evacuated & the seat of government will be Macon."[13]

Elizabeth Meriwether, whose husband was serving as a colonel in the Confederate army, shuddered at rumors that "Jeff Davis was to be hanged, his generals were to be shot and the private soldiers of his armies were to be imprisoned!" Small wonder Betty's nervous confession: "These rumors worried me."[14]

At first many Southerners scoffed at tales of Lee's surrender, thinking it a cruel joke. Kate Cumming told of a friend's coming and calmly announcing that "Lee and his whole army were captured. I was mute with astonishment, and looked at Mr. Moore, thinking I had seen our people take disasters coolly, but had never seen any thing to equal his coolness in telling of such a terrible one. After a while he laughed, and said he had frightened us enough; that such news had come by a lady from Chattanooga; she had seen it in the northern papers. He said it was one of the tales invented by the enemy to dismay us, but we were not to be so easily frightened."

A few hours later Kate, who had been reading some heartbreaking newspaper accounts of the fighting around Petersburg, was inclined to believe there possibly might be some truth to the report. Mr. Moore, however, would give no countenance to her concerns, convinced the story was preposterous, "a moral impossibility."

As the rumors continued to proliferate, including word that the French fleet had won a naval battle with the Federals and now occupied New Orleans, Kate Cumming derided the reports: "None of our people believe any of the rumors, thinking them as mythical as the surrender of General Lee's army. They look upon it as a plot to deceive the people." Finally, Kate admitted, "I cannot believe that we are subjugated, after enduring so much; but it is useless to be miserable about an uncertainty."[15]

It was easy to deny the rumors of Lee's capitulation when the next day yet another rumor contradicted the preceding day's report. Ellen House and her friends insisted, "We are not whipped, and never will be if the people of the South are true to themselves." When gentlemen in authority attempted to convince them the war "was over, not another gun would be fired, there would soon be a peace concluded," Ellen felt it "very humiliating," but still turned a deaf ear to the news: "We both gave it to him. We were not whipped we said." At last obliged to acknowledge the surrender, Ellen and most Southerners registered horror at the thought of rejoining the Union, as she wrote, "The people of the South are slaves—to the vilest race that ever disgraced humanity."[16]

Rumors of the defeat circulated around the Espy farm until finally Mrs. Espy received confirmation from "a soldier who says it is true that Gen. Lee has surrendered." (This almost three weeks after the fact!) "Capt. F. returned with the bad news of the downfall of the Confederacy, Gen. Johnston having also surrendered & given up the country east of the Chatahoochie river. He did not learn much of the terms of the surrender only that we are to go back in the Union as we were before the war. If this can be carried out, it will be well for us, but I much doubt it. The young folks feel badly, but finally concluded to go on with their party. Virginia came up this evening. She was surprised to see us so cast down; the people down her way are rejoicing at the prospect of peace."[17] Never the optimist, Mrs. Espy continued a few days later: "Soldiers are passing constantly on their way home; it looks like the war was indeed over for a time at least. I have fears that it is only 'a lull in the tempest' and will be resumed with added fury."[18]

Day after day, Catherine Edmondston had discredited the barrage of rumors that surrounded her, until on April 16, 1865, she could deny the truth no longer. "How can I write it? How find words to tell what has befallen us? *General Lee has surrendered!* Surrendered the remnant of his noble Army to an overwhelming horde of mercenary Yankee knaves & foreigners."[19]

Naturally, with news of the surrender, jubilation also reigned in the North and in various Union held Southern areas. On April 14, 1865, Mary Jane Chadick in Huntsville, Alabama, reported: "The firing has commenced. Cannon are booming from the Fort. The brass band is playing, town bells ringing. Railroad engines are shrieking out a prolonged doleful whistle, and the confusion is worse than confounded, and all, they say, for the surrender of Gen. Lee and that of the Northern Virginia army."

"The boys have gone upon the housetops," Mrs. Chadick wrote, "and the dogs have come into the house trembling with fear. Every boom comes to our ears like a knell, recalling our wandering soldiers. We have never yet learned the number that surrendered, as the papers are silent on that subject. Would we could know the truth. Bad as it may prove to be, it would be infinitely better than this suspense." Friends and neighbors stopped by to tell of "a great demonstration going on among the negroes."

For Mary Jane Chadick it must have been a day of unsettling mixed emotions: elation that the war was coming to an end, coupled with utter despair at the demise of their cause. After dinner Mary wound her way uptown, but then quickly retraced her steps upon hearing the Yankees had been given "until 6 o'clock to get drunk in." The soldiers were making the most of their time. "Came home heartsick and thoroughly disgusted with everything," she sighed.[20]

As for the surrender—and the war itself—the South's most famous diarist, Mary Chesnut, sarcastically concluded: "We fought to get rid of Yankees and Yankee rule. We had no use for Yankees down here and no pleasure in their company. We wanted to separate from them for aye. How different is their estimate of us. To keep the despised and iniquitous South within their borders, as part of their country, they are willing to enlist millions of men at home and abroad and to spend billions. And we know they do not love fighting per se—nor spending their money. They are perfectly willing to have three killed for our one. We hear they have all grown rich—shoddy—whatever that is. Genuine Yankees can make a fortune trading jack-knives."[21]

In a letter to Harriet Palmer, Beaufort Sims admitted: "You speak of the uprooting of our system. Yes, indeed, this is a terrible revolution. It has entirely upset everything that but for the strongest faith we must think ourselves a 'ruined people.' A hope remains that there still remains for us an 'abiding place' and perhaps that is all we ought to request in this trying world. It seems very hard to give up country, home, and everything we have been accustomed to hold dear for the gratification of a jealous, envious people. It seems impossible for me to convince myself that slavery is a thing of the past. Indeed we have not yet experienced the trial except in the demolition of our plantation which indeed is a grave exception."[22]

☯

The surrender also brought with it emancipation, a loss of the slave labor that revolutionized the Southland. For planters it was a tremendous financial loss; for many it was a relief from the responsibility of so many dependents. In either case it clearly added to the household drudgery of former slave-holding women.

For the former slaves, their freedom became the day of jubilee—that is for slaves whose masters informed them that they were free. Some slaves were held in bondage for months and even years after the surrender. Armaci Adams said that it was well over a year after the war before she learned she was free. Other ex-slaves testified to much longer periods of time before they were freed. Some ex–slave owners informed black children that although they were free they must remain with their former masters until they were twenty-one.[23]

In most cases, owners called their "hands" together and told them they were now free and that they could continue working on the plantation for a share of the crops or leave, as they wished. One former slave explained: "I was kinda lonesome and sad lak. Us slaves was lost, didn't know what to do or where to go."[24] Often, there was a mass exodus of former slaves who flocked to the cities, where they believed great opportunities awaited them. Many soon returned to their former owners, after finding that even the crude plantation slave quarters were far superior to the hovels and castaway board shacks that soon became their homes in the cities. Meager slave rations and a share of the crop were far better than starvation in the towns.

It was indeed a happy day when news came to the plantation where

Louise Bowes Rose was enslaved. Cries of "I'se free! Yes, my Jesus, I'se free!" reverberated through the quarters. "Daddy was down to de creek. He jumped right in de water up to his neck. He was so happy he jus' kep' on scoopin' up han'fulls of water and dumpin' it on his haid an' yellin', 'I'se free. I'se free! I'se free.'"[25]

News of emancipation on Susie Melton's plantation met wild exuberance: "Never will fergit dat night of freedom. I was a young gal 'bout ten years ole.... Old missus say dey warn't nothin' to it." When word of their freedom was confirmed by a passing soldier "all dat night de niggers danced an' sang...." "Nex' mornin' at day-break," according to Susie, "we all started out wid blankets an' clothes an' pots an' pans an' chickens piled on our backs, 'cause Missus said we couldn't take no horses or carts. An' as de sun come up over de trees de niggers all started to singin'."[26] Although Susie's description of their departure was supposedly prior to the end of the war, the same story was reenacted thousands of times in April and May of 1865.

On other plantations, news of their freedom had little effect on the "hands." Marriah Hines explained: "When master told us we was free, it didn't take much 'fect on us. He told us we could go were we pleased and come when we pleased—that we didn't have to work for him anymore 'less we wanted to. Most of us slaves stayed right there and raised our own crops. Master helped us much as he could. Some of us he gave a cow or a mule or anything he could spare to help us. Some of us worked on the same plantation and bought our own little farms and little log cabins, and lived there 'till master died and the family moved away." Fannie Nicholson remembered that her mother continued working for her former owner, but now she got paid.[27]

From later testimony of freed slaves it appeared that owners who had been good to their slaves and had given their former bondsmen a mule, equipment or a parcel of land had won the gratitude and cooperation of their former "hands," many of whom remained with them as sharecroppers until their deaths. Cruel owners watched their slaves disappear in droves, often accompanied by a barrage of "cussin' out" on the part of both owners and ex-slaves.[28]

While some owners were reluctant or delinquent in telling their "servants" they were free, other owners cursed their ex-slaves. Some shot at them with rifles. One freed black woman reported that her owner died shortly after the surrender: "She was so hurt that all the negroes was going to be free. She died hollering 'Yankee!' She was so mad that she just died." Beaufort Sims took the news of the emancipation of slaves resignedly: "The emancipation of the slaves is but a part of what we must now endure. Our tyrannical enemies will now try themselves and are very determined this must be a land of bondage."[29]

Finding domestic help became a great trial for women accustomed to "servants." Elizabeth Porcher complained to her sister: "Yesterday I had to dismiss my new maid servant. She proved such a lazy bulk and so much at her ease with us all. I am dependent upon the lodger in the kitchen who renders rather unwilling service but hope to hear today of a girl who I think will suit me very well. Housekeeping these days is a sore trial. Sometimes I wish we had no cooking to do but there would be the washing which I hate even more."[30]

For many Southern slaveholders, emancipation brought a relief, albeit more time at the ironing board and in the kitchen. Tryphena Fox considered slaves a tremendous responsibility: "Whether *they* are any happier *now*, I cannot say, I only know this, that *I* am happier & should be ten years younger, in looks & feelings had there never been such a thing as *slaves*."[31] Beaufort Sims disliked the kitchen work that had formerly been done by "servants" but also confessed: "For some reasons I am glad the institution is gone. The release from the responsibility which we ever considered very great is truly a relief. Many of our people are doing their own work, every servant having left, and hiring being a great trial, they thus make another attempt for independence"[32]

❦

As news of the surrender spread throughout the Southland, it resolutely sounded the death-knell to wishful thinking about a possible final victory and a separate Southern nation. Defeat is one thing, but for Southerners it was a traumatic defeat. Southerners had paid dearly for their struggle for independence. Their loss of homes, farms, bank accounts, household furnishings, and personal possessions, of course, paled in comparison with the devastating loss of loved ones. There was scarcely a woman but had lost one or more brothers, sons or loved ones. (In some areas, the demand for black mourning fabric exceeded the supply, and women were forced to forego wearing traditional funeral apparel.) Surely, the losses could not have been in vain. Defeat was an extremely bitter pill to swallow, particularly for true Southerners.

As with any defeat or loss, it was important to find a scapegoat. Who or what brought down the South? Where did the blame lie? Every Rebel had a candidate: President Davis, the Confederate Congress, the croakers, the monetary system, the stay-at-homes, the firebrands who fueled the war in the first place. As noted, some ex–Confederates and some later historians attribute an important role in the final surrender to women's unwillingness to make further sacrifices on the homefront. Others cite a general despair and feeling of hopelessness on the part of the South, in general, and the soldiers in particular. Certainly, the massive desertions in the latter months of the war give credence to the latter.

Kate Cumming, a Confederate hospital matron and author, wondered whether women—and also men—had done enough for the war effort and posed some challenging questions for her readers: "In a word have the women of the South done their whole duty and can the people of the South, as a whole, say they have done their duty? 'It is all over with,' some may say, 'and why bring these things in review before us?'" In the voice of truth, Kate cautioned: "It is not all over with! Men and women of the South, there is much yet to be done."[33]

As for villains, Zillah Brandon was absolutely certain there was no villain in history quite as evil as General Sherman. The trail of demolition wrought during his march to the sea and his parade through the Carolinas garnered not only Zillah's wrath but that of every Southerner in his path. Zillah vented her anger in her diary, in which she likened Sherman to Caligula, Nero, and one of the beasts of the Bible. (Grant and Lincoln were accorded similar vilification). The descent of Sherman's troops on Gaylesville in northeast Alabama and the ten-day pillaging of the area around her home fueled Zillah's hatred for the "arsonist." "I know not the number nor the heiniousness of the crimes committed within sound of the bugle where this modern Nero slept. Widows were robbed of their last meal, their furniture crushed, the beds on which their fatherless children slept ripped open and the feathers thrown to the winds. Sherman's pride and haughty brow did not conceal his determination to make these earthly Eden homes of ours a desert."

Zillah's vehement denunciation of Sherman continued unabated in her diary: "Sherman unmoved by orphans, tears, widows mourning, infancy or old age held us under his triumphal car, his favors if such form of speech is allowable were but galling chains. He left Gaylesville 30 October 1864, after firing the mill [probably her husband's mill] and bridge, leaving a guard around lest something should be saved. They stood until the last beam was borne off on the beautiful waters." After more outpourings of invective, Zillah asked, "But what say the advocates of this modern Nero, Sherman. God pity the man that traces glory in his wake or can sing a requiem to his sinking soul."[34] When Emma LeConte heard rumors that Sherman had been killed, she shrugged off the news, feeling, "that is far too good to be true."[35]

Ah, but there were heroes! While some chose to denigrate President Davis, Southerners tended to rally 'round the immensely popular Robert E. Lee. A Tennessee woman reported the jubilant celebrations by the Yankees over the surrender: "The bells began to ring furiously, bon fires were lighted about town and cannons boomed from the forts. The Yankees had another grand jubilee and forced illumination over the surrender of Gen. Lee with his staff and 20,000 men. How wretchedly it made us feel God only knows—yet I thought how small and insignificant must be our sorrow compared with that of the heroic Commander.... I have now really and in earnest given up the Confederate cause." Her praise of Lee echoed the ubiquitous admiration of Southerners for the famous General: "Lee—our great General has succumbed to circumstances. But oh! what a pride I have in that noble commander. He is grander surrendering an army than Grant or 40,000 like him—receiving a surrender. God bless him."[36]

◖◗

News of Lee's surrender had barely settled before word of Lincoln's assassination fostered fear in the minds of realists—who believed the South would be blamed for the murder—glee in the hearts of Lincoln-haters, and compassion in the souls of Southerners who believed they had lost a true friend in their time of need.

"The news of it [the surrender] came slowly to us," Jennie Stephenson wrote, "so cut off were we from intercourse with the outer world, and coming as it were in waves of truth, each incoming wave growing stronger, until the full anguish of engulfing gloom settled in and about us." She continued: "Blacker still seemed to grow the night of horror, when it was spread abroad that Lincoln had been assassinated. We felt that vengeance would be taken on an already conquered people. Only the consciousness of having done our best, sustained the crushed South. Honor was left."[37]

Unaware of Lincoln's death, Mary Jane Chadick "went to the provost marshal (Capt. Moore) this evening to get three letters approved." "While examining them," she later wrote, "he remarked to me, 'We have just got news that I fear will be worse for you Southern people than anything that has yet happened. President Lincoln was shot last night at the theatre in Washington and died this morning. Seward was stabbed, but it is thought will recover.' I asked him if it was supposed that a Southern man had done the deed. 'Oh, No' he replied, 'it was done by Booth!' I was exceedingly shocked, as well might be supposed, and felt in my heart that it must be bad news for the South, if Andrew Johnson was to succeed him. What startling events have crowded fast upon each other within the last few days!"[38]

Despite the fact that much of the nation truly grieved over Lincoln's death, Gertrude Thomas remained unmoved. Although she condemned Booth's attack on Lincoln, still her thoughts and loyalties continued to go with President Davis in his flight from Richmond: "I have no cause to love Lincoln. My womanly sympathys go out for Jeff Davis and I do hope and pray that he will escape. Not to save my right arm would I betray him if I knew where he was and yet I was beginning to think him despotic...."[39]

In addition to their mounting woes, Southerners looked upon the prospects of Andrew Johnson as president with little enthusiasm. A Georgia woman remarked in her diary: "Someone once remarked of Andy Johnson that 'his name stunk like carrion in the nostrils of the Southern people.' A strong expression but I know of none which will so well express my sentiments for the man who thus presumes to interfere in our domestic affairs...."[40]

Catherine Ann Devereux Edmondston, although reminding herself "Exult not over thine Adversary," wondered why, "if Booth intended to turn assassin why, O why, did he delay it for so long?" A sentence or so later she added, "Lincoln the rail splitter was bad enough, but Johnson, the renegade tailor, is worse."[41]

Many Southerners believed the North had made an extremely poor choice in electing Johnson vice president. Less than a month prior to Lincoln's death Mary Jane Chadick reported the Lincoln inauguration, secondhand from a Northern newspaper, in her diary: "It appears that Andy Johnson was most gloriously drunk and demanded to make his speech before taking the oath of office! The speech was, of course, incoherent, and he began by the announcement that President Lincoln was a plebian and himself was a plebian, and they both glorified in it. He disgraced his country and his cause. His friends hung their heads in shame. Most of the speech has been suppressed."[42]

While Northerners voluntarily draped their homes in black crepe, Southerners were ordered to do so. Numerous Southerners caustically correlated the preponderance of back crepe on the doors of Southern homes with the hypocrisy of the home's owner—the more crepe the less sincere the grief over Lincoln's demise. In addition, there were also many groups of conservative Southerners who, although distressed over his death, chastised Lincoln for being so wicked as to attend the theater in the first place.

ꙮ

For some fortunate Southerners, there were joyful homecomings. Although Federal soldiers were sent home by rail at government expense, the remnants of the Confederate army had to struggle home afoot. Day after day, eager eyes scoured the horizon for a glimpse of the dear, familiar face of a loved one among the little squads of two and three bedraggled, footsore men making their way home across the fields, stopping here and there to beg a cup of water or a crust of bread. Day after day, tens of thousands of grieving women, their loved ones asleep on some distant battlefield, struggled to suppress their envy of the families who lived with hope.

Following the war, Kate Cumming, a Confederate nurse, observed: "Hundreds of *rebels* were constantly passing. Some from Lee's army going south and others from the gulf department going north. Their demeanor, in general, a quiet submission to the inevitable. One band occupied an empty store near us, and sang hymns nearly all night. We saw General Allen and his staff pass and all had the same air of recognition."[43]

"Poor fellows," she continued "they appeared weary and ill, one having been wounded in the foot. At all times could be seen hundreds of Confederate Soldiers wending their way home; many of them in rags and barefooted—the sad remnant of a brave but unfortunate army!" The men, she wrote, "were determined to bear their present ills," rather than face "those they knew not."

On May 26, 1865, following Kirby Smith's surrender of the Confederate troops west of the Mississippi, Mary Jane Chadick breathed a sigh of relief to her diary. "A memorable day, for with it, ends all my suspense and anxiety with regard to the absence of the dear ones." Later, Mary Jane wrote, "soon after the whistle of the evening train, Sue came in and said 'Ma, Eddie has come and is on his way here in the omnibus!' It was no surprise, as we were looking for him; but we were not looking for W.D. [her husband] who got out of the omnibus at the same time, to our very great surprise. The meeting was one of great joy, mixed with sadness. When we thought of the painful weeks and months of separation, borne with patience and fortitude for the sake of the cause, and then the unfortunate result!"

With the safe return of her loved ones, Mary Jane closed her diary and attempted to put her dark thoughts of the past four years behind her: "The war being over and dear ones returned, there will be little more of interest for these pages. Therefore, you and I, dear journal, close friends as we have been, united by every bond of sympathy, must part. 'We have shared each other's gladness and wept each other's tears.'"

Homecomings often proved less than joyful for refugees returning home after months or years spent out of harm's way, a safe distance from the scenes of strife and carnage. Thousands of women found only crumbling ruins awaiting them—devastation they quickly added to their already lengthy list of grievances against the Yankees. Returning to their old home near Petersburg, Virginia, Jennie (Jane) Stephenson and her family were aghast to find it utterly demolished—barns, outhouses, timberland, fences, all gone. Only four bare walls of the old house still standing, only "The gapping, eyeless frame of a big house, porchless, doorless, windowless stood before us."[44]

"Not a dwelling to be seen in all that region of the country," Jennie despaired. Instead, clumps of graves (serving as ghastly reminders of the four years of sacrifice), "the coloring of the clothes still preserved, as we saw through the scant supply of earth upon these bodies." In the peach orchard were the graves of deserters, Jennie was told, "who had been court-martialed in the company chamber of the house, and were led out from that room, blind-folded, and shot on these spots."

Countless refugees returned only to find their homes occupied by their former slaves. One owner told of the servants, who welcomed him back enthusiastically, but announced "firmly and respectfully," "We own this land now. Put it out of your head that it will ever be yours again."[45]

When Frances Fearn and her husband came home from their refugee life in Europe, they found their plantation near New Orleans completely broken up. Her husband, unequal because of failing health to undertake the difficult work of reviving the plantation, found he must put it up for sale.[46] Thousands more like Mrs. Fearn found their homes unlivable, and lacking money and energy, they simply gave up, sold out, and moved on.

Few and far between were happy returnee stories. However, one feisty Memphis woman proved to be the exception. After the war, as Elizabeth Meriwether returned to their Memphis home with her three little children, she found the countryside "more and more desolate and dreary; the farm houses on the road side had been either deserted or burned to the ground. No inhabitants of the country did we see, nor human beings of any kind excepting occasionally we saw troops of Union soldiers marching northward. Some of those troops were black. They spoke no word to me, I spoke no word to them; their black faces and blue uniforms affrighted me."[47]

Understandably, Betty was skeptical about the condition of her home and about whether it might be still standing or whether it had been burned to the ground. In 1862, following a confrontation with Sherman, the general had banished Betty from the city. Would he have vindictively destroyed her home? After enduring trials she compared to those of Ulysses, Betty was one of the lucky Southerners who found her home intact. "House sitters" welcomed her home and quickly returned her property to her. It was another struggle, however, to discourage former slaves who were in the process of erecting a home on her front lawn. (These definitely were not the Meriwethers' former slaves, for Betty and her husband despised slavery and had freed their slaves years before.)

☙❧

For Southerners, their defeat was a crushing blow. Anxiety and grief were certainly no strangers to Southerners, who had suffered a traumatic loss of 258,000 men on the battlefield or from disease. An additional 129,000 men would be returning home with devastating physical or mental wounds. The surrender, however, marked the culmination of their grief. It constituted far more than an end to their hopes and dreams; it spawned the gut-wrenching realization that their loved ones had died in vain, that their sacrifices of homes, bank accounts, and creature comforts had been for naught. For a time an etherizing emptiness and foreboding cast a pall over the South.

The surrender prostrated Southerners. The Confederate government had been dissolved; banks had closed, taking with them their depositors' money and credit. Confederate bills were not worth the paper they were printed on. Thousands of homes and untold millions of bales of cotton had been consumed in the holocaust of war. The Confederacy had impressed horses and Northerners had stolen them, thereby wreaking havoc with Southerners' means of transportation and with the all-important backbone of farm work. Northern and Southern soldiers, foraging on the principle of "What's mine is mine, and what's yours is mine too," had denuded the countryside of chickens, milk cows, pigs, peaches, vegetables, fence rails, honey and, here and there, even the beehives themselves. Fields had been so murderously trampled by marching feet or annihilated by campsites that it would take years for them to become productive again. The blockade had rendered shoes a novelty, even basics such as pins and needles, a scarcity, and luxuries, a fantasy.

As time passed a quiet resignation set in, an acceptance of the outcome of the war as God's will and a recognition of the need to start over. Not surprisingly, scores of Southerners found comfort in their religion, oft repeating the conviction that although the Lord chasteneth and scourgeth his people, in the end one must submit to "Him who doeth all things well." Even the newspapers carried editorials acknowledging that grief "lies too deep for expression, as yet, by pen or by voice." For now, one editorial concluded, there could be no "utterance other than that of silent submission to the will of Him who doeth all things well...."[48]

Perhaps God was chastising them for holding slaves, or for being too proud, or too worldly, or too sinful. Kate Cumming confessed, "This is a severe ordeal; may God in his mercy give us comfort through it."

Instead of finding solace in their religion, other women discovered that the "lost cause" severely tested their religion. During the first days of relief that the fighting had ended, Gertrude Thomas told her diary: "Now that we have surrendered—are in a great degree powerless we can count with certainty upon nothing. Our Negroes will be freed our lands confiscated and imagination cannot tell what is in store for us but thank God I have an increased degree of faith—a faith which causes me to feel that all this will be for our good."[49] A short time later as reality sank in, however, she confessed: "Slavery was done away with and my faith in God's Holy Book was terribly shaken. For a time I doubted God. The truth of revelations, all—everything—I no longer took interest in the service of the church.... Our cause was lost. Good men had had faith in that cause. Earnest prayers had ascended from honest hearts—Was so much faith to be lost? I was bewildered—I felt all this and could not see God's hand."[50] Mary Goodwin begged for a strengthening of her faith: "Help me to believe that all is good. All is for the best."

The future would usher in a new life—for better or for worse. And it looked like for worse as bewildered Southerners contemplated what appeared to be an ominous future. What was to be their fate? Would their land be confiscated? Would high-ranking officers be hanged or imprisoned? Would the South be the victim of a vengeful North? Should they seek what might promise to be a better life in Brazil or Mexico or Europe? Would they be denied the right to vote or representation in Congress? Would they always be treated with contempt, as second class citizens? What would life be like without slaves? How could they ever recover economically? Would they be humiliated and cowed by a vindictive Northern government? How were their children to be educated? How were they to secure laborers without money to pay wages? How would the newly emancipated blacks behave? Would they be willing to work on shares or become indolent, believing that freedom meant never having to work at all? Would their former slaves' newly acquired freedom give rise to insurrections, rapes or murders? And yet, for many Southerners, the most immediate question was where their next meal would be coming from. Thus ran a partial list of the questions that plagued Southerners at the end of the war. Confused by these and a myriad of other perplexing problems, tens of thousands of Southerners struck out for the West, Chicago or New York City, or any place outside the Southland. Then, too, there were those who chose suicide, such as Edmund Ruffin and Henry Hartford Cumming, rather than living in what they believed would be subjugation.

Grace Elmore summed up the situation rather succinctly: "We cannot tell what the future holds, indeed human wisdom has been so utterly at fault, in all its deductions, with regard to this war and its results, that one dares not draw any conclusion, however plausible, from passing events. Our life for four years has been the 'baseless fabric of a vision,' and now we can only deal with the hard realities of the present."[51]

"Oh how different our feelings if we had won our 'cause.' With what spirit and heart," Grace persisted, "would we have gone to work, how willingly would loss of home and wealth have been borne for the sake of being free. But now we are forced to work; without hope for our country,—but that we might obtain bread."[52]

Tryphena Blanche Holder Fox, in calculating their losses during the war, confessed that she "would have been willing to have worn sack cloth could we have achieved our Independence, but now all the sacrifices we have made, seem of double weight."[53]

Deep gloom shrouded Mary Chesnut's days. "Blue-black is our horizon," she wrote. Rarely at a loss for words, Mary despaired: "A feeling of sadness hovers over me now, day and night, that no words of mine can express."[54]

In May of 1865, Sarah Espy wrote: "I look to the future with dread and think we have everything to fear if we are subjugated as I suppose we are. O! how dark looks all to me, & what is to be the end of it."[55] Sarah feared that there was little knowledge of "what our conquerors will do with us, but our situation for some years will be a hard one." Such was the thinking of untold numbers of Southern women. "It is a very sad thought connected with the past four years," one woman predicted, "that in addition to all the lives lost, so much beauty and fruitfulness have been laid waste in our dear country. It will be years before we shall recover entirely from the effect...."[56]

Marion Briscoe wrote gloomily: "In the postwar period the inhabitants of the little village of Boydton looked out on the same buildings and over the same green fields and pine forests, but the spirit behind those eyes was greatly changed from that of an earlier generation. Hope, ambition, and eager expectancy of the future had been laid low. Every step was groping in the dark. Every possession was swept away, the gardens and crops were gone, and there was no money and nothing to be bought if there were. The slaves now could not be worked without pay, and once again there was nothing with which to pay them. Between the neighbors there grew up an exchange of work. Mother would knit a baby sack if Mrs. Jones would make one of the children a little dress, and someone else would make candles if her neighbor would do a little quilting."[57]

Gertrude Thomas repressed thoughts of the war and the surrender, choosing instead to involve herself in reading and writing: "I make no plans for the future. It is impossible to indulge in golden day dreams."[58] While writing on May 1, 1865, Gertrude heard the tolling of a bell: "The bell which for so long a time has tolled to remind us to pray for the soldiers and alas by so many of us has been neglected—will toll no more— God help us. As an independent nation we will not exist—the bright dream of Southern independence has not been realized—The war is over and again we become a part of the United States—how united will depend alone upon treatment we receive from the hands of the North."

Upon returning to Georgia with her father to attempt to get their old plantation in some kind of working order, Frances Butler Leigh recorded despairingly the changes that had come about: "Our slaves had been freed; the white population was conquered, ruined, and disheartened, unable for the moment to see anything but ruin before as well as

behind, too wedded to the fancied prosperity of the old system to believe
in any possible success under the new. And even had the people desired
to begin at once to rebuild their fortunes, it would have been in most
cases impossible, for in many families the young men had perished in
the war, and the old men, if not too old for the labour and effort it
required to set the machinery of peace going again, were beggared, and
had not even money enough to buy food for themselves and their families, let alone their negroes, to whom they now had to pay wages as well
as feed them."[59]

"Besides this, the South was still treated as a conquered country,"
Frances continued. "The white people were disfranchised, the local government in the hands of either military men or Northern adventurers,
the latter of whom, with no desire to promote either the good of the
country or people, but only to advance their own private ends, encouraged the negroes in all their foolish and extravagant ideas of freedom,
set them against their old masters, filled their minds with false hopes,
and pandered to their worst passions, in order to secure for themselves
some political office which they hoped to obtain through the negro
vote."[60]

Zillah Brandon, in somewhat the same tone, believed the South,
although vanquished by superior numbers, should still take pride in its
legacy of truth and honor, "Though now crushed by overwhelming
numbers, despoiled of every right claimed by a free people, oppressed,
driven by a storm that caused our country to founder. Yet our enemies
cannot rob us of our birthright Truth and Honor. While we feel that we
have been conquered by might rather than right, we are not degraded.
The grand patriotism of '76 is burning in our souls as brightly as if it
had been of this hours kindling. We have just passed four years freighted
with historic interest, where scenes of ruthless violence and sin has desecrated our soil, our people have been insulted, our homes pillaged, our
churches destroyed, and at last our leading men have yielded to superior
force and to terms dictated by Federal officers whose record for Southern rights and privileges is only partly developed. God of heaven and
earth shield us from the spoilers forever; calm the storm that distracts
us as a people. Lead us our shepard. The oppressive tax imposed by the
Northern government is ruinous. Our rights as citizens are all taken from
us, our ancient landmarks removed, our states governed as territories.
Our sons denied the right to stand in the Cabinet, farm or field as
rulers."[61]

☙❧

Following the Armistice, and for months thereafter, the promise of
peace and a return to normalcy held little meaning for many unconscionable

Yankees, returning Confederate soldiers, blacks, "bummers," and stragglers—many of whom made violence and theft an everyday, every night, occurrence. Caroline Gilman told of a Yankee Raid in Greenville, South Carolina, as late as May 2, 1865. When Mrs. Gilman questioned the raids on non-combatants, especially during the Armistice, a Yankee lieutenant responded, "Oh, madam, the Armistice did not hold after Lincoln's death."[62]

The raiders, some two-hundred strong, then set about pillaging the town, opening the commissary stores, stealing over thirty thousand dollars from the bank, and plundering private homes. "Everything was rifled," Mrs. Gilman sighed, "books, costly plate, wines, pictures and bed linen thrown into the streets to be picked up by any passer-by. All the afternoon we saw white and black, laden with goods, passing by the house." Later, when Mrs. Gilman returned to her Charleston home, she discovered: "Books, private papers, and pictures are all stolen. The pillagers must have had some object beside robbery in their selection. Everything valuable as an autograph is gone."[63]

With the savage destruction of their homes and personal possessions by Union or Confederate troops—or gangs of stragglers—even wills had to be revised after the war. So great had been her loss of personal possessions, thanks to Yankee raids of their home that Caroline Gilman explained to her children: "I destroyed *my will* yesterday, 'circumstances having altered cases' as the copy book says. Caroline calls it *my won't*. It was with a very peculiar feeling that I ran over the items donated to all of you children and grandchildren, now either in possession of a Northern soldier, or destined to be sold for my temporary support."[64]

☙❧

"Forgive and forget?" Impossible: The wounds were far too deep. One Southerner announced that if forgiveness were required for admission to Heaven, he was sure he would be consigned to Hell. Although finally some feelings of resignation began to emerge with some Southerners—never with others—there still remained a deep-seated anger at the despoiling of their homes and property under Sherman's "scorched earth" policy, at the presence of troops of occupation—particularly black troops—at the enforced swearing to the detested oaths of allegiance following the bloody sacrifice of so many of their loved ones, at the required church prayers for the president of the United States, at a future in which they were sure they would suffer the vengeance and retaliation of the victorious North. It would be only natural that Southerners would find it difficult—if not impossible—to love their former enemies. As the carpetbaggers poured in and the scalawags took over, Southerners' hatred of Northerners boiled over. Ministers counseled Christian forgiveness, but there were no listeners.

Mary B. Goodwin wrote: "Alas! I fear I do not feel exactly as a Child of God should under the circumstances. Oh! will I *ever* get accustomed to our condition; *ever* be able to bear the thought of having been whipped, & being made once more a citizen of the U.S.? I fear not, for as time passes by I feel more & more repugnance to the thought, harder and harder to reconcile myself to being under the despised Yankees—and my hatred for them so far from diminishing seems to strengthen & increase as time passes on. Oh! that I were such a Christian as I ought to be! Then my feelings would not be so strong & I might be able to control them, & if I could not *love* the Yankees at least might *loathe* them less."[65]

⊖⊝

In time, anger gave way to resolution. Those unable to sublimate their anger, however, resolved to show their hatred of the "Blue Devils" by contemptuously ignoring them. Any neighbors who would be so despicable as to entertain a Yankee in their homes garnered the wrath of the entire neighborhood. The troops of occupation were given a cold shoulder by disdainful women in Richmond—and elsewhere throughout the South. Haughtily they turned up their noses as they passed the "Blue Devils" on the streets and gathered up their skirts for fear of accidentally touching one of the dispised Federals. On April 30, a Richmond lady wrote to her cousin: "We R[ichmond] people have grown calm some what. The young ladies keep themselves quietly at home, doing nothing to expose themselves to insult; and in all cases declining controversy with the U.S. officers, which I heartily approve.... For my own part I tread my own path, utterly ignoring them. I do not seem to see them, careful only not to expose myself to insult."[66]

Enraged Southerners vowed (as observed in Josephine LeConte's letters) to pass on to their children, their children's children, their children's children's children, their bitterness over the humiliation and indignities they had suffered at the hands of Northerners.

Southern men returning home seemed readier to accept the defeat than the women who had paid so dearly, having sacrificed such an appalling number of loved ones to a "lost cause." The cause might have been lost, but Southern women determined it would never be forgotten. Through their work in founding the ubiquitous memorial societies that immediately sprang up throughout the South, women could honor their fallen heroes and give immortality to their cause.

As the days and months passed, Southerners resolved to try to get on with their lives—to start over, to emerge from their straitened circumstances, to somehow raise the money for back taxes to retrieve their land, to make that land productive once again, to attempt to solve their drastic labor problems by sharecropping. For many women, it meant a resolve to provide the physical and moral support necessary to restore their incapacitated husbands to health or, failing that, to serve as farm managers or breadwinners for the family. Those fearing to live under Northern subjugation—or in a country with their former slaves their equals—determined to leave the country, find new homes in Mexico or Brazil, or set off for homesteads in the West.

Both whites and blacks faced a new world. For the blacks, there were the long overdue amendments that granted them freedom, citizenship, and suffrage. Former slaves set about legalizing their marriages, reuniting with family members who had been sold to distant plantations, learning to read and write, getting an education, organizing and building their own churches, and otherwise achieving an independent life for themselves.

The postwar era made way for a new world and a new life. For Josie LeConte and her family there was an exciting new beginning in California. Mary White gave up on the frustrations of the blockade and looked to friends, visits and parties at home—and eventually the bright promise of a happy marriage and a rewarding family life. Mary Lee never returned to live in Winchester but instead carved out a new, fulfilled life in Baltimore. Life would never be the same again for Sarah Duval, but she and her family experienced the euphoria of having survived the war and a traumatic refugee life. Nancy Jones, with her husband and son, came home from her temporary sanctuary in Canada. She gathered up her widowed daughter and her grandson in Texas, and with her entire family, Nancy discovered a life of tranquility and pleasure, in contrast to the fear and turmoil of Missouri's wartime chaos.

Having found that their wartime experiences—working in hospitals, conducting fairs, and taking care of businesses—had in many ways emancipated them from their traditional restricted sphere of family, home and church, many women were resolute about undertaking volunteer or paid work outside the home. In time, the women's suffrage movement, women's clubs, temperance societies, prison reform societies, hospital auxiliaries and philanthropic organizations took women out of the kitchen and into the mainstream. Their wartime services had conditioned many women to a certain amount of independence and an eagerness for more education.

◌◌

The war was over, the cannons were silent, and yet Southerners were doomed to face another cataclysmic struggle—Reconstruction— with its turmoil and upheaval that would last three times as long as the war itself. Ahead lay the rabid Radical Republicans, the influx of carpetbaggers, Southern cross-overs—the scalawags, the horrific race riots, the unrelenting violence carried out by stragglers, guerrilla bands, vigilante groups and the Ku Klux Klan, the Union Leagues, the loss of suffrage, homes and land, the scrounging for money to pay taxes, the almost insurmountable labor problems. But that, of course, is history.

For Southerners, the days of anxiety persisted with unabated regularity. It took years, even generations, for many Southerners to put the agony of defeat and the trauma of Reconstruction behind them. However, in time, the South did succeed in forging a new order of things, replete with new dimensions, a world alive with opportunity and challenge—and accomplishment.

In words addressed to men, but surely meant for women too, Jefferson Davis looked to a new day for Southerners: "Before you lies the future—a future full of golden promise, full of recompense for noble endeavor, full of national glory before which the world will stand amazed. Let me beseech you to lay aside all rancor, and all bitter sectional feeling, and take your place in the rank of those who bring about a conciliation out of which will issue a reunited country."[67]

Economic prosperity in the South proved to be a long way off. Pursuit of the basic needs of life occupied most southerners long after the war and Reconstruction had officially ended. Over the years, however, Southerners found they had not only survived, but had, indeed, overcome.

Notes

Chapter One

1. A copy of the handwritten diary of Mary Johnston White resides with James P. Beckwith, Jr., Durham, North Carolina, a native of Warrenton, North Carolina, a maternal great, great, great nephew of Mary White and a paternal cousin of Mary's husband, Edmund Ruffin Beckwith. At one time a copy of the diary was also presented to the authorities at the Southern Historical Collection at the University of North Carolina at Chapel Hill. A typescript of part of the diary containing very minor discrepancies (perhaps changes made by Mary herself at a later date as she reread her diary) is located in the Library of the Headquarters of the United Daughters of the Confederacy, Richmond, Virginia.

2. At least one account credited John White as having "perhaps the handsomest stock of dry goods and notions in North Carolina. Even families from Raleigh made the trip to Warrenton to purchase goods from Mary's father's store." Lizzie Wilson Montgomery, *Sketches of Old Warrenton, North Carolina: Traditions and Reminiscences of the Town and People Who Made It* (Spartanburg, South Carolina: The Reprint Company, Publishers, 1984), 85–6.

3. Dawson Carr, *Gray Phantoms of the Cape Fear: Running the Civil War Blockade* (Winston Salem, North Carolina: John F. Blair, 1999), 151.

4. Excellent discussions of the legality of the blockade are to be found in Robert Erwin Johnson's "Investment by Sea: The Civil War Blockade," *American Neptune*, 32 (January 1972): 34–57; Stephen R. Wise, *Lifeline of the Confederacy*

(Columbia: University of South Carolina Press, 1988), 24–5, and James Russell Soley, *The Blockade and the Cruisers* (Wilmington, North Carolina: Broadfoot Publishing Company, 1989), 26–38.

5. Bern Anderson, *By Sea and by River: The Naval History of the Civil War* (New York: Alfred A. Knopf, 1962), 303.

6. Shelby Foote, *The Civil War: A Narrative: Fort Sumter to Perryville* (New York: Random House, 1958), 741.

7. Soley, 156; Hamilton Cochrane, *Blockade Runners of the Confederacy* (Indianapolis: The Bobbs-Merrill Company, 1958), 172, and Wise, 106.

8. Soley, 155–6; Malcolm Ross, *The Cape Fear* (New York: Holt, Rinehart and Winston, 1965), 221–237; Dave Horner, *The Blockade-Runners: True Tales of Running the Yankee Blockade of the Confederate Coast* (New York: Dodd, Mead & Company, 1968), 5; and Frank E. Vandiver, *Blockade Running Through Bermuda, 1861–1865: Letters and Cargo Manifests* (Austin: The University of Texas Press, 1947), xv.

9. Horner, 13, and Foote, 741, reported similar although slightly different numbers.

10. Robert M. Browning Jr., *From Cape Charles to Cape Fear: The North Atlantic Blockading Squadron During the Civil War* (Tuscaloosa: The University of Alabama Press, 1993), 267; James Sprunt, *Chronicles of the Cape Fear River, 1660–1916* (Wilmington: Broadfoot Publishing Company, 1992), 454–5; Wise, 106.

11. James Sprunt, "Running of the Blockade," *Southern Historical Society Papers*, XXIV (January to December 1896), 158.

12. Marcus W. Price, "Ships That Tested the Blockade of the Georgian and

237

East Florida Ports, 1861–1865," *American Neptune* 15 (April 1955), 206–7.

13. For a more complete account see Wise, 105–6. The material is corroborated in Sprunt, CCFR, 454, and Cochran, 172.

14. Thomas E. Taylor, *Running the Blockade: A Personal Narrative of Adventures, Risks, and Escapes During the American Civil War* (New York: Charles Scribner's Sons, 1896), 44–45; Soley, 91–92; Browning, 220–221.

15. Johnson, 49–50; Soley, 9–19; and Anderson, 290–91.

16. Johnson, 52; Soley 94–5; Anderson 227–9.

17. Dave Page, *Ships Versus Shore: Civil War Engagements Along Southern Shores and Rivers* (Nashville, Tennessee: Rutledge Hill Press, 1994), 83.

18. George Cary Eggleston, *A Rebel's Recollections* (Bloomington: Indiana University Press, 1959. New York: Kraus Reprint Co, 1969), 99.

19. Taylor, 84–5; James M. Merrill, *The Rebel Shore: The Story of Union Sea Power in the Civil War* (Boston: Little, Brown and Company, 1957), 63; Ross, 230–31; Cochran 64.

20. Anderson, 222–23.

21. Cochran, 102.

22. On one occasion the *Advance*'s unusual cargo included three escapees from Johnson's Island. In a hair-raising adventure through the snowy fields, as they battled sub zero temperatures and a harrowing crossing of the partially frozen Detroit River, the escapees found their way to Montreal, secured passage to Bermuda, and finally made it home to North Carolina aboard the *Advance*. Charles E. Frohman, *Rebels on Lake Erie* (Columbus, Ohio: The Ohio Historical Society, 1965), 55–57.

23. Robert Carse, *Blockade: The Civil War at Sea* (New York: Rinehart Company, 1958), 19 and 148; Browning, 252.

24. Carr, 88.

25. Price, 201.

26. Stuart L. Bernath, *Squall Across the Atlantic: American Civil War Prize Cases and Diplomacy* (Berkeley: University of California Press, 1970), 4. For many seamen the excitement was as important—or even more important—an aspect as the financial rewards. William Watson concluded his memoirs by noting: "To those who took the active part, it was—although attended with some privation, danger, and anxiety—on the whole a rather enjoyable occupation, with something of the zest of yacht-racing—a kind of exciting sport of

the higher order, in which the participators regarded with more satisfaction some successful elusion of the enemy, a chase and excape, or other adventure, than any other emolument." William Watson, *The Adventures of a Blockade Runner; or, Trade in Time of War* (London: T. Fisher Unwin, 1898), 324.

27. Wise, 63 and 151; Horner, 11.

28. Horner, 11. Newspapers reported that the first dividend of the Bee Company in 1863 paid investors $5,000 per share; in August 1864 the dividend was only a shabby $2,000. Horner, 12.

29. Carr, 85, and Vandiver, *passim*. So lucrative were the blockade runners' returns that even novices were attracted to the business. Alexander Thom, a Richmond physician, detailed an interesting plan for a "get rich scheme" in letters to his brother that are detailed in "*My Dear Brother*": *A Confederate Chronicle* (Richmond, Virginia: The Dietz Press, 1952). By purchasing French silks, black sewing silk, ivory-handled cutlery, fine ladies' summer goods, Java coffee and other specialty items and sending them to Nassau and then to the Confederacy, Thom envisioned a financial killing for himself and his brother. Although his brother did not snap up Alex's plan, the physician's second scheme, to procure and send artificial limbs to ports in the Confederacy, actually warranted considerable merit. During the first year after the war, Mississippi, for example, devoted one fifth of its budget to securing artificial limbs for war, veterans. Other states made comparable expenditures.

30. Carse, 71, and Browning, 261–263.

31. Browning, 263; Cochran, 293; Wise, 205.

32. William W. Holden as leader of a movement advocating separate state action for peace was soundly defeated in the election by Governor Vance who actively supported the war. For a concise discussion of Holden's background, see Otto H. Olsen, ed., *Reconstruction and Redemption in the South* (Baton Rouge: Louisiana State University Press, 1980), 156–8. On May 29, 1865, Holden was appointed by President Andrew Johnson as Provisional Governor of North Carolina.

33. Long before the war, an amateur theatrical organization produced near-professional-caliber plays in the theater housed in the town hall. Actually, the Thalian Association productions seemed to continue even during the war years, for it was

rumored that one night a couple of Yankee officers sneaked in wearing civilian clothes, watched the show and emerged safely without being detected. Cochran, 168–9.

34. Watson, 324; Soley, 156.

35. J. Wilkinson, *The Narrative of a Blockade-Runner* (New York: Sheldon & Company, 1877), 199–200; Carr, 150.

36. Taylor, 4–5.

37. Carse, 163.

38. Soley, 94.

39. Browning, 264.

40. Soley, 166; Browning, 264.

41. The *Advance* could attain speeds of up to seventeen knots, although some sources indicated only twelve knots.

42. Sprunt, CCFR, 455.

43. Sometime later, half interest in the *Advance* was sold "in order to gain shipping rights on additional blockade runners." Wise, 212.

44. Cochran, 172; Wise, 105, 286, 199–200.

45. Hobart Pasha, *Sketches from My Life* (New York: D. Appleton and Company, 1887), 108 and Soley, 166.

46. Cochran, 236.

47. Browning, 265.

48. Anderson, 225.

49. Written August 8, 1864, but covering several days' experiences.

50. Taylor, 50.

51. Soley, 157; Browning, 250.

52. Browning, 249.

53. Augustus Charles Hobart-Hampden, *Hobart Pasha: Blockade Running, Slave Hunting and War and Sport in Turkey* (New York Outing Publishing Company, 1915).

54. Carr, 32; Soley, 158; Wilkinson, 165.

55. Soley, 94.

56. Cochran, 284.

57. Anderson, 218.

58. Sprunt, CCFR, 455.

59. Sprunt, CCFR, 455.

60. Carr, 64. James M. Merrill provides more detail on the torpedo boats in *The Rebel Shore: The Story of Union Sea Power in the Civil War* (Boston: Little, Brown and Company, 1957), 168. "Propelled at seven knots by a steam engine driving a screw propeller, these wooden- or iron-hulled cigar-shaped boats measured fifty feet in length, seven in breadth. The boiler was forward, the engine lay aft, and amidships was a cuddyhole for the captain, engineer, and crew. When assaulting the enemy, the craft was so well submerged that nothing was visible except her short stack and the hatch coaming. These boats carried their torpedo on a spar protruding from the bow, which could be raised or lowered by a line passing aft into the cuddyhole."

61. The *Little Hattie*, owned by Importing and Exporting Company of Georgia survived the war. Wise, 309.

62. Taylor, 97.

63. Wise, 127; Sprunt, CCFR, 287; Carr, 134.

64. Wise, 127; Sprunt, CCFR, 287; Carr, 136.

65. Taylor, 96–97.

66. Taylor, 97.

67. So virulent was the disease that some fiendish Confederate as a sort of nineteenth century "germ warfare" strategy, proposed spreading the fever among Northerners by sending what they considered to be infected clothing on ships headed northward. A stash of blankets, clothing and handkerchiefs suspected of harboring the disease was discovered in Bermuda in April, 1865; however, the rumored perpetrator was never convicted in Nassau or in Canada for insufficient evidence. Taylor, 130, and Dwight Franklin Henderson, ed., "The Private Journal of Georgiana Gholson Walker 1865 with Selections from the Post-war Years 1865–1876," *Confederate Centennial Studies*, No 25 (Tuscaloosa Alabama: Confederate Publishing Company, 1963), 25–26. The crew of the *Mary Celestia* suffered an unusual number of cases of the deadly fever. The pilot of the *Mary Celestia*, J. W. Anderson, died a hero's death on what was to be his last voyage in July 1864. Sick unto death with yellow fever when the ship left Nassau, he refused to allow the captain to turn back. When the ship was suddenly sighted and fired on by blockaders, Anderson returned from his deathbed to his position on the bridge and supported by two sailors, he determinedly, though feebly, directed the ship safely into port. Within minutes after the ship dropped anchor, J. W. Anderson was dead. Sprunt, SHSP, 161–2; Cochran, 290–1; Horner, 106–7.

68. The *Annie* later became a part of the U.S. Navy when it was purchased from Prize Court after having run aground near New Inlet scarcely three months later on November 1, 1864. Wise, 288.

69. Elisha Kent Kane was a famous Arctic explorer appointed in 1852 by the Secretary of the Navy to conduct an expedition to the Arctic. His two volume account of the expedition, entitled *Arctic*

Explorations in the Years 1853, '54, '55, was immensely popular and copies were said to be found in about every home in America. For more information see Oscar M. Villarejo, *Dr. Kane's Voyage to the Polar Lands* (Philadelphia: University of Pennsylvania Press, 1965).

70. Fortunately the Whites were not in the area in the summer of 1863 when one of the cannon balls landed in the middle of a ladies' croquet game. There were no fatalities; however, "several of the good ladies swooned and had to be revived with smelling salts and generous portions of blackberry cordial." Cochran, 180.

71. Henderson, 92.
72. Pasha, 118.
73. Pasha, 118–19.
74. Taylor, 86.
75. Carse, 119; Sprunt, CCFR, 288.
76. August 12, 1864.
77. August 12, 1864.
78. August 14, 1864.
79. September 4, 1864.
80. August 16, 1864.
81. Cochran, 180.
82. August 15, 1864.
83. August 16, 1864.
84. August 15, 1864.
85. August 16, 1864.

86. The flute and the guitar players appear to have been Sidney Lanier, later to achieve considerable fame as a poet, and his brother, Clifford Anderson Lanier, both talented musicians and serving with the Confederacy in August and September of 1864 as signal officers on blockade runners in Wilmington.

87. August 20, 1864.
88. August 23, 1864.
89. Browning, 257.
90. August 23, 1864.
91. August 24, 1864.
92. Wise, 309.
93. August 24, 1864.
94. August 25, 1864.
95. August 25, 1864.

96. The *Tallahasee*, as the *Atlanta*, was purchased by the Confederate Navy in July 1864, and was employed at various times under various names, as a raider and as a runner. Following the war the ship was turned over to the United States. It sank in 1869. Wise, 289. The ill-fated *Mary Celestia* returned to Bermuda but sank on September 26, 1864, after hitting a rock while leaving St. George Harbor. Wise, 312.

97. August 26, 1864.
98. See note 60.
99. August 29, 1864.

100. On April 9, 1864, the torpedo boat CSS *Squib* succeeded in pulling off a surprise attack on the Federal flagship USS *Minnesota* in the James River. The torpedo boat was a relatively new instrument of underwater warfare and the attack shocked the Confederate officials. Although the *Minnesota* was severely damaged it did not sink. For details see Louis Schafer, *Confederate Underwater Warfare: An Illustrated History*, 134–142, and *Official Records of the Union and Confederate Navies in the War of the Rebellion*, Series I, Vol. 9, 593–604.

101. The "rip" was a shifting sand bar, a bête noire for runners because of its constantly shifting tendencies. As for the *Coquette*, the Confederate Navy bought the ship in the fall of 1863 and sold her ten months later to J. R. Anderson and Company, who continued to run her until December 1865. Wise, 294.

102. Mr. Arrington was Mary's brother-in-law, the husband of Mary's sister, Hannah.

103. The *Mary Bowers* was owned by a Georgia company and was declared a complete loss when she ran into the wreck of the *Georgiana* just outside Charleston. Wise, 312.

104. The range lights were lights set to assist the runner in maneuvering the narrow channel via a signal from runner to shore and were closed down once the ship entered the river. Wilkinson, 153; Soley, 160.

105. September 4, 1864. The *City of Petersburg* was owned by a Virginia company and survived the war. Wise, 293.

106. Three weeks later, as the *Lynx* was attempting to leave Wilmington through New Inlet on September 25, 1864, she was "chased and destroyed" by three Yankee ships. Wise, 310.

107. It is interesting to note that the *Old Dominion*, owned by a Virginia Company, survived the war. Wise, 314.

108. September 5, 1864.

109. The incoming ship Mary referred to might possibly have been the *Elsie*, which was captured on September 5, 1864, about the time the Whites saw the flashes of gunfire. Apparently the *Elsie* was leaving Wilmington rather than coming in. Wise, 279.

110. September 6, 1864.

111. September 7, 1864. The *Will of the Wisp* continued to operate successfully until February 9, 1865, when Yankee vessels ran it aground off Galveston and destroyed it. Wise, 327. The *Owl* and, as

noted, the *Helen*, survived the war; the *Lynx* was destroyed September 25, 1864.

112. *The War of the Rebellion: A Compilation of the Official Records of the Union and Confederate Armies*, Series I, Vol. 42, Part 2-Correspondence, etc. (Washington: Government Printing Office, 1893), 794.

113. Governor Vance was incensed over the replacement of pilot Morse. In a scathing communication to Maj. Gen. Whiting following the capture of the *Advance*, Governor Vance intimated that it was common knowledge that the general "drank too much," and that the seizure of the pilot of the *Advance*, "and a drunken wretch sent in his place," contributed greatly to the loss of the ship. *War of the Rebellion*, 1299. Needless to say, experienced captains and pilots were at a premium. These skilled seamen became increasingly scarce during the latter months of the war as the North wisely incarcerated these men for lengthy stays following their capture. Often the Federal government refused to allow them to be exchanged. Less essential foreign seamen were often paroled after a short imprisonment; however, the captains, and particularly the pilots, so essential to effective penetration of the blockade, were too important to be quickly released and allowed to return to ply their trade once again. Confederate sailors often received much harsher treatment than foreign seamen. Captured aboard the *Lucy*, the future poet Sidney Lanier was incarcerated at Point Lookout, where during his three months' stay he developed tuberculosis and nearly starved to death. Wise, 108–9; Parks, *passim*. For a more benevolent prison experience see Wilkinson, 60–82.

114. September 8, 1864.

115. September 8, 1864.

116. Probably after midnight, thus making it September 10, 1864.

117. Wise, 200. An interesting rumor circulated that when the *Advance* was captured $40,000 in gold was tossed overboard.

118. The *Advance* was captured September 10 according to *Official Records of the Union and Confederate Navies*, Vol. 1 (Washington: Government Printing Office, 1896), 88.

119. It was interesting to note that James Maglenn, an Irishman and the chief engineer aboard the *Advance* when she was captured, escaped when the ship was sent to New Bern and, thanks to friends, made his way to Canada. Luckily, he narrowly avoided being recaptured on a train en route to Canada, when a guard came into his car inquiring how passengers were to vote in the coming elections. In a loud, enthusiastic response Maglenn answered, "I cast my vote for President Lincoln." It was the right answer and the officer slapped him on the shoulder, and approvingly acknowledged, "You are the right sort, my friend." Maglenn had successfully weathered the crisis. Sprunt, CCFR, 458.

120. Sprunt, CCFR, 456; Ross, 233; Wise, 200; Carr, 178–200. Governor Vance continued until the end of the war to barrage Confederate officials—and probably anyone who would listen—with his accusations over the allotment of poor coal to the *Advance*. For a more complete discussion of the coal issue, see Stephen R. Wise's *Lifeline of the Confederacy*, 200–201.

121. Wise, 200.

122. The *Virginia* survived the war.

123. May 2, 1865. General Lee had surrendered on April 9, 1865, leaving much of the Southeastern seaboard under Yankee control.

124. For an account concerning the fall of Fort Fisher written by Colonel Lamb himself, see "Fort Fisher: The Battles Fought There in 1864 and '65," *Southern Historical Society Papers*, XXI (January to December, 1893): 255–290.

125. Admiral David Porter, an important Union strategist in the capture of Fort Fisher, declared: "The capture of the defenses of Wilmington closed the last door through which the Southern Confederacy received their supplies of clothing, arms and ammunition; therefore when Fort Fisher fell, it was only a matter of a short time when the rebellion would collapse. No matter how brave an enemy may be, or how well commanded, he must have provisions and military stores; and at this time General Lee had not enough materiel of war to last him three months!" Quoted in Cochran, 329. Actually many naval historians point out that had the Federals not overestimated the strength of many of the Southern coastal cities, these coastal ports could have been captured much earlier in the war and the fighting brought to an end much sooner.

126. June 7, 1865. William Woods Holden was appointed provisional governor of North Carolina on May 29, 1865, was elected governor in 1868, and was impeached and removed from office in 1871 as a result of partisan turmoil involving Republicans, Democrats and the Ku Klux Klan.

127. May 3, 1865.
128. June 1, 1865.
129. *The War of the Rebellion: A Compilation of the Official Records of the Union and Confederate Armies*, Series 4, Vol. 3 (Washington: Government Printing Office), 1117.
130. Manly Wade Wellman, *The County of Warren North Carolina 1586–1917* (Chapel Hill: The University of North Carolina Press, 1959), 172.
131. June 7, 1865.
132. Robert E. Lee, Jr., *My Father General Lee* (New York: Doubleday & Company, 1960), 390–92. Following their brief visit in Warrenton, General Lee and Agnes found future crowds of well wishers far less subdued. Train stops in Raleigh, Charlotte, Wilmington and Charleston in the Carolinas, Augusta and Savannah in Georgia, and Jacksonville in Florida drew huge throngs of admirers. Adoring crowds stood in a pouring rain for Lee's fifteen minute train stop in Columbia. Bands, parades, speeches, receptions, and enthusiastic repetitions of the Rebel yell shattered Lee's attempt to recover his failing health by way of a quiet, relaxing vacation from the responsibilities of college administration. Tiny tot namesakes replete with huge bouquets of flowers and proffering small cards thronged the station platforms; old ladies thrust their heads through the train cars' windows to gain a glimpse of their hero. Food was sent to the train in such a preponderance that Agnes surmised, "I think we were expected to die of eating." Not a few acknowledged, "The greatest event in our lives had occurred— we have seen General Lee." Lee, 392, 410.
133. Wellman and Montgomery.
134. Wellman, 159.
135. Wellman, 163.
136. Wise, 221.
137. Walter Clark, ed., *Histories of the Several Regiments and Battalions from North Carolina in the Great War 1861–'65*, Vol. 1 (Raleigh, North Carolina: Published by the State, 1901), 34–5; and Sprunt, SHSP, 158.
138. Clark, 36.
139. For an excellent and concise discussion of the fate of the blockade-running firms see Wise, 222–226.
140. Sprunt, CCFR, 431.
141. Wilkinson, 162–63.
142. Sprunt, CCFR, 431.
143. Cochran, 258.
144. Sprunt, CCFR, 450–51.
145. Henderson, 40.
146. Carr, 57.

147. Carse, 199.
148. For a more detailed account of Rose Greenhow see Ishbel Ross's *Rebel Rose: The Life of Rose O'Neal Greenhow, Confederate Spy* (New York: Harper and Brothers, 1954). For more information on Belle Boyd see Ruth Scarborough's *Belle Boyd: Siren of the South* (Macon, Georgia: Mercer University Press, 1983).
149. Vandiver, xli.
150. Pasha, 139.

Chapter Two

1. Joseph LeConte and Caroline LeConte, *'Ware Sherman: A Journal of Three Months' Personal Experience in the Last Days of the Confederacy* (Berkeley: University of California Press, 1938) and *The Autobiography of Joseph LeConte*, edited by William Dallam Armes (New York: D. Appleton and Company, 1903); Earl Schenck Miers, ed. *When the World Ended: The Journal of Emma LeConte* (New York: Oxford University Press, 1957).
2. Richard LeConte Anderson, *LeConte History and Genealogy*, Vol. 2 (Macon, Georgia: Richard LeConte Anderson, 1981).
3. In his postwar travels in the South, Sidney Andrews cut to the heart of the situation as he observed: "There is a certain air of easy dignity observable among the people [of Columbia] that I have not found elsewhere in the State, not even in Charleston itself." This he attributed to "the existence of Columbia College." He noted that although the College had been closed during the war, some of the buildings were now being occupied by the military authorities and "partly by the professors and officers of the college." For the residents of Columbia Andrews saw "nothing but the beginning anew of life, on the strictest personal economy and a small amount of money borrowed in the city. It would be a benefit of hundreds of millions of dollars if the North could be made to practice half the economy which poverty forces upon this people." Andrews concluded his report: "The spirit of oppression still exists, however, and military authority cannot be withdrawn till the relation between employer and employed is put upon a better basis. On the one hand, the negro in the country districts must be made to understand, what he has already been taught in the city, that freedom does

not mean idleness. On the other hand, the late master should specially be made to understand that the spirit of slavery must go to the grave with the thing itself. It will not be an easy work to teach either class its chief lesson. We must have patience—patience, and faith that neither faints nor falters." Sidney Andrews, *The South Since the War as Shown by Fourteen Weeks of Travel and Observations in Georgia and the Carolinas* (Boston: Ticknor and Fields, 1866), 33–37.

4. Joseph LeConte, *Autobiography*, 206.

5. Josephine Graham LeConte (Josie), Letter, C-B 1014, LeConte Family Papers: Additions, 1856–1916, Manuscripts Division, Bancroft Library, University of California, Berkeley, February 28, 1865.

6. Josie LeConte, Letter, February 28, 1865.

7. Louis Julian LeConte, with the Confederate forces outside Columbia, confessed to his mother that he had learned from several sources that the fires "were set by our own troops." Julian LeConte, Letter, BANC MSS 70/24, Additions, 1862–1928, LeConte Family Papers, Manuscripts Division, Bancroft Library, University of California, Berkeley, May 19, 1864.

8. Several eyewitnesses compared the blowing cotton to a snowstorm when at first wisps and then "snowballs" of white escaped from the bales abandoned in the streets as the Confederates beat their speedy retreat from the city. (Two years after the holocaust in Columbia, a number of sympathetic New York firemen set about raising money to send a top-of-the-line hose carriage to Columbia as a peace offering. One hundred and thirty-five years later, the people of Columbia, in gratitude for the generosity of New Yorkers during South Carolina's time of need, reciprocated by raising over five hundred thousand dollars to purchase a fire engine for New York City after the devastation of 9/11.)

9. Mary Tallulah "Lula" LeConte, Letter, BANC MSS, LeConte Family Papers, Additions, 1862–1928, Manuscripts Division, Bancroft Library, University of California, Berkeley.

10. Josie LeConte, Letter, February 28, 1865.

11. Lula LeConte, Letter, February 28, 1865.

12. Mrs. Campbell Bryce, *The Personal Experiences of Mrs. Campbell Bryce During the Burning of Columbia, South Carolina by General W. T. Sherman's Army, February 17, 1865* (Philadelphia: Lippincott Press, 1899), 42–43.

13. Marion Brunson Lucas, *Sherman and the Burning of Columbia* (College Station: Texas A&M University Press, 1976), 110–11.

14. Bryce, 23.

15. Josie LeConte, Letter, February 28, 1865.

16. Josie LeConte, Letter, February 28, 1865.

17. Josie LeConte, Letter, February 28, 1865.

18. Josie LeConte, Letter, February 28, 1865.

19. Lillian Adele Kibler, *Benjamin F. Perry: South Carolina Unionist* (Durham, North Carolina: Duke University Press, 1946), 372.

20. Joseph LeConte, '*Ware Sherman*, xv.

21. Josie LeConte, Letter, February 28, 1865.

22. Lula LeConte, Letter, February 28, 1865.

23. Lula LeConte, Letter, February 28, 1865.

24. Josie LeConte, Letter, February 28, 1865.

25. Lula LeConte, Letter, February 28, 1865.

26. Andrews, 32–35.

27. John T. Trowbridge, *Picture of the Desolated South and the Work of Reconstruction 1865–1868* (Hartford, Connecticut: LeConte Stebbins, 1868), 563.

28. Trowbridge, 564. See also a portion of William Gilmore Simms's account of the Columbia fire in Richard B. Harwell, ed., *The Confederate Reader* (New York: Longmans, Green and Co., 1957), 346–359. For a discussion of the newspaper accounts of the fires and thefts in Columbia, see J. Cutler Andrews, *The South Reports the War* (Princeton, New Jersey: Princeton University Press, 1970), 490–496.

29. Francis Butler Simkins and Robert Hilliard Woody, *South Carolina During Reconstruction* (Chapel Hill: The University of North Carolina Press, 1932), 5.

30. Emma LeConte, 74.

31. Josie LeConte, Letter, February 28, 1865.

32. Josie LeConte, Letter, February 28, 1865.

33. Trowbridge, 568.

34. Lula LeConte, Letter, February 28, 1865.

35. Details of Joseph LeConte's escape can be found in his *Autobiography*, 206–225, and *'Ware Sherman*, 82–144.

36. Joseph LeConte, *Autobiography*, 225.

37. The new magazine, *The Nation*, in July of 1865 dispatched Northerner John Richard Dennett on a tour of the South for the purpose of objectively depicting "The South as It Is" in a series of articles for the magazine. His observations during his visit to Columbia merely underscored the LeContes' gloomy picture of the town and corroborated the shocking details of fellow journalist Sidney Andrews's report. Richmond and Charleston, according to Dennett, had suffered far less destruction than Columbia. "The city is, indeed, a melancholy sight.... In Columbia one is everywhere surrounded by ruins and silent desolation. Of the former great beauty of the city only so much remains as to cause one to regret the more that the work of destruction was so complete." The formerly beautiful tree-lined streets, he reported, had become wide swaths of devastation, bounded only by dead tree trunks and sentineled by black chimneys. "The hatred of the Northern people, which makes itself manifest more or less distinctly in nearly every Southern community, the Northern visitor is better able to bear with in Columbia than elsewhere. It need be so, for in no other city that I have visited has hostility seemed to me so bitter." John Richard Dennett, ed., *The South as It Is: 1865–1866* (New York: The Viking Press, 1965), 230. For more information on Sherman's troops in Columbia, see Burke Davis, *Sherman's March* (New York: Vintage Books, 1988), 156–184, and Lucas, *passim*.

38. Emma LeConte, 74.

39. LeConte relatives believe the all-important manuscript of Josie's husband's book was also destroyed in the firing of the supply wagons.

40. Emma LeConte, 79.

41. Josie LeConte, Letter, February 28, 1865.

42. Emma LeConte, 41.

43. Emma LeConte, 98.

44. Emma LeConte, 98–99.

45. Emma LeConte, 103.

46. Emma LeConte, 100–101.

47. Emma LeConte, 113.

48. Emma LeConte, 101.

49. Joseph LeConte, *Autobiography*, 236.

50. Caroline LeConte, *'Ware Sherman*, xvi.

51. Edwin LeConte Green, *A History of the University of South Carolina* (Columbia, South Carolina: The State Company, 1916), 400.

52. Charles Woodward Hutson in Green, 402.

53. Josie LeConte, Letters, C-B 1014 in LeConte Family Papers: Additions, 1856–1916, Bancroft Library, University of California, Berkeley, January 14, 1867, and April 29, 1867.

54. Dolly Dill, Letter, BANC MSS, LeConte Family Papers: Additions, 1862–1928, Manuscripts Division, Bancroft Library, University of California, Berkeley. November 10, 1865.

55. Caroline LeConte, *'Ware Sherman*, xvi.

56. Caroline LeConte, *'Ware Sherman*, xvi.

57. Josie LeConte, Letter, C-B 1014, LeConte Family Papers: Additions, 1856–1916, Bancroft Library, University of California, Berkeley, February 29, 1866.

58. At the end of the war, Mollie was able to return to the North.

59. Josie LeConte, Letter, C-B 1014, LeConte Family Papers: Additions, 1856–1916, Bancroft Library, University of California, Berkeley, February 4, 1866. Although it appears the date of the February 4 letter is 1864, it must had been careless penmanship—or the inability of readers to decipher Josie's numerals. The contents of the letter belie the date of 1864. Even 1865 would have been incorrect for Sherman and his troops did not appear in Columbia until February 17, of 1865. The contents of the letter indicate a date of 1866, and that date will be used throughout this chapter.

60. Emma LeConte, 107.

61. Emma LeConte names Hartwell; however, Lester Stephens credits Colonel Nathaniel Haughton, commandant of the garrison, with approaching Emma's father.

62. Emma LeConte, 112.

63. Josie LeConte, Letter, February 4, 1866.

64. Josie LeConte, Letter, C-B 1014, LeConte Family Papers: Additions 1856–1916, Bancroft Library, University of California, Berkeley, January 2, 1866.

65. Josie LeConte, Letter, January 2, 1866.

66. Josie LeConte, Letter, February 4, 1866.

67. Josie LeConte, Letter, C-B 1014, LeConte Family Papers: Additions, 1856–1916, Bancroft Library, University of California, Berkeley, December 4, 1865.

68. Josie LeConte, Letter, August 23, 1865.

69. Josie LeConte, Letter, January 2, 1866.

70. Josie LeConte, Letter, C-B 1014, LeConte Family Papers: Additions, 1856–1916, Bancroft Library, University of California, Berkeley, August 23, 1865.

71. Josie LeConte, Letter, August 23, 1865.

72. Emma LeConte, 117–118.

73. Emma LeConte, 117–118.

74. Josie LeConte, Letter, December 4, 1865.

75. Mary A. Graham (Mollie), Letter, C-B 70/24, LeConte Family Papers: Additions, 1862–1928, Manuscripts Division, Bancroft Library, University of California, May 19, 1867.

76. Graham, Letter, May 19, 1867.

77. Graham, Letter, May19, 1867.

78. Josie LeConte, Letter, C-B 1014, LeConte Family Papers: Additions 1856–1916, Bancroft Library, University of California, April 29, 1867.

79. Josie LeConte, Letter, January 2, 1866.

80. Joseph LeConte, *Autobiography*, 230.

81. Kibler, 391.

82. Simkins and Woody, 269. For more information on Reconstruction and its problems for Southern women, see Marilyn Mayer Culpepper, *All Things Altered: Women in the Wake of Civil War and Reconstruction* (Jefferson, North Carolina: McFarland & Company, Inc., Publishers, 2002).

83. Josie LeConte, Letter, C-B 1014, LeConte Family Papers: Additions, 1856–1916, Bancroft Library, University of California, Berkeley, September 17, 1865. Josie was correct in calling Benjamin Perry a Union man. Although a native of South Carolina, Perry held out against secession until finally giving in to the will of his fellow South Carolinians. Conceding defeat, he reluctantly declared, "You are all going to the devil, and I will go with you." Following the war Perry was famous for his attempts to create a peaceful merging of unreconstructed Southerners and zealous Northern radicals. Other important Unionists included James Petigru of South Carolina, Sam Houston of Texas, and William L. Sharkey and James L. Alcorn of Mississippi.

84. Kibler, 410.

85. *Chicago Tribune*, July 22, 1865.

86. Josie LeConte, Letter, September 17, 1865. For more details see Kibler, Chapter 21.

87. John William De Forest, *A Union Officer in the Reconstruction* (New Haven: Yale University Press, 1948), ix.

88. Josie LeConte, Letter, September 17, 1865. Particularly offensive to white Southerners were the colored troops of occupation. In response to the unending complaints of South Carolinians about the presence of the colored troops of occupation, Governor Perry begged Seward to remove the troops, insisting that the "troops are a great nuisance & that they do infinite mischief with the Freedmen.... They tell them that the lands are to be divided, that they are not to work for their employers, & that the white race is to be driven out of the Country or exterminated." Kibler, 400–401. William Gilmore Simms expressed his exasperation with the troops in the *Phoenix:* "For what good purpose these troops are kept in the country and scattered over it, it would be difficult to say. If a process were particularly required, for defeating all the hopes of the experiment at converting slave into free labor, and for driving the white population to madness, no better one could be devised." Kibler, 400–401.

89. Joseph LeConte, *Autobiography*, 236–7.

90. Josie LeConte, Letter, January 2, 1866. Adelbert Ames commanded the District of Western South Carolina from September 5, 1865, to April 30, 1866. He was named provisional governor of Mississippi on July 15, 1865, was a senator from Mississippi, and was elected governor in 1873. Nathaniel Haughton was commandant of the garrison of the troops of occupation.

91. Dill, November 10, 1865, and May 28, 1866.

92. Emma LeConte, 106.

93. Emma LeConte, 108–109.

94. Emma LeConte, 102.

95. Josie LeConte, Letter, January 2, 1866.

96. Josie, LeConte, Letter, February 4, 1866.

97. Josie LeConte, Letter, February 4, 1866.

98. Josie LeConte, Letter, February 4, 1866.

99. Josie LeConte, Letter, February 4, 1866.

100. Josie LeConte, Letter, February 4, 1866.

101. Josie LeConte, Letter, C-B 1014,

LeConte Family Papers: Additions, 1856–1916 Bancroft Library, University of California, Berkley, April 29, 1876.

102. Josie LeConte, Undated letter to Mollie, C-B 1014, LeConte Family Papers: Additions, 1856–1916, Bancroft Library, University of California, Berkeley.

103. Carpetbaggers were Northerners who came South with their carpetbags seeking political and economic gain. Many were adventurers who sought to make a killing raising cotton and then turned their attention to politics when their cotton fields failed to produce the riches they had envisioned. Native Southerners who allied themselves with the Radicals against their section and race gained an invidious reputation as "scalawags."

104. Josie LeConte, Letter, February 4, 1866.

105. Josie LeConte, Letter, C-B 1014, LeConte Family Papers: Additions, 1856–1916, Bancroft Library, University of California, Berkeley, November 22, 1865.

106. Josie LeConte, Letter, February 4, 1866.

107. Josie LeConte, Letter, August 23, 1865.

108. Josie LeConte, Letter, February 28, 1865.

109. Josie LeConte, Letter, C-B 1014, LeConte Family Papers: Additions, 1856–1916, Bancroft Library, University of California, Berkeley, July 14, 1865.

110. For further details on the wartime ravages of the property of John and Joseph LeConte in Liberty County, Georgia, see Lucinda H. MacKethan, ed., *Recollections of a Southern Daughter: A Memoir by Cornelia Jones Pond of Liberty County* (Athens: The University of Georgia Press, 1998), 71–79. Cornelia Jones Pond was a relative of the LeConte brothers and their sister Jane LeConte Harden. In several passages Cornelia refers to Joseph LeConte's harrowing trip to Georgia in December and January of 1864–65 to rescue his widowed sister, her two daughters and his own fourteen year old daughter, Sallie, from the devastation being wrought by Sherman's march to the sea. See Joseph LeConte's engrossing details of the experience in the early pages of '*Ware Sherman.*

111. Josie LeConte, Letter, July 14, 1865.

112. Josie LeConte, Letter, July 14, 1865.

113. R. Gage, Letter, BANC MSS 70/24, LeConte Family Papers: Additions, 1862–1928, Manuscripts Division, Bancroft Library, University of California at Berkley, February 14, 1867.

114. Gage, Letter.

115. Josie LeConte, Letter, January 2, 1866.

116. Jane Harden, Letter, BANC MSS 70/24, LeConte Family Papers: Additions, 1862–1928, Manuscripts Division, Bancroft Library, University of California at Berkeley. October 26, 1865. For more information about the LeConte Liberty County property, see Michael Golay, *A Ruined Land:The End of the Civil War* (New York: John Wiley & Sons, Inc., 1999).

117. Harden, Letter, BANC MSS 70/24, LeConte Family Papers: Additions 1862–1928, Manuscripts Division, Bancroft Library, University of California, Berkeley, December 13, 1865.

118. Harden, Letter, December 13, 1865. An interesting account of some of the female residents of Liberty County, Georgia, and their confrontations with the Federals may be found in Mary Sharpe Jones and Mary Jones Mallard, "Yankees A'Coming: One Month's Experience During the Invasion of Liberty-County, Georgia, 1864–1865," *Confederate Centennial Studies*, 12 (Tuscaloosa, Alabama: Confederate Publishing Company, 1959).

119. Harden, Letter, December 13, 1865.

120. Harden, Letter, December 13, 1865.

121. Harden, Letters, and Stephens, 94–96.

122. Josie LeConte, Letter, August 23, 1865.

123. Josie LeConte, Letter, January 2, 1866.

124. Josie LeConte, Letter, February 4, 1866.

125. Josie LeConte, Letter, April 29, 1867.

126. Josie LeConte, Letter, August 23, 1867.

127. Josie LeConte, Letter, July 14, 1865.

128. Josie LeConte, Letter, August 23, 1865.

129. Josie LeConte, Letter, August 23, 1865.

130. Dill, Letter, BANC 70/24 LeConte Family Papers: Additions, 1862–1928, Bancroft Library, University of California, Berkeley, July 31, 1866. How right both men were, for this was the setting for the July 30 New Orleans riots which resulted in the deaths of thirty-four blacks and three (some accounts noted four) whites with injuries to

more than one hundred people. Dolly also provided a vivid description of the riots observed from the vantage point of their house directly in front of Lafayette Square. For more information on the New Orleans and Memphis riots, see Eric Foner, *A Short History of Reconstruction 1863–1877* (New York: Harper & Row, Publishers, 1990), 261–263; Patrick W. Riddleberger, *1866: The Critical Year Revisited* (Carbondale: Southern Illinois University Press, 1979), 177–201; and George C. Rable, *But There Was No Peace: The Role of Violence in the Politics of Reconstruction* (Athens: The University of Georgia Press, 1984).

131. Emma LeConte, 112.

132. Josie LeConte, Letter, January 2, 1866.

133. Josie LeConte, Letter, January 2, 1877.

134. Emma LeConte, 115.

135. Josie LeConte, Letter, August 23, 1865.

136. Josie LeConte, Letter, C-B 1014, LeConte Family Papers: Additions, 1856–1916, Bancroft Library, University of California, Berkeley, May 27, 1867.

137. Josie LeConte, Letter, January 2, 1866.

138. The Freedmen's Bureau, created by Congress during the last months of the war as the Bureau of Refugees, Freedmen, and Abandoned Lands, was designed to help blacks (and white refugees) by providing food, clothing, medical care, possible resettlement and schooling. The life of the Bureau was extended over President Johnson's veto in February of 1866.

139. De Forest, xvi.

140. De Forest, xviii.

141. Josie LeConte, Letter, February 4, 1866.

142. Josie LeConte, Letter, February 4, 1866.

143. General Ralph Ely was the assistant commissioner of the Freedmen's Bureau in South Carolina and was assigned supervision over fifteen districts in the northern part of the state. He was very nearly court-martialed on the grounds of incompetence.

144. Dill, Letter, November 10, 1865.

145. For an interesting analysis of the subject of loyalty oaths, see "Oaths, Amnesties and Rebellion" in *Debow's Review* (January–June 1866): 283–303, and Harold Melvin Hyman, *Era of the Oath: Northern Loyalty Tests During the Civil War and Reconstruction* (Philadelphia: University of Pennsylvania Press, 1954).

146. Josie LeConte, Letter, April 29, 1867.

147. Emma LeConte, 107–108. Some of these laws were later declared unconstitutional. Also it should be noted that in some areas the signing of the Loyalty Oath by former Confederates was mandatory, while in other areas the requirement was casually observed or even overlooked. In 1868 general amnesty was granted for all. Some men by virtue of their property holdings or their rank or service to the Confederacy had earlier been excluded from amnesty. According to Josie's letters there were job offers for her husband, but those would have required his taking the Iron Clad Oath: "Of course it was impossible for any true Southern man to think of taking it...." Josie LeConte, Letter, May 27, 1867. It would seem there was no other choice, however, for Josie's husband, but to take the less demanding Loyalty Oath.

148. Emma LeConte, 110–111.

149. Helen Kohn Henning, ed., *Columbia: Capital City of South Carolina 1786–1936* (Columbia, South Carolina: The State-Record Company, 1966), 31–32. For more information about the "Great Bazaar" and its purposes, see the circulars enlisting contributions of everything from bales of cotton, to preserves and handiwork in Harwell, 327–330, and in the South Carolina newspapers.

150. Emma LeConte, 12–13.

151. Josie LeConte, Letter, C-B 1014, LeConte Family Papers: Additions, 1856–1916, Bancroft Library, University of California, Berkeley, December 11, 1866.

152. Josie LeConte, Letter, December 11, 1866.

153. Josie LeConte, Letter, C-B 1014, Additions, 1856–1916, LeConte Family Papers: Additions, 1956–1916, Bancroft Library, University of California, Berkeley, September 30, 1867.

154. Emma LeConte, 107–110.

155. Josie LeConte, Letter, August 23, 1865.

156. Josie LeConte, Letter, August 23, 1865.

157. Trowbridge, 564.

158. Daniel Walker Hollis, *University of South Carolina: College to University*, Vol. 2 (Columbia: University of South Carolina Press, 1956), 21.

159. Hollis, 19–21.

160. Josie LeConte, Letter, January 2, 1866.

161. Requests for much needed repair work on the faculty houses were

ignored in favor of more pressing needs, and professors had to pay for improvements out of their own pockets. The LeConte home was the newest (completed in 1860) and apparently the most comfortable faculty home; however, in 1866 the contractor began pressing for remuneration for the $3,000 still owing him from before the war. Hollis, 25.

162. Green, 83–93; Hollis, 25–43.

163. One veteran years later acknowledged, "There were very few verdant greenhorns among us…. There were a number of boys who had only one arm, some were on crutches with only one leg, while a large number had been seriously or slightly wounded. And some had languished for months in prison. The experiences through which many of us had passed gave us a decided advantage over the ordinary greenhorn we nowadays find at College." Green, 402–403.

164. Hollis, 45.

165. Joseph LeConte, *Autobiography*, 239.

166. John S. Reynolds, *Reconstruction in South Carolina* (Columbia, South Carolina: The State Company, 1905), 237, and Simkins and Woody, 441.

167. Josie LeConte, Letter, February 4, 1866.

168. Josie LeConte, Letter, C-B 1014, LeConte Family Papers: Additions, 1856–1916, Bancroft Library, University of California, Berkeley, March 16, 1867.

169. Hollis, 41 and 25–28.

170. Joseph LeConte, *Autobiography*, 237–238.

171. Other Southern colleges suffered from many of the same problems that rocked South Carolina College. On April 26, 1861, the University Greys, a company made up of most of the student body of the University of Mississippi, was mustered into the Confederate service. In short order, all but five of the students had also left the campus, and that group was hourly expected to leave. Thinking the war would be of short duration, the officials attempted to open school in September of 1861. Four students appeared for classes, and the University closed for the duration. A single blank page representing the four-year-and-eight-day interval between the faculty minutes that concluded on September 18, 1861, and resumed on September 26, 1865, marked the Civil War period at the University of Mississippi. Chancellor Barnard and five professors resigned. The professor of chemistry was dismissed because of

his Northern sympathies, and the remaining three chairs were declared vacant. (Following Barnard's resignation he traveled to Norfolk and then on to Washington, D.C., where he openly professed his Union sympathies. In 1864 Columbia College in New York City selected Barnard as their new president. In recognition for his accomplishments during his presidency, which lasted for over a quarter of a century, Barnard College, Columbia's "sister" college across the street, was named in his honor.)

As was true of South Carolina College, several of the buildings at the University of Mississippi were used as hospitals during the war. Following the war, professors were appointed, and in the 1865-1866 session ninety-three students, many wearing remnants of their CSA uniforms (most of them had served with the Confederate army—their professors also), were enrolled at the University. Special instruction was provided for students who were ill prepared for college as a result of the interruption of their earlier education by the war, a burden which necessitated increased teaching loads for the faculty. Allen Cabaniss, *The University of Mississippi: Its First Hundred Years* (Hattiesburg: University & College Press of Mississippi, 1971), *passim*, and John K. Bettersworth, ed., *Mississippi in the Confederacy: As They Saw It* (Baton Rouge: Louisiana State University Press, 1961), 333–334.

In 1865 Louisiana State Seminary (renamed Louisiana State University in 1870) bravely reopened its doors to a student body of four. (See reports of the hardships of that University's professors and president in Walter LeConte Fleming, *Documentary History of Reconstruction: Political, Military, Social, Religious, Educational, and Industrial 1865 to 1906*, Vol. 2 (New York: McGraw-Hill Book Company, 1966), 199–202. The University of Georgia resumed classes in January of 1866. In North Carolina the university was taken over by the Radicals in 1868, and the student body dwindled to so few students that the university was closed for five years. E. Merton Coulter, *A History of the South*, Vol. 8 (Baton Rouge: Louisiana State University Press, 1947), 319–320.

172. Josie LeConte, Letter, C-B 1014, LeConte Family Papers: Additions, 1856–1916, Bancroft Library, University of California, Berkeley, December 17 (?), 1866.

173. Emma LeConte, 110.

174. Josie LeConte, Letter, September 30, 1867.

175. Josie LeConte, Letter, August 23, 1865.

176. Josie LeConte, Letter, January 2, 1866.

177. Josie LeConte, Letter, February 4, 1866.

178. Josie LeConte, Letter, February 4, 1866.

179. Josie LeConte, Letter, February 4, 1966.

180. Josie LeConte, Letter, February 4, 1866.

181. "The American Colony in Mexico," *De Bow's Review*, Vol. 1 After the War Series (January–June 1866), 623–630.

182. Josie LeConte, Letter, February 4, 1866.

183. Emma LeConte, 107–108.

184. Stephens, 104–105.

185. Andrew F. Rolle, *The Lost Cause: The Confederate Exodus to Mexico* (Norman: University of Oklahoma Press, 1965), 131–144. By the spring of 1867 the Cordova colony was "a thing of the past," its demise carefully recaptured in Rolle's book.

186. Caroline LeConte, '*Ware Sherman*, xvii.

187. Caroline LeConte, '*Ware Sherman*, xvii.

188. Caroline LeConte, '*Ware Sherman*, xx.

189. Caroline LeConte, '*Ware Sherman*, xix.

190. Caroline LeConte, '*Ware Sherman*, xx.

191. Josie was told by Mrs. Barton Alexander that "if it had not been for the deep anguish of my letters [Josie's] to the General that worked upon his sympathies *so that he could not refuse* we might still have been in Carolina but that he could not resist *my* appeal." Barton Alexander, C-B 1014, LeConte Family Papers: Additions, 1856–1916, Bancroft Library, University of California, Berkeley, June 20, 1869. (Barton Stone Alexander, 1819–1878, U.S. Military Academy graduate, brevetted General in U.S. Army, 1865.)

192. Caroline LeConte, '*Ware Sherman*, xxv.

193. Caroline LeConte, '*Ware Sherman*, xxvii.

194. Josie LeConte, Letter, C-B 1014, LeConte Family Papers: Additions, 1856–1916, Bancroft Library, University of California, Berkeley, May 9, 1869.

195. Josie LeConte, Letter, May 9, 1869.

196. Caroline LeConte, '*Ware Sherman*, xxviii.

197. Caroline LeConte, '*Ware Sherman*, xxix.

198. Joseph LeConte, "Biographical Memoir of John LeConte, 1818–1891," in *Biographical Memoirs, National Academy of Sciences*, 3 (1895), 371–393.

199. Anderson, 906.

200. Caroline LeConte, '*Ware Sherman*, xxx.

201. Stephens, 206.

202. Stephens, 42.

203. W. LeConte Stevens, "Sketch of Prof. John LeConte," *The Popular Science Monthly*, Vol. 36 (November 1889–April 1890), 114.

204. Joseph LeConte, Memoir, 375.

Chapter Three

1. For a concise discussion of Missouri's divided citizenry, see James M. McPherson, *Battle Cry of Freedom: The Civil War Era* (New York: Ballantine Books, 1988), 290–293.

2. Michael Fellman, *Inside War:The Guerrilla Conflict in Missouri During the American Civil War* (New York: Oxford University Press, 1989), xvi.

3. McPherson, 292.

4. James C. Neagles, *Confederate Research Sources: A Guide to Archive Collections* (Salt Lake City: Ancestry Publishing, 1986), 200, and Shelby Foote, *The Civil War: A Narrative: Fort Sumter to Perryville* (New York: Random House, 1958), 53–54.

5. McPherson, 291–3, and Neagles, 200–3. Actually Jackson, after departing Jefferson City, set up a pro-southern legislature at Neosho, on the state's southwestern border, which despite lacking a quorum passed an ordinance of secession. On November 28 the Confederate Congress welcomed Missouri into the Confederacy, and senators and representatives were dispatched to Richmond. Shortly thereafter, however, the Jackson government was forced out of Missouri. McPherson, 293, and Ralph R. Rea, *Sterling Price: The Lee of the West* (Little Rock, Arkansas: Pioneer Press, 1959), 62–3.

6. Neagles, 203, and McPherson, 293.

7. Boonville, Missouri, was apparently named in honor of Daniel Boone.

8. Nancy Chapman Jones's letters to her daughter, Mary, constitute the framework for this chapter. The letters are

held by Nancy's great, great granddaughter and namesake, Nancy Simmons Berger, of Dimondale, Michigan, and are used with her permission. Additional information has been obtained from a family history written by Nancy Jones's grandson, William J. McCarthy, which is also held by Nancy Simmons Berger. In this manuscript the dated endnotes, unless otherwise specified, refer to Nancy Chapman Jones's letters to her daughter.

9. May 4, 1861. Justin McCarthy is mentioned frequently in the early pages of the James Fremantle diary (written by the Englishman during his three months' visit to the Southland in 1863.) The two men were traveling companions on a journey from Brownsville, Texas, to Justin and Mary's home in San Antonio. During the three week trip the two men became fast friends as Justin volunteered to squire the Englishman through the south of Texas. Apparently Fremantle (as well as Mary) found Justin most personable, for as Fremantle left for Houston, he wrote, "To my extreme regret, I took leave of my friend Mc'Carthy this evening whose hospitality and kindness I shall never forget." As he piloted the English visitor around San Antonio, Justin pointed out his store, "which is a very large building but now desolate, everything having been sold off." While in San Antonio, Fremantle also met Mary, and noted: "Mrs. M'Carthy was thrown into a great state of agitation and delight by receiving a letter from her mother, who is in Yankeedom. Texas is so cut off that she only hears once in many months." For more information about Justin and his business, see Walter Lord, ed., *The Fremantle Diary: Being the Journal of Lieutenant Colonel James Arthur Lyon Fremantle, Coldstream Guards on His Three Months in the Southern States* (Boston: Little Brown and Company, 1954), 5–45.

10. Fellman, 201.

11. George Graham Vest was a law partner of Nancy and Caleb's son-in-law, William Muir, and James Wellington Draffen. Vest served in the Confederate Congress and later in the United States Congress.

12. April 22, 1861.

13. May 4, 1861.

14. May 20, 1861.

15. Brigadier General Nathaniel Lyon, according to Shelby Foote, was "A hard-bitten, capable New Englander, forty-three years old, well acquainted with violence and well adapted for countering that par-

ticular brand of it being met with in Missouri." Foote, 91.

16. August 25, 1861.

17. May 20, 1861.

18. August 27, 1861.

19. March 27, 1861.

20. December 11, 1863.

21. May 27, 1861.

22. June 25, 1861.

23. October 3, 1861.

24. June 14, 1861.

25. Confederate Major General Sterling Price, known as "Old Pap" to his men, was fifty-two years old and a veteran of the Mexican war.

26. McPherson, *Battle Cry*, 292.

27. May 20, 1861.

28. See McPherson, Foote, or Rea for a more detailed description of the St. Louis action.

29. June 25, 1861.

30. June 25, 1861.

31. Historians disagree somewhat on the number of casualties. Some report two dead on each side, while other reports dismiss exact figures, merely noting "minimal losses" for both sides.

32. June 25, 1861.

33. *Harper's Weekly* reported that fifty rebels had died in the encounter. In one account *Harper's* stated that "Lyon once had State troops in a position where he could have mowed them down with terrible effect, but that he ordered the firing to stop just at that time and proceeded to make prisoners." After the battle, General Lyon issued a proclamation (carried in *Harper's*) in which he assured the people of Missouri that "his mission is not to invade their private rights as citizens or to interfere with their business occupations, and he implores all loyal citizens to return to their ordinary avocations in which they shall be protected." The eighty men and boys who were taken prisoners, he said, were mostly youths who admitted they were confused and misled and were released. "He reminds the people, however," *Harper's* pointed out, "that the clemency of the Government can not be too far relied upon in the case of persons taken in array against its authority" (July 6, 1861).

34. June 25, 1861.

35. June 25, 1861.

36. June 25, 1861.

37. July 11, 1861.

38. July 11, 1861.

39. June 25, 1861.

40. July 11, 1861.

41. August 25, 1861. Five days later all of Missouri was declared under martial law by General John Frémont, the Federal commander at St. Louis.
42. August 25, 1861.
43. August 25, 1861.
44. August 25, 1861.
45. Francis P. Blair, Jr., son of a Lincoln adviser and brother of the U.S. Postmaster General, was intricately tied to the Lyon operations.
46. June 25, 1861.
47. May 20, 1861.
48. April 22, 1862.
49. May 11, 1861.
50. June 25, 1861.
51. Fellman, 95.
52. October 3, 1861.
53. October 16, 1862.
54. July 11, 1861.
55. July 11, 1861.
56. April 13, 1863.
57. March 6, 1862.
58. June 25, 1861.
59. October 3, 1861.
60. Fellman, 199–200.
61. October 3, 1861.
62. March 6, 1862.
63. April 22, 1862.
64. October 16, 1862.
65. April 22, 1862.
66. October 16, 1862.
67. McPherson, 786; Fellman, 95; Neagles, 203.
68. Missouri Division, United Daughters of the Confederacy, *Reminiscences of the Women of Missouri During the Sixties* (Jefferson City: The Hugh Stephens Printing Company, 1920), 263.
69. Brigadier General Thomas Ewing was Commander of the District of St. Louis and also Sherman's brother-in-law.
70. May 27, 1861.
71. July 11, 1861.
72. August 25, 1861.
73. November 12, 1861.
74. August 25, 1861.
75. December 11, 1863.
76. December 11, 1863.
77. December 11, 1863.
78. December 11, 1863.
79. April 1, 1865.
80. Fellman, 101.
81. General Henry Wagner Halleck was General-in-Chief of all the armies of the North for two years before Grant was appointed Supreme Commander, in March 1864, at which time Halleck was given the position of Chief-of-Staff.
82. In 1864 the State Constitution of Missouri required that "No person shall practice law, be competent as bishop, priest, deacon, minister, elder, or other clergyman of any religious persuasion, sect, or denomination, teach, preach, or solemnize marriage until such person shall have first taken the oath required as to voters."
83. Martra Lockett Avary, *Dixie After the War* (Boston: Houghton Mifflin Company, 1937), 127, but also see Hilary A. Herbert *et al.*, *Why the Solid South? Or Reconstruction and Its Results* (Baltimore: R. H. Woodward & Company, 1890), 287.
84. March 27, 1862.
85. April 22, 1862. Even months earlier Nancy and her fellow Missourians must have read the handwriting on the wall when John C. Frémont, appointed by Lincoln as Commander of the Western Department, had taken it upon himself to issue a proclamation in August of 1861 that "freed the slaves of all Confederate activists in Missouri." This rash act of emancipation so angered President Lincoln that he revoked Frémont's order and removed General Frémont from his command.
86. December 11, 1863.
87. May 11, 1861. It is interesting to note that Ann, despite being a slave, had been taught to read and write.
88. July 11, 1861.
89. Undated letter.
90. April 6, 1861.
91. April 6, 1861.
92. April 6, 1861.
93. April 22, 1861.
94. August 25, 1861.
95. March 27, 1862.
96. October 16, 1862.
97. June 14, 1861.
98. March 6, 1862.
99. October 16, 1862.
100. March 27, 1862.
101. April 1, 1865.
102. May 17, 1861.
103. July 11, 1861.
104. July 11, 1861.
105. May 20, 1861.
106. May 4, 1861.
107. April 22, 1862.
108. March 9. 1863.
109. May 11, 1861.
110. October 3, 1861.
111. October 3, 1861.
112. October 3, 1861.
113. November 12, 1861.
114. March 27, 1862.
115. March 6, 1862.

116. May 18, 1863.
117. March 6, 1862.
118. March 27, 1862.
119. March 27, 1862.
120. April 13, 1863.
121. April 13, 1863.
122. July 11, 1861.
123. March 27, 1862.
124. March 27, 1862.
125. May 27, 1861.
126. May 11, 1861.
127. May 18, 1863.
128. October 3, 1861.
129. April 6, 1861.
130. May 18, 1863.
131. June 23, 1865.
132. April 1, 1865.
133. May 11, 1861.
134. April 22, 1861.
135. April 22, 1861.
136. March 27, 1862.
137. October 16, 1862.
138. March 6, 1862.
139. September 21, 1864.
140. April 1, 1865.
141. September 21, 1864.
142. September 21, 1864.
143. Mexico was a popular destination for hundreds of frightened, apprehensive Missourians. In the "Incomplete and Tentative List of Confederate Immigrants Going to Mexico in 1865 and 1866," found in W. C. Nunn's *Escape from Reconstruction*, some fifty of the 257 names included were from Missouri, including two former U.S. senators and two Confederate generals. In addition, scores of names were listed without identifying a home state. W. C. Nunn, *Escape from Reconstruction* (Westport, Conn.: Greenwood Press, 1956. Reprint), 129–136.
144. September 21, 1864.
145. Earlier, Caleb had sold his farm and home, "Waverly," to a Mr. Brown; however, when Mr. Brown wished to pay off in greenbacks the fifty-five hundred he still owed, Caleb took back the farm (March 1863).
146. September 21, 1864.
147. June 23, 1865.
148. June 23, 1865.
149. In 1877 Mary entered Willie at Notre Dame. Later, Willie toured the country as an actor, and in 1927 took a position with the Western and Southern Life Insurance Company. Caleb Jones died in 1883. Nancy Jones died in 1878.

Chapter Four

1. Sarah Dandridge (Cooke) Duval, "Recollections of 1864," found in The Virginia Historical Society, Richmond, Virginia, 7. Excerpts are used thanks to permission from the Virginia Historical Society.
2. Page 7.
3. Page 9.
4. Page 9.
5. Page 10.
6. Page 11.
7. Page 12.
8. Pages 13–15.
9. Page 15.
10. Page 17.
11. Pierre Gustave Toutant Beauregard, Confederate Army general. In the spring of 1864 he halted a Union advance on Richmond and held off Northern attacks on Petersburg in June.
12. George E. Pickett, a CSA general, a veteran of the Mexican war, was part of the Gettysburg disaster, and served under Lee in the Petersburg campaign.
13. Benjamin Franklin Butler, a Union general, was made military governor of New Orleans when the city fell. In the spring of 1864 he failed in his assignment to cut the railroad lines between Richmond and Petersburg and attack Richmond. His force was stymied in May in the Bermuda Hundred peninsulas.
14. Pages 17–18.
15. Pages 18–19.
16. Pages 19–20.
17. Pages 19–21.
18. Libby Prison for captured Northern soldiers in Richmond, Virginia.
19. Pages 21–22.
20. Pages 23–25.
21. Page 25. Sallie was referring to the Battle of the Crater where Union forces dug a huge tunnel under the enemy. The explosion proved a fiasco and constituted a great loss of lives.
22. There is little additional information about Sallie Duval. The December 15, 1887, issue of the *Richmond Dispatch* noted that she died in Lexington, at the age of 61, on December 14, 1887, and that the funeral would be held at Hollywood Cemetery in Richmond on the evening of December 15.

Chapter Five

1. Mary Greenhow Lee (Mrs. Hugh), Diary, manuscript found in the

Stewart Bell Jr. Archives Room, Handley Regional Library, Winchester, Virginia, 454 and 444. It should be noted that Mary Lee's diary is some 900 pages long, and the selections chosen for this chapter constitute only a very small portion of her diary.

2. Laura Lee, "The History of Our Captivity" Diary, March 1862 to April 1865, is located in the Manuscripts and Rare Books Department, Swem Library, College of William and Mary, Williamsburg, Virginia. A photocopy is found in the Stewart Bell Jr. Archives Room, Handley Regional Library, Winchester, Virginia.

3. Mary's half-brother, Robert Greenhow, Jr., had married Rose O'Neal, who following her husband's death became famous for her Confederate espionage activities. Known as "Rebel Rose," Rose Greenhow was imprisoned as a spy and was sent through the lines to Richmond. As she attempted to return to the South following a diplomatic mission to Europe, she was drowned while trying to run the blockade.

4. Laura Lee, April 7, 1862 and Shelia Phipps, "132 North Cameron Street: 'Secesh Lives Here,'" *Winchester-Frederick County Historical Society Journal* 8 (1993): 30.

5. Mary Greenhow Lee, 30. A detailed study of the Lees' next door neighbors David and Fanny Barton is to be found in Margaretta Barton Colt, *Defend the Valley: A Shenandoah Family in the Civil War* (New York: Orion Books, 1994). Colt's book consists of a charming collection of Barton family letters and the particulars of Winchester war activities. The book also includes information on the Baldwin family, the Lees' next door neighbors, on what was then Market Street.

6. Mary Greenhow Lee, 18 and 12.

7. Mary Greenhow Lee, 783.

8. Mary Greenhow Lee, 776. This gathering convened despite the fact that the Federals forbade more than two Rebels to talk on the street together! Cornelia McDonald, a fellow Winchester resident, complained that, in contrast, the Negroes were free to gather in any numbers they wished. She believed the Negroes were given an undue share of liberty. Cornelia McDonald, *A Diary with Reminiscences of the War and Refugee Life in the Shenandoah Valley 1860–1865* (Nashville: Cullom & Ghertner Co., 1935), 138.

9. Laura Lee, 26.

10. Gertie Miller, Diary, Stewart Bell Jr. Archives Room, Handley Regional Library, Winchester, Virginia, April 7, 1863.

11. Colt, 219.

12. McDonald, 151.

13. McDonald, 153.

14. Mary Greenhow Lee, 312.

15. McDonald, 137.

16. Colt, 239.

17. Laura Lee, 35.

18. Mary Greenhow Lee, 102. General Benjamin Butler, incensed over the ill-treatment of his troops by the women of New Orleans, issued his famous Order Number 28 that "when any female shall, by word, gesture, or movement, insult or show contempt for any officer or soldier of the United States, she shall be regarded and held liable to be treated as a woman of the town plying her avocation." Naturally, the Order universally stirred up the wrath of Southerners and not a few Northerners as well.

19. Union General William Wood Averell, 1832–1900, quarreled with Sheridan when Averell did not act aggressively enough after Fisher's Hill.

20. Mary Greenhow Lee, 448.

21. Colt, 125.

22. Mary Greenhow Lee, 12. Rose Greenhow was Mary Lee's half-brother's widow. She was imprisoned for suspected espionage activity. For more information, see Ishbel Ross, *Rebel Rose: Life of Rose O'Neal Greenhow, Confederate Spy* (New York: Harper & Brothers, 1954).

23. Mary Greenhow Lee, 554. General Richard Stoddert Ewell, 1817–1872, was wounded at Gettysburg and fought strapped to his saddle. He was captured at the Battle of Saylor's Creek in April of 1865.

24. Mary Greenhow Lee, 739.

25. McDonald, 48.

26. McDonald, 43.

27. Mary Greenhow Lee, 314.

28. Mary's secret mail service was directly benefitting Jackson and his officers.

29. Mary Greenhow Lee, October 27, 1862.

30. Mary Greenhow Lee, October 28, 1862, 249–250.

31. McDonald, 99 and 112.

32. McDonald, 68.

33. Mary Greenhow Lee, May 23, 1862.

34. Laura Lee, 13.

35. Mary Greenhow Lee, 102.

36. Portia Baldwin Baker, diary, September 19, 1859–January 8, 1863, Stewart Bell Jr. Archives Room, Handley Regional Library, Winchester, Virginia.

37. McDonald, 53–56.

38. Julia Chase, wartime diary, Stewart Bell Jr. Archives Room, Handley Regional Library, Winchester, Virginia, 94.

39. McDonald, 141.

40. McDonald, 141 and 149.

41. Mary Greenhow Lee, 739.

42. Laura Lee, 99.

43. Mary Greenhow Lee, 26.

44. Laura Lee, March 20, 1862, 14.

45. Mary Greenhow Lee, 53.

46. Laura Lee, 99.

47. McDonald, 169.

48. Kate Sperry, diary, Stewart Bell Jr. Archives Room, Handley Regional Library, Winchester, Virginia, 22. Kate was living with her grandfather, Peter Graves Sperry, and her aunt, Mary W. Sperry, in Winchester.

49. Mary Greenhow Lee, 620.

50. Laura Lee, 50.

51. Laura Lee, 14.

52. James M. McPherson, *Battle Cry of Freedom: The Civil War Era* (New York: Ballantine Books, 1988), 405.

53. Mary Greenhow Lee, May 24, 1862.

54. Mary Greenhow Lee. May 24, 1862.

55. General Philip H. Sheridan, appointed by Grant in August of 1864 as Commander of the Army of the Shenandoah. It was hoped he would be able to thwart the activities of Jubal Early and also destroy the farms in the valley that were providing much of the food supplies for the Confederate armies. He was successful on both counts.

56. Laura Lee, 3.

57. Mary Greenhow Lee, 776.

58. General Jubal A. Early, 1816–1894, was defeated in the battles of Winchester and Fisher's Hill in September 1864. General John Brown Gordon, 1832–1904, was famed for his action in the Wilderness Campaign and fought in Early's Valley Campaign in 1864.

59. Mary Greenhow Lee, 314.

60. Mary Greenhow Lee, 783.

61. Mary Greenhow Lee, 783.

62. Mrs. Tuley was the Lees' neighbor who had rented the Barton home after the death of Fanny Barton's husband.

63. Mary Greenhow Lee, 788.

64. Laura Lee, 3.

65. Mary Greenhow Lee, 783.

66. At one time the Lees had four female "servants"; however, by this time one or two may have left with the Federals.

67. Laura Lee, 2.

68. The banishment of Ellen Renshaw House has many similarities to the Lees' banishment: for example, the vague charge, the hosts of well-wishers, and the search of the baggage. See Daniel F. Sutherland, ed., *A Very Violent Rebel: The Civil War Diary of Ellen Renshaw House* (Knoxville: The University of Tennessee Press, 1996), 107–137. For other accounts of just a few of the women ordered "through the lines" for their "disloyal acts," see Ross; G. Glenn Clift, ed., *The Private War of Lizzie Hardin: A Kentucky Confederate Girl's Diary of the Civil War in Kentucky, Virginia, Tennessee, Alabama, and Georgia* (Frankfort: The Kentucky Historical Society, 1963); and Rosa Postell, "Sherman's Occupation of Savannah: Two Letters," *Georgia Historical Quarterly*, 50 (1966): 109–115.

69. Laura Lee, 4. Mr. Sherrard was an officer of the Farmer's Bank in Winchester. The Sherrards were intimate friends of the Lees and were banished along with the Lees.

70. Mary Greenhow Lee, 739.

71. Laura Lee, 14.

72. Colt, 358.

73. Mary Greenhow Lee, 804 and 824. John Singleton Mosby, 1833–1916, was the leader of a band of partisan rangers who were successful in wreaking havoc with the Union armies' supply lines. The Crook-Kelley fiasco involved the capture, in their hotel room in Cumberland, Maryland, of General George Crook and General B. F. Kelley, both U.S. generals, by Confederate guerrillas. The raiders succeeded in kidnapping them and taking them to Libby Prison in Richmond. Southerners, of course, rejoiced in their embarrassment. See Shelby Foote, *The Civil War: A Narrative: Red River to Appomattox* (New York: Random House, 1974), 804.

74. Laura Lee, 5.

75. Laura Lee, 7.

76. Dr. Francis Taliaferro Stribling and his family were good friends of the Lees in Staunton where Dr. Stribling was superintendent of the Western Lunatic Asylum from 1840 to 1874.

77. Scarlett O'Hara's concluding remarks in *Gone with the Wind* tended to echo Mary Lee's despairing words: "What tomorrow may bring, we cannot tell & I will try not to think of it." 809.

78. Mary Greenhow Lee, 808.

79. Mary Greenhow Lee, 810. General Fitzhugh Lee, 1835–1905, was the nephew of General Robert E. Lee and was

wounded at the Battle of Winchester in 1864.

80. Mary Greenhow Lee, 809.
81. Mary Greenhow Lee, 810.
82. Mary Greenhow Lee, 813.
83. Mary Greenhow Lee, 814.
84. Mary Greenhow Lee, 315 and 818.
85. Mary Greenhow Lee, 815.
86. Mary Greenhow Lee, 810.
87. Mary Greenhow Lee, 813.
88. For a more complete analysis of this argument, see Drew Gilpin Faust, "Altars of Sacrifice: Confederate Women and the Narratives of War," *Journal of American History*, 76, No. 4 (March 1990): 1200–1228.
89. Mary Greenhow Lee, April 5, 1865.
90. Mary Greenhow Lee, 816.
91. Mary Greenhow Lee, 820 and 823.
92. Mary Greenhow Lee, 818 and 817.
93. Mary Greenhow Lee, 314.
94. Mary Greenhow Lee, 817.
95. Mary Greenhow Lee, 819.
96. Mary Greenhow Lee, 824.
97. Mary Greenhow Lee, 826.
98. Mary Greenhow Lee, 809. General Winfield Scott Hancock, U.S. 1824–1886. Commander of 1st Veteran Volunteer Corps (November 27, 1864–February 27, 1865) and Commander of Middle Military Division (February 27–June 27, 1865).
99. *War of the Rebellion: A Compilation of the Official Records of the Union and Confederate Armies*, Series 1, Vol. 43, pt. 1, 37; James I. Robertson, Jr., *Civil War Virginia: Battleground for a Nation* (Charlottesville: University Press of Virginia, 1991), 160–161; Edward H. Phillips, *The Shenandoah Valley in 1864: An Episode in the History of Warfare* (Charleston: The Citadel: The Military College of South Carolina, May 1965), 22.
100. Mary Greenhow Lee, 813 and 819.
101. Mary Greenhow Lee, 824.
102. Mary Greenhow Lee, 825.
103. General Isaac Hardin Duval, 1824–1902, a division commander under Sheridan, fought at Third Winchester and later was brevetted major general.
104. Mary Greenhow Lee, 825.
105. Mary Greenhow Lee, 825.
106. Mary Greenhow Lee, 819.
107. Mary Greenhow Lee, 823.
108. Mary Greenhow Lee, 827.
109. Mary Greenhow Lee, 827.

110. Hattie H. Griffith, diary, Stewart Bell Jr. Archives Room, Handley Regional Library, Winchester, Virginia, 14.
111. Chase, 73.
112. Chase, 104.
113. Chase, 91.
114. Chase, 92.
115. "Rebecca Wright: Her Role at 3rd Winchester," *Winchester Evening Star*, September 16, 1964; Sylvia G. L. Dannett, "Rebecca Wright—Traitor or Patriot?" *Lincoln Herald*, 65, No. 3 (Fall 1963): 103–112; McPherson, 777.
116. *Winchester Evening Star*; Dannett; and McPherson. Sheridan, himself, notes his debt to Rebecca in his *Personal Memoirs*, Vol. 2 (New York: Charles L. Webster & Company, 1888).
117. Phipps, 381.

Chapter Six

1. Mary Burrows Fontaine, Letters, Eleanor S. Brockenbrough Library, The Museum of the Confederacy, Richmond, Virginia. May 7, 1865.
2. Fannie E. Dickinson (Taylor), diary, Virginia Historical Society, Richmond, Virginia. April 4, 1865.
3. Kate Cumming, *Kate: The Journal of a Confederate Nurse*. Edited by Richard Barksdale Harwell (Baton Rouge: Louisiana State University Press, 1959), 268. April 6, 1865.
4. Catherine Ann Devereux Edmondston, *"Journal of a Secesh Lady": The Diary of Catherine Ann Devereux Edmondston 1860–1866*. Edited by Beth G. Crabtree and James W. Patton (Raleigh, North Carolina: Division of Archives and History, 1979), 691. April 6, 1865.
5. Sarah Rodgers Rousseau Espy, diary (SPR 2), Alabama Department of Archives and History, Montgomery, Alabama. April 22, 1865.
6. Espy, diary, April 27, 1865.
7. Richard Addison Wood and Joan Faye Wood, "For Better or for Worse," in *The Women's War in the South: Recollections and Reflections of the American Civil War*, Charles G. Waugh and Martin H. Greenberg, eds. (Nashville, Tennessee: Cumberland House, 1991), 252.
8. Virginia Ingraham Burr, ed., *The Secret Eye: The Journal of Ella Gertrude Clanton Thomas, 1848–1889* (Chapel Hill: The University of North Carolina Press, 1990), 263. May 2, 1865.
9. John Rozier, ed., *The Granite*

Farm Letters: The Civil War Correspondence of Edgeworth & Sallie Bird (Athens: The University of Georgia Press, 1988), 246. April 22, 1865.

10. Tirza Willson Patterson, papers, Tennessee State Library and Archives, Nashville, Tennessee.

11. Mary Jane Chadick, diary, Rare Book, Manuscript, and Special Collections Library, Duke University, Durham, North Carolina. April 12–13, 1865.

12. Espy, diary, April 6, 1865.

13. Espy, diary, April 16, 1865.

14. Elizabeth Avery Meriwether, *Recollections of 92 Years 1824–1916* (Nashville, Tennessee: The Tennessee Historical Commission, 1958), 164.

15. Cumming, *Kate*, 271–275. April 17–April 30, 1865.

16. Daniel E. Sutherland, ed., *A Very Violent Rebel: The Civil War Diary of Ellen Renshaw House* (Knoxville: The University of Tennessee Press, 1996), 161.

17. Espy, diary, May 6, 1865.

18. Espy, diary, May 17, 1865.

19. Edmondston, 694. April 16, 1865.

20. Chadick, diary, April 14, 1865.

21. Woodward, *Mary Chesnut's Civil War*, 789. April 19, 1865.

22. Louis P. Towles, ed., *A World Turned Upside Down: The Palmers of South Sante, 1818–1881* (Columbia: University of South Carolina Press, 1996), 489–90. November 3, 1865.

23. Paul Escott, *Slavery Remembered: A Record of Twentieth Century Slave Narratives* (Chapel Hill: University of North Carolina Press, 1979), 132–4.

24. Escott, 129.

25. Charles L. Perdue, Jr., Thomas E. Barden, Robert K. Phillips, eds., *Weevils in the Wheat: Interviews with Virginia Ex-Slaves* (Bloomington: Indiana University Press, 1980), 242.

26. Perdue *et al.*, 212.

27. Perdue *et al.*, 142 and 218.

28. Escott, 136.

29. Towles, 478. July 10, 1865.

30. Towles, 487. October 1965.

31. Tryphena Blanche Holder Fox, *A Northern Woman in the Plantation South: Letters of Tryphena Blanche Holder Fox 1856–1876*. Edited by Wilma King (Columbia: University of South Carolina Press, 1993), 146. July 15, 1865.

32. Towles, 490. November 3, 1865.

33. Kate Cumming, manuscript, *Gleanings from the Southland* (LPR 164), Alabama Department of Archives and History, Montgomery, Alabama.

34. Zillah Brandon, diaries (SPR 262), Alabama Department of Archives and History, Montgomery, Alabama. Reminiscence, July 7, 1869.

35. Emma LeConte, *When the World Ended: The Diary of Emma LeConte*, edited by Earl Schenck Miers (New York: Oxford University Press, 1957), 79. March 14, 1865.

36. Virginia L. French, diary, Tennessee State Library and Archives, Nashville, 227. April 17, 1865.

37. Jane F. Stephenson, "My Father and His Household, Before, During and After the War," Blanton Family Papers, Virginia Historical Society, Richmond, Virginia, 38.

38. Chadick, diary. April 15, 1865.

39. Burr, 266. May 8, 1765.

40. Burr, 277. October 8, 1875.

41. Edmondston, 702. April 23, 1865.

42. Chadick, diary, March 19, 1865. Actually Johnson had taken a couple of stiff drinks to steel himself against the pressures of the inauguration, and unfortunately, the fiery liquor had gone straight to his head.

43. Cumming manuscript.

44. Stephenson, 40.

45. Woodward, 827. June 12, 1865.

46. Frances Fearn, *Diary of a Refugee* (New York: Frances Fearn, 1910), *passim*.

47. Meriwether, 164.

48. *New Orleans Daily Picayune*, April 20, 1865.

49. Burr, 264–65. May 8, 1865.

50. Burr, 277. October 8, 1865.

51. Grace Brown Elmore, diary, South Caroliniana Library, University of South Carolina, Columbia, 92. June 24, 1865.

52. Elmore, 95. July 4, 1865.

53. Fox, 143. June 12, 1865.

54. Woodward, 782 and 814. April 7, 1865, and May 16, 1865.

55. Espy, diary, May 9, 1865.

56. Elisa Gates, letter to Jennie Parsons, Parsons Collections, Alabama Department of Archives and History, Montgomery, Alabama.

57. Marion Knox Goode Briscoe, memoir, Virginia Historical Society, Richmond, Virginia, 186.

58. Burr, 257. March 29, 1865.

59. Frances Butler Leigh, *Ten Years on a Georgia Plantation Since the War 1866–1876* (Savannah: Beehive Press, 1992), 1.

60. Leigh, 2.

61. Brandon, diary, July 6, 1865.

62. Caroline H. Gilman, "Letters of a Confederate Mother: Charleston in the Sixties," *Atlantic*, 137 (April 1926): 512.

63. Gilman, 512–15. December 12, 1865.

64. Gilman, 511. No month indicated, 1865.

65. Mary B. Goodwin, diary, 1860–1867, and papers, 1877–1890 (Accession 27846), Personal Papers Collection, Research Services, The Library of Virginia, Richmond, Virginia. June 11, 1865.

66. Fontaine, letter. April 30, 1865.

67. Myrta Lockett Avary, *Dixie After the War* (Boston: Houghton Mifflin Company, 1937). (Opposite Publisher's Note.)

Bibliography

Anderson, Richard LeConte. *LeConte History and Genealogy.* Vol. 2. Macon, Georgia: Richard LeConte Anderson, 1981.

Andrews, J. Cutler. *The South Reports the War.* New Jersey: Princeton University Press, 1970.

Andrews, Sidney. *The South Since the War as Shown by Fourteen Weeks of Travel and Observations in Georgia and the Carolinas.* Boston: Ticknor and Fields, 1866.

_____. "Three Months Among the Reconstructionists." *Atlantic Monthly* 17 (February 1866): 237–245.

Avary, Myrta Lockett. *Dixie After the War.* Boston: Houghton Mifflin Company, 1937.

Baker, Portia Baldwin. Diary, September 19, 1859–January 8, 1863. Stewart Bell Jr. Archives Room, Handley Regional Library, Winchester, Virginia.

"Barnard, Frederick A. P." *American National Biography.* Vol. 1. New York: Oxford University Press, 1999.

Bettersworth, John K., ed. *Mississippi in the Confederacy: As They Saw It.* Baton Rouge: Louisiana State University, 1961.

Brandon, Zillah. Diaries (SPR 262). Alabama Department of Archives and History. Montgomery, Alabama.

Briscoe, Marion Knox Goode. Memoir. Virginia Historical Society. Richmond, Virginia.

Bryce, Mrs. Campbell. *The Personal Experiences of Mrs. Campbell Bryce During the Burning of Columbia, South Carolina by General W. T. Sherman's Army, February 17, 1865.* Philadelphia: Lippincott Press, 1899.

Burr, Virginia Ingraham, ed. *The Secret Eye: The Journal of Ella Gertrude Clanton Thomas, 1848–1889.* Chapel Hill: The University of North Carolina Press, 1990.

Cabaniss, Allen. *The University of Mississippi: Its First Hundred Years.* Hattiesburg: University & College Press of Mississippi, 1971.

Chadick, Mary Jane. Diary. Rare Book, Manuscript, and Special Collections Library. Duke University. Durham, North Carolina.

Chase, Julia. Wartime diary. Stewart Bell Jr. Archives Room, Handley Regional Library, Winchester, Virginia.

Clark, Walter, ed. *Histories of the Several Regiments and Battalions from North Carolina in the Great War 1861–'65.* Vol. 1. Raleigh, North Carolina: Published by the State, 1901.

Clift, G. Glenn, ed. *The Private War of Lizzie Hardin: A Kentucky Confederate Girl's Diary of the Civil War in Kentucky, Virginia, Tennessee, Alabama, and Georgia.* Frankfort: The Kentucky Historical Society, 1963.

Colt, Margaretta Barton. *Defend the Valley: A Shenandoah Family in the Civil War.* New York: Orion Books, 1994.

Coulter, E. Merton, and Wendell Holmes Stephenson, eds. *A History of the South.* Vols. 7–8. Baton Rouge: Louisiana State University Press, 1947.

Cumming, Kate. (manuscript) *Gleanings from the Southland* (LPR 164); Alabama Department of Archives and History. Montgomery, Alabama.

_____. *Kate: The Journal of a Confederate Nurse.* Edited by Richard Barksdale Harwell. Baton Rouge: Louisiana State University Press, 1959.

Dannett, Sylvia G. L. "Rebecca Wright—Traitor or Patriot?" *Lincoln Herald*, 65, No. 3 (Fall 1963): 103–112.

Davis, Burke. *Sherman's March.* New York: Vintage Books, 1988.

De Forest, John William. *A Union Officer in the Reconstruction.* New Haven: Yale University Press, 1948.

Dickinson, Fannie E. (Taylor). Diary. Virginia Historical Society. Richmond, Virginia.

Edmondston, Catherine Ann Devereux. *"Journal of a Secesh Lady": The Diary of Catherine Ann Devereux Edmondston 1860–1866.* Edited by Beth G. Crabtree and James W. Patton. Raleigh, North Carolina: Division of Archives and History, 1979.

Elmore, Grace Brown. Diary. South Caroliniana Library. University of South Carolina. Columbia, South Carolina.

Escott, Paul. *Slavery Remembered: A Record of Twentieth Century Slave Narratives.* Chapel Hill: University of North Carolina Press, 1979.

Espy, Sarah Rodgers Rousseau. Diary (SPR 2). Alabama Department of Archives and History. Montgomery, Alabama.

Faust, Drew Gilpin. "Altars of Sacrifice: Confederate Women and the Narratives of War." *Journal of American History,* 76, No. 4 (March 1990): 1200–1228.

Fearn, Frances. *Diary of a Refugee.* New York: Frances Fearn, 1910.

Fellman, Michael. *Inside War: The Guerrilla Conflict in Missouri During the American Civil War.* New York: Oxford University Press, 1989.

Foner, Eric. *Nothing but Freedom: Emancipation and Its Legacy.* Baton Rouge: Louisiana State University Press, 1983.

_____. *A Short History of Reconstruction 1863–1877.* New York: Harper & Row, 1990.

_____, and Olivia Mahoney. *America's Reconstruction: People and Politics After the Civil War.* New York: Harper Collins, 1995

Fontaine, Mary Burrows. Letter. Eleanor S. Brokenbrough Library. The Museum of the Confederacy. Richmond, Virginia.

Foote, Shelby. *The Civil War: A Narrative: Fort Sumter to Perryville.* New York: Random House, 1958.

_____. *The Civil War: A Narrative: Red River to Appomattox.* New York: Random House, 1974.

Fox, Tryphena Blanche Holder. *A Northern Woman in the Plantation South: Letters of Tryphena Blanche Holder Fox 1856–1876.* Edited by Wilma King. Columbia: University of South Carolina Press, 1993.

French, L. Virginia. Diary. Tennessee State Library and Archives. Nashville, Tennessee.

Gates, Elisa. Letter to Jennie Parsons. Parsons Collections. Alabama Department of Archives and History. Montgomery, Alabama.

Gilman, Caroline H. "Letters of a Confederate Mother: Charleston in the Sixties." *Atlantic,* 137 (April 1926): 503–15.

Golay, Michael. *A Ruined Land: The End of the Civil War.* New York: John Wiley & Sons, 1999.

Goodwin, Mary B. Diary, 1860–1867, and papers, 1877–1890 (Accession 27846). Personal Papers Collection, Research Services, The Library of Virginia. Richmond, Virginia.

Green, Edwin L. *A History of the University of South Carolina.* Columbia, South Carolina: The State Company, 1916.

Griffith, Hattie H. Diary. Stewart Bell Jr. Archives Room, Handley Regional Library, Winchester, Virginia.

Harper's Weekly. July 26, 1861.

Harwell, Richard B., ed. *The Confederate Reader*. New York: Longmans, Green, 1957.

Hennig, Helen Kohn, ed. *Columbia: Capital City of South Carolina 1786–1936*. Columbia, South Carolina: The State-Record Company, 1966.

Herbert, Hilary Abner, *et al. Why the Solid South? Or, Reconstruction and Its Results*. Baltimore: R. H. Woodward, 1890.

Hilgard, Eugene W. "Biographical Memoir of Joseph LeConte 1823–1901." Read Before the National Academy of Sciences, April 18, 1907.

Hollis, Daniel Walker. *University of South Carolina: College to University*. Vol. II. Columbia: University of South Carolina Press, 1956.

Hyman, Harold Melvin. *Era of the Oath: Northern Loyalty Tests During the Civil War and Reconstruction*. Philadelphia: University of Pennsylvania Press, 1954.

Jones, Mary Sharpe, and Mary Jones Mallard. "Yankees A'Coming: One Month's Experience During the Invasion of Liberty-County, Georgia, 1864–1865." *Confederate Centennial Studies*. 12. Tuscaloosa, Alabama: Confederate Publishing, 1959.

Jones, Nancy Chapman. Letters. Privately held by Nancy Simmons Berger. Dimondale, Michigan.

Kibler, Lillian Adele. *Benjamin F. Perry: South Carolina Unionist*. Durham, North Carolina: Duke University Press, 1946.

LeConte, Emma. *When the World Ended: The Diary of Emma LeConte*. Edited by Earl Schenck Miers. New York: Oxford University Press, 1957.

LeConte, Joseph. *The Autobiography of Joseph LeConte*. New York: D. Appleton, 1903.

_____. "Biographical Memoir of John LeConte, 1818–1891." *Biographical Memoirs, National Academy of Sciences*, 3 (1895): 371–393.

_____, and Caroline LeConte. *'Ware Sherman: A Journal of Three Months' Personal Experience in the Last Days of the Confederacy*. Berkeley: University of California Press, 1938.

LeConte Family Papers. Additions: 1856–1916. Manuscripts Division, Bancroft Library. University of California, Berkeley. Letters written by Eleanor Josephine LeConte, C-B 1014: 23 August 1865, 17 September 1865, 4 December 1865, 28 February 1865, 14 July 1865, 22 November 1865, 11 December 1866, 2 January 1866, 4 February 1866, 17 December 1866, 29 December 1866, 16 March 1867, 29 April 1867, 27 May 1867, 30 September 1867, 9 May 1867, 20 June 1869, (nd.). Letter written by Barton Alexander: 20 June 1869.

_____. Additions: 1862–1928 BANC MSS 70/24. Letters written by Mary A. Graham. Manuscripts Division, Bancroft Library, University of California, Berkeley: 3 December 1865, 19 May 1867.

_____. BANC 70/20. Letter written by Louis Julian LeConte: 19 May 1864.

_____. BANC MSS 70/20. Letter written by Mary Tullulah LeConte: 28 February 1865.

_____. BANC MSS 70/20. Letter written by R. Gage: 14 February 1867.

_____. BANC MSS 70/20. Letters written by Dolly Dill: 10 November 1865, 28 May 1866, 31 July 1866.

_____. BANC MSS 70/20. Letters written by Jane Harden: 26 October 1865, 13 December 1865.

Lee, Laura. "The History of Our Captivity," Diary. March 1862 to April 1865. Manuscripts and Rare Books Department, Swem Library, The College of William and Mary, Williamsburg, Virginia. A photocopy is found in the Stewart Bell Jr. Archives Room, Handley Regional Library, Winchester, Virginia.

Lee, Mary Greenhow (Mrs. Hugh). Diary. Stewart Bell Jr. Archives Room, Handley Regional Library, Winchester, Virginia. It should be noted that Mary Lee's diary is some 900 pages long, and the selections chosen for this chapter constitute only a very small portion of her diary.

Leigh, Frances Butler. *Ten Years on a Georgia Plantation Since the War 1866–1876.* Savannah: Beehive Press, 1992.

Lord, Walter, ed. *The Fremantle Diary: Being the Journal of Lieutenant Colonel James Arthur Lyon Fremantle, Coldstream Guards on His Three Months in the Southern States.* Boston: Little, Brown, 1954.

Lucas, Marion Brunson. *Sherman and the Burning of Columbia.* College Station: Texas A&M University Press, 1976.

Lupold, John Samuel. "From Physician to Physicist: The Scientific Career of John LeConte, 1818–1891." Ph.D. diss., University of South Carolina, 1970.

McDonald, Cornelia. *A Diary with Reminiscences of the War and Refugee Life in the Shenandoah Valley 1860–1865.* Nashville: Cullom & Ghertner, 1935.

Mac Kethan, Lucinda H., ed. *Recollections of a Southern Daughter: A Memoir by Cornelia Jones Pond of Liberty County.* Athens: The University of Georgia Press, 1998.

McPherson, James M. *Battle Cry of Freedom: The Civil War Era.* New York: Ballantine Books, 1988.

Maury, Matthew Fontaine. "The American Colony in Mexico." *De Bow's.* Series 2 (January–June 1866): 622–630.

Meriwether, Elizabeth Avery. *Recollections of 92 Years 1824–1916.* Nashville, Tennessee: The Tennessee Historical Commission, 1958.

Miers, Earl Schenck, ed. *When the World Ended: The Journal of Emma LeConte.* New York: Oxford University Press, 1957.

Miller, Gertie. Diary. Stewart Bell Jr. Archives Room, Handley Regional Library, Winchester, Virginia.

Missouri Division, United Daughters of the Confederacy. *Reminiscences of the Women of Missouri During the Sixties.* Jefferson City: The Hugh Stephens Printing Co., 1920.

Moore, John Hammond. *Columbia and Richland County: A South Carolina Community 1740–1990.* Columbia: University of South Carolina Press, 1993.

Neagles, James C. *Confederate Research Sources: A Guide to Archive Collections.* Salt Lake City, UT: Ancestry, 1986.

Nunn, W. C. *Escape from Reconstruction.* Westport, CT: Greenwood, 1956. (Reprint.)

"Oaths, Amnesties and Rebellion." *Debow's Review* (January–June 1866): 283–303.

"Our Women and the War": The Lives They Lived; The Deaths They Died. Charleston, South Carolina: The News and Courier Book Presses, 1885.

Page, Dave. "A Fight for Missouri." *Civil War Times Illustrated,* 34 (July/August 1995): 34–38.

Parsons, Jeanette Hepburn. Papers (7N/Box 178). Alabama Department Archives and History. Montgomery, Alabama.

Patterson, Tirza Willson. Papers. Tennessee State Library and Archives. Nashville, Tennessee.

Perdue, Charles L., Jr., Thomas E. Barden, Robert K. Phillips, eds. *Weevils in the Wheat: Interviews with Virginia Ex-Slaves.* Bloomington: Indiana University Press, 1980.

Phillips, Edward H. *The Shenandoah Valley in 1864: An Episode in the History of Warfare.* Charleston: The Citadel: The Military College of South Carolina, May 1965.

Phipps, Shelia. "132 North Cameron Street: 'Secesh Lives Here.'" *Winchester-Frederick County Historical Society Journal,* 8 (1993): 51–68.

Postell, Rosa. "Sherman's Occupation of Savannah: Two Letters." *Georgia Historical Quarterly,* 50 (1966): 109–115.

Rable, George C. *But There Was No Peace: The Role of Violence in the Politics of Reconstruction.* Athens: The University of Georgia Press, 1984.

Rea, Ralph R. *Sterling Price: The Lee of the West.* Little Rock, Arizona: Pioneer, 1959.

"Rebecca Wright: Her Role at 3rd Winchester." *Winchester Evening Star*. September 16, 1964.

Reynolds, John S. *Reconstruction in South Carolina*. Columbia, S.C: The State Co., 1905.

Riddleberger, Patrick W. *1866: The Critical Year Revisited*. Carbondale: Southern Illinois University Press, 1979.

Robertson, James I., Jr. *Civil War Virginia: Battleground for a Nation*. Charlottesville: University Press of Virginia, 1991.

Rolle, Andrew F. *The Lost Cause: The Confederate Exodus to Mexico*. Norman: University of Oklahoma Press, 1965.

Ross, Ishbel. *Rebel Rose: Life of Rose O'Neal Greenhow, Confederate Spy*. New York: Harper & Brothers, 1954.

Rozier, John, ed. *The Granite Farm Letters: The Civil War Correspondence of Edgeworth & Sallie Bird*. Athens: The University of Georgia Press, 1988.

Saville, Julie. *The Work of Reconstruction: From Slave to Wage Laborer in South Carolina, 1860–1870*. Cambridge: Cambridge University Press, 1944.

Scudder, Samuel H. "John Lawrence LeConte: A Memoir." Read to the National Academy of Sciences, April 17, 1884.

Sheridan, Philip. *Personal Memoirs*, Vol. 2. New York: Charles L. Webster & Company, 1888.

Silver, James W. *Mississippi in the Confederacy as Seen in Retrospect*. Baton Rouge: Louisiana State University Press, 1961.

Simkins, Francis Butler, and Robert Hilliard Woody. *South Carolina During Reconstruction*. Chapel Hill: The University of North Carolina Press, 1932.

Sperry, Kate. Diary. Stewart Bell Jr. Archives Room, Handley Regional Library, Winchester, Virginia.

Stephens, Lester D. *Joseph LeConte: Gentle Prophet of Evolution*. Baton Rouge: Louisiana State University Press, 1982.

Stephenson, Jane F. "My Father and His Household, Before, During and After the War." Blanton Family Papers. Virginia Historical Society. Richmond, Virginia.

Stevens, Le Conte W. "Sketch of Prof. John Le Conte." *The Popular Science Monthly*, Vol. 36 (November 1889–April 1890): 112–118.

Sutherland, Daniel E., ed. *A Very Violent Rebel: The Civil War Diary of Ellen Renshaw House*. Knoxville: The University of Tennessee Press, 1996.

Towles, Louis P., ed. *A World Turned Upside Down: The Palmers of South Sante, 1818–1881*. Columbia: University of South Carolina Press, 1996.

Trowbridge, John T. *The Desolate South 1865–1866: A Picture of the Battlefields and of the Devastated Confederacy*. Boston: Little, Brown, 1956. (Another copy cites Gordon Carroll, ed. Freeport, N.Y.: Books for Libraries Press, 1956.)

_____. *Picture of the Desolated South and the Work of Reconstruction 1865–1868*. Hartford, CT: L. Stebbins, 1868.

War of the Rebellion: A Compilation of the Official Records of the Union and Confederate Armies. Series 1, Vol. 43, pt. 1 (Washington: Government Printing Office).

Wellman, Manly Wade. *The County of Warren North Carolina 1856–1917*. Chapel Hill: University of North Carolina Press, 1959.

Wood, Richard Addison, and Joan Faye Wood. "For Better or for Worse." *The Women's War in the South: Recollections and Reflections of the American Civil War*. Charles G. Waugh and Martin H. Greenberg, eds. Nashville, Tennessee: Cumberland House, 1999.

Woodward, C. Vann, ed. *Mary Chesnut's Civil War*. New Haven: Yale University Press, 1981.

Index